7/05

Gypsy

D1073521

DATE DUE

WITHDRAWN

Gypsy Law

Romani Legal Traditions and Culture

EDITED BY

Walter O. Weyrauch

UNIVERSITY OF CALIFORNIA PRESS

Berkeley   Los Angeles   London

"Autonomous Lawmaking: The Case of the 'Gypsies' " by Walter O. Weyrauch and Maureen Anne Bell reprinted by permission of The Yale Law Journal Company and Fred B. Rothman & Company from the *Yale Law Journal*, vol. 103 (November 1993), pp. 323–399.

Chapter 1 and chapters 3-11 first appeared in a slightly different form in the *American Journal of Comparative Law*, vol. 45, no 2 (spring 1997).

University of California Press
Berkeley and Los Angeles, California

University of California Press, Ltd.
London, England

Library of Congress Cataloging-in-Publication Data

Gypsy law : Romani legal traditions and culture / edited by Walter O. Weyrauch.
    p.   cm.
Includes bibliographical references and index.
ISBN 0-520-22185-0 (cloth : alk. paper)—ISBN 0-520-22186-9 (pbk. : alk. paper)
    1. Law, Gypsy.   2. Gypsies—Legal status, laws, etc.   I. Weyrauch, Walter O. (Walter Otto), 1919–

K197.G97 2001
346.01'3—dc21   00—46710

The paper used in this publication meets the minimum requirements of ANSI/NISO Z39.48-1992 (R 1997) (*Permanence of Paper*). ♾

Contents

Editor's Note on Terminology

The term "Gypsies," as used in the title of this volume, corresponds to common English usage. It originates from past mistaken beliefs that the Romani people came from Egypt. The term was imposed on the Roma by outsiders to their culture who were unaware of the Roma's Indian roots. Even the terms "Rom" (singular) and "Roma" (plural) lend themselves to misunderstandings because they seem to imply descent from Romania; in fact, these terms connote "man" or "husband" in the Romani language, which is related to Sanskrit. Further complications may arise from externally imposed terminology. The result may be to include persons who, because of their customs, are erroneously believed to be Roma. The German Sinti have insisted on their own separate identity as "Roma and Sinti."

These problems of language are sensitive because they reflect and reinforce conflicting modes by which the Romani people identify themselves and how they are identified by others. An ideal solution that is accepted by all the people concerned has not yet been found. Moreover, the problem is not unique to the Romani people. The term "Eskimo," for example, was imposed on the people concerned by their Native American neighbors. Its meaning of "people who eat raw meat" had disparaging connotations, yet the increasingly used term "Inuit" covers only a small segment of the population. Similarly, the French term "Allemands" for Germans covers only a small segment of the German population bordering France. The term "Nemtsy," used for Germans in Russian and in derivative forms in Slavic languages, had originally negative connotations of mute people who are incapable of communicating in any articulate way.

Related problems are created by the use of the term "host country" for the nation-state where Roma are present. This term, too, touches upon sensitivities that relate to Romani identity. The Sinti legitimately claim that they have been located in Central Europe for six hundred years and that they are entitled to be called Germans as much as anybody else in Germany. To call them mere guests in a host country is inappropriate and insulting. (Indeed, Germany has its own problems resulting from the pervasive persecution of the Roma throughout its history, culminating in the organized mass killings of the Nazi era. As a consequence, the term "Zigeuner," which was once customary in Germany for the Romani people, is no longer used.) Some Roma consider reference to host countries as offensive because of biological connotations that they are "parasites" on a host. Even the alternative term "majority population" for host country is not fully acceptable to all Roma. It may imply that the Roma, as a minority, are subject to discriminatory conditions that are dictated by the majority.

Usage of terms in this volume is not uniform or consistent. For example, chapter 2 by Weyrauch and Bell, "Autonomous Lawmaking: The Case of the 'Gypsies,'" was first published in 1993 as an article in the *Yale Law Journal*. Although that essay provided the stimulus to the 1997 Gypsy Law Symposium in the *American Journal of Comparative Law* and the present book, it still used the term "host country," which was then common in the literature.

These and related terminological dilemmas pervade this volume, and the contributors have dealt with them in a variety of ways.

Foreword

Angela P. Harris

'In a riddle whose answer is chess, what is the only prohibited word?'
I thought a moment and replied, 'The word chess.'
JORGE LUIS BORGES, "THE GARDEN OF FORKING PATHS"

The contributors to this book struggle throughout with a problem that they do not name but that surrounds their thoughtful and informative essays like a mist: the problem that arises when the academic enterprise and unequal power relations meet. Roma have for many centuries been the target of discrimination, persecution, stereotyping, forced assimilation, and violence.[1] Survival for cultural groups in this situation becomes what Native American scholar Gerald Vizenor calls "survivance," for survival through resistance; and the primary Romani tactic of survivance has historically been invisibility. As the essays in this book document, Roma have been able to maintain an impressive degree of cultural integrity not only by absolutely excluding *gadje* [non-Gypsies] from their private lives, their law, their personal practices, and their values, but by excluding them even from knowledge about Romani language and social institutions. While the subordination of other "people of color" in the United States—notably African Americans, Native Americans, Asian Americans, and Latino/as—has resulted in a complex cultural interchange with European America, the Roma have been able to remain a people apart, largely invisible both to the dominant culture and to other racialized minorities.

As the publication of this book also suggests, however, this situation is changing. Walter Weyrauch notes that "[t]he appearance of *Romaniya* or Gypsy law in legal literature is of extraordinary moment for jurisprudence and the comparative study of law." With this unprecedented visibility come new opportunities and new pitfalls, and a series of strategic choices. In this essay I do not attempt to predict how Roma will choose to negotiate their increased visibility; rather, I briefly sketch

I am grateful for comments on previous versions of this essay by Dick Buxbaum, Ian Hancock, Colin Samson, and Walter Weyrauch.

1. See Edward W. Said, *Culture and Imperialism* (1993).

some possible implications for survivance in a world in which "Gypsy law" has entered the legal literature.

One strategy of increased visibility this book might represent could be called the "folklore" approach. Here, the purpose of introducing Gypsy law to legal scholars would be simply to enlighten the curious about an obscure and interesting corner of the jurisprudential world. This approach leaves the word "power" unspoken; the assumption is that knowledge for its own sake is an unqualified good.

One danger inherent in the process of gathering and publishing information about a hitherto invisible group is, of course, the possibility of getting it wrong. Weyrauch notes that many aspects of purity and pollution in Gypsy law were not known to *gadje* until female anthropologists were able to establish intimate relationships with Romani women. To the extent that talking about certain issues is both taboo within the community and discouraged as a way to keep outsiders out, outsiders may receive a partial, misleading, or even false impression of much of Romani culture.

A second problem of scholarship in this context involves the inherent distortions in trying to capture an oral tradition within a written tradition. Weyrauch and Bell, for example, are attentive to the role of memory in Gypsy law—a role that memory does not play in Western literate cultures. Third, even assuming that an outsider gains total access to all aspects of a given Romani culture, how can that culture be rendered accurately within a system of representation whose terms already construct Roma as inferior? For example, Weyrauch and Bell discuss the problem of whether Gypsy law should be recognized as law when Western society identifies law with the presence of a state. Leaving this assumption unquestioned guarantees that Gypsy law will be thought of as a primitive form of social regulation, a conclusion that may hinder full understanding.

A deeper problem with the "folklore" approach, however, is that its lack of attention to relations of oppression and privilege tends to perpetuate those relations. Anne Sutherland's essay, for instance, shows how Gypsy law includes not only the norms and institutions that characterize relations among Roma but also the way Roma are stereotyped, persecuted, and labeled as criminal within the dominant criminal justice system. Sutherland gives one chilling example: her own work on Romani cultural practices was incorporated into an article recycling the grossest of stereotypes and titled "Gypsies, the People and Their Criminal Propensity," and then used by an assistant district attorney in prosecuting a Romani man. Weyrauch gives another, more subtle example: one reaction to the article he originally published with Maureen Bell in the *Yale Law Journal* was the suggestion that Gypsy law oppresses women and that human rights law should be used to change it. When the object of academic study is an oppressed group, a little knowledge may be a dangerous thing.

A second possible strategy of greater Romani visibility might be the one Weyrauch himself champions. Weyrauch uses as a central image in his essay Jonathan Swift's vivid story of the moment when the fabled traveler Gulliver, after having treated the Yahoos as an alien and repulsive species, realizes that he himself is a Yahoo—or at least so close in resemblance as to be taken for one by a Yahoo woman. As used by Weyrauch, the story represents the relationship between Roma and *gadje* as a problem of unacknowledged similarities: Gulliver has supposed himself wholly different from the despised Yahoos, and suddenly is forced to see himself as akin. Weyrauch's own goals in writing about Gypsy law are similar. As he tells us, the purpose of his work is not to criticize Gypsy law but rather to force Westerners to notice how their own legal culture resembles that of the supposedly alien, "foreign" Roma. This sudden shift in perspective promises at least two valuable effects: Westerners may begin to recognize the extent of their own "private lawmaking" within an officially state-based legal culture; and Westerners may exercise a new tolerance toward the Roma and their Gypsy law.

These effects are two of those traditionally sought by cultural anthropologists: to gain insights into our own culture through the technique of seeing it through a foreigner's eyes, and to stay the hands of the missionaries, traders, and monarchs who would prefer that the native culture disappear. Weyrauch is quite explicit about his commitment to these goals. Central to his essay is the caution that "[t]he objective of the original article on Gypsy law was less concerned with changing the Roma in any way and more with creating an awareness of submerged patterns of private lawmaking in the American legal culture." Under this view, for example, it may or may not be the case that gender-based rules of *marimos* [pollution] are unjust to women. The point is that such a determination cannot be made unless the opposition between "us" and "them" is destabilized and the machinery of cultural projection dismantled.

The problem, however, is even more daunting than Weyrauch's use of the Gulliver story suggests. It is as if Gulliver, rather than being a hapless and solo traveler, were the herald of a conquering army, or a missionary to a newly discovered country of heathens. Western lawyers have the power and ability to revise their understanding of the relationship between state and non-state law if they choose to; but they also have the power and ability—and perhaps the inclination—to decline the invitation. Indeed, even when a dominant group sincerely wishes to revise its opinion of itself, things may go awry. As literary critic Arnold Krupat argues in the context of criticizing indigenous American (Indian) literature:

> For all that ethnocriticism [by which Krupat means literary criticism across vastly different cultures] wishes to engage on an equal footing with Native literary practice, it cannot help but do so in a context of vastly unequal power relations. Thus, for all that the ethnocritic may decently and sincerely attempt to inquire into and learn from the Otherness of ongoing Indian literary performances, the sociopolitical context being what it is, she or he cannot help but threaten to swallow, submerge, or obliterate these performances. This is not to say that nothing can be done; but good-will or even great talent alone cannot undo the current differential power relations between dominant and subaltern cultural production.[2]

2. Arnold Krupat, *Ethnocriticism: Ethnography, History, Literature* 186 (1992).

Thus, the history of anthropology has made clear that the project of gathering knowledge about the Other—even when greater mutual understanding and tolerance is avowedly the goal—has often been tainted with the attitudes and goals of the group doing the gathering. Margaret Mead's classic study, *Coming of Age in Samoa*, for example, was originally directed at forcing Americans to rethink their own rites of adolescence and rules of gender in a critical light; yet the book now is held up by many as an example of bad anthropology, condescension, and cultural projection. The problem is not necessarily wrong information, incomplete information, or mistranslation of many different kinds; nor is it the assumption that knowledge gathered about "others" has no possible implications for "us." Rather, the pursuit of knowledge is inevitably saturated with both the blindnesses and the desires and repulsions of the pursuers; and when the pursued are a minority group in a hostile society, encouraging that society to reexamine itself is a dicey proposition.

So what should be done? Krupat takes seriously the argument that the best thing to do in such a situation is to keep silent. He ultimately chooses to speak, however, in the hope that if there can be no "nonviolent criticism of the discourse of Others," there can at least be "a rather less violent knowledge."[3] Toward this end, he tries to construct a third approach to increased visibility. Krupat argues that the work of describing and critiquing minority cultural practices must take a "multicultural" approach, by which he means an approach that "engages the other in such a way as to provoke an interrogation of and a challenge to what we take as ours."[4] Krupat then goes further: he argues that the goal should be neither the neutral pursuit of truth nor increased understanding of the other through a new understanding of oneself. Rather, the point of translating a culture understood as foreign must be to make an anti-imperialist critique of one's own culture, to blur the supposed distinctions between "us" and "them" in order to reveal and condemn the power relations that make visibility dangerous to oppressed peoples.

In the academic legal world, sustained efforts of this kind have issued for the last ten years under the rubric of "critical race theory" and "Indian law." Critical race theorists—primarily African American, Asian American, and Latino/a scholars—have concerned themselves with achieving "equality" as minorities within the larger American society; native scholars and activists working with Indian law have worked primarily toward achieving some form of sovereignty, or self-determination. Both literatures have in common, however, the explicit theme of power and the way power corrupts both group political relations and the quest for knowledge itself.

This third approach to the politics of visibility—the "critical" approach—suggests the possibility of an intellectual dialogue and political solidarity that might be forged between Roma and other racialized peoples. Roma, perhaps by being

---

3. Krupat, *Ethnocriticism*, at 6.
4. *Id.* at 236–37.

attached neither to a political-legal nation-state nor to a geographical land base, have escaped to a large extent the colonization of their political-legal system, their economic system, and their culture. They point up the extent to which African Americans, Latino/as, Asian Americans, and Indians, in contrast, are the unwilling products of colonialism. It would change the conversation immeasurably to include within the intellectual and political debate peoples who both survived colonialism and avoided the "melting pot."

This third strategy of visibility, however, has its own perils. Both the equality and the sovereignty path, given the reality of the greater size and strength of the dominant society, ultimately rely on moral pressure to realign the pernicious relationship between "white" and "nonwhite" that has sustained inequality for so long. Meanwhile, the sustained effort to present one's case as a wronged people, entitled to compensation under the dominant society's own rules, can be damaging. Gerald Vizenor, for example, attacks "professional Indians" whose uses of the rhetoric of victimhood and the stereotypes of the noble, wise Indian only serve to make more invisible the real struggles of contemporary native people, while "simulations" of "real Indians" proliferate.[5] The history of other racialized groups in the United States—at least those considered visually "nonwhite"—suggests that the search for respect by the dominant society is a kind of Tar Baby, both irresistible and (possibly) futile.

A fourth and final approach to the politics of visibility is perhaps less a strategy than an attitude. Vizenor's work, for example, embraces postmodern thought as one intellectual approach to the problem of native survival in a world overrun with "Indians." In his writing on native Americans, Vizenor's watchwords are irony, humor, cynicism, and the rejection of a victim identity. Vizenor calls attention to the unequal power relations between Indians and whites, but not in service of the demand that whites make things right; his goal is the trickier one of keeping the native spirit alive. Toward this end, Vizenor works constantly to undermine the relationship between native peoples and the "Indians" that are everywhere in American popular culture and history; he undermines even the word "Indian" itself, by writing it in italics and lowercase, to constantly remind the reader that Indians and Indian cultures as the West knows them are inventions. Vizenor also resists "identity politics"; ceding all rights to the label "Indian," he supports instead a "postindian" identity, one that "stands for an active, ironic resistance to dominance, and the good energy of native survivance."[6]

Vizenor's writings encourage his readers to be tricky, evasive, combative; not to pursue a politics of "authenticity" with its concern for telling "true" from "false" members of the group, but to be aware that "the native" is always the unnameable. Vizenor does not ignore everyday injustices to native people; but his focus is inward

---

5. See Gerald Vizenor, *Fugitive Poses: Native American Indian Scenes of Absence and Presence* (1998).
6. Gerald Vizenor and A. Robert Lee, *Postindian Conversations* 85 (1999).

toward natives rather than outward toward whites. Indeed, Vizenor's proposals suggest an affinity with the inward-looking strategies of survivance Roma have practiced over the centuries.

How will the Roma negotiate their relationship to the dominant society in the next millennium? As Ronald Lee notes at the end of his essay, at least some Roma—the American and Canadian Rom-Vlach—"are becoming more of an ethnic minority in urbanized North America than a people apart. . . . Yet, in order to survive as a culture, the Rom will need to develop some form of representation in the future where they can have a voice in defining who they are." The emergence of "Gypsy law" as represented by this book signals the beginning of this process. The nature of the ongoing balance between academic exploration and the politics of "survivance," however, is still in the making.

ONE

Romaniya: An Introduction to Gypsy Law

Walter O. Weyrauch

The appearance of *Romaniya* or Gypsy law in legal literature is of extraordinary moment for jurisprudence and the comparative study of law. This autonomous body of law, existing unnoticed among dominant legal systems, has been invisible to legal scholarship and provides a considerable challenge to established ways of thinking.

This volume contains ten essays that describe aspects of *Romaniya*. Much of the presentation has testimonial character, for example, accounts of past field research in Finland, as told by Martti Grönfors, or of giving expert testimony in a criminal trial involving a Gypsy who had used a wrong social security number, as related by Anne Sutherland.[1] Two of the contributors belong to the Romani people: Ian Hancock, who provides a glossary of Romani terms, and Ronald Lee, who gives an ac-

---

Helpful suggestions by Gunther Arzt and Lynn LoPucki are gratefully acknowledged. Research assistance by Rosalie Sanderson is deeply appreciated.

Reference to "Gypsies" in the title and text is not free of problems. The term continues to be widely used in the English language, as illustrated by the Journal of the Gypsy Lore Society. The corresponding designation taken from the Gypsy language, "Roma," has gained wide acceptance, but is disfavored by some Gypsy groups. The Sinti in Germany, for example, prefer separate reference to "Sinti and Roma." Historically the Roma had no common name for themselves, although a contemporary movement among them advocates universal adoption of this name. All terms originating from non-Gypsy sources are somewhat in doubt, although not as much as the German word, "Zigeuner," which should not be used at all because of disparaging connotations from the times of the Nazi persecutions. Although this essay still refers to "Gypsies," it applies the term interchangeably with "Roma" to reflect that custom is in flux. It follows in these respects the mixed usage as applied in the writings of Ian Hancock, Professor of Linguistics and English at the University of Texas in Austin. Hancock, whose Romani name is O Yanko Le Redžosko, is a Rom of British-Hungarian extraction.

1. Grönfors, "Institutional Non-Marriage in the Finnish Roma Community and Its Relationship to Roma Traditional Law," chap. 7; Sutherland, "Complexities of U.S. Law and Gypsy Identity," chap. 10.

count of the workings of *Romaniya* and the *kris* proceedings that may occur in cases of violations.[2] The unique value of their contributions consists in validating and often qualifying earlier anthropological accounts given by outside observers.

The reader should not expect uniformity of viewpoints. These essays deal with a legal culture that for about one thousand years has been based on oral tradition, and contradictions are inevitable. Lee points out that the various branches of the Romani people know little about each other.[3] Thus generalizations based on accounts from one particular group are bound to be misleading, as stressed by Thomas Acton, Susan Caffrey and Gary Mundy.[4] Even spelling of terms within the volume is not uniform, although efforts at standardization of *Romani*, the Gypsy language, are currently under way.

The absence of a common sovereign or territory may contribute to misconceptions. Commonly used terms, such as "law," "courts," or "sanctions," are impliedly based on the presence of a state that prescribes rules about responsibilities and individual rights. Much of this is not applicable to the Gypsies. Yet the Romani people have survived as a distinct culture, although dispersed throughout the world, under conditions of often ferocious persecution. Their legal culture, perhaps strengthened through persistent external threats, appears to have been largely responsible for this miraculous feat. The vitality of this culture and the function of law in its survival make comparisons with legal notions familiar in the Western world particularly stimulating.[5]

Although this volume encourages a wide variety of analyses, a search for common threads reveals three themes that have recurred with some frequency: first, the link between the law and the human body in *Romaniya*, with consequences for the conduct of daily life, as distinct from a legal system based on abstract rules; second, the arbitrariness of many rules of *Romaniya* that seem to defy any form of explanation or purpose; and third, the frequent criminalization of the Romani people under the dominant legal systems that, even though externally imposed upon them, in subtle ways appears to be related to their internal legal culture. For purposes of discussion these three themes are presented under the headings of sexuality, irrationality, and criminalization. I will try to show that, while these labels have shock value, they represent a reality that is amorphous and complex. Although I suggest a few theories of my own, I do not intend to preclude other forms of analysis.

2. Hancock, "A Glossary of Romani Terms," chap. 8; Lee, "The Rom-Vlach Gypsies and the *Kris-Romani*," chap. 9. For an alternative spelling of *Romaniya*, see Hancock supra at 184.

3. Lee, supra n. 2, at 217 n. 31.

4. Acton, Caffrey & Mundy, "Theorizing Gypsy Law," chap. 3.

5. For a broad definition of law, as used in this volume, see Weyrauch, "Oral Legal Traditions of Gypsies and Some American Equivalents," chap. 11, at 248 n. 20. See also Weyrauch & Bell, "Autonomous Lawmaking: The Case of the 'Gypsies'," chap. 2, at 15 (quoting Thomas A. Cowan & Donald A. Strickland, *The Legal Structure of a Confined Microsociety*, at i, University of California, Berkeley, Space Sciences Laboratory, Working Paper No. 34, 1965).

I. SEXUALITY

The curious link between the human body, intimate body functions, and the law is described in various manifestations by the contributors. Sexuality, procreation, and marriage seem to be perceived in *Romaniya* as fundamental notions that sustain law. In a loose way one may view them as an equivalent to a constitution that is unwritten and gains its strength and binding force by not being articulated. The very foundation of law is protected by taboos that, although they are adhered to, prevent their discussion and explanation. To the outside observer these taboos, especially those relating to sexuality and procreation, are difficult, if not impossible, to understand. Gender is an important factor. An appearance of male dominance conceals the powerful position of women. Women have the power to curse and to pollute, in particular Gypsy men.[6] They are also the guardians of law, because they communicate the taboos to their offspring from early infancy.

Grönfors' field research on the Finnish Kaale Gypsies is truly astounding.[7] They have retained archaic notions in their pure form, having been cut off from other Romani groups for four hundred years. To the Kaale the concepts of marriage and even of virginity are already polluting because they imply sexual conduct, or the significance of its absence. Rituals have been developed that permit procreation without acknowledging that it has ever taken place. Yet he posits that the absence of marriage among the Kaale is an essential element in the ways in which their legal system operates. Marriage establishes loyalties that could become burdensome in cases of serious conflicts. Since the Kaale have no judicial proceedings, like the *kris* of the Vlach Gypsies, blood feuding becomes an issue.[8] Openly acknowledged affinity relations create loyalties that could be problematical in cases of blood feuding and even disturb those mechanisms that have been developed to avoid this most serious sanction.

In his searching comparison of *Romaniya* with Jewish law, Calum Carmichael suggests a trend toward "desexing of ancient customs."[9] The traditional custom of a Gypsy woman tossing her skirt in order to defile a possible transgressor, once perceived as a means to bring about the need for a *kris* proceeding, is becoming increasingly discredited. The woman and her family, as also described by Lee,[10] may become themselves impure by resort to what was earlier perceived to be legitimate behavior. This evolution may find a parallel in the characteristic of contemporary law, common in Western cultures, to rely on abstract rules as a primary source of

6. Weyrauch, supra n. 5, at 261–69 (discussing the power of Gypsy women).

7. Grönfors, supra n. 1.

8. Martti Grönfors, *Blood Feuding Among Finnish Gypsies* (University of Helsinki Department of Sociology, Tutkimuksia Research Reports No. 213, 1977); Acton, Caffrey & Mundy, supra n. 4, at 99 (suggesting that the *kris* may have developed under conditions of chattel slavery of Vlach Gypsies in Romania).

9. Carmichael, "Gypsy Law and Jewish Law," chap. 5, 135.

10. Lee, supra n. 2, at 203.

law. Judicial proceedings, accordingly, are meant to be as neutral as possible by minimizing references to personal factors, including sexuality.[11] Exclusionary rules of
evidence and conceptions of relevance, unknown in Romani proceedings, support
these policies. Theoretical constructs originating from the state may be felt to be
necessary to govern effectively in multiethnic and industrialized societies. Yet what
may be necessary under modern conditions may also suggest why, in terms of vitality and survival power, Gypsy law has been superior to the law of the state.

On the other hand, even in the laws of the dominant cultures, the laws of the
family and of gender distinctions, although embroiled in controversy, may have an
increasingly recognized role in the functioning of law. For instance, the relationship between family law and commercial law is again being explored.[12] Practicing
lawyers, in applying broad concepts of relevance in legal counseling, are aware
that any controversy, regardless of the specialization involved, has a personal dimension.[13] Furthermore, the trend toward "desexing" of law, as described by
Carmichael, is not likely to be fully effective. Unrecognized oral legal traditions
continue to compete with the law of the state and often determine the outcome of
cases. What is disparaged by legal scholarship as mere strategy may be one form
for oral legal traditions to rival the supposedly neutral law of the state. To be effective, these strategies can only be hinted. If a lawyer were to refer to them openly,
the strategy would become as damaging as the articulation of taboos in the Gypsy
culture. Loss of credibility or, in more serious cases, violation of professional ethics,
would bring about this result.[14]

II. IRRATIONALITY

Many of the rules of *Romaniya* or, as Lee calls it, the *marimé* code,[15] make no sense
to the outside observer. The rule that the presence of women on higher floors of a
house pollutes the occupants of lower floors appears to be irrational. In some of
the rules the possible explanation is so farfetched to Western thinking that they are
felt to be absurd. One could explain the replacement of used sinks and toilets with
new facilities in rented premises by reference to extreme hygienic precaution.[16] Yet

---

11. See, e.g., John T. Noonan, *Persons and Masks of the Law: Cardozo, Holmes, Jefferson, and Whythe as Makers of the Masks* (1976); Weyrauch, "Law as Mask: Legal Ritual and Relevance," 66 *Cal. L. Rev.* 699 (1978).

12. Walter O. Weyrauch, Sanford N. Katz & Frances Olsen, *Cases and Materials on Family Law: Legal Concepts and Changing Human Relationships* 3–156 (1994); Olsen, "The Family and the Market: A Study of Ideology and Legal Reform," 96 *Harv. L. Rev.* 1497 (1983).

13. See, e.g., Harrop A. Freeman & Henry Weihofen, *Clinical Law Training: Interviewing and Counseling* (1972) (containing counseling materials from all fields of law, as reported by attorneys).

14. Weyrauch, supra n. 5, at 255; Weyrauch & Bell, supra n. 5, at 70–74, 85–87.

15. Lee, supra n. 2, at 203–4.

16. Id. at 216 (discussing women on higher floors), 205 (discussing replacement of used sinks and toilets).

a frame of mind that requires such extreme measures approaches irrationality to ordinary thinking. However, to speak of arbitrariness or irrationality implies that some absolute standards exist that permit final value judgments. The doubtful nature of such assumptions can easily be shown. They are expressions of ethnocentrism. To the equally ethnocentric Gypsy the validity of the rules of *Romaniya* is beyond dispute. Their "rationality" is as self-evident as their irrationality is to the outside observer. To this frame of mind further explanations are offensive, as the following illustration shows.

Romaniya prohibits the articulation of intimate sexual matters, especially in mixed company. A Gypsy woman to whom passages on these matters were read reacted with the caustic statement that this was "trash." To her it was obvious that no further explanation was needed. In fact, any attempt at giving reasons, both for the read materials and her response, would have violated the same rule, thus aggravating the offense. Whenever one is faced with this form of an impasse, including in our legal system, it is possible that the outer bounds of comprehension have been reached. Thus what is declared to be clear could sometimes have elements of the opposite. The purportedly self-evident, combined with an unwillingness to engage in further discourse, could mean that the matter concerned is not obvious at all.[17] One is faced with unknown and therefore threatening issues. Social taboos may have the function of warding off further inquiries.

An added complication relates to the efficacy of legal rules. One would assume that irrational rules are less effective than rational ones. However, this assumption may not be accurate. The effectiveness of *Romaniya* over a millennium may have been largely due to the religious factors that are inextricably tied to law, but inimicable to rational explanation. The whole distinction between rationality or irrationality of rules may be irrelevant for the Roma. Even if one were to call these rules irrational, their binding force is perceived to be tied not to human reasoning, but to divine forces. A rule is there, so to say, because "it is." The *gaje* who look for explanations only demonstrate their fundamental ignorance. They are not "in the know." Even Gypsies from a different branch of the Roma, with somewhat different rules, merely prove that they are not "our kind of Gypsies."[18] Orthodox beliefs, among the Roma as well as Judeo-Christian cultures, will resist attempts to explain the reasons for a given rule, but merely insist that it is to be strictly followed. As Lee explains, *Romaniya* is really based in an ancient folk religion going back to Indian sources,[19] and efforts to explain it contain the seeds of doubt. As soon as rules are perceived to require a rational basis, they can be attacked by examining their elements. A flaw in a single element of a rule of law may destroy the logic of

17. Daube, "The Self-Understood in Legal History," in *Collected Studies in Roman Law* 1277, 1285 (David Cohen & Dieter Simon eds., 1991). See also Carmichael, supra n. 9, at 000–000.

18. Lee, supra n. 2, at 197.

19. Id. at 209 n. 24. Cf. Carmichael, supra n. 9, at 128–31 (discussing supposedly irrational rules in Jewish law).

the whole. Resorting to science could be especially damaging because scientific knowledge is constantly modified and revised.

Within the American legal culture these factors are not unknown. Any attorney has experienced that efforts to sustain a view by legal reasoning are often felt to be irritating by those who are listening. To rely on rational explanation may be intuitively felt by them to be a sign of weakness that may undermine the majesty of the law. On the other hand, pure invocation of irrationality is not likely to work under contemporary conditions either. The belief systems in a modern state are too heterogeneous for this form of power exercise. A system of law that stresses the protection of individual rights, if necessary against the family and the state, is bound to insist on attempts at rational explanation and thus, in comparison to *Romaniya*, may be relatively vulnerable. A possible question is whether attempts at rationality in law are really hiding continued irrational factors that paradoxically either may be deplorable or may add to the stability of the system, depending on one's point of observation.

III. CRIMINALIZATION

Caffrey and Mundy, Lee, Sutherland, and I variously refer to the criminalization of the Gypsies by the dominant society.[20] Since criminalization is not a trait of the described group, but the result of a characterization imposed from the outside, one might wonder whether this aspect is beyond the scope of this volume. Yet it is no accident that this topic comes up in descriptions of Gypsy law. Much of the so-called criminal propensity ascribed to the Gypsies is based on disregard or ignorance of the rules of *Romaniya* that are followed by the Roma. Even if these rules are pointed out by expert witnesses, they tend to be dismissed as irrelevant by the police or the courts or, as Grönfors and Sutherland document, are used to sustain convictions.[21] These essays contain examples of this dilemma.

Use of multiple names, misuse of social security numbers, or otherwise inadequate means of identification, easily explainable under Gypsy law as not being based on illegal motives, are taken routinely as evidence of criminal intent.[22] There is an overwhelming pressure on Gypsies to confess to deeds that were not committed, to avoid consequences that are unbearable to them. As Sutherland explains, a prison term for a Gypsy, being deprived of any association with his family and peers, amounts to the equivalent of solitary confinement. Gypsies are on a starvation diet in prison because they do not eat food that, under their notions, is wrongly prepared

20. See, e.g., Caffrey & Mundy, chap. 4 "Informal Systems of Justice: The Formation of Law Within Gypsy Communities," chap. 4; Lee, supra n. 2, at 299–300; Sutherland, supra n. 1, at 238; Weyrauch, supra n. 5, at 250–52.

21. Grönfors, *Finnish Roma*, supra n. 1, at 154 n. 13; Sutherland, supra n. 1, at 237–39.

22. Lee, supra n. 2 at 198–99 (explaining use of different names); Sutherland, supra n. 1, at 233–35 (explaining alleged misuse of social security number).

and served under conditions that are polluting.[23] The whole prison environment, being conceived and administered by non-Gypsies, is severely polluting, although the criminal sentence as such carries no stigma to the Roma. The pollution is so serious that a separate formal proceeding before a Gypsy court (*kris*) may be required to reinstate the convicted Rom to full status among his fellow Gypsies.[24]

Under *Romaniya* any contact with dogs is polluting, dogs (and cats) being perceived as inherently unclean animals. The potential physical contact with police dogs is consequently viewed as a frightening threat, not because of fear of attack as the police may surmise, but because of concern of being polluted.[25] The presence of a police dog during investigation or detention, as far as the Roma are concerned, may amount to torture. A strip search may be experienced as a permanent impairment. Danger of detection is not the issue, but concern about being polluted. It may severely impair the marital chances of unmarried young Gypsy women.[26] Any of these and related incidents is likely to trigger responses from the Gypsies that, to the police, confirm their suspicions of a guilty conscience. Sources from other jurisdictions confirm this state of affairs.

Martti Grönfors has described the problem of criminalization of Gypsies, based on extensive field research in Finland.[27] His hypotheses and conclusions, although couched in general terms, relate mainly to his observations in 1975. Citing Émile Durkheim, he suggests that any society, regardless of its political or economic conditions, needs its criminals.[28] The dominant group within any society, in looking toward potential threats, is likely to focus on those segments of the population that are least able to defend themselves. Because of this focus of attention, Grönfors

23. Sutherland, supra n. 1, at 240.

24. Id. at 240–41.

25. See Lee, supra n. 2, at 208 (discussing dogs and cats as polluting); Grönfors, infra n. 34 and accompanying text (discussing use of police dogs during interrogations). See also Judith Okely, *The Traveller Gypsies* 91–97 (1983) (explaining animal symbolism, including of dogs and cats, among Gypsies).

26. See Dowling & Gomex, "Gypsies," *Life*, Oct. 1992, at 47–53; Morlin & Nappi, "Gypsy Daughters Say 1986 Search Violated Culture," *Spokane Spokesman Rev.*, Sept. 18, 1992, at A1. On the same case, see State v. Marks, 790 P.2d 138, 142 (Wash. 1990) (mentioning "egregious behavior" of the investigating police). See also Weyrauch & Bell, supra n. 5, at 54 n. 184.

27. Martti Grönfors, *Ethnic Minorities and Deviance: The Relationship Between the Finnish Gypsies and the Police* (University of Helsinki Sociology of Law Series No. 1, 1979) [hereinafter Grönfors, *Helsinki Report*]. This monograph is an abridged version of Martti Grönfors, *Finnish Gypsies and the Police: An Examination of a Racial Minority and Its Relationship with Law Enforcement Agents* (1979) (unpublished Ph.D. thesis, London School of Economics and Political Science) (on file with the London School of Economics Library). See also a further abridged version, id., "Police Perception of Social Problems and Clients: The Case of the Gypsies in Finland," 9 *Int'l J. Soc. L.* 345 (1981). Because the research on police attitudes by Grönfors is not contained in this symposium, I have attempted to summarize his complex findings in the following paragraphs. However, for a full authentication of his evidence and conclusions, reading of the actual *Helsinki Report* or at least of the article on police perception is suggested.

28. Grönfors, *Helsinki Report*, supra n. 27, at 32, citing Durkheim, "The Normal and the Pathological," in *The Sociology of Crime and Delinquency* 11–14 (Marvin E. Wolfgang, Leonard Savitz & Norman Johnston eds., 2d ed. 1970).

maintains, it is inevitable that these minorities have the highest rate of crimes and constitute the highest proportion of the prison population.[29] Police statistics of arrests are misleading because, as the Finnish experience shows, they tend to validate preconceived notions on criminality held by police officers and the general public.

Since the police are charged with maintaining law and order, many of their attitudes and conduct, Grönfors suggests, are occupational hazards that to some extent are unavoidable. The police force is charged with defending established values in situations that often permit only limited time for reflection. Its members tend to be moved by a spirit of "moral indignation" that is likely to be directed toward outgroups, such as the Gypsies.[30] Close observation and higher police presence result in inflated arrest statistics. Grönfors stresses that criminality occurs in any group or population, but he documents special circumstances in regard to the Finnish Gypsies.

Based on information gathered from the Helsinki Criminal Investigation Bureau, Grönfors found that the police reports on crime often related to the same group of Gypsies. These persons were held in low repute as deviants within their own Romani communities. A closer examination revealed that the Gypsies involved had been taken from their families in early infancy and, after having spent their formative years in institutions, had lost contact with the values as reflected in *Romaniya*. Yet their multiple crime sprees inflated the police statistics, seemingly supporting the charge that Gypsies have a general propensity for crime.[31] Similar observations were made by Lee for Canada. Young Gypsy men who were arrested and convicted for robbery were mostly from marriages in which the mother was a non-Gypsy, or had been raised in foster homes by non-Gypsies.[32]

Independently, Grönfors conducted interviews with Finnish police officers. They overwhelmingly reported that they target the Kaale Gypsies for observation. They

29. Grönfors, *Helsinki Report,* supra n. 27, at 33. For comparative references on blacks and Mexican-Americans in the United States, Indians in the United States and Canada, and Maoris in New Zealand, see id. at 13–36. Similar findings have been reported from Germany and Switzerland. See Angelika Pitsela, *Straffälligkeit und Viktimisierung ausländischer Minderheiten in der Bundesrepublik Deutschland* 146–51 (1968) (reporting on xenophobia as a source of criminalization of foreign minorities); letter from Gunther Arzt, Professor of Criminal Law and Criminology, University of Bern, Switzerland, to Walter O. Weyrauch (June 9, 1994) (on file with author) (relating to the criminalization of Gypsies).

30. See, e.g., Grönfors, *Helsinki Report,* supra n. 27, at 44–52 (background and moral dilemma of police), 139 ("moral indignation").

31. Id. at 58–65.

32. Lee, supra. n. 2, at 211. As reported, more than six hundred Gypsy children were taken from their parents by a Swiss welfare agency (*Pro Juventute*) between 1926 and 1973 and placed in foster homes and institutions for their "well-being." According to a Swiss lawyer, Stephan Frischknecht, "many of the children wound up in prisons, mental institutions or juvenile detention centers." Some of the children, without being integrated into Swiss society, no longer identified with their Gypsy parents. The President of Switzerland, Alphons Egli, issued a formal apology to the Swiss Gypsy community in 1986 for the past government-supported program. Netter, "Swiss Gypsies: A Tale of Vanishing Children," *N.Y. Times,* June 9, 1986, at A9. Actually, Jenische seem to have been mostly involved in the Swiss program, although Gypsy children may have shared the same fate. The Jenische are not Gypsies, but are often confused with them. See Angus Fraser, *The Gypsies* 254, 296–97 (1992).

stop cars driven by Gypsies, ask for identification, and detain the Gypsies concerned to check whether any charges are outstanding. Since overnight detentions are a frightening experience to Gypsies, Grönfors concludes that many confessions are given for the sole purpose of being released after posting bail or paying a fine.[33] The interviewed officers were aware of Gypsy peculiarities, such as their claustrophobia and their fear of dogs. Without knowing the reasons for these attitudes, they may have used them to facilitate arrests and confessions.[34] The police maintained that they treat the public equally, but that in case of the Gypsies special considerations should apply. One interviewee stated that "[i]f one wants to look closely enough, something can always be found."[35] The actual wording of statements contained often a curious mixture of claims to objectivity and claims to superior knowledge based on rumor. Other interviews stated that Gypsies should be forced to work, put in detention camps, sent back to where they came from, or worse.[36]

Reported reactions of Gypsies to police behavior, according to Grönfors, were largely confirmed by statements made independently by police. Essentially, police expectations of Gypsy criminality corresponded to Gypsy expectations that they were going to be treated in a discriminatory and violent way.[37] One may disagree with Grönfors' presentation, and he notes himself in this volume that complete neutrality is not possible.[38] It coincides, however, with observations that can be made in other countries. Police publications in the United States, as well as reports on supposed Gypsy criminality in the media, seem to confirm similar attitudes.[39] Whatever one may think about my highly condensed summary of the relation between the Finnish Kaale and the police, as described in the Helsinki Report, at a minimum it should make anyone cautious before assuming an innate criminality of the Romani people.

33. Grönfors, *Helsinki Report*, supra n. 27, at 95–96, 111–12, 124–26 (stopping of cars driven by Gypsies and checking for outstanding arrest warrants), 115 (securing confessions from Gypsies).

34. Id. at 114 (reporting police statements about Gypsy claustrophobia and weight loss in prison), 117 (reporting police interviews stating that Gypsies are "as amenable as sheep" and "don't resist arrest usually," if dogs are present).

35. Id. at 95.

36. Id. at 102 (alleged proclivity of Gypsies for stealing, based on hearsay), 83–84 (reproducing police interviews mentioning forced labor, detention camps, deportation, and even killing).

37. Finnish Gypsies questioned by Grönfors seemed to have taken the view that they had not been sufficiently on guard toward the police and, to that extent, had to blame themselves for whatever misfortune befell them. See Grönfors, *Helsinki Report*, supra at 27, at 120–30.

38. Grönfors, supra n. 1, at 151, n. 6.

39. Police publications and manuals are characterized by a law-and-order orientation and tend to assume a criminal propensity of Gypsies. They often include detailed descriptions of scams attributed to Gypsies. See, e.g., John B. McLaughlin, *Gypsy Lifestyles* (1980); Roy House, *Introduction to Investigations Involving the Rom* (a.k.a. Gypsies) (n.d.) (unpublished typescript, mimeographed, on file with the author). In a chapter, *Gypsy Criminality as Seen by the Police*, Grönfors comes to different conclusions, deploring the absence of reliable research. Grönfors, *Helsinki Report*, supra n. 27, at 88–119. The chapter contains a detailed examination of alleged stealing, shoplifting, and pickpocketing, crimes commonly said to be practiced by Gypsies. Id. at 98–105. For media representation of Gypsies, see, e.g., Ian Hancock, *The Pariah Syndrome; An Account of Gypsy Slavery and Persecution* 143–62 (1987).

IV. SOME THEORETICAL CONSIDERATIONS

On the general level of legal theory I can see a possible relationship between criminal law and conflict of laws. Conflicts can be viewed as a branch of legal knowledge that is willing to recognize the autonomy of a foreign legal system. This spirit of tolerance may result in the application of foreign law in local courts, except in extreme cases in which public policy demands otherwise. The fundamental nonrecognition or ignorance of a foreign legal system, as is the case with Gypsy law, is likely to result in the criminalization of that foreign legal culture. This consequence is almost unavoidable because the local powers, in the absence of conflict rules, are bound to express official disapproval or "moral indignation." Angus Fraser's article shows the historical basis for this view. He demonstrates that Gypsies were accorded considerable autonomy in the early phases of their history in Europe. At a later time systematic persecutions were substituted, evolving in some areas into chattel slavery.[40] Lee reports attempted recognition of Gypsy law in some Southern California courts, but these efforts appear to have been unsuccessful and would, in any event, relate to an isolated incident.[41]

Also of import is the relationship between autonomy and assimilation. Demands for assimilation to the values of a dominant culture are antithetical to the conception of autonomy. The Finnish experience indicates that assimilation of Gypsies can sometimes become the source of genuine, as distinguished from imagined, criminality. This result seems to follow from the fact that adherence to the traditional Romani family values and *Romaniya* is weakened, while corresponding recognition within the dominant society is not forthcoming.[42] In these instances the benefits of the original legal culture are no longer fully accessible, yet the substituted legal culture remains dominant—in other words, insists on its inherent superiority. Individual minorities might react differently to this situation, but social deviance appears to be a possible result.

For positive judicial reactions toward Gypsies in the United States, see Saint Francis College v. Al-Khazraji, 481 U.S. 604, 612 (1987) (dictum by Justice White referring to Gypsies as a group entitled to constitutional protection); Janko v. Illinois State Toll Highway Auth., 704 F. Supp. 1531 (N.D. Ill. 1989) (ruling in favor of Gypsy plaintiff in Title VII employment discrimination suit, relying on *Saint Francis College*); Spiritual Psychic Science Church of Truth v. Azusa, 703 P.2d 1119 (Cal. 1985) (holding that municipal ordinance aimed at Gypsies that prohibited fortune-telling and any related activity violated Cal. Const. art. I, § 2); State v. Marks, 790 P.2d 138 (Wash. 1990) (ruling in favor of Gypsy plaintiffs in a matter relating to a police search). Traditionally, Gypsies have refrained from addressing non-Gypsy authorities with their grievances; thus, these few instances may have a significance beyond their number.

40. Fraser, "Juridical Autonomy Among Fifteenth and Sixteenth Century Gypsies," chap. 6.
41. Lee, supra n. 2, at 228.
42. Grönfors, *Helsinki Report,* supra n. 27, at 63–64, 139–44.

TWO

Autonomous Lawmaking: The Case of the "Gypsies"

Walter O. Weyrauch and Maureen Anne Bell

This essay is a study of the laws and legal processes of the Romani people, traditionally known as Gypsies.[1] The account of the autonomous legal system of the Romani people provided here may appear so incredible that some readers may believe that it is based not on research but on insupportable construction. In fact, this account finds its support in the extensive and amorphous nonlegal literature and from the few Romani sources available.

The essay discusses the highly developed internal laws of the Gypsies to illustrate how private lawmaking is central to the everyday workings of society. The Vlax Roma, the largest Gypsy group in the United States, have laws that are generations old, administered by their own courts (*kris*) and judges (*krisnitorya*). For centuries, their courts have functioned autonomously virtually without regard for those

We are indebted to Frank Allen, Gunther Arzt, Stanley Ingber, Lynn LoPucki, and Rosalie Sanderson for their valuable suggestions. Special thanks are due to Ian Hancock, a British-Hungarian Rom and Professor of Linguistics at the University of Texas, for his numerous comments and valuable critique on earlier drafts of the manuscript.

1. The terminological difficulties regarding the word "Gypsy," and the conceptual problems resulting from them, are described in detail in Part II, *infra.* "Gypsy" is a designation used by non-Gypsies to describe the ethnic people who call themselves "Roma." English-language scholarship still refers widely to "Gypsies" rather than "Roma." *See* Jan Yoors, *Gypsy,* 13 ENCYCLOPEDIA AMERICANA 646, 646 (Int'l ed. 1989) [hereinafter Yoors, AMERICANA]; *Gypsy,* 5 NEW ENCYCLOPEDIA BRITANNICA 593 (15th ed. 1990). Difficulties exist in other languages as well. The German word *Zigeuner* is no longer used in scholarly writings. A German author reports that, consequently, she began using the word "Roma" in her writings, Rumanian Gypsies, however, objected to this usage. They preferred to be called *Zigeuner.* Herta Müller, *Der Staub ist blind—die Sonne ein Krüppel,* FRANKFURTER ALLGEMEINE ZEITUNG, May 4, 1991, Bilder und Zeiten at 1, 2 (postscript to article).

This essay uses the term "Gypsy" interchangeably with the term "Roma" to reflect the fact that its research depends on both Gypsy and non-Gypsy sources. Gypsy authors such as Ian Hancock have used the term "Gypsy" when addressing a non-Gypsy audience. *See* IAN HANCOCK, THE PARIAH

of the host country. Although these judicial gatherings are not officially recognized and, if noticed, tend to be misunderstood, they effectively impose sanctions within their own communities. A detailed examination of the Gypsy legal system can sensitize us to the private lawmaking that takes place in American society.

Analysis of law usually focuses on the law of the state. This essay, however, uses the law of the Gypsies as an example of an autonomous legal system, one which operates outside the parameters of state law. It argues that in most cases in which the autonomous legal system of the Gypsies clashes directly with the law of the host country, the private legal system of the Gypsies prevails. More frequently, however, autonomous legal systems and state law interact in a more subtle manner. Even when they do not come into conflict, each can powerfully influence the other. Thus, the norms of any legal system, public or private, may only be preserved intact through a cultural isolation which is nearly impossible to achieve.

Apart from its central concern with autonomous private lawmaking, this essay is timely for its consideration of the relationship between ethnicity and law. Contemporary ethnic tensions have been a major factor in recent bitter confrontations around the world. Bosnia-Herzegovina, the Near East, Armenia and Azerbaijan, South Africa, India, and Sri Lanka, for example, all have been affected by ethnic confrontation. Within the United States, the 1992 Los Angeles riots may have been fueled in part by perceptions of the relationship between ethnicity and law. The Gypsies themselves are increasingly targets of persecution in Eastern Europe, where the collapse of communism has revived not only nationalism and ethnic pride, but also fanaticism and racial hatred. That hatred is often directed against the Gypsies, who, as scapegoats, are blamed for many past and present ills of society.[2] Some of this racial animosity may stem from ignorance and misinterpretation of the Gypsies' internal norms, which set them apart from other cultures.

Part I of this chapter discusses the concept of autonomous lawmaking and how it has been neglected in legal scholarship. It then explains why the Gypsies provide an optimal example for examining private law. Part II describes how problems of terminology and language render terms originating from non-Gypsy sources inadequate and misleading. It then traces the severe persecution of the Romani people from the Middle Ages to the present times, and discusses how this persecution has permanently affected the willingness of the Gypsies to collaborate with any structured inquiry into their culture, especially their law.

SYNDROME: AN ACCOUNT OF GYPSY SLAVERY AND PERSECUTION (1987) [hereinafter HANCOCK, PARIAH SYNDROME]. Throughout this Article we use the alternative spelling "Rumania" for Romania to stress that the term "Roma" for Gypsies is not linguistically related to Rumanian. This spelling is used by Hancock for the same reason.

2. Don Pavel, *Wanderers: Romania's Hidden Victims: New Assaults upon the Gypsy Minority*, NEW REPUBLIC, Mar. 4, 1991, at 12 (Juliana G. Pilon trans.); Carol J. Williams, *Gypsies Feel Curse of Hatred*, L.A. TIMES, Dec. 20, 1991, at A1.

Part III presents the essential features of Romani law, including its sanctions. It discusses the significance of Romani law for the survival of Romani culture. Part IV analyzes some crucial features shared by Gypsy law and other forms of private lawmaking in our own legal culture. It examines the roles of oral legal traditions, language, and legal strategies as they relate to the substance of law. In addition, it discusses how the laws of evidence in private lawmaking operate. Part V concludes the chapter by suggesting a concise theoretical framework to better understand private lawmaking and its relationship to state law.

I. INTRODUCTION: SOURCES OF LAW

State Law vs. Private Lawmaking

Commonly held assumptions about lawmaking have profound theoretical and practical consequences. The traditional view is that law originates with the state.[3] Even if we recognize contracts as a form of private lawmaking, it is assumed that we make formal agreements essentially with delegated state power.[4] According to these notions, the legitimacy of lawmaking depends on the authority of the state, or at least on the degree to which the state tolerates private lawmaking. This view of the primacy of state law is of relatively recent origin. It can be traced to times of absolutism, when monarchs were perceived to be the ultimate lawgivers.[5] Created by the monarch for self-serving purposes, this conception of law reflects ideas that may no longer be applicable under contemporary standards and values. The time is ripe to reexamine this limited view of law and to broaden its scope.

Eugen Ehrlich suggested that in the Middle Ages, prior to the rise of monarchies when state authority as we understand it arose, most lawmaking took place in a variety of autonomous institutions and groups, such as cities and guilds, leav-

---

3. *See, e.g.,* W. FRIEDMANN, LEGAL THEORY 120–22, 258–60 (5th ed. 1967) (discussing theories of Thomas Hobbes and John Austin); *see also* H.L.A. HART, THE CONCEPT OF LAW 49–76 (1961) (discussing relationship between sovereign and society); HANS KELSEN, GENERAL THEORY OF LAW AND STATE 181–207 (Anders Wedberg trans., 1945); JULIUS STONE, LEGAL SYSTEMS AND LAWYERS' REASONINGS 63–136 (1964) (discussing theories of John Austin and Hans Kelsen). The jurisprudential conception of legal positivism often mentioned in this context is less clear than commonly assumed. *See* Helen Silving, *Positive Natural Law*, 3 NAT. L.F. 24, 27–30 (1958).

4. *See, e.g.,* HART, *supra* note 3, at 94 ("We have already described in some detail the rules which confer on individuals power to vary their initial positions under the primary rules. . . . The kinship of these rules with the rules of change involved in the notion of legislation is clear, and as recent theory such as Kelsen's has shown, many of the features which puzzle us in the institutions of contract or property are clarified by thinking of the operations of making a contract or transferring property as the exercise of limited legislative powers by individuals."); *see also* KELSEN, *supra* note 3, at 204 (noting delegation of power to contract from legal order).

5. EUGEN EHRLICH, FUNDAMENTAL PRINCIPLES OF THE SOCIOLOGY OF LAW 14–38 (Walter L. Moll trans., 1936).

ing large geographic areas unregulated.[6] Without an effective central government, private organizations could maintain considerable autonomy in making rules to govern their own affairs.[7]

Even though the modern state reaches across broad swaths of territory, its regulations do not always penetrate all social ordering. The modern equivalent of the laws of autonomous medieval groups is the informal lawmaking which takes place whenever people join in groups, associations, or institutions to pursue common ob-

6. *Id.* at 14–38. For an analysis of Ehrlich's theories about the evolution of law, see William H. Page, *Professor Ehrlich's Czernowitz Seminar of Living Law, in* 1914 PROC. ASS'N. AM. L. SCH. 46, *reprinted in* READINGS IN JURISPRUDENCE 825 (Jerome Hall ed., 1938). The theories of von Savigny similarly argue that law, like language, forms within peoples "by internal silently-operating powers, not by the arbitrary will of a law-giver." FRIEDRICH KARL VON SAVIGNY, OF THE VOCATION OF OUR AGE FOR LEGISLATION AND JURISPRUDENCE 30 (Abraham Hayward trans., spec. ed, 1986) (1814). Ehrlich also acknowledged his indebtedness to Otto von Gierke for his writings about the internal ordering of associations. EHRLICH, *supra* note 5, at 24 (referring to OTTO VON GIERKE, DAS DEUTSCHE GENOSSENSCHAFTSRECHT [1868]). For further background on Gierke's political philosophy, see generally OTTO VON GIERKE, POLITICAL THEORIES OF THE MIDDLE AGES (Frederic W. Maitland trans., 1900).

Contemporary scholarship has focused primarily on microlegal systems, which include small groups, aggregated units that are characterized by little or no commonality of purpose, and even casual encounters between individuals. *See generally* THOMAS A. COWAN & DONALD A. STRICKLAND, THE LEGAL STRUCTURE OF A CONFINED MICROSOCIETY (University of California, Berkeley Working Paper No. 34, 1965); GROUP DYNAMIC LAW: EXPOSITION AND PRACTICE (David A. Funk ed., 1988); LEOPOLD J. POSPISIL, ANTHROPOLOGY OF LAW: A COMPARATIVE THEORY (1971) [hereinafter POSPISIL, ANTHROPOLOGY OF LAW]; WALTER O. WEYRAUCH, THE LAW OF A SMALL GROUP (University of California, Berkeley Working Paper No. 54, 1967) [hereinafter WEYRAUCH, THE LAW OF A SMALL GROUP]; Walter O. Weyrauch, *The "Basic Law" or Constitution of a Small Group,* 27 J. SOC. ISSUES 49 (1971), *reprinted in* LAW, JUSTICE, AND THE INDIVIDUAL IN SOCIETY 41 (June L. Tapp & Felice J. Levine eds., 1977) [hereinafter Weyrauch, *Basic Law*]; Walter O. Weyrauch, *Law in Isolation—the Penthouse Astronauts,* TRANSACTION, June 1968, at 39 [hereinafter Weyrauch, *Law in Isolation*]; Michael Reisman, *Lining Up: The Microlegal System of Queues,* 54 U. CIN. L. REV. 417 (1985) [hereinafter Reisman, *Lining Up*]; Michael Reisman, *Looking, Staring and Glaring: Microlegal Systems and Public Order,* 12 DENV. J. INT'L L. & POL'Y 165 (1983) [hereinafter Reisman, *Looking, Staring and Glaring*]; Michael Reisman, *Rapping and Talking to the Boss: The Microlegal System of Two People Talking, in* CONFLICT AND INTEGRATION: COMPARATIVE LAW IN THE WORLD TODAY 61 (Institute of Comparative Law in Japan ed., 1988) [hereinafter Reisman, *Rapping*].

Stewart Macaulay has written numerous articles about the development of informal legal culture using examples in the United States. *E.g.,* Stewart Macaulay, *Images of Law in Everyday Life: The Lessons of School, Entertainment, and Spectator Sports,* 21 LAW & SOC'Y REV. 185 (1987); Stewart Macaulay, *Noncontractual Relations in Business: A Preliminary Study,* 28 AM. SOC. REV. 55 (1963); Stewart Macaulay, *Popular Legal Culture: An Introduction,* 98 YALE L.J. 1545 (1989). Recently scholars have pointed to the Jewish legal tradition as expressed in the Torah to provide further support for their argument that law should be defined by communal acceptance rather than by reference to the law of the state. *E.g.,* Robert M. Cover, *The Supreme Court, 1982 Term—Foreword: Nomos and Narrative,* 97 HARV. L. REV. 4, 11–19 (1983); Suzanne L. Stone, *In Pursuit of the Counter-Text: The Turn to the Jewish Legal Model in Contemporary American Legal Theory,* 106 HARV. L. REV. 813, 865–72 (1993) [hereinafter Stone, *Counter-Text*].

7. For a discussion of autonomy in German law, see JOHN C. GRAY, THE NATURE AND SOURCES OF THE LAW 158–59, 325–28 (2d ed. 1921); *see also* Cover, *supra* note 6, at 26–33 (discussing origin of legal meanings in insular autonomous communities).

jectives. This essay adopts the broad definition of law proposed by Cowan and Strickland in 1965:

> Law is an existential condition in which men are carriers of rights and duties, privileges and immunities. No formal structure supporting the system of law need be visible. Those accustomed to seeing law only in its formal institutions, in terms of statutes, decisions, judges, legislators and administrators miss the point. Law can be found any place and any time that a group gathers together to pursue an objective. The rules, open or covert, by which they govern themselves, and the methods and techniques by which these rules are enforced, is the law of the group. Judged by this broad standard, most law-making is too ephemeral to be even noticed. But when conflict within the group ensues, and it is forced to decide between conflicting claims, law arises in an overt and relatively conspicuous fashion. The challenge forces decision, and decisions make law.[8]

This description covers a wide range of human activities in a continuum that encompasses tribal law and other examples of informal lawmaking, as well as the more formal charters and bylaws of corporations.

The extent to which such laws are visibly formalized may affect the relationship between private lawmaking authority and state law. If private lawmaking is more visible, the state will assume control by legislation and regulation. Less de facto autonomy will remain in the hands of the private organization. Frequently, the visible forms of private lawmaking such as charters and bylaws coincide with unwritten customs which are enforced by sanctions. Thus, quite independently from the mandates of the state, various levels of private law may either supplement or conflict with each other. Any corporate lawyer is aware of corporate customs supported by sanctions that supplement but sometimes conflict with the more formal laws of the state. These customs may relate to corporate etiquette, career patterns, or entertainment expenses, or to such matters as maintaining corporate secrets or making payments to foreign officials. Other forms of private lawmaking may have an even broader range. Recent scholarship maintains that fleeting human encounters do not take place in a legal void, but are governed by culturally determined understandings and customs which cause them to be more rigidly enforced than the laws of the state.[9]

---

8. COWAN & STRICKLAND, *supra* note 6, at i. Fuller has described informal lawmaking under the rubric of "implicit law," which he distinguishes from "made law," i.e., a statute passed under the authority of the state. LON L. FULLER, ANATOMY OF LAW 43–49 (1968) [hereinafter FULLER, ANATOMY]. This conceptualization of informal lawmaking may include the rules governing a camping trip of friends, *id.* at 48–49, the custom of merchants, *id.* at 45, or tribal law, *id.* at 74–75.

9. Reisman has described microlegal systems that govern encounters on the street, the act of waiting in lines, and communications between subordinates and superiors. *See generally* Reisman, *Lining Up, supra* note 6; Reisman, *Looking, Staring and Glaring, supra* note 6; Reisman, *Rapping, supra* note 6. It should come as no surprise that related legal dynamics govern both microlegal and macrolegal systems. Both systems try to maximize their efficacy within limits imposed by circumstances such as competing legal systems.

Nevertheless, there are still many intellectual obstacles to acknowledging these forms of private lawmaking. Some view private lawmaking as interference with the autonomy of the individual and as lacking fairness and due process.[10] Private lawmaking also challenges the authority of the state. The many competing interests that characterize contemporary life inspire apprehension that chaos would ensue if any single group of participants was recognized as having autonomous rule-making powers,[11] but that does not mean that such rules no longer exist or have lost their effectiveness. The effectiveness of state-sponsored laws in statute books or appellate court opinions depends in part on how well they incorporate common understandings of private laws and customs.[12]

10. Perceived injustice commonly occurs in microlegal systems such as the family, schools, and the workplace. *See* Allen Barton & Saul Mendlovitz, *The Experience of Injustice as a Research Problem*, 13 J. LEGAL EDUC. 24, 30 (1960). One aspect related by Melitta Schmideberg concerned parent-child relations:

> A child may be punished for something which was passed over yesterday and is joked about to-morrow; it is blamed for things its parents do without qualms. Adults usually have some neat explanation at hand to cover up their inconsistent and unjust behavior against which children are helpless. Whenever trouble arises the child is likely to be held responsible, and there are very few adults who would ever admit to a child that they had been in the wrong. Justice between parents and children does not exist because there is no equality, and those in authority are judges in their own cause. The nursery is like a fascist state; a great parade is made of justice but it depends on the good-will of the authorities whether they dispense justice or punish whoever dares to complain.
>
> The fact that men may prefer death to a life without freedom and justice shows how bitterly they must have resented the lack of these in their childhood.

Melitta Schmideberg, *On Querulance*, 15 PSYCHOANALYTIC Q. 472, 488 (1946). For a critical description of the romantic view of private lawmaking as more just and democratic than any other form of law imposed by a ruler or the state, see FULLER, ANATOMY, *supra* note 8, at 70.

11. Fuller argues against the notion that autonomous private lawmaking necessarily results in chaos. LON L. FULLER, THE MORALITY OF LAW 124–29 (1964) [hereinafter FULLER, MORALITY]. *See generally Developments in the Law—Judicial Control of Actions of Private Associations*, 76 HARV. L. REV. 983 (1963).

12. Sometimes appellate courts openly admit the significance of private laws and customs, for example when usage (private lawmaking) has supplanted statutory provisions. *See, e.g.*, Spurgeon v. Jamieson Motors, 521 P.2d 924 (Mont. 1974). Usage in the Wisconsin lumber industry played a significant role in the application of contract law. JAMES W. HURST, LAW AND ECONOMIC GROWTH: THE LEGAL HISTORY OF THE LUMBER INDUSTRY IN WISCONSIN 1836–1915, at 290 (1964); *see also* E. ALLAN FARNSWORTH, CONTRACTS §§7.13–.14 (1982); FULLER, ANATOMY, *supra* note 8, at 57–59 (arguing that interpretation acts as a means to adjust "made law" to "implicit law").

With respect to the First Amendment, Ingber maintains that "communal values" should be recognized and protected within institutional settings. Stanley Ingber, *Rediscovering the Communal Worth of Individual Rights: The First Amendment in Institutional Contexts*, 69 TEX. L. REV. 1, 98–102 (1990). A constitutional document, like any other written enactment, tends to be interpreted and supplemented by an unwritten body of private law. Weyrauch, *Basic Law, supra* note 6, at 52–53. Indeed, the laws of associations, groups, and institutions have been characterized as a body of unwritten constitutional law that has grown outside of the written constitution. FULLER, MORALITY, *supra* note 11, at 128–29 (citing Charles E. Wyzanski, *The Open Window and the Open Door*, 35 CAL. L. REV. 336, 341–45 [1947]); *see also* Thomas C. Grey, *The Constitution as Scripture*, 37 STAN. L. REV. 1 (1984); Thomas C. Grey, *Do We Have an Unwritten Constitution?*, 27 STAN. L. REV. 703 (1975); Thomas C. Grey, *Origins of the Unwritten Constitution:*

Mechanical application of the law often creates perceptions of injustice and meets with substantial opposition.[13] This injustice results when written law lacks the support of unwritten laws and custom. Unwritten rules often have greater vitality and power than the traditional public laws that originate in the cerebral and abstract reasoning of the courts and legislatures. Decision makers work under a continuing pressure to incorporate customary rules into their decisions. Such incorporation takes place subtly. For instance, a court's formalistic application of law may be reversed on appeal as an abuse of discretion or a violation of established canons of interpretation. Yet, in their written opinions appellate courts rarely articulate that the basis for their decision rests at least as much on the amorphous body of private law as on public laws. Appellate judges may not even be aware that this is their source of law.[14]

At trial, in appellate courts, and in negotiations, a skillful lawyer avoids referring directly to private lawmaking. Instead an attorney merely hints that his case draws support from private lawmaking, while overtly reasoning in terms of state-made law. Indeed, lawyers' pleas to juries not to leave their common sense at the

---

Fundamental Law in American Revolutionary Thought, 30 STAN. L. REV. 843 (1978). Grey's theory of an "unwritten Constitution" appears mostly aspirational, invoking fundamental rights and natural law. The unwritten constitution described in Weyrauch, *Basic Law, supra* note 6, attempts to reflect reality rather than ideals. This form of unwritten law, although very powerful and to some extent beyond human control, can bring benefits. But it can also discriminate and oppress.

13. *See, e.g.,* Dred Scott v. Sandford, 60 U.S. 393 (1856) (using jurisdictional argument to dispose of issue of major national significance, citizenship of African Americans); *In re* Civil Rights Cases, 109 U.S. 3 (1883); Plessy v. Ferguson, 163 U.S. 537 (1896).

14. Most appellate courts do not explicitly recognize private lawmaking as such and are not conscious of its underlying dynamics. *But see* Marvin v. Marvin, 557 P.2d 106, 109 n.l (Cal. 1976) (recognizing that eightfold increase in nonmarital cohabitation called for decisive statement of law on this subject). Furthermore, private lawmaking has even greater influence in nonlitigative contexts, such as negotiations, and in the lower courts, especially when appeals are unlikely. Although empirical evidence is rare, many lawyers attest that trial judges adhere to precedent and statutory authority loosely and essentially dispose of cases according to inarticulate standards and hunches which reflect an immense and amorphous body of informal law. *See, e.g.,* KARL LLEWELLYN, THE CASE LAW SYSTEM IN AMERICA 78–80 (Paul Gewirtz ed. & Michael Ansaldi trans., 1989); Joseph C. Hutcheson, *The Judgment Intuitive: The Function of the "Hunch" in Judicial Decision,* 14 CORNELL L.Q. 274, 286–88 (1929); Willard M. McEwen, *What is Never in the Record but Always in the Case,* 8 ILL. L. REV. (1914).

Arzt has queried:

Quite generally one may ask, according to what rules do we conduct ourselves, because we normally do not consult the written law beforehand. . . . We are controlled in vast areas by reason, decency . . . and conformity. The latter functions differently in small groups, such as a faculty, than in larger settings. Viewed this way, perhaps the difference between oral and written concretization [of law] disappears?!

Letter from Gunther Arzt, Professor, University of Bern, Switzerland, to Walter O. Weyrauch, translated from German (Jan. 26, 1993) (on file with authors). The broad definition of law proposed by Cowan and Strickland, *supra* text accompanying note 8, may encompass some aspects of the phenomenon described by Arzt.

door can be understood as an appeal to interpret public law in conformity with private law. Lawyers may not be fully aware of this strategy and often credit "experience" for success.[15] The emphasis of legal education on the state's law makes it unlikely that a lawyer will be conscious of private lawmaking. Nevertheless, a good lawyer instinctively avoids arguing only legal technicalities because doing so often creates the impression that the case is weak. Lawyers instead stress social context, communal values, and public policies, which are often veiled references to private forms of lawmaking. This essay argues that private lawmaking often prevails over state law in direct conflicts between the two.[16]

In practice, private lawmaking pervasively influences the legal process. The sensitivity of lawyers and policymakers to private social norms often determines whether legislation is effective, whether cases are won or lost, or whether a legal argument is persuasive. Yet, legal theory and practice generally ignore this vast body of law. Bar examinations concentrate on traditional laws of the state, which, in their literal form, have only limited practical significance. Such an approach underestimates the importance of private law. Although lawyers do acknowledge the existence of private-law rules, they dismiss them as rules of expediency rather than accept them as coherent systems.[17]

These views treat the most important part of the legal process as purely a matter of common experience that is inevitably subservient to officially sanctioned laws. Law is divided into two spheres, the conscious laws of the state and the unconscious private laws, the latter of which are in fact substantially more important. If scholars can sensitize people to the pivotal role of private lawmaking by exposing its basic dynamics, legal theory will present a more accurate picture of legal re-

---

15. JEROME FRANK, LAW AND THE MODERN MIND 111 n.2 (1970) ("All successful lawyers are more or less consciously aware of this technique. But they seldom avow it even to themselves.").

16. See Walter O. Weyrauch et. al., *The Family as a Small Group, in* GROUP DYNAMIC LAW: EXPOSITION AND PRACTICE *supra* note 6, at 153, 156 [hereinafter Weyrauch, *Family*], where the following partly overlapping hypotheses are developed in detail. First, informal lawmaking has more vitality than the traditional law of the state. Second, in a clash between traditional state law and informal private law, the latter is likely to prevail. Third, legal characterizations are likely to be of little effect, unless supported by informal private law. Fourth, a result supported exclusively by the law of the state is likely to be perceived as inhumane and unjust. Fifth, an argument is likely to be persuasive if it can be supported by both the law of the state and informal private law. Sixth, discretionary decisions are likely to be based on informal private law. Seventh, discretionary decisions that violate the norms of private lawmaking are prone to be reversed on appeal. Eighth, legal counseling and planning must take account of informal law. For illustrations, see *infra* text accompanying notes 243–54, 266–69. In a conflict between the laws of the state and "folk norms" in negotiations, the latter tend to govern. Herbert Jacob, *The Elusive Shadow of the Law*, 26 LAW & SOC'Y REV. 565, 566–67 (1992).

17. *See* WALTER O. WEYRAUCH & SANFORD N. KATZ, AMERICAN FAMILY LAW IN TRANSITION 507–08 (1983) (discussing unwritten standards in adjudication of child custody disputes which deal with sexual taboos that "cannot be openly acknowledged"); *see also* Boroff v. Boroff, 250 N.W.2d 613, 617–18 (Neb. 1977) (noting trial court's improper refusal to award custody of twelve-year-old daughter to her divorced father because she should "get up to her maturity with the mother"), *infra* note 243.

ality. The dichotomy between the law in the books and the law in action,[18] the latter of which is based mostly on private lawmaking, would disappear.

Fostering Respect for Private Lawmaking

PARALLELS BETWEEN PRIVATE LAWMAKING AND TRIBAL LAW

This essay uses an intensive study of tribal laws[19] to illustrate how scholars can increase awareness of private lawmaking.[20] There are important parallels between legal cultures based on oral traditions and the unwritten laws within institutions such as courts, corporations, and university faculties.[21] In addition to the practical importance of these forms of lawmaking, legal scholars should not overlook the relevance of private law to theory. "Tribal" aspects of private law illuminate larger issues. This chapter does not maintain that contemporary institutions, such as law firms,[22] legislative committees,[23] juries and appellate

---

18. *See* EHRLICH, *supra* note 5, at 486–506 (discussing need for study of "living law" in addition to "legal propositions"); Roscoe Pound, *Law in Books and Law in Action*, 44 AM. L. REV. 12 (1910) (discussing relationship between public thought, feeling, and law in action).

19. For the purposes of this essay, "tribal law" means the norms of a homogeneous ethnic group, mostly based on oral tradition and supported by communal sanctions, which aim to regulate life and promote the common good. The use of the terms "tribe" or "tribal" does not impute any sense of primitiveness. The terms are useful for the limited purposes of this essay because they demonstrate that our law has numerous characteristics that also could be called tribal. These elements of our legal system lend themselves to comparisons with the laws of the Roma, as will become increasingly apparent as the chapter progresses. But see the references to "primitive law" in E. ADAMSON HOEBEL, THE LAW OF PRIMITIVE MAN 18–28 (1954); KARL. L. LLEWELLYN & E. ADAMSON HOEBEL, THE CHEYENNE WAY: CONFLICT AND CASE LAW IN PRIMITIVE JURISPRUDENCE 41–63 (1941).

20. In his comparative law classes Weyrauch found that students were persistently more interested in tribal law than in the laws of western Europe. The materials included, among others, HOEBEL, *supra* note 19, at 67–99 (discussing legal norms of "Eskimo" villages); JOHAN HUIZINGA, HOMO LUDENS: A STUDY OF THE PLAY ELEMENT IN CULTURE 84–86 (1950) (discussing legal culture of Inuit); and J.F. Holleman, *Disparities and Uncertainties in African Law and Judicial Authority: A Rhodesian Case Study*, 17 AFR. L. STUD. 1 (1979). The Holleman article has significant contemporary relevance. Holleman describes the effects of a conflict between colonial law and preexisting tribal norms. As faith in the existing tribal legal order was undermined, violent forms of self-help emerged that outwardly invoked earlier law. The resulting social disorder was combined with excessive demands for redress. Although the article is confined to African tribal history, the parallels to American urban riots are evident. Compare Holleman, *supra*, with reports of the Los Angeles riots in May 1992 following the Rodney King verdicts. *See, e.g., Understanding the Riots Part I: The Path to Fury*, L.A. TIMES, May 11, 1992, at T-1. See also reports of the Miami riots in May 1980, occurring after an all-white jury acquitted four white policemen who had beaten a black motorist to death. *See, e.g.,* BRUCE PORTER & MARVIN DUNN, THE MIAMI RIOTS OF 1980: CROSSING THE BOUNDS (1984), *reviewed by* Anthony Chase, *In the Jungle of Cities*, 84 MICH. L. REV. 737, 751–59 (1986).

21. *See* sources cited *supra* note 6.

22. *See generally* Walter O. Weyrauch, *An Anthropological Study of the Legal Profession: Erwin O. Smigel, The Wall Street Lawyer*, 113 U. PA. L. REV. 478 (1965) (book review) [hereinafter Weyrauch, *Legal Profession*].

23. The Clarence Thomas Senate confirmation hearings, in particular the televised hearings before the Senate Judiciary Committee involving Anita Hill, resembled a tribal court in numerous

courts,[24] university faculties,[25] corporations,[26] and families,[27] are "tribal," but merely suggests that they share characteristics with societies that are commonly referred to as tribes. There are close analogies between tribal lawmaking and informal private law in our daily lives. Thus, if we understand tribal law, we can better comprehend the operation of our own legal system.

The present analysis focuses on a tribal system that is operating autonomously within our society, largely unnoticed: the internal laws and procedures of the population known as "Gypsies." Perhaps the term "nation" would be more appropriate for Gypsies than "tribe,"[28] although the Gypsies lack many features usually attributed to nations, such as common territory and centralized government. The Gypsies do share, however, a common identity and ethnic origin, a common language, and an identifiable culture. A legal system of common basic characteristics also exists, even though it may differ in some respects among various ethnic subdivisions of the Roma.

---

respects: (1) the adjudicators were all male; (2) the standards applied were based on oral tradition; (3) no clear distinctions between facts and opinion were maintained; (4) no distinctions between procedure and substance were observable; (5) standards of relevance tended to be interpreted in the widest possible sense; (6) no exclusionary rules of evidence were applied; (7) the adjudicators and witnesses played to the wider audience; (8) the audience, although not physically present, played a major role in the adjudication, in that the presumed reaction of the audience affected all participants. *Cf.* Holleman, *supra* note 20, at 5–9 (characterizing tribal adjudication); *see also* Dennis E. Curtis, *The Fake Trial,* 65 S. CAL. L. REV. 1523 (1992) (analysis of Thomas/Hill hearings).

24. With respect to courts, see generally Walter F. Murphy, *Courts as Small Groups,* 79 HARV. L. REV. 1565 (1966); Eloise C. Snyder, *The Supreme Court as a Small Group,* 36 SOC. FORCES 232 (1958). With respect to juries, see generally Mortimer R. Kadish & Sanford H. Kadish, *The Institutionalization of Conflict: Jury Acquittals,* 27 J. SOC. ISSUES 199 (1971); Fred L. Strodtbeck & L. Harmon Hook, *The Social Dimensions of a Twelve-Man Jury Table,* 24 SOCIOMETRY 397 (1961).

25. *See generally* William L. Richard, Note, *Faculty Regulations of American Law Schools (A Survey),* 13 CLEV-MARSHALL L. REV. 581 (1964).

26. For a discussion of legal and sociological approaches to various such groups, see generally Joseph Taubman, *Law and Sociology in the Control of Small Groups,* 13 U. TORONTO L. REV. 23 (1959).

27. *See generally* Herma H. Kay, *The Family and Kinship System of Illegitimate Children in California Law,* 67(6) AM. ANTHROPOLOGIST 57 (1965); Weyrauch, *Family, supra* note 16.

28. The Romani Union, an international organization located in Hamburg, Germany, links national Gypsy organizations and has consultative status within the Economic and Social Council of the United Nations. The consultative status enables the Romani Union to speak as a nongovernmental organization at Economic and Social Council meetings. *List of Non-Governmental Organizations in Consultative Status with the Economic and Social Council in 1989: Note by the Secretary General,* U.N. ESCOR E/1989/INF/11 (1989); *see also* ANGUS FRASER, THE GYPSIES 315–18 (1992).

In the United States, Gypsies have been recognized as a distinctive ethnic group deserving protection under antidiscrimination law. Saint Francis College v. Al-Khazraji, 481 U.S. 604, 612 (1987) (dictum by Justice White referring to Gypsies in suit brought by person of Arab descent); Janko v. Illinois State Toll Highway Auth., 704 F. Supp. 1531 (N.D. Ill. 1989) (ruling in favor of Gypsy plaintiff in Title VII employment discrimination suit, relying on *Saint Francis College*).

REASONS FOR SELECTING GYPSY LAW

This essay focuses on the Roma because the conspicuous absence of legal scholarship on their laws and courts, amidst an otherwise vast body of literature, demonstrates that the academy is oblivious to the existence of embedded autonomous legal systems. The very idea that an autonomous, cohesive society with its own language and legal system exists in the United States (and elsewhere) surprises most theorists, and highlights the extent to which Gypsies have successfully maintained their invisibility within a larger host society.[29] Traditional legal scholarship presumes that different regionally identifiable legal systems may coexist and be compared. They may also conflict with each other; the ornate doctrine of conflict of laws has been developed to resolve these clashes. Yet, legal scholars have consistently failed to acknowledge the possibility that our legal system is permeated by other autonomous legal systems. These coexisting autonomous legal systems are fundamentally "foreign" to the laws of the state, and the study of those systems remains foreign to much of current legal scholarship.[30]

This essay resists examining a more remote tribal society, because distance in time and space encourages detachment. The Gypsies living among us help reinforce the thesis that autonomous private legal systems have a pervasive influence on daily life. Indeed, the Romani legal system coexists with the host legal order wherever Gypsies are present. Legal and political theories, because they concentrate on the laws of the state, have limited intellectual apparatus with which to recognize such coexisting legal systems. A broader conception of law is necessary to account for the flow of "tribal" law that emanates from associations, groups, and institutions.

29. *Cf.* HANCOCK, PARIAH SYNDROME, *supra* note 1, at 130 (noting that American Gypsies have learned to hide their identity in order to avoid discrimination); ANNE SUTHERLAND, GYPSIES: THE HIDDEN AMERICANS 290 (Reissue 1986) (1975) (commenting that most non-Gypsies are ignorant of or doubt the existence of Gypsies in United States); Albert W. Vogel, *The Least Known Minority,* CIV. RTS. DIG., Fall 1978, at 35; *see also* RONALD LEE, GODDAM GYPSY 9 (1971) [hereinafter LEE, AUTOBIOGRAPHY] ("The greatest strength of the Gypsies is their invisibility. It is not without good reason that many people consider them to be extinct, for the Roms themselves do everything in their power to perpetuate the myth of their non-existence.").

30. Some authors whose work is more related to the social sciences than to traditional legal research have commented upon the manner in which legally distinct subgroups may interact with a larger, enveloping society. *See* POSPISIL, ANTHROPOLOGY OF LAW, *supra* note 6, at 97–126, referring with qualifications to EHRLICH, *supra* note 5, at 24, 36–38; LLEWELLYN & HOEBEL, *supra* note 19, at 27–28; MAX WEBER ON LAW IN ECONOMY AND SOCIETY 17 (Max Rheinstein ed. & Edward Shils & Max Rheinstein trans., 1969); Laura Nader & Duane Metzger, *Conflict Resolution in Two Mexican Communities,* 65 AM. ANTHROPOLOGIST 584 (1963). *See also* LEOPOLD POSPISIL, THE ETHNOLOGY OF LAW, 54 (2d. ed. 1978) ("[T]here are in a society as many legal systems as there are functioning subgroups"); Weyrauch, *Basic Law, supra* note 6, at 49 ("Law can be viewed as a network of small group interaction. Basic characteristics of legal systems govern the interaction and permeate each individual small group."). In the Middle Ages the Gypsies were recognized as an *imperium in imperio,* with jurisdiction over their own affairs. FRASER, *supra* note 28, at 127.

II. IMPEDIMENTS TO RESEARCH ON GYPSY LAW

Impact of Terminology

The terminology used by non-Gypsies to describe the Romani people reflects hidden value judgments. The term "Gypsy" as used in scholarly writings and encyclopedias supports misconceptions that all Gypsies are migratory, roam the countryside, and are engaged in questionable or illegal activities, as exemplified by slang terms like "to gyp" (meaning to swindle) and "gyp joints."[31] It is only natural that many Roma, therefore, view the word "Gypsy" as offensive. The term also perpetuates the misconception that the people originated in Egypt. In French, *bohémien* and *tsigane*, and in German, *Zigeuner*, have similar meanings and connotations. Like "Gypsy," these terms reinforce incorrect perceptions that the Gypsies originally came from Bohemia (or in the case of *tsigane*, from Phrygia in Asia Minor and Thrace).[32] The term "Sinti" refers to a part of the Gypsy population that resides mainly in Germany.[33] To attach universal meaning to the word "Gypsy" is inappropriate.

Nevertheless, non-Gypsies (*gajé*) use the term "Gypsy" to describe all Romani people and their descendants, who are believed to have left northern India about a thousand years ago.[34] Despite the generic label "Gypsy," the Romani people actually comprise many different groups bound together by notions of purity and pollution, and by Gypsy law. The research that forms the basis for this essay deals overwhelmingly with Vlax Gypsies from Wallachia, Rumania—in particular, the Mačvaya, Kalderasha, and Lovara.[35] The Vlax is the largest identifiable group of Gypsies in the United States, although precise estimates of the size of its population are elusive. Because the Romanichals, Bashalde, and Sinti have quite different customs, in spite of cultural similarities, academic literature neglects them.[36] Therefore, unavoidably, so does this essay.

---

31. WEBSTER'S THIRD NEW INTERNATIONAL DICTIONARY 1015, col. 3 (unabr. ed. 1986) [hereinafter, WEBSTER'S THIRD]. There is a corresponding slang term among American Roma, to "get gadged," meaning to be cheated by non-Gypsies (*gajé*). Notes by Ian F. Hancock, Professor of English and Linguistics at the University of Texas, Austin, on manuscript draft of this Article (Jan. 1993) at 6 n. 69 (on file with authors) [hereinafter Hancock, Notes].

32. Yoors, AMERICANA, *supra* note 1, at 647 (referring to Michael J. de Goeje and Franz von Miklošić).

33. WALTER O. WEYRAUCH, GESTAPO V-LEUTE 66 (1989); *see also* REIMER GRONEMEYER & GEORGIA A. RAKELMANN, DIE ZIGEUNER: REISENDE IN EUROPA 9–11 (1988). The designation as "Sinti" probably originates from the German word *Zinn* (tin). Hancock, Notes, *supra* note 31, at 2 n.31. This word likely originated at a time when many German Gypsies worked as tinsmiths.

34. *See supra* note 1 (terminology); *infra* note 57 and accompanying text (history and migrations).

35. The reader is therefore cautioned against making generalizations about all Gypsies based on the information presented here.

36. *See* Thomas Acton, *Academic Success and Political Failure: A Review of Modern Social Science Writing in English on Gypsies*, 2 ETHNIC & RACIAL STUD. 231, 234–35 (1979); *see also* Ian F. Hancock, *Gypsies in the United States*, 8 ETHNIC F., 72, 73–75 (1988) (reviewing MARLENE SWAY, FAMILIAR STRANGERS: GYPSY LIFE IN AMERICA 6–13 (1988)) [hereinafter Hancock, *Review*]. Anthropologists in particular have mistakenly assumed that Kalderash informants, belonging to the Vlax group, have informed on customs that apply to

The literature's ignorance of Romani terminology parallels the legal scholarship's ignorance of Romani law. The Gypsies call themselves "Roma" (singular "Rom," meaning man or husband), but this word is little known outside Gypsy communities.[37] Its similarity to "Romania," especially in the adjectival form "Romani," leads to the misconception that Gypsies and Rumanians are identical or related. Words of Gypsy origin, descended from Sanskrit sources, are essentially unknown among non-Gypsies. Even the growing literature of Gypsy scholars uses the term "Gypsies" interchangeably with "Roma" due to the non-Gypsy world's ignorance of the Romani language.

These misconceptions about the Roma can result in confusion among non-Gypsy authors. The deeply ingrained notion that all Gypsies are nomadic overlooks the fact that the Vlax in Wallachia and Moldavia (which are now parts of Rumania and Moldova) were enslaved until 1856. Indeed, the Vlax were bound to their owners' homes and farms for about five hundred years.[38] Among the Vlax, the forced sedentary life of serfdom seems to have preserved internal Gypsy law and strengthened the culture as a whole, although some of their cultural characteristics probably were acquired from the host population.[39] The large-scale migration of the descendants of these Gypsies to the United States may have revived ancient nomadic patterns only to the extent necessary to avoid local hostility.

Impact of Past Persecution

Negative characterizations of the Romani people create corresponding problems in research efforts, especially those concerning Gypsy law. Most literature on Gypsies has been produced by non-Gypsy scholars who relied on the writings of other non-Gypsies and ultimately on Gypsy informants.[40] The Gypsies' views, and their responses to scholarly inquiries, reflect a long and continuing history of suffering and worldwide persecution, including the murder of an unknown number of Gypsies

---

all American Gypsies. These misconceptions are so frequent that Acton has coined the term "Kalderashocentric." Acton, *supra* at 234–36.

Although the name "Vlax" comes from "Wallachia," many modern Vlax populations do not identify with that region in Rumania, but with an intermediate country or location to which they migrated at a later time, For example, the Mačvaya mention a Serbian town, Mačva, as theirs, Hancock, Notes, *supra* note 31, at 1 n.12. The spelling of names of different Romani ethnic groups, such as the Mačvaya, varies. We have followed the spellings suggested by Hancock, although cited authors may have used different spellings.

37. At the First World Romani Congress in 1971, the delegates adopted the term "Roma" as a collective name for all Gypsies. FRASER, *supra* note 28, at 316.

38. *See* FRASER, *supra* note 28, at 57–59; Ian F. Hancock, *The Romani Diaspora Part One*, 1989 WORLD & I 612, 617 [hereinafter Hancock, *Diaspora I*].

39. Hancock, *Diaspora I*, *supra* note 38, at 617.

40. *See* Acton, *supra* note 35, at 234–37; HANCOCK, PARIAH SYNDROME, *supra* note 1, at 125–27.

in Nazi concentration camps.[41] Fearing further persecution, the Gypsies are inclined to distrust all non-Gypsies.

Tellingly, the Gypsies use the term *gaje* to refer to all non-Romani people without differentiating among them. *Gaje* has pejorative connotations. It originally meant peasants, or uncivilized and uneducated persons, but it also had connotations comparable to "barbarians" in English. In contemporary usage, *gaje* has a more neutral meaning: "non-Gypsy."[42] The *gaje* (singular *gajo*) are subject to ridicule and disdain because, from a Gypsy perspective, they do not conform to norms of

41. Estimates of the number of Gypsies who fell victim to the Nazis vary because not all Roma were brought to concentration camps. Some were shot or hanged as partisans at the Russian front, while others were summarily executed as "asocials." Moreover, classifications within concentration camps were not uniform. While Kogon posits that only an "insignificant remnant" of the Romani population survived the Holocaust, EUGEN KOGON, THE THEORY AND PRACTICE OF HELL: THE GERMAN CONCENTRATION CAMPS AND THE SYSTEM BEHIND THEM 39 (Heinz Norden trans., 1950), Döhring suggests that 20–45% of the German Gypsy population died as a result of the Holocaust, HANS J. DÖHRING, DIE ZIGEUNER IM NATIONALSOZIALISTISCHEN STAAT 191–92 (1964). Estimates of a million Gypsies killed are probably too conservative. *See* Ian Hancock, *"Uniqueness" of the Victims: Gypsies, Jews and the Holocaust,* 1988 WITHOUT PREJUDICE; EAFORD INT'L REV. RACIAL DISCRIMINATION 45, 55–56 [hereinafter Hancock, *Holocaust*]. *But cf.* Yoors, AMERICANA, *supra* note 1, at 647; ULRICH KÖNIG, SINTI UND ROMA UNTER DEM NATIONALSOZIALISMUS; VERFOLGUNG UND WIDERSTAND 87–88 (1989) (estimating over 500,000 killed).

The attitude of the German population toward Gypsies continues to be overwhelmingly negative. A poll taken in the 1960's in a city outside of which a Gypsy camp had long existed indicated that of 200 respondents, 180 expressed hostile sentiments. Luc Jochimsen, *Zigeuner hierzulande, in* MINDERHEITEN IN DER BUNDESREPUBLIK 21, 49 (Bernhard Doerdelmann ed., 1969). German news reports, while critical of xenophobia, tend to be ambivalent toward Gypsies, especially those who have recently arrived from other countries. *See, e.g.,* Ariane Barth, *"Hier steigt eine Giftsuppe auf,"* DER SPIEGEL, Oct. 14, 1991, at 118; Sabine Rückert & Michael Schwellen, *Die Zigeuner sind da!,* DIE ZEIT, Sept. 25, 1992, at 11. For responses from the United States, see, for example, Andrei Codrescu, *Gypsy Tragedy, German Amnesia,* N.Y. TIMES, Sept. 23, 1992, at A27 (criticizing Germany's policy of repatriating Roma to Rumania); Marc Fisher, *Germany's Gypsy Question: Haunting Echoes as a Hated Minority Gets "Retransferred,"* WASH. POST, Nov, 1, 1992, at F1 [hereinafter Fisher, *Germany's Gypsies*]; Carol J. Williams, *For Gypsies, No Place To Call Home. Ethnic Tension: The Refugees Being Repatriated from Germany Face an Unfriendly Reception in Romania,* L.A. TIMES, Oct. 12, 1992, at A8. A recent German constitutional revision has severely restricted asylum rights. GRUNDGESETZ [Constitution] [GG] art. 16a (Germany). The revision, although couched in general language, primarily applies to Gypsy refugees from Eastern Europe. Stephen Kinzer, *Bonn Parliament Votes Sharp Curb on Asylum Seekers,* N.Y. TIMES, May 27, 1993, at A1, A4 ("More than half of the foreigners now arriving in Germany in search of asylum are from Rumania and Bulgaria, and most of them are Gypsies."); *see also supra* note 2. For an exhaustive treatment of German law relating to Gypsies, *see* Michael M. Jansen, *Sinti and Roma: An Ethnic Minority in Germany, in* THE PROTECTION OF ETHNIC AND LINGUISTIC MINORITIES IN EUROPE 167 (John Packer & Kristian Myntti eds., 1993). Concerns have been expressed that recent German legislation is specifically aimed at repatriating Gypsy refugees to Rumania, *Id.* at 182.

42. *See* GRONEMEYER & RAKELMANN, *supra* note 33, at 9 (defining *gaje* as peasants, fools); JAN YOORS, THE GYPSIES 16 (1967) [hereinafter YOORS, GYPSIES] ("All non-Gypsies or outsiders are called 'Gaje,' which he translated as 'peasants.' He looked me in the eyes as he said it, but there was a slight hesitation in his voice and I sensed the pejorative connotation.") (footnote omitted). According to Hancock the term *gaje* refers to male non-Gypsies. HANCOCK, PARIAH SYNDROME, *supra* note 1, at 137. Hancock asserts that the term is not necessarily pejorative. However, the context in which the word is used and

proper behavior. The Gypsies generally view the *gaje* as having no sense of justice or decency. Even behavior that is "law-abiding" by *gajïkane*[43] standards can be considered inherently indecent. Furthermore, not only do the Gypsies consider non-Gypsies polluted, they also believe that Gypsy names and rituals lose their magical effectiveness if uttered to *gaje*.[44] Consequently, the Gypsies believe they should approach and respond to the *gaje* with caution,[45] especially if the *gaje* profess good intentions, claim to serve the best interest of the Gypsies, or propagate some abstract ideals of non-Gypsy origin, such as the scholarly pursuit of truth. Romani reservations apply equally to *gajïkane* notions of due process, civil rights, and neutrality of law.

As a result of such reservations, persons inquiring into the operation of the Gypsy legal system cannot count on cooperation. Distortions of reality are inevitable and they permeate almost every aspect of non-Gypsy scholarship on the Gypsies. As a further impediment to accuracy in studies of the Gypsies, *gajïkane* scholars have failed to wrestle with their own deeply ingrained beliefs in the superiority of their cultural values, including the notions that objective scholarship and science are possible and that some neutral concept of merit[46] can determine the value of other cultures. *Gajïkane* scholars implicitly and paradoxically assume that *gajïkane* standards of measurement are useful in evaluating the Gypsy culture.

---

the intonation may result in a negative meaning. Following Hancock, who stresses the essentially neutral contemporary meaning of *gaje*, this chapter uses the term interchangeably with the term "non-Gypsy." This interchangeable use helps to effect the incorporation of a Romani perspective into the essay. It corresponds to the interchangeable use of the term "Gypsy" (which also may have pejorative connotations) with the term "Roma." *See supra* note 1. Absolute neutrality, unfortunately, is not possible because the linguistic means to express it are inherently flawed. *Cf.* Walter O. Weyrauch, *Limits of Perception: Reader Response to Hitler's Justice*, 40 AM J. COMP. L. 237, 251–54 (1992) (discussing reader-response school of literary theory). Some authors capitalize the term *gaje*. We have consistently used capital letters for Rom and Gypsy, but not for *gaje*. The latter term is all-encompassing and does not refer to any distinct ethnic group or nationality.

43. *Gajïkano* is the singular adjectival form of *gaje*. The plural adjectival form is *gajïkane*. We are indebted to Ian Hancock for this clarification; *see also* IAN HANCOCK, NOTES ON ROMANI GRAMMAR 15–16 (4th ed. 1992).

44. MARTIN BLOCK, GYPSIES 13 (1939); JEAN-PAUL CLÉBERT, THE GYPSIES 132 (Charles Duff trans., 1963) (describing "secular taboo" that prevents disclosure of religious ritual to non-Gypsy world).

45. *See* SUTHERLAND, *supra* note 29, at 21 (describing how author encountered vehement cursing, feigned imbecility, pretense of mental retardation, polite imperviousness, alleged deafness and blindness, mocking lies, and panic in response to tape recording); Vogel, *supra* note 29, at 36 (noting extreme suspicion against any form of structured questioning). The evasionary strategies of Gypsies toward non-Gypsies are ingenious. Yoors reports veiled ridicule, seeming childlike admiration, and an endless stream of questions meant to induce the non-Gypsies to reply rather than ask questions themselves. If questions cannot be avoided, multiple inconsistent answers might be given. Gypsies may start scratching themselves persistently, implying the presence of vermin, or they may cough violently, suggesting a contagious lung ailment. YOORS, GYPSIES, *supra* note 42, at 50–51.

46. The concept of merit is essentially culturally determined. One of the coauthors has defined merit as the "ability to act 'responsibly' and to fit and operate well within an existing institutional

Scholars do not characterize themselves as non-Gypsy; indeed, there is no corresponding word for *gaje* in our vocabulary. Yet other cultures that have experienced persecution or that are insular have words corresponding to the Gypsy term *gaje*, such as *goyim* for everyone who is not a Jew and *haole* for all non-Hawaiians. All these terms share disparaging connotations and reflect barriers to communication.[47] Thus, widespread failure to confront the difficulties of *gajikane* scholars studying Gypsies has resulted in a subtle yet pervasive cultural insensitivity in most literature on the Gypsies.

A Suggested Method for the Study of Gypsy Law

To some extent, this essay faces the same problems as other scholarship by non-Gypsy authors. Partially to offset any hidden bias, it tries to recognize the perspectives that the Romani people have about themselves and about non-Gypsies. Although these standards undoubtedly reflect the Gypsies' own ethnocentrism, they nevertheless articulate viewpoints often neglected in non-Gypsy scholarship. If this creates an appearance that we are overly sympathetic to the Gypsies, the basic purpose of our presentation should be kept in mind. It is less focused on solving the social problems that may result from the steadfast refusal of an ethnic people to be assimilated and more concerned with gaining insight into the workings of customary oral traditions in law, including our own.

Any study of the internal laws of the Gypsies must inevitably reflect the research difficulties associated with studying Gypsies generally. Not only is it incorrect to project the legal customs of some Gypsies onto the whole population, but the memory of severe persecution may affect the willingness of Gypsies to share confidential information on their law. To the Gypsies, the purity of their law plays a crucial role in maintaining cultural identity and integrity against an onslaught of foreign cultural influences that may be well motivated, but often are of doubtful

---

framework." Walter O. Weyrauch, *Governance Within Institutions*, 22 STAN. L. REV. 141, 151 (1969) [hereinafter Weyrauch, *Governance*]. It tends inevitably to disadvantage some ethnic minorities, such as Gypsies, because they adhere to values different from those of the ruling majority who determine institutional frameworks. From that perspective, the traditional educational process can indeed damage cultural identity. *See infra* note 204. Whether Gypsy children who have been forced into the *gajikano* educational system are capable of exercising genuine choice to remain with the Romani people or go elsewhere is at least subject to debate. *But see* W. Michael Reisman, *Autonomy, Interdependence, and Responsibility*, 103 YALE L.J. 401, 416–17 (1993) [hereinafter Reisman, *Comment*]. No doubt, the Romani people are now better off in the United States than in many other countries, but the American liberal democratic state is in some respects aspirational and, in spite of major progress in the last decades, not fully realized, particularly in areas of race relations.

47. LEO ROSTEN, THE JOYS OF YIDDISH 141–42 (1968) (defining *goy:* "1. A Gentile, i.e., anyone who is not a Jew. . . . 2. Someone who is dull, insensitive, heartless"); WEBSTER'S THIRD, *supra* note 31, at 1030 (defining *haole:* "one who is not a member of the native race of Hawaii; *esp:* a member of the white race").

value, if not destructive.[48] While these impediments to the study of Gypsy law leave unanswered numerous questions, traditional scholarship on Gypsies nevertheless has value because it does provide some accurate and detailed information which is otherwise unavailable to non-Gypsies and points to fruitful areas for further research. The writings of Gypsy authors also have value in that they demonstrate that many stereotypes of Romani culture may be unfounded. To the extent that existing uncertainties affect this essay, cautionary signals alert the reader that our presentation, especially with regard to the particularities of Gypsy law, is not meant to be conclusive.

The research method employed here is similar to the one Thomas Acton employed.[49] Many case studies of Gypsies already exist. Typically these studies focus on a small group of Gypsies and then make generalizations about all Gypsies. Thus, Acton argued that another such project would add little to the state of knowledge on Gypsies; instead he favored a synthesis of the existing data. Although he rarely quoted it in his work, Acton used his field research primarily as an aid to analyze the existing literature.[50] Similarly, this essay uses the emerging literature of Romani scholars for critical insights into the writings of *gajikane* authors.

III. GYPSY LAW[51]

An important goal of this essay is to demonstrate that the Gypsy legal system not only protects the Gypsies from external and internal threats, but also serves as a code that organizes Gypsy society. In particular, Gypsy law has evolved to insulate Gypsies from the host society, and thus to maintain its own insularity from the host legal system.

---

48. Sutherland suggests that the concepts of religion, tradition, and law, as embodied in the term of *romaniya*, are interrelated. Accordingly, a person's identification as a Rom appears to depend on the unquestioning acceptance of these spiritual values rather than on external factors, such as ethnic origin. SUTHERLAND, *supra* note 29, at 17–18, 29.

Sutherland reports also in the new preface to her book, reissued in 1986, that the scholarly information in the earlier 1975 edition was misused by the police to prosecute Gypsies. ANNE SUTHERLAND, THE HIDDEN AMERICANS, at xii (Waveland Press, Inc. 1986) (1975).

49. THOMAS A. ACTON, GYPSY POLITICS AND SOCIAL CHANGE 2–3 (1974). Acton argues that even inconsistent or inaccurate existing studies could be useful if supplemented by his own field research.

50. *Id.* at 3.

51. This discussion of Gypsy law deals primarily with Vlax Gypsies of Rumanian origin, the largest identifiable group of Roma in the United States. Other Gypsies, such as the Romanichals from northern Europe and the British Isles, adhere to similar notions of purity and pollution, but have less formalized procedures. *See* Ronald Lee, *The* Kris Romani, ROMA, July 1987, at 19, 19–20 [hereinafter Lee, Kris].

Much of the factual information is based on the works of authors such as Jean-Paul Clébert, Rena C. Gropper, Ian Hancock, Ronald Lee, Jean-Pierre Liégeois, John B. McLaughlin, Carol J. Miller, Judith Okely, Matt T. Salo, Sheila M. Salo, Carol Silverman, Anne Sutherland, Marlene Sway, Carl-Herman Tillhagen, Elwood B. Trigg, and Jan Yoors, as cited in this section. Because of the multitude of detailed facts and parallel observations, for example, on *marime* and the *kris*, references have been grouped together and all relevant references may not be given in each individual instance.

Historical Origins and Ethnic Setting

There are anywhere from three to fifteen million Gypsies living in forty countries today.[52] Although research in linguistics suggests a common Indian source, the origins of the Gypsy people remain unclear because their history is largely unrecorded. Some social scientists attribute this lack of recorded history to the high rate of illiteracy among the Gypsies. Interestingly, Gypsy illiteracy may have been purposeful.[53] Gypsies share a fervent belief in their own uniqueness, and ethnocentricity has kept them from violating their prohibition against cultural integration. Likewise, myths surrounding the Gypsies and their origins might have been a matter of faith, or perhaps were devised to mislead non-Gypsies, and thus to support their own cultural insularity.[54] A history of persecution has further reinforced this isolationism. As a result of suspicion and hostility, countries in western and central Europe have tried for centuries to rid themselves of the Roma. State-sponsored discriminatory measures have included forced assimilation and slavery, as well as the systematic murder of Gypsies in Nazi concentration camps.[55] In spite of this persecution, or perhaps because of it, Gypsies have succeeded remarkably in retaining their cultural identity, often by engaging in the migratory behavior characteristic of the nomads of Asia.[56]

The precise reasons why the Roma left their homeland remain uncertain. Current research suggests that the Roma are descendants of the Dravidians who inhabited India before the arrival of Indo-European populations. They appear to have left northern India between A.D. 1000 and 1025 during a period of frequent invasions of the Sind and Punjab regions by Islamic forces. Although the ethnic and caste origins of the Roma may have been mixed, prolonged separation from the Punjab weakened their identification with the subcontinent and eventually re-

---

52. World estimates vary significantly and are highly unreliable. *See, e.g.,* JEAN-PIERRE LIÉGEOIS, GYPSIES: AN ILLUSTRATED HISTORY 45–46 (1986) (12–15 million); MARLENE SWAY, FAMILIAR STRANGERS: GYPSY LIFE IN AMERICA 6 (1988) (8–10 million); Mary Lou Fulton, *'King of the Gypsies' Seeks New Image for His People,* L.A. TIMES, May 28, 1989, § 2, at 1 (3–5 million). Liégeois suggests that political motives, and the dominant populace's attitude toward the Romani population, have led to denials, underestimates, and even exaggerations of statistical census data. LIÉGEOIS, *supra,* at 45. Equally important is the desire of the Roma to protect themselves by concealing ethnicity from a dominant, hostile host country. Hancock estimated the American Romani population at between 750,000 and 1,000,000. Hancock, *Diaspora I, supra* note 38, at 613. The true figure may be higher than any of the estimates because of the traditionally high birthrate of Gypsies. The U.S. Census figure of about 1,600 Gypsies in the United States for 1980 is absurdly low. *See id.,* Yoors, AMERICANA, *supra* note 1, at 650.

53. *See* CLÉBERT, *supra* note 44, at 132–33; *see also infra* notes 192, 203–4 and accompanying text.

54. SWAY, *supra* note 52, at 39.

55. *Id.* at 44; Toby F. Sonneman, *Buried in the Holocaust,* N.Y. TIMES, May 2, 1992, at A17. For a discussion of the systematic lack of recognition given the Romani holocaust, see generally Sybil Milton, *The Context of the Holocaust,* 13 GERMAN STUD. REV. 269 (1990). For further details, see *supra* note 41.

56. CLÉBERT, *supra* note 44, at 201–02. This does not apply to the Vlax who were enslaved in Rumania for 500 years and thereby compelled to stay in a designated location. *See supra* note 38 and accompanying text.

sulted in a culturally distinct population. Linguistic evidence supports this theory, but a more detailed historical foundation is still lacking.[57]

No reliable sources document the arrival of the Gypsies in the United States or their departure from other countries.[58] An initial handful may have come with Columbus, and later England deported others.[59] A significant number of Gypsies arrived in the United States with the immigration waves of the nineteenth and early-twentieth centuries. In the United States, the Gypsies were not identified as such for quite some time, for several reasons. First, the United States, with its vast size and mobile population, offered a favorable environment for a population that often does not adhere to a sedentary life. Second, Gypsies commonly do not identify themselves as Gypsies, but merely indicate their last host home as their nationality.[60] Finally, the presence of other non-white population groups helped the Roma to blend in unnoticed.[61]

Functions of Concepts of Impurity (Marime)

The Gypsies' determination not to assimilate into the dominant society has been crucial to their survival as a separate population. This drive stems in part from the Roma's belief that non-Gypsies are in a state of defilement because of their ignorance about rules on purity and impurity. Gypsy society relies heavily on distinctions between behavior that is pure (*vujo*) and polluted (*marime*).[62] The *marime* con-

---

57. Hancock, *Diaspora I, supra* note 38, at 615; Ian Hancock, *On the Migration and Affiliation of the Dōmba: Iranian Words in Rom, Lom and Dom Gypsy* (Occasional Papers, Int'l Romani Union, Series F, No. 8, 1992); *see also* DONALD KENRICK & GRATTAN PUXON, THE DESTINY OF EUROPE'S GYPSIES 14–15 (1972). For theories on the origins of Gypsies, *see* BLOCK, *supra* note 44, at 32–47; CLÉBERT, *supra* note 44, at 15–23, 26–42; FRASER, *supra* note 28, at 25–29, 33–40; SWAY, *supra* note 52, at 31–33; YOORS, GYPSIES, *supra* note 42, at 9–10; John Sampson, *On the Origin and Early Migrations of the Gypsies,* 2 J. GYPSY LORE SOC'Y 156, 159 (1923).

58. *See* JOHN B. MCLAUGHLIN, GYPSY LIFESTYLES 3 (1980).

59. Reportedly, Gypsies entered the Americas with Columbus on his third voyage in 1498. England began deporting Romanichal Gypsies in 1544. Large numbers of Gypsies were sent from England to Virginia and Georgia in 1695. Queen Christina of Sweden had Gypsies deported to her colony in Delaware in 1648. Gypsies from Germany escaped "Gypsy hunts" that had been legalized after the Thirty Years War by coming to America. Ian F. Hancock, *The Romani Diaspora Part 2,* 1989 THE WORLD & I 644 [hereinafter Hancock, *Diaspora II*].

60. Vogel, *supra* note 29, at 35 ("Rom from Germany are listed as Germans."); *see also* MCLAUGH-LIN, *supra* note 58, at 3. According to Hancock, the United States adopted immigration policies in the 1880's restricting entrance of Gypsies. Hancock, *Diaspora II, supra* note 59, at 646–47; *see also* Ian F. Hancock, *Gypsies, in* HARVARD ENCYCLOPEDIA OF AMERICAN ETHNIC GROUPS 440, 441 (1980) [hereinafter Hancock, *Gypsies*]. On the history of American immigration law, especially the aggressive xenophobia advocated in the nineteenth century by the political movements of Native Americanism and the Know-Nothings, *see* FRANK G. FRANKLIN, THE LEGISLATIVE HISTORY OF NATURALIZATION IN THE UNITED STATES 184–300 (1906).

61. Hancock, *Diaspora II, supra* note 59, at 647.

62. SWAY, *supra* note 52, at 46–59; *see also* HANCOCK, PARIAH SYNDROME, *supra* note 1, at 115–16; JU-DITH OKELY, THE TRAVELLER-GYPSIES 77–78 (1983) [hereinafter OKELY, TRAVELLER]; YOORS, GYPSIES,

cept has powerful significance for Gypsies. *Marime* has a dual meaning: it refers both to a state of pollution as well as to the sentence of expulsion imposed for violation of purity rules or any behavior disruptive to the Gypsy community. Pollution and rejection are thus closely associated with one another.[63] The *marime* rules minimize and regulate association between Gypsy and non-Gypsy. Although the notion of *marime* supports the Roma's desire for autonomy, Gypsy pollution taboos evolved in part to prevent dissension and disease among people living in deprived and unstable conditions.[64]

According to *romaniya*,[65] or Gypsy law, the human body is both pure and impure. The waist is the equator, or dividing line. The lower body is *marime* because the genital areas and the feet and legs may cause pollution and defilement.[66] The upper body is fundamentally pure and clean. Any unguarded contact between the lower and upper bodies is *marime*.[67] Rituals of purification preserve the power attributed to the upper half of the body and the health of the Gypsy concerned.[68]

---

supra note 42, at 150; Carol J. Miller, *American Rom and the Ideology of Defilement, in* GYPSIES, TINKERS AND OTHER TRAVELLERS 41, 45–46 (FARNHAM REHFISCH ED., 1975) [hereinafter Miller, *Defilement*] (noting that *gajikane* living habits confuse pure and impure and invite spreading of contagious disease, especially venereal disease); Judith Okely, *Gypsy Women: Models in Conflict, in* PERCEIVING WOMEN 55, 59–60 (Shirley Ardener ed., 1975) [hereinafter Okely, *Gypsy Women*]; *cf.* JACOB NEUSNER, THE IDEA OF PURITY IN ANCIENT JUDAISM 108 (1973) (discussing purity and impurity as metaphors for moral and religious behavior relating to sex and unethical conduct).

63. SWAY, *supra* note 52, at 53; FRASER, *supra* note 28, at 245–47; Carol J. Miller, *Mačwaya Gypsy Marimé* 5 (1968) (unpublished M.A. thesis, University of Washington [Seattle]) [hereinafter Miller, Thesis]; Miller, *Defilement, supra* note 62, at 40. Miller's pathbreaking field research dealt only with Mačwaya families that belong to the Rom-Vlax group. According to Hancock *marime* is a Vlax word, unknown to other Romani populations. Some populations have no word for ritual pollution; other groups use a variation of the Indian-derived word *makhardo*, meaning smeared. Hancock, *Review, supra* note 35, at 74–75. Not all Gypsy groups adhere to the precise beliefs and practices discussed in this chapter, although most Gypsies employ concepts of "pollution" in one form or another.

The notion of pollution exists in most cultures, but it usually does not have the same crucial religious and legal significance as in the case of the Gypsies. Lawrence S. Kubie, *The Fantasy of Dirt*, 6 PSYCHOANALYTIC Q. 388 (1937) (describing dirtiness as cultural construct); *see also* Martha G. Duncan, *In Slime and Darkness: The Metaphor of Filth in Criminal Justice*, 68 TUL. L. REV. 725 (1994).

64. MCLAUGHLIN, *supra* note 58, at 19. *But see* OKELY, TRAVELLER, *supra* note 62, at 78–83 (stressing concern with inner purity).

65. SUTHERLAND, *supra* note 29, at 101–02, 263–64, 319 (defining *romaniya* in Glossary as "the laws and traditions of the Rom"). *Romaniya* in essence means that which is considered right, true, correct, and acceptable regarding all aspects of living. Hancock, *Gypsies, supra* note 60, at 443. It covers relationships between Gypsies and with non-Gypsies, including matters of health, food, and morality, as well as procedures and rituals. *Id.* The antithesis of *romaniya* is *marimos*, meaning defilement, pollution, or banishment. If something is *marime*, it is in violation of Gypsy law. *Id.*

66. Hancock, *Gypsies, supra* note 60, at 443; Miller, *Defilement, supra* note 62, at 41–42.

67. SUTHERLAND, *supra* note 29, at 258, 264; SWAY, *supra* note 52, at 53; Miller, *Defilement, supra* note 62, at 42.

68. *See* SUTHERLAND, *supra* note 29, at 255–87; Miller, *Defilement, supra* note 62, at 42–43.

Only the hands may transgress the boundary line between the upper and lower parts of the body.[69]

Notions of purity and impurity follow the life cycle. Gypsies consider children *marime* for six weeks after birth because the birth canal is a polluting site.[70] After this six-week period, children enjoy a privileged status in society until puberty, when they become subject to *marime* taboos.[71] Following the onset of puberty, women remain in a latent stage of impurity until they reach menopause.[72] In old age, Gypsies believe that one regains some of the innocence of childhood. As one scholar has noted, Gypsies consider elders "close to the gods and the ancestors."[73] Postmenopausal women do not have the power to pollute by tossing their skirts (as they can before they reach menopause), because they no longer menstruate or bear children.[74]

Pollution taboos vary from group to group and often among smaller Romani units.[75] Nevertheless, Gypsies define themselves in part by their adherence to these cleanliness rituals.[76] There may be class distinctions among some Roma, based on how strictly individuals or families maintain distinctions between purity and impurity.[77] All these taboos involve rules that are aspirational. The actual behavior of

---

69. Miller, *Defilement, supra*, note 62, at 43. Washing rituals must be performed assiduously after contact with the lower body, especially before food preparation or religious rituals. *Id.; see also* Miller, Thesis, *supra* note 63, at 9–14.

70. SUTHERLAND, *supra* note 29, at 262; *see also* Miller, *Defilement, supra* note 62, at 42–44 ("three days . . . to several weeks").

71. SUTHERLAND, *supra* note 29, at 262.

72. *See* Miller, *Defilement, supra* note 62, at 44; *see also* ELWOOD B. TRIGG, GYPSIES, DEMONS AND DIVINITIES 55 (1973); Aparna Rao, *Some Mānuš Conceptions and Attitudes, in* GYPSIES, TINKERS AND OTHER TRAVELLERS, *supra* note 62, at 139, 154–55. The power of the female's lower body to pollute accounts for the segregation of males and females following puberty. *See* Rao, *supra*, at 155; Carol Silverman, *Negotiating "Gypsiness": Strategy in Context*, 101 J. AM. FOLKLORE 261, 264 (1988) [hereinafter Silverman, *Gypsiness*]. An exception to sexual segregation occurs while Gypsies watch television, Rao, *supra*, at 155.

73. Miller, *Defilement, supra* note 62, at 44. Miller notes that elders are believed no longer to have an interest in sex. *Id.* at 44 n.10. The conception of age among Gypsies appears to be different from that of non-Gypsies. The advent of old age is signalled by the arrival of the second or third grandchild. *See* SUTHERLAND, *supra* note 29, at 263. Many Roma do not know their exact age, so they judge by life cycles (puberty, adulthood and marriage, old age) and visible factors, such as the presence or absence of wrinkles and gray hair. McLAUGHLIN, *supra* note 58, at 12; *see also* SUTHERLAND, *supra* note 29, at 150–51.

74. Miller, *Defilement, supra* note 62, at 44 (noting that older women lose power to contaminate by "tossing the skirt"); *id.* at 51–52 (discussing skirt-tossing as symbolic power to pollute); *see also infra* note 79 and accompanying text.

75. *See* Hancock, *Gypsies, supra* note 60, at 443.

76. *See* OKELY, TRAVELLER, *supra* note 62, at 83. The *marime* taboos are not completely known or understood by non-Gypsies, who adhere to different and often incompatible notions of cleanliness.

77. SUTHERLAND, *supra* note 29, at 260; *see also* Hancock, *Gypsies, supra* note 60, at 442; MATT T. SALO & SHEILA M. SALO, THE KALDERAS IN EASTERN CANADA 115–16 (Canadian Centre for Folk Culture Studies Paper No. 21, 1977). According to LIÉGEOIS, *supra* note 52, at 76, the *marime* code enables Gypsy subgroups to distinguish among themselves, and also helps maintain their separation from non-Gypsies. Gypsies use peer pressure to point out behavior that amounts to impurity. They then take action to maintain separation from the behavior to avoid becoming polluted.

the Gypsy people is likely to fall short of the communal expectations expressed in the taboos.

According to Elwood Trigg, the *marime* rules fall into four overlapping categories: (1) taboos directly or indirectly related to the fear of being contaminated by women; (2) sexual taboos; (3) things considered to be dirty or unhygienic; and (4) disdain of socially disruptive behavior.[78] Adherence to these ritual purity laws is central in setting Gypsies apart from their host cultures.

CONTAMINATION BY WOMEN[79]

Women may contaminate men in a number of ways.[80] Because of menstruation and childbirth, the Gypsies consider the female genitalia impure. A severe state of *marime* befalls any man if a woman lifts her skirt and exposes her genitals to him ("skirt-tossing").[81] A woman must never walk by a seated man because her genitals would be at

78. TRIGG, *supra* note 72, at 55. Trigg's work focused largely on European Gypsy populations. He uses the term *mokadi*, as distinguished from *marime*, in his book. It is probably a derivation of the word *makhardo* (smeared) of Indian origin. The term *marime* is derived from Greek and used only by the Vlax. Hancock, *Review, supra* note 35, at 74–75.

79. It should be noted that many of the elements of Gypsy law described in this essay have come to light only recently, significantly through the efforts of female scholars. The guardians of *romaniya* are primarily Gypsy women who orally transmit knowledge to their children. *Gajikane* males could not have obtained this confidential information, because Gypsy women would never reveal many important aspects of Gypsy law, including those which relate to sexual taboos and other highly intimate matters, to a non-Gypsy man. SUTHERLAND, *supra* note 29, at xiii (crediting female scholars with discovery of the Gypsy "moral code"). Women scholars have also noted the problems of scientific ethics connected with gathering intimate and confidential information. RENA C. GROPPER, GYPSIES IN THE CITY: CULTURE PATTERNS AND SURVIVAL at ix (1975) (noting promises made to Gypsy informants and invasion of privacy); SUTHERLAND, *supra* note 29, at xii (noting danger of use by police). These same concerns apply to this essay, which disseminates confidential information to a wider public.

Problems similar to those posed by Gypsy law find parallels in other areas of religious law. Female legal scholars have been concerned with reexamining ancient notions of purity and pollution as contained in Jewish and Christian tradition from a feminist perspective. *See, e.g.,* Mary E. Becker, *The Politics of Women's Wrongs and the Bill of "Rights": A Bicentennial Perspective,* 59 U. CHI. L. REV. 453, 466–67 (1992); Jeanne L. Schroeder, *Feminism Historicized: Medieval Misogynist Stereotypes in Contemporary Feminist Jurisprudence,* 75 IOWA L. REV. 1135, 1190–95 (1990).

80. *See* TRIGG, *supra* note 72, at 55; Miller, *Defilement, supra* note 62, at 42. The *gaji* (a non-Gypsy female) normally cannot defile a Rom, and as such is perceived as being outside the scope of the Romani legal system. SALO & SALO, *supra* note 77, at 125.

81. Miller, *Defilement, supra* note 62, at 51–52. According to Miller, a woman may toss her shoe at a man's face with the same effect. *Id.* at 51 n.20. Because of the severe consequences for the man, in all likelihood neither of these things ever happen. If they did occur, the defiled male Rom would be cast out of the society permanently. *Id.* at 52. In most cases, after a period of time the woman would simply deny that it ever happened or say that it was a mistake if it is doubtful that the defilement could be proven. To attempt to deny a man forgiveness under such uncertain circumstances would eventually deadlock a Gypsy judicial proceeding. Miller, Thesis, *supra* note 63, at 22–23.

A Gypsy male will often take his wife with him when meeting an unknown Gypsy. This assures him that in the event of a squabble he is armed. Miller, *Defilement, supra* note 62, at 51–52 n.20; *see also* YOORS,

the same height as his face.[82] A man may not walk under a clothesline where women's clothes are hanging.[83] Women cover their legs when they sit down and, in mixed company, single women keep their legs together when seated. These stringent rules may explain the traditionally long and wide skirts worn by Gypsy women.[84] Especially in the United States, clothing has changed among Gypsy women, but skirts typically are still long. Slacks have also become acceptable apparel for women.[85]

Historically, *marime* taboos were quite strict. For example, if a woman stepped into a stream, no one could drink from it for several hours because the water had been exposed to her genitals.[86] The same taboo extended to food and dishes, all of which were thrown out if a woman stepped over them.[87] Even today, some Roma will not rent a lower floor apartment for fear that a woman living upstairs will at some point pollute them by walking overhead.[88] Similarly, a woman may get out of the car if her husband has to look under it because of mechanical trouble.

When a Gypsy woman goes to the toilet, special precautions must be taken to prevent any man from entering. Even a married couple will not share the bathroom at the same time.[89] A man can become *marime* by using a toilet seat that a woman

---

GYPSIES, *supra* note 42, at 151. Interestingly, tossing the skirt has been successful in combating the *gaje*. In one case, police officers attempting to arrest Gypsy males were distracted when " 'one of the women lifted her dress over her head'. . . . 'While the cops stared at her, her companions had time to flee.' " Stanley Penn, *Gypsy Gangs Range Across the Country, Stealing Rugs, Gems,* WALL ST. J., Dec. 15, 1988, at A1, A10 (quoting Chicago police detective Donald Kuchar).

82. MCLAUGHLIN, *supra* note 58, at 20; SALO & SALO, *supra* note 77, at 122; SUTHERLAND, *supra* note 29, at 151; TRIGG, *supra* note 72, at 58; *see* Thomas W. Thompson, *The Uncleanness of Women Among English Gypsies,* I J. GYPSY LORE SOC'Y 15, 23 (1922). In an interview with a Mačvaya couple, one investigator was told that many young women do not observe this rule. Marie W. Clark, *Vanishing Vagabonds: The American Gypsies,* TEX. Q., Summer 1967, 204, 205–06.

83. MCLAUGHLIN, *supra* note 58, at 20.

84. *Id.;* SWAY, *supra* note 52, at 54; TRIGG, *supra* note 72, at 58; Okely, *Gypsy Women, supra* note 62, at 63; Thompson, *supra* note 82, at 22.

85. *See* MCLAUGHLIN, *supra* note 58, at 20 (observing that Gypsy women sometimes wear blue jeans or slacks); OKELY, TRAVELLER, *supra* note 62, at 207; SUTHERLAND, *supra* note 29, at 27 (noting that Gypsies sometimes wear "American clothes" in public places); Okely, *Gypsy Women, supra* note 62, at 63. On the question of whether the women's movement has had any effect on Gypsy households, Hancock notes that when Romani women speak of feminism they usually are talking about non-Gypsy women, because some changes due to feminism are seen as contradicting *romaniya* (Gypsy law). Letter from Ian Hancock, Professor of Linguistics, University of Texas, to Maureen A. Bell (July 8, 1989) (on file with authors).

86. MCLAUGHLIN, *supra* note 58, at 20.

87. Rao, *supra* note 72, at 151; *see* GROPPER, *supra* note 79, at 92–93; MCLAUGHLIN, *supra* note 58, at 20; SWAY, *supra* note 52, at 54; TRIGG, *supra* note 72, at 56; YOORS, GYPSIES, *supra* note 42, at 150; Okely, *Gypsy Women, supra* note 62, at 64; Thompson, *supra* note 82, at 21.

88. SWAY, *supra* note 52, at 55; Hancock, *Gypsies, supra* note 60, at 442; David W. Pickett, *The Gypsies of Mexico,* 45 J. GYPSY LORE SOC'Y 6, 12 (1966).

89. MCLAUGHLIN, *supra* note 58, at 20. Many ritual behaviors focus around the bathroom in Mačvaya households. Miller, Thesis, *supra* note 63, at 14. The strict prohibitions may even survive mixed

has sat on. To avoid this problem, Gypsies prefer to rent or buy residences that have two bathrooms.[90] Among some groups, a woman cannot comb her hair or let it down in the presence of a man.[91] A wife must undress with her back to her husband and get into bed before him. She must also rise in the morning before he does.[92]

During her menstrual cycle, a woman is *marime* and must avoid contact with others. Among some groups, a menstruating woman must eat alone and cannot prepare food that will be eaten by a man.[93] In addition, she must not sleep with her husband, or he will become polluted.[94] With the onset of menstruation at puberty, a girl's clothing cannot be washed with men's, boys', or premenstrual girls' clothing. Some researchers have indicated that much of the Gypsies' fixation with menstruation originates in India.[95]

Pregnancy also signals danger of pollution for others. A pregnant woman may not prepare food for other Gypsies. She is expected to eat by herself and her food must

---

marriages. *See, e.g.,* Letter from Patti J. Jeatran to Walter O. Weyrauch (Nov. 21, 1990) (on file with authors) [hereinafter Jeatran Letter].

90. SWAY, *supra* note 52, at 55; *see also* Jeatran Letter, *supra* note 89. *Romaniya* makes no distinction between custom and law. *See supra* note 65. Furthermore, many Gypsy customs have direct legal consequences. *See, e.g.,* LEE, AUTOBIOGRAPHY, *supra* note 29, at 37 ("Plumbing is a trade forbidden to Gypsies by their own law. A Gypsy man would be defiled by handling toilet fixtures and would run the grave risk of being socially ostracized.").

Germans often complain that Gypsy refugees urinate and defecate outdoors. *See, e.g.,* Fisher, *Germany's Gypsies, supra* note 41, at F1 (quoting aide of German Chancellor Helmut Kohl). Gypsy asylum seekers may prefer the outdoors to the polluted facilities provided, which they cannot use without becoming *marime.* The German and Romani notions of legal behavior directly conflict with one another.

91. MCLAUGHLIN, *supra* note 58, at 21; TRIGG, *supra* note 72, at 58; *see* Thompson, *supra* note 82, at 23–24.

92. LEE, AUTOBIOGRAPHY, *supra* note 29, at 45–47 (describing bed rituals). Gypsies traditionally sleep on the floor. Hancock, Notes, *supra* note 31, at 4 n.43; *see also* YOORS, GYPSIES, *supra* note 42, at 17–19, 37 (observing that Gypsies traditionally sleep in open air when climate permits).

93. MCLAUGHLIN, *supra* note 58, at 20; TRIGG, *supra* note 72, at 61; Okely, *Gypsy Women, supra* note 62, at 65; Thompson, *supra* note 82, at 38–39. Some Gypsy branches prohibit menstruating women from handling "red" meat or any meat. *Id.* at 27, 37.

94. KATHARINE ESTY, THE GYPSIES: WANDERERS IN TIME 73–74 (1969); MCLAUGHLIN, *supra* note 58, at 20. In former times, even mentioning menstruation in mixed company would place men in danger of being polluted. Okely, *Gypsy Women, supra* note 62, at 65; Thompson, *supra* note 82, at 38. "Sexual intercourse during the proper time of the month (12th day of [female] cycle to onset of menstruation) is not a polluting act. Sex during a woman's period is very marime." Letter from Marlene Sway to Maureen A. Bell (June 30, 1989) (on file with authors). For an interesting parallel in Mosaic law, see *Leviticus* 15:24 (man impure for seven days if he lies with a woman during her period). Bleeding in consummation of marriage is a matter of great pride as evidence of virginity. SUTHERLAND, *supra* note 29, at 226–27.

95. GROPPER, *supra* note 79, at 92–93 (separate laundering); MCLAUGHLIN, *supra* note 58, at 20; Okely, *Gypsy Women, supra* note 62, at 65; Thompson, *supra* note 82, at 28. The distinction between *melyardo* (soiled) and *marime* (polluted or unclean) is applicable to garments worn and separated for washing. *See infra* note 113. For example, clothing worn above the waist can be *vujo* if it is clean and *melyardo* if it is soiled, but clothing worn below the waist is *marime*. Children's clothing can at worst be *melyardo*. SUTHERLAND, *supra* note 29, at 268. Regarding the taboos surrounding menstruation in India, see

be cooked in her own pots and pans.[96] She cannot share a bed with her husband.[97] Even after birth, there is still a period of time, up to six weeks, during which a woman is unclean. In former times, a pregnant woman's clothing, bedding, utensils, and even her tent were burned. Today, Gypsies view childbirth in hospitals as a convenience because the *gaje* dispose of the polluted items.[98] In public, couples strictly observe *marime* taboos, but privately husbands and wives may relax the standards somewhat.[99]

SEXUAL TABOOS

Sexual taboos have great importance in Gypsy law. The potential for defilement is greatly heightened at marriage because Gypsies perceive it as the end of a woman's innocence.[100] Traditionally (though *Gajïkano* influence may have undermined the practice),[101] marriage for Gypsies has occurred early, after age nine but usually before age fourteen.[102]

McLAUGHLIN, *supra* note 58, at 20; GABRIELLE TYRNER-STASTNY, THE GYPSY IN NORTHWEST AMERICA 14 (1977). On the other hand, menstruation and the capacity of women to pollute also has been of intense concern in Jewish and Christian religious law. Becker, *supra* note 79, 466 (discussing menstruation and childbirth as polluting). *See generally* BLOOD MAGIC: THE ANTHROPOLOGY OF MENSTRUATION (Thomas Buckley & Alma Gottlieb eds., 1988).

96. McLAUGHLIN, *supra* note 58, at 21; OKELY, TRAVELLER, *supra* note 62, at 210–11; TRIGG, *supra* note 72, at 59; Thompson, *supra* note 82, at 26, 32.

97. McLAUGHLIN, *supra* note 58, at 21. Among the Mačvaya and Kalderasha, sexual intercourse between husband and wife is not taboo during a pregnancy as long as there is no vaginal spotting and bleeding. Letter from Marlene Sway, *supra* note 94.

98. SALO & SALO, *supra* note 77, at 131; Okely, *Gypsy Women, supra* note 62, at 66–67. According to McLaughlin, at the end of this untouchable period, a woman who has given birth "must undergo an elaborate ceremony to cleanse herself. She must destroy everything that she wore during her period of defilement, and she must wait another 40 days before resuming sexual relations with her husband." McLAUGHLIN, *supra* note 58, at 21; *see also* Becker, *supra* note 79, at 466 (discussing purification by ritual bath after menstruation and childbirth in Jewish tradition).

99. SUTHERLAND, *supra* note 29, at 266. Generally, autonomous systems can exist within other autonomous systems. Thus, the Gypsy family, in relaxing otherwise binding restrictions of *romaniya* within its jurisdiction, may enjoy a certain degree of autonomy within the larger autonomous legal system of the Gypsies.

100. Miller, *Defilement, supra* note 62, at 43–44.

101. TRIGG, *supra* note 72, at 65.

102. *See generally* McLAUGHLIN, *supra* note 58, at 14–15; Marna F. Fisher, *Gypsies,* in MINORITY PROBLEMS 50, 51 (Caroline B. Rose & Arnold M. Rose eds., 1st ed. 1965) [hereinafter Fisher, *Gypsy Minorities*]. According to Sutherland, a first marriage ideally occurs before the eighteenth birthday. SUTHERLAND, *supra* note 29, at 223. Marital age among the Kalderasha in Canada has risen to an average age of eighteen, although marriage between fourteen-year-olds is not uncommon. SALO & SALO, *supra* note 77, at 144–45. Among the urban Gitanos in Spain, most men wed between seventeen and twenty-two. Women wed between fifteen and seventeen years of age, which is young in comparison with the Spanish non-Gypsy population. Teresa San Román, *Kinship, Marriage, Law and Leadership in Two Urban Gypsy Settlements in Spain,* in GYPSIES, TINKERS AND OTHER TRAVELLERS *supra* note 62 at 169, 182. For similar observations among the Gypsy population in Britain, see OKELY, TRAVELLER, *supra* note 62, at 153.

Sexual mores are rigorously enforced and a wife's complaint of "shameful practices" is ground for annulment as well as a sentence of *marime* and banishment of the husband. Gypsy law considers oral sex, sodomy, and homosexuality crimes against nature and prohibits them, although these acts may occur in secrecy.[103] Moreover, even "appropriate" sexual activity between husband and wife may be "tinged with shame."[104] Merely making implicit references to genitals, defecation, or sexual intercourse brings shame, especially when both sexes are present. In addition, Gypsies consider yawning or looking sleepy shameful, because they suggest that one is thinking about going to bed.[105]

In spite of myths of Gypsy immorality, most Roma follow strict rules of sexual behavior. Prostitution and infidelity are unusual.[106] *Marime* rules are particularly harsh on women. For example, if a Gypsy male marries a *gaji* (non-Gypsy female), his community will eventually accept her, provided that she adopts the Gypsy way of life. But it is a worse violation of the *marime* code for a Gypsy female to marry a *gajo* (non-Gypsy male), because Gypsy women are the guarantors for the survival of the population.[107] Gypsies expect females to be virgins when they marry and to

---

Premarital sex reduces the amount of the bride price drastically. *See* SWAY, *supra* note 52, at 64. Yet abortion is exceedingly rare among Gypsies. CLÉBERT, *supra* note 44, at 162. According to Hancock, Gypsy boys typically date non-Gypsy girls (*raklia*). It is through these encounters that they acquire sexual expertise. Nonetheless, adult Gypsies discourage romantic involvement with *raklia*. Hancock, *Review, supra* note 35, at 77–78.

103. CLÉBERT, *supra* note 44, at 175; TRIGG, *supra* note 72, at 64–65; Miller, *Defilement, supra* note 62, at 42. No distinction is made between married or single Gypsies in regard to these prohibitions.

104. Silverman, *Gypsiness, supra* note 72, at 263. Silverman does not explain this observation. Okely indicates that loss of virginity even within marriage is viewed as a loss of purity, an unclean act. OKELY, TRAVELLER, *supra* note 62, at 209. The Romani word for "deflowered" is *porradi*, which means "spread apart," "split open," or "broken." Hancock, Notes, *supra* note 31, at 4 n.49. Parallels exist in Christianity. *See* 1 *Corinthians* 7:7–9 (stating Paul's admonition that staying unmarried is preferable to marriage, although marriage is permissible for those who cannot contain themselves); *see also* Schroeder, *supra* note 79, at 1190–95 (discussing views of medieval theologians that female sexuality is ritually polluting).

105. Miller, *Defilement, supra* note 62, at 42 n.3. Roma avoid the word *pato* for bed and use the euphemism *than* (place) instead. Hancock, Notes, *supra* note 31, at 4 n.48.

106. CLÉBERT, *supra* note 44, at 175; TRIGG, *supra* note 72, at 62–64. But it is not unusual, and sometimes even encouraged, for a Gypsy male to have clandestine sexual relations with a *gajikani* female. He must act with utmost discretion, because if he were found out he and his family would be *marime*. See Miller, Thesis, *supra* note 63, at 32–34; SUTHERLAND, *supra* note 29, at 262–63; *see also* San Román, *supra* note 101, at 193.

107. Miller suggests that the temporary period of *marime* for the *gajikani* wife lasts for approximately three to four months. During this time the *gaji* is taught proper washing and avoidance behavior. Miller, Thesis, *supra* note 63, at 15. Intermarriage remains rare. Hancock, *Gypsies, supra* note 60, at 442. According to a Romani source, intermarriage may have undesirable results because the mixed couple loses the full support of the Roma without gaining the respect of *gajikano* society. LEE, AUTOBIOGRAPHY, *supra* note 29, at 104, 117. Concern about intermarriage has also been raised in Jewish communities. *See* R. Gustav Niebuhr, *Keeping the Faith: Marriage and Family No Longer Are Ties That Bind to Judaism,* WALL ST. J., Aug. 8, 1991, at A1. According to Jewish law, which is matrilineal, the religion of the mother determines whether the child is born Jewish. *Id.* at A6.

remain faithful to their husbands until death. Infidelity in marriage historically has had serious consequences for the wife, including mutilation or a sentence of *marime*.[108]

HYGIENIC MATTERS

Complex rules also govern tangible items considered dirty or unhygienic.[109] In Romani society, food preparation is replete with ritual. A woman must serve a man from behind and guard against reaching across or in front of him. Gypsies use the dining table exclusively for eating and keep it immaculately clean. In the past, women wore full white aprons when preparing meals or mending men's clothing in order to protect the food or clothing from the "dirt" of their dresses.[110] Gypsies guard their dishes and utensils closely and generally do not share them with their *gajikane* guests. Visitors have to provide their own. If necessary, their hosts provide them with a set which traditionally must be destroyed afterwards or saved for other non-Gypsy visitors. Today, Gypsies use paper or plastic plates and tableware for this purpose. Silverware may regain purity after being soaked in bleach. Food in which a hair has been found must be discarded. Blowing one's nose or sneezing

---

With regard to marriages of Gypsy women to *gajikane* men, see SUTHERLAND, *supra* note 29, at 247–53; Miller, *Defilement*, *supra* note 62, at 45. Such a marriage is likely to be perceived as a rejection of *romaniya* (Gypsy law). The character and quality of a Gypsy woman is largely judged by whether she is perceived to be respectable, which is determined by whether she follows Gypsy laws and customs. LEE, AUTOBIOGRAPHY, *supra* note 29, at 57.

108. CLÉBERT, *supra* note 44, at 175–76; TRIGG, *supra* note 72, at 62–64. Quintana and Floyd assert that Gypsy females in Spain strongly support the double standard as well as the punishments. The Gitana maintain that their fidelity is further proof of their superiority. BERTHA B. QUINTANA & LOIS G. FLOYD, ¡QUÉ GITANO! GYPSIES OF SOUTHERN SPAIN 36 (1972).

109. Trigg groups various Romani taboos under the heading *mokadi*. TRIGG, *supra* note 72, at 54–55. The Vlax Roma distinguish between things that are *melyade* (visibly dirty) and things that are *marime* (ritually polluted). These concepts are perceived differently by the Vlax Roma and the non-Gypsies. The *gaje* focus on visible dirt. The Roma, however, are concerned with inward cleanliness. Each perceives the other as dirty or polluted. GROPPER, *supra* note 79, at 91. An untidy or unkept home would not be *marime*, assuming adherence to *marime* regulations regarding washing and preparation of food. Instead, the home would be considered *melyade*. Untidiness can generate much gossip, even heated debate within a *kumpania* (a group of Roma living or travelling together). A house, however, that has been occupied only by Roma, even if it is *melyade*, is still considered "cleaner" than a home formerly occupied by non-Gypsies or by a banished Roma family. The Gypsies consider the latter two *marime*. SUTHERLAND, *supra* note 29, at 270; *see also supra* note 62.

The Vlax also have a concept of *pokelime* for something that is already defiled. *Gajikane* movies, literature, mass communication, and advertisements are *pokelime*, because they were polluted at their inception. Hancock, *Review*, *supra* note 35, at 74–75 (noting also the differences in terminology among various Romani populations).

110. MCLAUGHLIN, *supra* note 58, at 21 (discussing eating rituals). According to Okely, small aprons are still worn today and symbolize "a true Gypsy." OKELY, TRAVELLER, *supra* note 62, at 208; *see also* TRIGG, *supra* note 72, at 56–57; Thompson, *supra* note 82, at 19, 24.

would pollute the food and make the offender *marime*, as would neglecting to wash one's hands before eating. A man who touches a woman's skirt should not handle food without washing his hands first.[111] Even a shadow can pollute food.[112]

A kitchen sink cannot be used for washing hands or clothes, only for cleaning dishes and silverware. A Rom who accidentally washes his hands in a basin for washing dishes is *marime*. Dishes that are mistakenly washed in a "polluted" place, regardless of their apparent cleanliness, must be destroyed or soaked in bleach. Gypsies divide their living quarters into *marime* and *vujo* areas. The front of the house could be *marime* unless protective measures are taken, since this is where the *gaje* may enter. Gypsies often reserve one chair for *gajikane* visitors. A Rom must never sit in this chair, for if he does, he will be deemed *marime*. Today, other furniture is protected from pollution with plastic covers. Gypsies never permit *gaje* in the back of the house.[113]

The division between pure and impure extends to bodily by-products. Gypsies consider tears, spit, and even vomit clean because they emanate from the top half of the body, whereas emissions from the lower half of the body are polluting. Gypsies will take extreme measures to conceal the fact that they need to urinate.[114]

Marime taboos extend to animals as well, from the edibility of certain types of meat to pet ownership. For example, dogs and cats, as opposed to horses, are considered polluted because of their unclean living habits. Gypsies consider cats particularly unclean because they lick their paws after burying their feces. The critical concern (as with dogs licking themselves) is that the uncleanliness of the external world may defile the purity of the inner self if it is permitted to enter the body through the mouth. Cats are also a sign of impending death. If a cat sets foot in a Gypsy's house, trailer, or automobile, a purification ceremony is required. Dogs

---

111. McLAUGHLIN, *supra* note 58, at 21–22; SALO & SALO, *supra* note 77, at 120–21; *cf.* RAV ZVI COHEN, TEVILATH KELIM: A COMPREHENSIVE GUIDE 17, 37, 115 (1988) (discussing Judaic laws that require ritual washing of utensils acquired through purchase or gift from non-Jewish sources); MOSHE MORGAN, A GUIDE TO THE LAWS OF KASHRUS 107 (discussing whether it is permissible to use refrigerator which has been used by non-Jew). The reader is cautioned that rules in communities of different ethnic backgrounds, even if outwardly comparable, may be based on substantially different rationales.

112. The shadow of the *gaje* is particularly polluting. Judith Okely, *Why Gypsies Hate Cats but Love Horses*, 63 NEW SOC'Y 251, 252 (1983) [hereinafter Okely, *Cats*].

113. On cleanliness and visitors, see generally McLAUGHLIN, *supra* note 58, at 21–22; YOORS, GYPSIES, *supra* note 42, at 150; Okely, *Gypsy Women*, *supra* note 62, at 60; Thompson, *supra* note 82, at 20. If used and washed properly, items commonly used for food preparation such as tablecloths, dish towels, and dishes can become *melyade*. They do not become *marime* unless prohibited contact is made, for example, when a towel falls on the floor. SUTHERLAND, *supra* note 29, at 266–69. When moving into a house that has been occupied by *gaje*, Gypsies may board up sinks or replace them with new ones for fear that the original facilities were used for improper purposes, in particular urination. OKELY, TRAVELLER, *supra* note 62, at 82; SALO & SALO, *supra* note 77, at 120.

114. SUTHERLAND, *supra* note 29, at 265–66; YOORS, GYPSIES, *supra* note 42, at 30. According to Vogel, *supra* note 29, at 37, even flushing the toilet can be embarrassing for many Roma. Among the Gitanos in Spain, however, many of these taboos have virtually disappeared. MERRILL McLANE, PROUD OUTCASTS 48 (1987).

are also unclean, but to a lesser extent. Dogs are tolerated outside the house because of their value as watchdogs.[115]

Socially disruptive behavior may result in legal sanctions, including a sentence of *marime*. In addition to strong taboos against exploiting or stealing from a fellow member of the Gypsy community, Gypsies consider crimes of violence and noncommercial association with *gaje* as crimes against Romani society as a whole and therefore *marime*.[116] A *marime* label can be removed by the forgiveness of the offended party, the passage of time, or by a Gypsy legal proceeding called *kris Romani*. Readmission to Gypsy society following a sentence of *marime* is cause for celebration.[117]

In all cases of *marime*, enforcement depends primarily on a superstitious fear of the consequences of violating the *marime* rules. The individual who violates a *marime* prohibition has succumbed to powers of evil and destruction that are so frightening that even his own family shuns him for fear of contamination. Such an individual becomes tainted and can be redeemed only by making the prescribed amends.[118]

Administration of Justice

Because of the general lack of territorial boundaries, each Gypsy group can determine its own form of adjudication. Although there are many words for "group" in the

---

115. MCLAUGHLIN, *supra* note 58, at 22; OKELY, TRAVELLER, *supra* note 62, at 91–97; TRIGG, *supra* note 72, at 69; Okely, *Cats, supra* note 112, at 253 (describing rejection of cats for being polluted). The Biblical rules, *Leviticus* 11:2–22; *Deuteronomy* 14:4–21, prohibit eating dogs and cats. For many people, regardless of their religious or ethnic affiliation, these prohibitions have become rules of oral legal tradition.

116. GROPPER, *supra* note 79, at 90, 106; SUTHERLAND, *supra* note 29, at 257–58; SWAY, *supra* note 52, at 78; YOORS, GYPSIES, *supra* note 42, at 176–79 (describing a Gypsy trial relating to theft); Miller, *Defilement, supra* note 62, at 46 (discussing noneconomic association with *gaje*); San Román, *supra* note 101, at 191–94 (describing substantive criminal law among Gitanos in Spain). Much behavior that is acceptable to and commonplace among non-Gypsies is taboo for the Roma. Consequently, any exchange with *gaje* entails a risk of pollution. LIÉGEOIS, *supra* note 52, at 76.

117. MCLAUGHLIN, *supra* note 58, at 20 (noting ways in which one can remove oneself from *marime* state).

118. TRIGG, *supra* note 72, at 55. Trigg uses the term *mokadi* instead of *marime*. The terms vary depending on the particular Romani population involved. The fear of being declared *marime* is a powerful means of social control. Letter from Marlene Sway, *supra* note 94 ("Even if a Gypsy is tried on a *marime* charge and is cleared by the *kris*, the stigma or cloud of doubt lingers for his or her entire lifetime."). Some observers have suggested similar aspects in our own proceedings that prevent rehabilitation. Goffman notes that "barbarous ceremonies" in our society, such as criminal trials and courts-martial, have the sole purpose of preventing the accused from saving face. Erving Goffman, *On Cooling the Mark Out: Some Aspects of Adaptation to Failure*, 15 PSYCHIATRY 451, 462 (1952). Disclosure of arrest records, whether the accused was convicted or not, are required on immigration and naturalization applications, applications for law schools, and applications for taking the bar examination and for being admitted to the practice of law. For example, see Florida Board of Bar Examiners, Application for Admission to the Florida Bar, form 1, revised Dec. 1992, Question No. 20 a:

Gypsy language, four primary associations can be identified: *natsia,* meaning nation; *kumpania,* an alliance of households not necessarily of the same *natsia* but of the same geographic area bound together for socioeconomic reasons; *vitsa,* or clan; and *familia,* which consists of the individual extended family.[119] Each associational unit is involved in the administration of justice, beginning with the smallest, the *familia,* which informally settles minor disputes, and extending to the larger units with increasing formality.

ROLE OF CHIEFS

Gypsies have no kings in the traditional meaning of the term.[120] Every *vitsa* has a *rom baro,* literally meaning "Big Man," commonly referred to as the chief. The chief is elected for life, and the position is not inheritable.[121] If a chief dies or falls into disgrace, another chief is chosen to replace him. The main criteria for chiefdom are intelligence and a sense of fairness. Wealth and large physical stature are not required, although they help. Most chiefs are literate.[122] Elders are considered particularly suited to this role because they have greater knowledge of *romaniya* and

---

List all instances in your entire life (including while you were a juvenile) in which you have been arrested, detained or restrained, given a warning or taken into custody or accused, formally or informally, of the violation of a law, or ordinance, or accused, formally or informally, of committing a delinquent act and attach a detailed explanation of the facts and the subsequent actions taken by the authorities.

A preamble clarifies in greater detail that no expunging or sealing of records, or dismissing, vacating, or setting aside any arrest "shall excuse less than full disclosure, irrespective of any advice from any source that such information need not be disclosed." *See also* Michelson v. United States, 335 U.S. 469, 482 (1948) ("Arrest without more may nevertheless impair or cloud one's reputation."); Menard v. Mitchell, 430 F.2d 486, 491 n.24 (D.C. Cir. 1970) ("Presumably the fact of arrest indicates some possibility that the individual concerned engaged in the criminal activity with which he was charged.").

119. *See also* SUTHERLAND, *supra* note 29, at 10–13, 32–34, 181–205; SWAY, *supra* note 52, at 61; YOORS, GYPSIES, *supra* note 42, at 134–35; Anne Sutherland, *Gypsies: The Hidden Americans,* 12 SOCIETY 27, 28 (1975); LIÉGEOIS, *supra* note 52, at 57–66. Within each *kumpania,* there are further divisions called *wortacha* (partners). These groups are formed between members of the same sex who work together. They may include fathers and sons, or mothers and daughters. SUTHERLAND, *supra* note 29, at 66–68. *But see* Hancock, *Gypsies, supra* note 60, at 442 (noting that Romanichals only divided into clans and families). The Lovara do not use the term *vitsa.* Hancock, Notes, *supra* note 31, at 5 n.56.

120. On the absence of law enforcement, see YOORS, GYPSIES, *supra* note 42, at 174. On the absence of kings, see SWAY, *supra* note 52, at 61. According to Yoors, "kings" existed among the European Lovara, but not as portrayed by the media. These kings were actually informal intermediaries between the real chiefs and the local *gajikane* authorities. YOORS, GYPSIES, *supra* note 42, at 114–16. GROPPER, *supra* note 79, at 70–72, indicates that these false "kings" do not exist in the United States. For an illustration of how the label "king" was attached to a Gypsy spokesman by a reporter, see LEE, AUTOBIOGRAPHY, *supra* note 29, at 111–21.

121. CLÉBERT, *supra* note 44, at 126–28. Yet GROPPER, *supra* note 79, at 71, notes that one of the sons of a former chief typically becomes the next leader.

122. With regard to the Roma, see CLÉBERT, *supra* note 44, at 126. Some authors suggest that the *rom baro* is self-appointed and not selected or elected. *See* McLAUGHLIN, *supra* note 58, at 16; SALO & SALO,

are believed to be less susceptible to the temptations of violating the *marime* code. The chief chairs the council of elders, generally the patriarchs of the extended families. He is held accountable if he himself violates Gypsy law or ignores the other chiefs. All chiefs have equal authority and decide jointly about when the larger group should migrate.[123]

There is a female counterpart to the chief. Her power is unofficial but substantial. The Vlax call her *mami, daki-dei,* or *dadeski-dei.* Other Gypsy groups use the term *phuri-dae* (old mother). She is the guardian of the moral code and helps decide matters involving women and children. In important affairs involving the entire *kumpania,* she is the spokeswoman for Gypsy women.[124]

The tribal chiefs are not necessarily aware of all the laws; not only are the laws too numerous, but many laws have been lost because they have never been written down. The Gypsies interpret laws according to contemporary custom. Former rationales and interpretations of laws gradually may be revised as the needs of the community evolve. The exclusive reliance on oral transmission has led to a high degree of flexibility. Nevertheless, there is a shared, though not necessarily realistic, feeling that the law is clearly defined. Few ever challenge this notion. This strict adherence to the law in part accounts for the continued cohesion of the Gypsies in spite of their persecution and forced migration. Secrecy surrounds Gypsy law; unauthorized disclosure to the *gaje* may lead to sanctions.[125]

Each chief handles all day-to-day conflicts within his population. When conflict emerges between Gypsies of different *vitsi* or *kumpaniyi* (singular *kumpania*), a *divano* may assemble.[126] A *divano* is an informal proceeding in which the chiefs of the

---

supra note 77, at 55–56. According to SUTHERLAND, *supra* note 29, at 116, a *rom baro* should ideally be tall and have a large body frame and head. Literacy may be desirable or even necessary because of the *rom baro*'s role as a liaison between the Roma and the *gajikane* authorities. On literacy see GROPPER, *supra* note 79, at 71; SWAY, *supra* note 52, at 61.

123. CLÉBERT, *supra* note 44, at 126–28. *See generally* GROPPER, *supra* note 79, at 70–80, 102. According to SUTHERLAND, *supra* note 29, at 104, there is a positive correlation between age and knowledge of *romaniya* (Gypsy law).

124. CLÉBERT, *supra* note 44, at 128; SWAY, *supra* note 52, at 61–62. According to BLOCK, *supra* note 44, at 170–71, the old mother traditionally had some formal powers. For example, although the chief had to be present at weddings, it was the old mother who performed the ceremony. If the chief was unavailable for dispute consultation, it was the old mother who made the final adjudication. So powerful was her presence that even her glance and cry, "I am old, I am old," struck fear in all, because she had the power to inflict curses and bring bad luck. *See also* Rao, *supra* note 72, at 143–44.

125. CLÉBERT, *supra* note 44, at 131–32 (discussing secrecy); GROPPER, *supra* note 79, at 98 (discussing flexibility of *romaniya* and oral tradition).

126. LEE, AUTOBIOGRAPHY, *supra* note 29, at 68; McLAUGHLIN, *supra* note 58, at 22–23. According to Pickett, *supra* note 88, at 6–7, the Gypsies of Mexico successfully used the *divano* for dispute resolution. *But see* Jan Yoors, *Lowari Law and Jurisdiction,* 26 J. GYPSY LORE SOC'Y 1, 2 (1947) [hereinafter Yoors, *Lowari Law*] (noting that *divano* may perpetuate quarrels and result in interminable discussions).

The Emirate of Kuwait has an institution called *diwaniya.* In regularly scheduled meetings, headed by the Crown Prince, friends and members of the extended family gather to discuss grievances. John

various clans try to mediate a dispute. The parties themselves are not required to attend—and they are not technically bound by the chiefs' suggestions. But the contestants sometimes do bow to peer pressure and settle the case. Blatant disregard for the chiefs' recommendations could cost them the respect of the community.[127]

ROLE OF COURTS (*KRIS*)

When the Roma cannot settle a controversy amicably in a *divano*, a *kris* may become necessary.[128] In former times, the *kris* usually adjudicated three kinds of cases: property losses, matters of honor, and moral or religious issues, including nonobservance of *marime* taboos.[129] Brawls, demands by parents for return of their married daughters, defaults in payments of debts, *marime* violations, and personal retribution all required the attention of the *kris*.[130] In the United States today, the *kris* calendar is largely occupied by divorce cases and economic disputes.[131]

Divorce cases are complex. Even today, most Gypsy marriages (which may not be legal marriages according to *gajikano* law) are arranged, and the groom's family

---

Kifner, *After the War: Emir Disparaged at Kuwaiti Forums*, N.Y. TIMES, Mar. 27, 1991, at A8. The word *divano* is of Persian origin and means council of state or court of justice. Lee, Kris, *supra* note 51, at 20 n.1.

127. MCLAUGHLIN, *supra* note 58, at 23; *see also* SUTHERLAND, *supra* note 29, at 131. According to a Gypsy saying, "It's better to part as friends from a *divano* than as enemies from a *kris*." Hancock, Notes, *supra* note 31, at 5 n.59.

128. SWAY, *supra* note 52, at 77. For an excellent description of the *kris* and the applicable law, see Lee, Kris, *supra* note 51. Lee cites with approval GROPPER, *supra* note 79, and SALO & SALO, *supra* note 77. *See also* David J. Nemeth, *Gypsy Justice in America*, I J. GYPSY LORE SOC'Y 3 (1974): David J. Nemeth, *Field Notes from 1970: A Kris in River City*, in 100 YEARS OF GYPSY STUDIES 117 (Matt T. Salo ed., 1990) [hereinafter Nemeth, *Field Notes*]. The word *kris* is not of Indian origin. The term derives from the Greek word *krisis*, meaning judgment. FRASER, *supra* note 28, at 56; Lee, Kris, *supra* note 51, at 19. The *kris* as a judicial institution exists among the Vlax, the most numerous Romani group in the United States. It appears that the conditions of slavery in Rumania, under which the Vlax lived for five centuries, helped to preserve the *kris* as part of their distinct culture. *See* Hancock, *Diaspora I, supra* note 38, at 617. The Vlax *kris* may be modeled after a council of elders of non-Gypsy villagers in Rumania that also settled disputes. Hancock, Notes, *supra* note 31, at 5 n.59. The Romanichals (British Gypsies) and the descendants of Balkan Gypsies, who were not enslaved, do not have the *kris*. Lee, Kris, *supra* note 51, at 19.

129. Yoors, *Lowari Law, supra* note 126, at 3. During *kris* proceedings the litigants agree to a truce. *Id.* at 11. According to GROPPER, *supra* note 79, at 82, a judge will not accept a case for a *kris* unless the litigants take an oath promising to abide by the decision. *See also* MCLAUGHLIN, *supra* note 58, at 23.

130. C.-H. Tillhagen, *III. Conception of Justice Among the Swedish Gypsies*, 38 J. GYPSY LORE SOC'Y 18, 19 (1959) [hereinafter Tillhagen, *III*]. A detailed list of controversies falling under the jurisdiction of the *kris* is also contained in Lee, Kris, *supra* note 51, at 21–22. *See also* SUTHERLAND, *supra* note 29, at 292–304 (giving account of two Gypsy trials: (1) *kris Romani* in New Orleans and (2) *divano* in Wichita, reported by John Marks, party to proceedings).

131. According to GROPPER, *supra* note 79, at 85–91, four kinds of cases dominate the *kris* calendar in the United States: (1) work related, e.g., unfair division of profits; (2) divorce; (3) feuding between extended families and bands; and (4) matters similar to our criminal cases, e.g., murder, rape, theft (*marime* violations). See also *Salo & Salo, supra* note 77, at 59, for parallels to Kalderasha in Canada.

pays a bride price. If the marriage ends in divorce, a *kris* may be called to determine how much, if any, of the bride price should be returned to the groom's family.[132]

Economic cases, on the other hand, cover such issues as who has the right to engage in fortune-telling in a specific territory. Gypsies believe that every Gypsy has the right to work. Accordingly, groups divide territory into economic units. Controversies may result when some Gypsies poach on others' turf, and then a *kris* is called. A first-time offender may receive a warning by the *kris*. Repeated violations result in a sentence of *marime*.[133]

In all cases, it is the aggrieved party who must request the *kris*, which is then held at a neutral *kumpania*. If the alleged victim is old, sick, or very young, the victim's nearest male relative brings the case to the *kris*. If the welfare of the community demands joint action, the entire clan may be a plaintiff.[134]

The elders of the tribes then hold a meeting and select one or more men to act as the *krisnitorya* (singular *krisnitori*), or judges. The plaintiff is allowed to choose the judge who will preside over his case, but the defendant has a right to veto that choice.[135] Among the Roma in the United States it is not unusual for more than one judge to preside.[136] The senior judge is surrounded by the members of the *kris*

---

132. GROPPER, *supra* note 79, at 88–89; SWAY, *supra* note 52, at 73. According to Hancock, *Gypsies, supra* note 60, at 442, arranged marriages are fairly common among both the Romanichals and the Roma (Gypsies of eastern and southern Europe, principally the Mačvaya, Kalderasha, Churara, and Lovara). Sometimes the marriage agreement, arranged by the parents, is completed prior to the child's birth.

A Gypsy woman may occasionally use the *gajikane* courts to get a more favorable divorce settlement. But this is a violation of *romaniya* (Gypsy law) and may result in a *kris*. It appears that Gypsy marriages and divorces are de facto recognized by the *gajikano* legal system. This tolerance may be due to official indifference, or it may be due to American state-law presumptions of what constitutes marriage. *See* Walter O. Weyrauch, *Informal Marriage and Formal Marriage: An Appraisal of Trends in Family Organization,* 28 U. CHI. L. REV. 88, 105–08 (1960). Moreover, some states still recognize common-law marriage. The requirements for the presumption of marriage and common-law marriage are identical: cohabitation and the repute of being married. The minimum ages for a valid common-law marriage were, and in some states still are, twelve for the female and fourteen for the male. HOMER H. CLARK, THE LAW OF DOMESTIC RELATIONS IN THE UNITED STATES 49–50 (on cohabitation and repute of being married), 89 n.8 (on age limits) (2d ed. student ed., 1988).

133. SWAY, *supra* note 52, at 88–89.

134. MCLAUGHLIN, *supra* note 58, at 23; SUTHERLAND, *supra* note 29, at 134; Yoors, *Lowari Law, supra* note 126, at 3–9 (noting that Romani group may act as plaintiff if victim fails to complain about an act that shames community as whole, e.g., adultery; winner pays for feast following *kris*). According to SUTHERLAND, *supra* note 29, at 132, the public and not the litigants decide to have a *kris*, in serious civil matters as well as in criminal matters.

In the United States, calling a *kris* involves notifying the parties, renting a "court room" or hall, and making provisions for food and beverage for all in attendance. The guilty party pays all the costs including travel expenses. GROPPER, *supra* note 79, at 96; SWAY, *supra* note 52, at 78.

135. Tillhagen, *III, supra* note 130, at 21 (describing selection of judge for Swedish *kris*). The procedure for the American *kris* is probably similar because it requires the parties to agree on the judge, usually after protracted haggling. *See* Lee, *Kris, supra* note 51, at 26, 29.

136. MCLAUGHLIN, *supra* note 58, at 23. No firm rule suggests when more than one judge should be selected. YOORS, GYPSIES, *supra* note 42, at 174, states that without a permanent judicial cadre, the

council, who act as associate judges.[137] Generally, five or more men from both sides, usually the elders, form the council. In the United States, the council may have as many as twenty-five members.[138]

The audience of a *kris* was once largely male. Women and unmarried or childless men were allowed to attend only if they were needed as witnesses. It is now acceptable, if unusual, to have the entire family present for support.[139] Witnesses may speak freely about the case, for the Gypsies believe there can be no justice without hearing the matter out to its fullest.[140] Exaggerated claims and ornate stories referring to folktales and mythology are common.[141] When members of the audience think the witness is not being truthful or responsive, they hiss or make jokes.[142] In some delicate matters, such as adultery, the public and witnesses can be excluded.[143] At a *kris* only Romani may be spoken, and participants discourage lapses into English by shouting and hissing. Furthermore, arguments are often presented in a special oratory that differs grammatically from ordinary Romani and resembles a legal jargon.[144] When the accused testify on their own behalf they are ex-

---

selection of judges would depend upon the number of qualified men available. Lee refers to the *krisnitorya* as an advisory body sitting together with the judge or judges. Since these men appear to be "associate judges" rather than a jury, they may sometimes have been mistakenly counted as judges. Lee, Kris, *supra* note 51, at 26.

137. CLÉBERT, *supra* note 44, at 130.

138. McLAUGHLIN, *supra* note 58, at 23. It should be remembered that the *kris* procedure is based on oral tradition and may vary from case to case and depending on what particular Romani group is involved. YOORS, GYPSIES, *supra* note 42, at 174.

139. GROPPER, *supra* note 79, at 83 (noting that no Gypsy would be denied admission to *kris*); Yoors, *Lowari Law, supra* note 126, at 6. Among the Swedish Gypsies, women accompanied their husbands to the *kris*. Tillhagen, *III, supra* note 130, at 21. The Gitanos in Spain do not tolerate the presence of women. *See* QUINTANA & FLOYD, *supra* note 108, at 73. Their presence at the *kris* is also not permitted in Canada, except in the capacity of witness. Lee, Kris, *supra* note 51, at 26.

Jeatran, the daughter of a Lovara Rom and a *gajikani* woman, has studied American Gypsies and reports that women may attend the *kris*, although they are not permitted to speak unless they are litigants or witnesses. A Romani informant has told Jeatran that "because we are in America now, so we have to respect the 'Women's Lib.' " Patti J. Jeatran, Disputing and Social Control Among American Gypsies 22 (Nov. 14, 1990) (unpublished paper, University of Illinois Department of Criminal Justice, on file with authors) [hereinafter Jeatran, Social Control]. According to Jeatran's informant, women are not allowed to participate in the *kris* because "if an old one speaks, a young one will start arguing with her and disrupt everything." *Id.* at 26. Hancock stresses that he has never been to a *kris* where women were let into the hall. Hancock, Notes, *supra* note 31, at 5 n.60.

140. GROPPER, *supra* note 79, at 81–84.

141. McLAUGHLIN, *supra* note 58, at 23–24.

142. SWAY, *supra* note 52, at 78 (noting hissing and joking as informal sanctions). Tillhagen, *III, supra* note 130, at 24, reports that Swedish Gypsies did not tolerate such disruptions. The European Lovara also adhered to strict rules of behavior. *See* Yoors, *Lowari Law, supra* note 126, at 11.

143. Yoors, *Lowari Law, supra* note 126, at 6. In cases of exclusion, the *kris* scrutinizes the evidence of defilement and publicly pronounces the defendant as either clean or *marime*.

144. GROPPER, *supra* note 79, at 84–85; Lee, Kris, *supra* note 51, at 28. According to Jeatran, Social

pected to be truthful.[145] The *kris* can further insure their honesty by invoking the magic power of the dead with an oath. If the witnesses must swear an oath, an altar of justice consisting of icons of the clans present is erected.[146] In complex situations, the judge may ask for expert opinions from tribal chiefs or the elders. Nonetheless, only the judge decides guilt and punishment.[147]

The judge declares the verdict in public to those who are present. In former times, if the accused Rom was found guilty, a married Gypsy woman was symbolically called on to tear a piece of cloth from her dress and throw it at the Rom, but this ritual is no longer practiced. If the accused is found innocent, there is a celebration and an oath of peace is sworn. The decision of the *kris* is final and binding.[148] Even in countries such as Spain and the United States, where the Roma are considered by some *gajikane* scholars to be semi-assimilated, the verdict of an official state trial is not final: a *kris* will still be held. Beyond its judicial function, the *kris* plays an important role in maintaining the customs of the Gypsy people.[149]

Recent developments suggest the possibility of cooperation between the Romani and American judicial systems. By March 1987, local Roma in Southern California had reportedly established eighteen territorial jurisdictions, each with its own judge. The idea was that these *kris* would receive case referrals from the Cal-

---

Control, *supra* note 139, at 26, some young Gypsy men in the United States ridicule the formal oratory and prefer telephone "conference calling" to settle their disputes, perhaps as a preliminary step to a *divano*.

145. C.-H. Tillhagen, *V. Conceptions of Justice Among the Swedish Gypsies*, 38 J. GYPSY LORE SOC'Y 127, 131 (1959) (quoting Romani source on honesty among Gypsies) [hereinafter Tillhagen, *V*]. *But see* Yoors, *Lowari Law, supra* note 126, at 13 (accused tries to elude questions and attempts to make the crime seem less serious). The Roma present their own case, husbands answering for their wives. Yet, spokesmen, the equivalent of lawyers, can be employed to plead the case for the parties. They may be young men who test their rhetorical skills and their capacity for leadership. GROPPER, *supra* note 79, at 82–84; MCLAUGHLIN, *supra* note 58, at 23–24; Yoors, *Lowari Law, supra* note 126, at 3. Jeatran, Social Control, *supra* note 139, at 20, describes two exceptional cases in which non-Gypsies attended a *kris:* a local *gajikano* attorney acting as informal counsel in a child custody matter and a California social worker appearing at the Gypsies' request for informational purposes.

146. CLÉBERT, *supra* note 44, at 130; YOORS, GYPSIES, *supra* note 42, at 177–79; *see also* Yoors, *Lowari Law, supra* note 126, at 17 (describing solemn oath, *solax,* administered when no decision can be reached). According to GROPPER, *supra* note 79, at 83, a new trial must be held if the *krisnitorya* cannot reach a decision. Parties may also swear an oath before the *kris,* agreeing to abide by the decision. SUTHERLAND, *supra* note 29, at 134–35.

147. CLÉBERT, *supra* note 43, at 130. As long as the *kris* has not proceeded beyond hearing from the witnesses and final instructions, either the plaintiff or the defendant may request permission to settle the case outside the *kris.* Yoors, *Lowari Law, supra* note 126, at 14. After hearing from both sides, but before giving the decision, an impartial elder may emerge to attack the litigants' arguments. *Id.* at 16. Among the Lovara, if a judge appears to be wrong on a point of law, the council can ask him to justify his decision. *Id.* at 4.

148. SUTHERLAND, *supra* note 29, at 132. *But see* Yoors, *Lowari Law, supra* note 126, at 5 (observing that appeals are allowed among European Lovara, but severely frowned upon); *see also* CLÉBERT, *supra* note 44, at 130 (oath of peace).

149. *Cf.* CLÉBERT, *supra* note 44, at 130–31; GROPPER, *supra* note 79, at 180.

ifornia state courts of civil and domestic disputes involving only Gypsies. The local *kris* would then refer nonbinding recommendations back to the California courts.[150] In another recent development, over two hundred Roma gathered for an advisory *kris* in Houston to discuss improving the rights of divorced women under the Romani legal system, to keep pace with developments in American law and to remove the incentive for Gypsy women to appeal to the American legal system for a stronger remedy.[151] These developments could conceivably lead to the establishment of standing Romani courts within each state.[152] But it is unclear how the American legal system would respond to such a system, since it does not recognize Romani law as binding. Gypsies, too, might find it difficult to abandon their traditional distrust of American courts.

LEGAL SANCTIONS

The *kris* imposes punishment according to the seriousness of the offense. The death penalty, once an acceptable option, is now virtually unknown[153]—possibly because of the Gypsies' fear of spirits and belief that the angry ghost of the deceased will take revenge upon the executioner. In times when the death penalty was still employed, the entire community would participate in the execution to prevent revenge by the spirit. The Roma seemed to feel a joint undertaking was safer, although today

---

150. Lee, Kris, *supra* note 51, at 32. We were not able to confirm that this procedure, if approved, was ever implemented, but the Gypsies' desire for any affiliation with the American court system is unprecedented. Telephone Interview with Barry A. Fisher, Attorney-at-Law, Los Angeles, Cal. (Mar. 8, 1993), who has represented Romani interests in the past.

151. Lee, Kris, *supra* note 51, at 32–33. Hancock, who participated in a Houston *kris* that dealt with the topics of child support and divorce, reports:

> The issue was that divorced women were going to the *gajikane dukaturya* (non-Gypsy lawyers) for relief because the *kris* wasn't satisfactory. The main concern was that by going to the *gaje*, the power of the *kris* was being undermined. In order for it to maintain its strength (*krisaki putyerya*) it would have to provide better resolutions to divorcees (divorced according to Romani tradition, not American tradition). So control cuts both ways. The decision was to enforce more responsibility on the part of the father.

Letter from Ian F. Hancock, Romani Union, Professor of Linguistics, University of Texas, to Walter O. Weyrauch, at 5 n.46 (July 1990) (on file with authors) [hereinafter Hancock, Letter].

Hancock also describes a *kris* in California that debated the issue of whether Romani women could wear jeans. He adds that European Roma think that this topic is too trivial to require a *kris* and that a *divano* would have been more appropriate. *See also* SUTHERLAND, *supra* note 29, at 131–32 (*divano* involving many *vitsi* may decide matters of general policy). These consultative functions of the *kris* or *divano* resemble the *Weistum* in medieval Germany, in which learned authorities gave legal advice. In the contemporary American context, these functions resemble the opinions of the attorneys general. On the *divano*, see *supra* notes 126–27 and accompanying text.

152. Lee, Kris, *supra* note 51, at 34.

153. CLÉBERT, *supra* note 44, at 130.

they rarely test this belief.[154] Nowadays, the *kris* relies primarily on such sanctions as fines, corporal punishment, and banishment. The responsibility to pay a *kris*-imposed fine, called *glaba*, falls collectively on the wrongdoer's lineage.[155] Corporal punishment, rarely employed today, is typically used only in cases of a wife's infidelity.

A sentence of *marime*, or banishment, is today considered the most severe punishment. *Marime* stigmatizes all wrongdoers as polluted and justifies their expulsion from the community. No one will eat with them. If they touch an object it must be destroyed, no matter what the value. Nobody will even attempt to kill them, for fear of contamination. When they die, no one will bury them, and they will not have a funeral. They will soon be forgotten.[156] No marriages are arranged for those stigmatized as *marime*, and without marriage in Gypsy society one's economic and social life is over.[157] In other words, permanent banishment is the equivalent of social death. Such punishment is rare and used only for serious crimes such as murder. An escape into *gajikano* society is not an alternative for the banished wrongdoer, however. Disdain for the non-Gypsy world, acquired in early infancy, maintains its hold over most Roma even after their expulsion from the community.

A temporary *marime* sentence may be imposed for less serious crimes. If a Gypsy steals from another Gypsy, for example, the thief is publicly shamed and banished from the community until he or she has repaid the victim. The *kris* may impose a

---

154. GROPPER, *supra* note 79, at 100–02. Gropper also notes that a permanent sentence of *marime* is seen as equivalent to a death sentence; the permanent outcast, in fact, often commits suicide. A death sentence thus becomes unnecessary, and the sentence of *marime* also provides a form of sanctuary against revenge of the spirit. *Id., see also* FRASER, *supra* note 28, at 243 (fear of spirits). Reisman comments that interviews with Gypsy defectors could be the subject of an interesting follow-up study. Reisman, *Comment, supra* note 46, at 404. In Canada, resettling outside the Gypsy community has occurred. *See infra* note 160.

155. LIÉGEOIS, *supra* note 52, at 76–77. In her study of Gitano urban populations, San Román, *supra* note 101, at 192–93, divides "wrongs" in Gypsy society into two categories: (1) wrongs that have consequences for the wrongdoer's lineage and the victim's lineage, and (2) wrongs that have consequences only for the wrongdoer and the victim's lineage. The first category of wrongs consists of serious offenses like murder, bloodshed, serious assault, and "naming the dead" (insults directed toward a deceased relative). Bloodshed and assault may or may not be avenged. These wrongs are generally dealt with on the spot by a fight among members of the respective lineages present. However, murder and "naming the dead" are crimes that must be addressed by the *kris Romani*. Murder is extremely rare because of the Gypsies' fear of ghosts.

The second category of wrongs involves mostly sexual offenses such as rape and incest. In Gitano society, the male is held primarily responsible for these wrongs. Women are held less accountable because of their assumed inferiority. Nonetheless, depending on the group, infidelity may carry serious penalties for a female. QUINTANA & FLOYD, *supra* note 108, at 35, report that among the Gypsies in Spain punishments may include facial disfigurement and other mutilation, public beatings, and death.

156. CLÉBERT, *supra* note 44, at 124–25 (quoting Mateo Maximoff). A person who receives a permanent sentence of *marime* is treated very much like someone in today's society who is diagnosed with an infectious disease. *See also* SUTHERLAND, *supra* note 29, at 98–99. Hancock reports that a Rom with AIDS committed suicide in New York City three years ago because of the shame (*lajav*) associated with the illness. Hancock, Notes, *supra* note 31, at 6 n.66.

157. *Cf.* SWAY, *supra* note 52, at 118.

form of "community service" and require the *marime* Rom to work for an indefinite time without pay in order to compensate Gypsy society for violating the taboo of stealing from another Gypsy. Temporary sentences of *marime* are also imposed for offenses such as familiarity with the *gaje* or failure to pay a debt on time.[158]

The entire Gypsy community is responsible for enforcing sanctions. Gypsies have no police or prisons; they have no "law enforcement" in the *gajikano* sense. Peer pressure fanned by gossip and communal knowledge of the verdict tend to ensure the wrongdoer's compliance.[159] The Gypsy community may place a curse on the guilty party to insure that he or she accepts the chosen punishment, and it appears that this practice is still effective. Only in rare cases, when the Roma have difficulty enforcing a judgment by the *kris*, do they turn to the *gajikano* penal system. The *kris* may ask the *gajikane* authorities to arrest the renegade, and if necessary will employ false charges as a basis for the arrest. At this point, the wrongdoer will usually accept the punishment and the charges will be dropped. Should the wrongdoer persist, however, he or she might be forced to endure a *gajikano* court trial.[160]

Conflict Between Host Legal System and Gypsy Law

Gypsy sources consistently assert the superiority of their legal system, noting the following three elements:

(1) Gypsy law acts as a cohesive force serving to protect Gypsy interests, rights, traditions, and ethnic distinctiveness; (2) Gypsy law is more democratic than any other law because it does not discriminate against individuals without financial or other influence; and (3) because Gypsy law has maintained its basic form, even though older methods of punishment have given way largely to banishment or social ostracism, it must be more nearly perfect than other laws, which appear to be undergoing constant change.[161]

---

158. TRIGG, *supra* note 72, at 70–71.

159. SWAY, *supra* note 52, at 119; YOORS, GYPSIES, *supra* note 42, at 174; *see also* Anne Sutherland, *Gypsies, The Hidden Americans,* SOCIETY, Jan.–Feb. 1975, at 30 (discussing gossip as means of social control).

160. GROPPER, *supra* note 79, at 103–05; McLAUGHLIN, *supra* note 58, at 24; SWAY, *supra* note 52, at 82. According to BLOCK, *supra* note 44, at 172, in former times the defendant who did not show up at the *kris* became an outlaw. There were special signs (*patrin*) that this Gypsy was being hunted. Any Rom who saw the signs was obliged to help in the search. An accused who resisted when caught could be shot. *Gajikane* authorities who investigated would learn only of a tragic accident. The potential ineffectiveness of the *kris* under contemporary conditions in Eastern Canada is discussed in Lee, Kris, *supra* note 51, at 31–32 (describing how Rom can evade Gypsy law and resettle outside Gypsy communities). Lee points out that the *kris* remains effective in the United States.

161. QUINTANA & FLOYD, *supra* note 108, at 38–39. Although the quotation relates to Gitanos in Spain, it seems to represent the ways most Romani people feel about their laws. Quintana and Floyd merely convey the subjective ideas of their sources; they express no opinion on the accuracy of these views. The authors also note that it is extremely difficult to get Gypsy informants to discuss their laws. *Id.* at 37–38. Fully one-third of the sample refused to answer. Typical responses were: " 'I do not think of these things. Are you being paid to find out?' 'It is better not to answer. Who knows what may come of it.' "

These attitudes have an impact on how the Gypsies approach conflicts with the *gajikano* legal system. *Romaniya* has no equivalent to the concept of conflict of laws. Gypsy law is self-contained and cannot incorporate rules of a foreign legal system. Consequently, severe clashes of inherently incompatible legal notions occasionally occur. The *gajikano* legal system is equally insular so far as *romaniya* is concerned. But unlike the *gaje* who know nothing about *romaniya*, Gypsies are necessarily aware of non-Gypsy law. They may tolerate it or violate it, all the while maintaining that their own law is the only true law.

Studies indicate that the most frequent violations of the host countries' laws by Gypsies are theft and fraud.[162] Some have interpreted this phenomenon as a reflection of a Gypsy penchant for lawlessness. The Gypsies, however, have no moral objections to these activities so long as one does not victimize another Gypsy, causes no physical harm,[163] and takes no more than is necessary to survive.[164] Thus what is permissible under *romaniya* may be criminal under the host legal system. Other sources have argued that, to a Gypsy, stealing from a *gajo* is even praiseworthy because of the skill and courage involved. Moreover, subsistence theft may be permitted under Gypsy law because the *gaje* are seen as overindulgent and exploitative; thus there is nothing wrong in taking from them what they do not need.[165]

So-called swindling is considered a common means for Gypsies to make a living.[166] There is a danger, however, that the dominant culture can use the term

162. San Román, *supra* note 101, at 188–89. San Román's work deals with the urban Gitano population. According to Hancock, *Diaspora II, supra* note 59, at 654, subsistence stealing largely occurs in the United States among recent European Gypsy immigrants. Most American Roma abhor this behavior because it results in stereotyping of the whole population. It should be noted that much of the information on alleged Gypsy criminality has been collected by law enforcement agencies, and this reflects the perspective of the host legal system.

Thomas Acton, as quoted in Ian Hancock, *The Roots of Inequity: Romani Cultural Rights in Their Historical and Social Context*, IMMIGRANTS & MINORITIES, Mar. 1992, at 3, 7, has maintained that the emphasis on Gypsy crime is misplaced: "Compared with the massive record of murder, theft, kidnapping and other crimes by non-Gypsies against Gypsies (throughout history), Gypsy crime against non-Gypsies pales almost into insignificance, so that to prioritize the study of the latter over the former shows a twisted sense of values." For example, more than six hundred Gypsy children were kidnapped by the Swiss Pro Juventute program between 1926 and 1973. Thomas W. Netter, *Swiss Gypsies: A Tale of Vanishing Children*, N.Y. TIMES, June 9, 1986, at A9. The scandal resulted in a formal apology by Alphons Egli, President of Switzerland. After the fall of the Ceauşescu regime in Rumania, persecution and poverty left thousands of Gypsy children homeless or housed in orphanages. Kathleen Hunt, *Romania's Lost Children: A Photo Essay by James Nachtwey*, N.Y. TIMES, June 24, 1990, § 6 (Magazine), at 28; *see also* Pavel, *supra* note 2, at 12 (detailing Gypsy persecution under new government). Efforts of U.S. citizens to adopt some of these children were thwarted because parental consent was missing or flawed. *Battle over Romanian Adoptions Continues*, 70 INTERPRETER RELEASES 561 (1993).

163. San Román, *supra* note 101, at 188–89.

164. YOORS, GYPSIES, *supra* note 42, at 34; *see also* Fisher, *Gypsy Minorities, supra* note 101, at 51–52.

165. TRIGG, *supra* note 72, at 72–73. For a detailed discussion of Romani rules on theft, see Linnet Myers, *Circling the Wagons*, CHI. TRIB., Dec. 27, 1992, at C1.

166. San Román, *supra* note 101, at 189. See the account of a minor fraud perpetrated by a Gypsy in LEE, AUTOBIOGRAPHY, *supra* note 29, at 26–27. The Rom's explanation in this case was, "The non-Gypsy is a fool" (*"Gazho si dilo"*).

"swindling" ethnocentrically to stigmatize minority groups. A host culture may tolerate essentially fraudulent advertising and sales practices—for example, in so-called clearance sales and "bait-and-switch" schemes—as long as they are employed by people who are perceived as members of the dominant culture and who meet the minimum standards of local custom.[167] When ethnic minorities such as Gypsies use comparable sales techniques, the doctrine of *caveat emptor* no longer applies and the whole group becomes stigmatized. Thus, claims of Gypsy criminality must be examined in comparison to the host culture which criminalizes those activities. While the dominant culture may overlook its own members' transgressions, it notes the Gypsy practice with indignation and may even prosecute it. The host society's occasional leniency toward such Gypsy behavior may be due not to ideas of fairness but to difficulties in communicating with alien people or to limited resources. Realistically, prosecution of Gypsies often results not from their violation of the formal laws of the host culture (which members of the host culture may also violate), but instead from Gypsies' adherence to their own informal laws which conflict with the host nation's informal laws.

Host countries often view fortune-telling, a traditional occupation of Gypsy women, as swindling. Not practiced among the Roma themselves, fortune-telling involves the use of ritual and charms meant to dazzle the *gajikano* customer. Many host countries have reacted to this traditional Gypsy practice by banning fortune-telling, although authorities often do not enforce these laws against the Gypsies with the same stringency they do other laws.[168] Indeed, the dominant culture has reluctantly begun to recognize that its own cultural values are not necessarily absolute. Cultural defenses have been increasingly permitted in American trials.[169] In

---

167. ARTHUR A. LEFF, SWINDLING AND SELLING 134–37 (clearance sale), 143–46 (bait-and-switch) (1976). In discussing his theory that swindling and selling are based on essentially similar dynamics, Leff contends that the so-called Gypsy switch is related to most forms of selling. The "Gypsy switch" involves an exchange in which something of value is offered but, by a sleight of hand, something of no or little value is substituted. Leff suggests that in successful selling, particularly advertising, the seller tends to promise more than he can deliver. Leff concludes that somehow a "switch," in other words, a form of confidence game, has been pulled. *Id.* at 12–13, 155–57.

168. Roma have successfully challenged state laws banning fortune-telling. *See, e.g.,* Spiritual Psychic Science Church of Truth v. Azusa, 703 P.2d 1119 (Cal. 1985); *see also* Dan Morain, *State High Court Rules Out Ban on Fortune-Tellers,* L.A. TIMES, Aug. 16, 1985, pt. 1, at 3. On fortune-telling, see generally LEE, AUTOBIOGRAPHY, *supra* note 29 (autobiographical account containing illustrations and explanations of tarot cards); SUTHERLAND, *supra* note 29, at 85–89; TRIGG, *supra* note 72, at 74–75: San Román, *supra* note 101, at 189.

169. *See, e.g.,* Mull v. United States, 402 F.2d 571, 575 (9th Cir. 1968), *cert. denied,* 393 U.S. 1107 (1969) (dictum) (noting claim that Native American may lack criminal intent because of cultural beliefs); State v. Curbello-Rodriguez, 351 N.W.2d 758, 770 (Wis. Ct. App. 1984) (Bablitch, J., concurring) (stating that sexual customs of Cuban culture should be considered when sentencing for rape); People v. Kimura, No. A-091133 (Los Angeles City Super. Ct. filed Apr. 24, 1985), *cited in* Spencer Sherman, *Legal Clash of Cultures,* NAT'L L.J., Aug. 5, 1985, at 1 (considering Japanese custom in murder case); *see also* Paul J. Magnarella, *Justice in a Culturally Pluralistic Society: The Cultural Defense on Trial,* J. ETHNIC STUD., Fall 1991, at 65; Note, *The Cultural Defense in the Criminal Law,* 99 HARV. L. REV. 1293 (1986); Rorie Sherman, *"Cultural" Defenses Draw Fire,* NAT'L L.J., Apr. 17, 1989, at 3.

addition, some courts have considered the issue under *gajikano* law of whether a fortune-teller who believes in magic and ancient healing powers can form a criminal intent.[170] Thus the American host legal system has taken some steps to accommodate Gypsy practices.

The issue of fortune-telling is actually more complex than it appears. On the one hand, Gypsies believe in their magical powers, as exemplified by their use of curses and the practice of fortune-telling. On the other hand, they practice fortune-telling not among themselves but only for the benefit of *gaje*. Thus their beliefs in their own magical powers may appear to stand on shaky ground. This apparent paradox has a relatively simple explanation. The concept of fortune-telling contains several independent elements that are misleadingly grouped together. One element is foretelling the future. Perhaps because of its inherent dangerousness, this activity is not practiced internally among Gypsies. Another element, according to Sanskrit sources, relates to "making well" and healing powers, which the Gypsies do practice among themselves.[171] The healing elements of fortune-telling are reflected in Gypsy references to fortune-telling as "advising." Both elements are based on a belief in magic, although they often appear to the non-Gypsy world as scams.

In addition to fortune-telling and healing, Gypsies engage in deliberately fraudulent practices. In Spain, Gypsies have been reported to misrepresent goods and trade unfit horses. In the United States, there have been reports of used car scams and home repair deceptions. These scams reflect the disdain that many Gypsies are said to have for the *gaje*.[172] In the United States, many Gypsies consider welfare to be the ultimate scam, as it proves the naiveté of the *gaje*.[173] One study gives a detailed account of the strategies Gypsies use to obtain benefits from welfare agencies.[174] Gypsy women aggressively negotiate with social workers, while the men stand by passive and mute, often pretending to be mentally retarded and unemployable. One Gypsy explained how he was able to score low on a test:

> The trick is never to protest anything but act like you are doing everything right and are, you know, simple-minded and goodhearted about it. Anything she asks me I just

---

170. *Azusa,* 703 P.2d at 1126 ("[S]ome persons believe they possess the power to predict what has not yet come to pass. When such persons impart their beliefs to others, they are not acting fraudulently."). On the difference between advising and fortune-telling, see Ian F. Hancock, *The Gypsies, Indian World Citizens, in* GLOBAL MIGRATION OF INDIANS: SAGA OF ADVENTURE, ENTERPRISE, IDENTITY AND INTEGRATION (Jagat K. Motwani ed., forthcoming winter 1993–94) (manuscript at 5, on file with authors) [hereinafter Hancock, *World Citizens*].

171. Hancock, *World Citizens, supra* note 170 (manuscript at 5) (noting Sanskrit sources of fortune-telling).

172. San Román, *supra* note 101, at 189 (Spain); McLAUGHLIN, *supra* note 58, at 51–56, 71 (United States). Since most of these scams are widely practiced by non-Gypsies as well, and to some extent condoned, the focus on the Gypsies may be an expression of xenophobia. *See* HANCOCK, PARIAH SYNDROME, *supra* note 1, at 115–28 ("Anti-Gypsyism"), 143–62 ("Media Representation of Gypsies").

173. LIÉGEOIS, *supra* note 52, at 82. Gypsies may not realize, however, that in some cases they may be entitled to public assistance and thus are not committing a crime under host-country law.

174. SUTHERLAND, *supra* note 29, at 75–85.

give some wrong answer. For instance there was a picture of this doll, and I was supposed to connect the arms and legs. Well I put the legs in the armholes and the arms below. She kept trying to help me but I stuck with that like I was sure it must be right.[175]

Under Gypsy law, theft and fraud are crimes only when perpetrated against other Gypsies. These actions severely violate the basic Romani tenets of mutual cooperation,[176] and may result in a *kris* and stringent sanctions. When the victim is a non-Gypsy, however, a *kris* and sanctions are unlikely to result. To that extent, the *kris* is ethnocentric because it is limited to parties and participants who are Gypsies. The *gaje* may take no part in these proceedings. Victimized Gypsies may be sued and have standing to complain in *gajikane* courts. Yet victimized non-Gypsies may only sue in non-Gypsy courts. These victims have no standing to complain by way of a *kris*. In other words, Gypsies would have to invoke the jurisdiction of *Romani* courts on behalf of non-Gypsies, a procedural impossibility because *romaniya* is only meant to protect the Gypsy community. No Rom would be likely to accept a judgeship in a case that an outsider attempted to bring.

It is imaginable, although probably more hypothetical than real, that in instances of extreme misconduct toward non-Gypsies, the jurisdiction of a *kris* could be invoked. The complainants, however, would be other Roma who were endangered or subjected to persecution, and thus victimized, as a result of the reckless conduct of a fellow Gypsy toward *gaje*. Even under these circumstances, though, a *kris* might not occur because community members would fear the attention it could draw. Substantively, the crime involved would be reckless endangerment of other Gypsies, rather than violation of the rights of the *gaje*.

The host country and Gypsy systems inevitably conflict. Nevertheless, host authorities often do not interfere with Gypsy society and in many respects are unequipped to deal with Romani culture when conflict occurs. But local *gajikane* authorities do intervene in cases of serious crimes, like murder. Even then, Gypsy law has a way of asserting itself.[177] A study of urban Gitano populations provides two examples.[178] In the first, a Gypsy murdered another Gypsy and was sentenced to death by a *gajikano* court. While in prison, the convicted Gypsy died after eating food that other Gypsies had brought to him. This may be one of the rare instances

---

175. *Id.* at 81; *see also* SWAY, *supra* note 52, at 11. Field research of this type presents a professional dilemma. The information gained is likely to become known to law enforcement and welfare agencies who then are prone to use it to the detriment of those attempting the "revealed" practices. On the other hand, if a researcher is not able to obtain the confidence of Romani informants, the information is worthless and only adds to a growing pool of similar "evidence." SUTHERLAND, *supra* note 29, at ix–x, xii.

176. The fundamental spirit of cooperation is exemplified by the Romani word *pal*, meaning close friend, brother, or accomplice, now in American usage but of Sanskrit origin, *See* WEBSTER'S THIRD, *supra* note 31, at 1622.

177. *See* Fisher, *Gypsy Minorities, supra* note 101, at 51.

178. San Román, *supra* note 101, at 190.

in which a Romani population imposed and executed a death sentence. On the other hand, the convict may have eaten the poisoned food willingly, in order to commit suicide. In either case, the Romani law prevented the *gajikane* authorities from executing their death sentence. Gypsy law prevailed over the law of the host country without the Spanish authorities' knowledge.

The second example in the study describes cases in which a Romani chief has committed a crime under *gajikano* law. The elders will decide that, if there is a police investigation, a younger member of the group, usually the son of the actual culprit, will accept blame for the crime. This subterfuge protects the chief, who is more important to the group as a whole. If the *gaje* imprison the young man, members of the group will visit him in prison and give him any convenience possible. By the time of his release, he will have gained the gratitude and respect of the group. As in the first case, Gypsy law has effectively circumvented the host country's justice system.

According to a study of the Gypsy population in Sweden, if a Gypsy is called before a *gajikano* tribunal, a crowd of Gypsies escorts the individual. In so doing, the Gypsies hope either to show support for the accused or to influence the judge. If neither works, the Gypsies may utter magic curses to interfere with evidence taking or sentencing. Gypsy women disrupted one trial by chewing bread, spitting it out in their palms, and kneading the bread as they whispered curses. One Gypsy commented that at a *gajikano* trial "we tell lies, we make up stories, we pretend to forget things, so that in the end no one knows which is front and which is back!"[179]

Most Roma learn their native language, Romani, and may use it strategically to create confusion and indirection.[180] Spoken by millions of Gypsies, Romani is known to only a few researchers.[181] In addition, Gypsies from some groups may have several names: a secret name used in rituals, a name given at baptism and used among brethren, and one or more names reserved for the *gaje*. According to a study written by a non-Gypsy, Gypsies do not record births, marriages, or divorces; they do not file income taxes; they do not pay property taxes; they rarely maintain bank accounts; and they often obtain credit for short periods of time

---

179. Tillhagen, *V, supra* note 145, at 131–32.

180. CLÉBERT, *supra* note 44, at 191 (noting Sanskrit origin of Romani); Beverly N. Lauwagie, *Ethnic Boundaries in Modern States: Romano Lavo-Lil Revisited*, 85 AM. J. SOC. 310, 321 (1979); Carol Silverman, *Everyday Drama: Impression Management of Urban Gypsies*, 11 URB. ANTHROPOLOGY 377, 382–83 (1982) [hereinafter Silverman, *Impression Management*]. The Romanichals, Gypsies of English origin, have adopted English surnames, such as Ronald Lee, while the Vlax group originating from Wallachia uses Romani names in addition to surnames common in the host country. Hancock, *Gypsies, supra* note 60, at 442. For example, Ian Hancock's Romani name is O Yanko Le Redžosko, 1 WHO'S WHO IN AMERICA 1427 (47th ed. 1992–1993).

181. YOORS, GYPSIES, *supra* note 42, at 7 ("When approached directly, they show a total disregard for consistency and may become totally incomprehensible about any matter they do not want to discuss. . . ."). Some characteristics of Romani may facilitate hiding information from the rare outsiders who understand the language. It contains 'loan' words from many countries, enabling the speaker to express the same content in different ways. GROPPER, *supra* note 79, at 84–85.

under aliases.[182] These practices would make Gypsies difficult to track and would prevent authorities from gaining access to information. Romani sources, however, dispute such stereotypes.[183]

Gajikane legal authorities consequently face unusual problems obtaining evidence and have often chosen to ignore the Roma rather than prosecute them for minor offenses. Unfortunately, in some cases where the police have become active, they have seriously violated the Roma's civil rights under American law.[184] Such violations appear to be due not merely to frustration and difficulties in obtaining evidence, but also to the assumption that Gypsies are so universally despised that nobody will come to their aid. The police are more likely to engage in official misconduct when they know that Gypsies do not customarily complain to non-Gypsy authorities about abuses and do not seek legal redress from the host sys-

182. McLAUGHLIN, *supra* note 58, at 78; *see also* CLÉBERT, *supra* note 44, at 166–67 (discussing multiple names).

183. The Romani sources note that numerous Gypsies adhere to the laws of their host countries, pay taxes, and are professionals, authors, or entertainers; and that Gypsies regularly have a lower violent crime rate than their hosts. *See, e.g.,* HANCOCK, PARIAH SYNDROME, *supra* note 1, at 111–14 (criticizing authors of law enforcement orientation). Hancock also gives an account of the literature and media reporting that have reflected negative stereotyping of Gypsies. *Id.* at 115–62; *see also supra* note 162. Gypsies generally do not engage in crimes of violence (murder, rape, robbery, and assault and battery) in order to gain money. McLAUGHLIN, *supra* note 58, at 86–87. Hancock stresses that prominent respected Romani Americans are known within their Gypsy communities, but avoid drawing attention to their ethnic origin. Hancock, *Diaspora II, supra* note 59, at 653–54.

184. On June 18, 1986, the Spokane Police Department and Sheriff's Office raided a local Gypsy home without a proper search warrant. The officers seized $1.6 million in cash held in trust for the Gypsy Church of the Northwest and more than six hundred pieces of jewelry. The seized property has been ordered to be returned but is still partly unrecovered. Members of the family, including women and young children, were body searched. The state supreme court declared that the police had engaged in "egregious behavior." State v. Marks, 790 P.2d 138, 142 (Wash. 1990).

In a subsequent federal suit for civil rights violations, which is still pending, the Gypsies sought $40 million in damages. The city and county admitted liability and agreed that they would accept a ruling by Judge Robert McNichols regarding the amount of damages, provided that the Gypsies agreed not to seek punitive damages. Ian Hancock was asked to testify as an expert witness on the damage caused by the illegal police search. In addition to losing the unreturned property, the whole family has become *marime* (outcasts to other Roma), because the family's chief, Grover Marks, lost credibility and because its members have been contaminated through physical contact with *gajikane* men. The marital prospects of the young Romani girls, in view of the intimate body search by the police officers, look very dim. The settlement is now being questioned because Judge McNichols, who heard the evidence, died, and the case has been reassigned to a new judge. For details on this case, see Claudia G. Dowling & Linda Gomez, *Gypsies,* LIFE, Oct. 1992, at 47–53; Timothy Egan, *Police Raid and Suit Open Window into Gypsy Life,* N.Y. TIMES, Apr. 14, 1992, at A16; Bill Morlin, *New Judge Takes Over Gypsy Case: McNichols Too Ill To Continue,* SPOKANE SPOKESMAN REV., Dec. 16, 1992, at A1; Bill Morlin & Rebecca Nappi, *Gypsy Daughters Say 1986 Search Violated Culture,* SPOKANE SPOKESMAN REV., Sept. 18, 1992, at A1.

The Spokane litigation is a rare instance of Roma invoking the jurisdiction of host courts. The personality of Judge McNichols may have influenced the family in their decision to sue in the American system. He was a highly respected jurist and known for his compassion. *See* Bill Morlin, *U.S. District Judge Robert McNichols Dies,* SPOKANE SPOKESMAN REV., Dec. 22, 1992, at B1.

tem.[185] Gypsies believe they cannot expect sympathy or even neutrality from the host country,[186] an attitude that undoubtedly affects some of their conduct.

Although Gypsy law sometimes conflicts with statutory or common law, it is virtually impossible for it to violate the U.S. Constitution. The Constitution primarily restrains the activities of state actors, not private parties or autonomous legal systems. Even when Gypsy law establishes repressive regimes or violates what would be called due process in the state system, it cannot be considered "unconstitutional." These actions may be tolerated by authorities because Gypsy law is not visible to the state or because the state does not perceive Gypsies as "lawmakers." The situation is analogous to that of the informal rules established within the family which are authoritarian and violate democratic ideals, but nevertheless go unchallenged by the state.[187] The state may occasionally try to regulate what goes on in the family, just as it may also try to regulate Gypsy practices such as fortune-telling. In either case, however, the regulations are likely to be held to violate constitutional rights.[188] Thus, the state is practically incapable of regulating at this level of private lawmaking.

Previous Attempts at Theory

SOME TRENDS IN THE NONLEGAL LITERATURE

Most scholars do not analyze Gypsy law's legal significance but rather its general cultural significance. Their scholarship focuses on customs, traditions, norms, and

---

185. According to HANCOCK, PARIAH SYNDROME, *supra* note 1, at 105–06, local laws discriminating against Gypsies were still in effect in 1987. Despite some changes in recent years, Gypsies remain reluctant to bring their grievances to *gajikane* courts. If these discriminatory laws are not challenged, however, they may remain in effect indefinitely. For a contemporary illustration, see N.J. STAT. ANN. § 40: 52-1 (West 1991) ("The governing body may make, amend, repeal and enforce ordinances to license and regulate: . . . k. Roving bands of nomads, commonly called gypsies. . . .").

Hancock states that attempts to strike such laws have been successful but slow. He reports that when these laws were brought to the attention of the Federal Office of Civil Rights in 1986, the Office said that the term "living like a Gypsy" referred to all those living a nomadic life and was not targeted against the Gypsies as an ethnic minority. Hancock, *Diaspora II, supra* note 59, at 647–48. For corresponding problems under English law, see FRASER, *supra* note 28, at 2–7.

186. In national opinion polls taken both in 1964 and 1989, Gypsies had the lowest social standing of fifty-eight ethnic minorities included in the surveys. *See* Tamar Lewin, *Study Points to Increase in Tolerance of Ethnicity,* N.Y. TIMES, Jan. 8, 1992, at A12.

187. *See* Schmideberg, *supra* note 10.

188. *Compare, e.g.,* Griswold v. Connecticut, 381 U.S. 479 (1965) (holding Connecticut statute prohibiting use of contraceptives unconstitutional as violating right of marital privacy) *with* Spiritual Psychic Science Church of Truth v. Azusa, 703 P.2d 1119 (Cal. 1985) (holding city ordinance prohibiting fortune-telling violative of California Constitution's freedom of speech clause). Without a stimulus such as oppressive state legislation, however, it is unlikely that members of the Gypsy community will bring complaints.

In many respects, private lawmaking, including Gypsy law, is beyond the practical reach of any state authority. Government does not have the economic resources, personnel, and expertise to regulate on this amorphous level. This inactivity is due to a lack of power and knowledge and not necessarily an intent to foster private lawmaking. *But see* Reisman, *Comment, supra* note 46, at 409–10.

rules. As a consequence, it does not devote significant attention to legal institutions as such. Even if the literature refers to legal terms, such as "procedure" and "courts," these terms inevitably have connotations different from those used in law.[189]

The literature has sometimes described the Gypsy mode of life as "primitive,"[190] or has stressed the alleged illiteracy of the Gypsies.[191] These characterizations, however, have little analytical value. The often incomprehensible conduct of the non-Gypsy world, as seen by a Gypsy, could with equal justification be characterized as "primitive," in the sense that the *gajikane* values may appear to be rudimentary and irregular to anybody who does not share them. Similarly, one could maintain that the non-Gypsies are illiterate because they are ignorant of the Romani language and of fundamental skills needed for effective communication, as seen from a Gypsy perspective.[192] In other words, from a Gypsy's point of view the *gaje* are uncivilized.

In so-called primitive societies, as characterized by Jonathan Turner, laws are typically not recorded, and are steeped in custom, religion, and tradition. Yet, there are traces of a distinction between substantive and procedural law.[193] In terms of the characteristics ascribed by Turner to primitive legal systems, substantive law in Gypsy society consists largely of the *marime* taboos, which specify pure and impure acts and things. Procedurally, enforcement occurs through informal social control via the *divano*, the *kris*, and the dreaded *marime* sanction. Mediation and the courts, such as the *divano* and the *kris*, are summoned in an ad hoc fashion as conflicts arise, and owe their existence only to the specific case. At least two clearly identifiable legal actors participate within these "courts": judges or *krisnitorya*, who decide on both facts and law; and the parties, who have sworn an oath to respect the authority of the *krisnitorya*.

Although the Roma's legal system seems in many ways to fit into this scheme, Turner's primitive legal systems are generally "typical of hunting and gathering

189. *See generally* Thomas A. Cowan, *What Law Can Do for Social Science, in* LAW AND SOCIOLOGY EXPLORATORY ESSAYS 91 (William M. Evan ed., 1962).

190. *See, e.g.,* C.-H. Tillhagen, *Conception of Justice Among the Swedish Gypsies,* 37 J. GYPSY LORE SOC'Y 82, 83 (1958) [hereinafter Tillhagen, *II*]. In recent years, characterization of population groups as "primitive" is found less frequently in the literature. *See, e.g.,* Dell Hymes, *The Use of Anthropology: Critical, Political, Personal, in* REINVENTING ANTHROPOLOGY 3, 27 (Dell Hymes ed., Vintage Books 1974) (1972) (criticizing use of the term "primitive").

191. *See, e.g.,* SWAY, *supra* note 52, at 124.

192. Indeed, a Romani source declares, perhaps facetiously, that people who are illiterate are better off and that an inevitable result of literacy is stupidity. LEE, AUTOBIOGRAPHY, *supra* note 29, at 27–28; *see also* Sally F. Moore, *Treating Law as Knowledge: Telling Colonial Officers What To Say to Africans About Running "Their Own" Native Courts,* 26 LAW & SOC'Y REV. 11, 26–27 (1992) (stating that emphasis on literacy not always helpful when dealing with foreign cultures).

193. JONATHAN H. TURNER, PATTERNS OF SOCIAL ORGANIZATION 216–18 (1972) (describing primitive legal systems); *see also* HOEBEL, *supra* note 19, at 114.

and simple agrarian societies."[194] The Gypsies' dependence on the dominant host economy makes them different from other societies; their need for ongoing relations with the *gaje* is an essential feature of their culture.[195] This dependence is not confined to economic matters. The threat of *gajikane* authorities and their legal system reinforce the Romani way of life and culture. These unique characteristics of the Roma invite comparisons with other forms of private lawmaking that are neglected in legal scholarship. Yet the link between tribal law and private lawmaking seems to be insufficiently noted in the nonlegal literature as well.

Many researchers have attempted to find a framework in which they can place Gypsies, a group that most host countries regard as an anomaly. For example, Robert Redfield has described what he calls an idealized primitive or "folk society," which he contrasts with urban society.[196] He conceives of the Roma as having retained many of the traits of his ideal folk society, in spite of their continuing migration throughout the world.[197] He perceives the Roma as isolated, nonliterate, and homogeneous, motivated by a pervasive feeling of group identity— characteristics typical of a folk society. In addition, folk societies and Gypsies are governed by strict rules of convention that can be neither effectively challenged by individual members nor controlled by outsiders. These conventions do not depend on discipline but are internalized among the members of the society, who conform to them in a consistent way and without much reflection. Consequently, there is no need for legislation.[198] The members of Redfield's folk society act not as individuals but spontaneously and uncritically according to tradition and as members of the clan.[199] Religion and conceptions of status prevail in all phases of life.[200]

Redfield calls rules of convention or coherent patterns "culture,"[201] although this essay would call them "law." The difference is not merely a matter of terminology.[202] Reference to law as a cultural phenomenon strips it of centuries of meanings that are attached to the term "law." Although some detachment is gained by looking at law as a pattern, the change of terms demystifies law and alters its meaning in a negative fashion. In addition, reference to Gypsy laws as rules of convention and cultural patterns insulates them from comparison with the concepts of law that are traditionally employed in legal scholarship. Stressing that *romaniya* is law therefore is an important clarification of an historical distortion.

Many authors wrestle with the problem, also faced here, that identifying commonalities among all Gypsies is difficult. The stress on literacy (which varies

---

194. TURNER, *supra* note 193, at 216, 217–18 (scheme of courts in primitive legal systems).
195. OKELY, TRAVELLER, *supra* note 62, at 28–29.
196. Robert Redfield, *The Folk Society*, 52 AM. J. SOC. 293 (1947).
197. *Id.* at 296.
198. *Id.* at 299–300.
199. *Id.* at 301.
200. *Id.* at 305.
201. *Id.* at 299–300.
202. *See supra* note 189 and accompanying text.

substantially among different Romani groups) seems to compound the problem.[203] Illiteracy, according to Marlene Sway, is assumed to bar the Roma from
entering any middle-class or professional occupation. On the other hand, the
low-level positions available to them, such as factory work, conflict with the
Gypsies' sense of dignity and need for autonomy. Illiteracy also prevents the cultural and intellectual values of the *gaje* from infiltrating and undermining traditional Gypsy society.[204] Basic tenets of *marime* would begin to crumble with
exposure. These conceptions of supposedly universal Gypsy illiteracy, combined
with our own society's illiteracy in *romani* (Gypsy language) and ignorance of *romaniya* (Gypsy law), contribute to the difficulties experienced by *gajikane* legal authorities.

Some have compared Gypsies with other ethnic minority groups. But such comparisons may be confusing as they tend to oversimplify similarities and differences
between groups. A correlation between the Gypsies and the Amish has been suggested.[205] Both the Amish and the Roma are unusual minority groups because they
have successfully separated themselves from the outside community. According to
this view, the Amish are like the Roma in that they have their own rules of behavior, which in the case of the Amish are moral values and beliefs derived from the
Bible.[206] In Amish society, anyone who violates the rules may be shunned or even
excommunicated. The shunned person may be asked to leave the community to
prevent the stigma from tainting other family members. The punishment is not indefinite, and the wrongdoer can return to the fold after making prescribed amends.
Likewise, the Amish have strict social boundaries isolating them from non-Amish,[207]
as well as clearly delineated rules for attire, language use, sexual roles, and prac-

203. *See, e.g.,* SUTHERLAND, *supra* note 29, at 290–91; SWAY, *supra* note 52, at 124.

204. *Id.* Hancock, a noted linguist and Romanichal-Lovara Rom, in reviewing Sway's book, ob-
jects to her emphasis on illiteracy, and provides numerous examples of literate Romani professionals.
Hancock, *Review, supra* note 35, at 73, 79–80. Hancock acknowledges, though, that the majority of Gypsies feel uneasy about schooling because Romani children are kept uncomfortably close to *gajikane* children for hours. Hancock, *Gypsies, supra* note 60, at 444.

Among the Vlax Roma the conception of *marime* appears to be a critical factor in forming attitudes
toward schooling and literacy. According to Vogel, the arrangements in public schools almost inevitably
lead to pollution. Eating in lunchrooms, use of public bathrooms and shower facilities, integration of
adolescent boys with girls, and programs of sex education are so problematic for some Gypsies that
they prefer to keep their children out of school altogether. Vogel, *supra* note 29, at 37. For a Romani
voice, see LEE, AUTOBIOGRAPHY, *supra* note 29, at 131 ("They were all too ready to give us . . . their own
brand of lobotomizing education, but they would never give us equality of culture."). *Cf.* Grumet v.
Board of Educ., 62 U.S.L.W. 2045, 1993 WL 241389 (N.Y. July 6, 1993) (New York school district established for Hasidic Jews).

205. SUTHERLAND, *supra* note 29, at 5–7. Sway compares Romani culture and Jewish culture. SWAY,
supra note 52, at 47–48, 54–55; *see also supra* notes 47, 62, 79, 94–95, 98, 107, 111, 115, 206, and *infra* notes
286, 303 (references to Jewish tradition). *But see* Hancock, *Review, supra* note 35, at 75–76 (noting strained
comparisons of Romani with Jewish culture).

206. SUTHERLAND, *supra* note 29, at 6.

207. *Id.* at 5–6.

tices. Respecting elders and avoiding contact with outside institutions are two other similarities between the Amish and the Roma.[208]

While a comparison of the Roma with other ethnic groups is interesting, it can also be misleading. Apparently similar practices may serve entirely different functions and have completely separate histories. What appears to be a similarity may be coincidental. Comparisons here may also detract from the primary focus of attention, Gypsy law.

INTEGRATION, ASSIMILATION, AND ADAPTATION

The literature has contributed the concepts of integration, assimilation, and adaptation, which prove to be helpful terms when analyzing to what extent the Roma can be classified as an autonomous group. As the essay progresses, it will become increasingly apparent that true isolation is not possible, even for the Romani people. Autonomy and isolation are interrelated concepts. The degree of isolation determines the level of autonomy which a group can claim. Assimilation and integration undermine isolation and, therefore, group autonomy. Adaptation, however, is a form of adjustment to the greater environment which preserves the inner character of an autonomous system.

Indeed, a key problem in understanding Romani culture in its relation to non-Romani cultures, including that of the United States, could be the distinction between assimilation and adaptation. The two concepts are not synonymous. Assimilation implies the demise of a distinct culture, or at least its merger into a dominant culture. Adaptation, on the other hand, implies the survival of a minority culture, despite conscious adjustments by its members to cope with a surrounding environment that is different and often hostile. Assimilation and adaptation are not necessarily exclusive of each other in practice, although conceptually they seem to be.[209] Hancock's observation that gradual integration may lead in time to assimilation acknowledges this possibility.

Although the anthropological literature does not provide distinct legal analysis, it does explore the concepts of integration, assimilation, and adaptation in a form that could prove to be useful for legal scholars. Sutherland suggests that the success of a minority group's integration into American culture can be measured by the degree to which members identify themselves as American and the degree to which they participate in a main aspect of social structure.[210] She finds that Gypsies are less integrated into and identified with American society than are other ethnic groups.[211]

---

208. *Id.* at 6.

209. Lee speaks of "incognito Gypsies," Roma who have adapted enough to pass as *gaje,* but are in danger of losing their identity. LEE, AUTOBIOGRAPHY, *supra* note 29, at 82–83, 116.

210. *Id.* at 290.

211. *Id.*

A Romani source confirms that Gypsies do not identify with American society. Accordingly, most Gypsies born in the United States refer to Americans as though they themselves were not included in this group and perceive American values as conflicting with their own beliefs.[212] Sutherland adds that although the Gypsies have largely adapted to living surrounded by a foreign culture, their social organization fosters the separation of Gypsy from non-Gypsy. This separation places Gypsies at a greater disadvantage than other, less separatist ethnic groups. For example, African Americans and Latinos have suffered from discrimination in a number of areas, such as the educational system, but the Roma have tended to stay apart by choice. Although illiteracy (according to *gajikane* standards) may help the Roma preserve their ethnic identity by isolating them, it also handicaps them in the modern bureaucratic state.[213] Yet according to Hancock, many Roma are slowly integrating and participating in the mainstream of American culture without compromising their identity.[214] He concedes that over time integration could lead to assimilation.[215]

It has been increasingly difficult for Gypsies to maintain a separate cultural identity, especially with the advent of mass media. Television follows them even if they migrate. Perhaps the closely knit Romani family and the presence of older women provide some measure of immunity to these "foreign" influences. These traditional Gypsies may accept television programs as no more than entertainment. If children watch the programs with adults, the latter are bound to comment on what is shown according to traditional Gypsy values. Furthermore, to the extent that television signals a shift from writing and print toward oral communication, it may move American culture closer to the oral traditions which have been longstanding features of Gypsy culture.

Although Gypsies have inevitably been exposed to popular culture as much as any other ethnic group, their reactions have differed from those who more closely

212. Hancock, *Diaspora II, supra* note 59, at 651. According to Hancock, this is even true of most fourth- and fifth-generation American-born Gypsies. Hancock stresses that Gypsies have for centuries adapted to their host cultures. *See infra* notes 214–16 and accompanying text.

213. SUTHERLAND, *supra* note 29, at 290–91.

214. Hancock, *Diaspora II, supra* note 59, at 651–52. Silverman, too, notes that American Gypsies have successfully adapted to their environment without losing their identity. In her view, the appearance of assimilation may actually be a cover that hides a robust Romani culture from the non-Gypsy world. Gypsies may encourage and exaggerate *gajikane* stereotypes about themselves, thereby concealing their culture. Silverman, *Gypsiness, supra* note 72, at 266. Quoting Jan Yoors, she somewhat facetiously suggests that the large volume of college-educated people in the United States "prepares them for psychoanalysis—and for fortune telling." *Id.* at 270. Gypsies have also been adept at using modern technology to support their culture. Telephones, for example, are extensively used by Gypsies for communication with other Roma, for news about business opportunities, and for lucrative fortune-telling. The telephone encourages the orality of Romani culture. *Id.* at 271, Silverman gives numerous other illustrations of how "Gypsiness" has been used innovatively to adapt to an American setting. In an earlier article she maintained that close proximity to non-Gypsies and economic dependence on them forces Gypsies to adapt as a means of survival. Silverman, *Impression Management, supra* note 180.

215. HANCOCK, PARIAH SYNDROME, *supra* note 1, at 130.

identify themselves as American. Indeed, minority status, civil rights, and integration are terms that do not necessarily have the same meaning for the Romani people as for African Americans, Latinos and Native Americans.[216] In the case of the Gypsies, centuries of often vicious persecution seem to have strengthened the insularity of the culture, counteracting influences toward assimilation. As Sutherland observes, Gypsies have participated less in American social processes than have other minority groups.[217] They have little inclination to contribute actively to the politics of non-Gypsies. African Americans and Latinos, on the other hand, have sought to increase their participation in American society, turning to highly visible civil rights litigation when their efforts have been rebuffed. If the Romani people move down the road of adaptation to American culture, it is likely that they, too, will bring increased demands for civil rights under the host legal system.

The operative and autonomous legal system governing Gypsy society has played a central role in promoting the astounding survival and integrity of Gypsy culture. Indeed, it is that law-related aspect of the problem that makes a study of Gypsy law, existing in our midst unnoticed, so vitally interesting. A close examination of the Gypsies' autonomous legal system sheds new light on aspects of American private lawmaking that have been overlooked.

IV. CENTRAL FEATURES OF GYPSY LAW
AND OTHER FORMS OF PRIVATE LAWMAKING

All forms of private lawmaking share certain basic features. Some of these features have parallels in state-made law and some do not. This part first describes the centrality of the oral tradition to private lawmaking, discussing the natural progression of private lawmaking, from the memorization, storage, and retrieval of rules to their eventual expression and qualification. The oral character of private law is closely intertwined with the types of procedures the Gypsies have adopted. These procedures reinforce the importance of oral advocacy, thus encouraging the use of allusion. This part next turns to the evidentiary rules of the Gypsies and draws lessons about our own legal system. Whether they are all-inclusive or exclusionary, rules of evidence have a critical effect on the outcome of legal controversies. Such rules determine whether only a narrow issue of dispute has been settled or whether a more searching inquiry into the roots of the controversy will be undertaken.

---

216. On some possible disadvantages of adaptation, especially if it results in greater visibility to American-style bureaucracies, see SUTHERLAND, *supra* note 29, at 290–91. In contrast, Hancock views adaptation positively. He maintains that throughout their history Gypsies have adapted successfully to their environment without assimilation. Trading with horses, for example, shifted to trading with cars. Similar changes among non-Gypsies, he notes, would be called progress. Hancock cautions that reasoning against adaptation might "keep Roma in a time capsule, or in a compound as a protected species!" Hancock, Letter, *supra* note 151, at 8 nn. 100 and 102.

217. SUTHERLAND, *supra* note 29, at 290–91.

Oral Legal Tradition

Reliance on orally transmitted tradition characterizes Gypsy law as well as other forms of private lawmaking.[218] This feature distinguishes private law from the laws of the state, which are contained in printed sources. Even the invocation of state law occurs mostly non-orally, for example, by filing a written complaint. While printed or written sources—such as charters and bylaws of corporations or contracts—exist in private lawmaking, most private law never reaches this level of articulation. Yet private law still regulates conduct effectively by creating informal and implicit understandings that determine behavior and result in sanctions if violated.[219] There can be little doubt that Gypsy law and adjudication, as employed in the *kris* of the Vlax people, is effective. What factors account for this high degree of effectiveness of oral legal traditions? A comparison of oral and printed law may furnish clues.

LEGAL FUNCTIONS OF MEMORY

Private lawmaking relies largely on memory and, as a result, encourages development of the mental capacity to retain information. Knowledge of past private lawmaking, to the extent that it is based on oral traditions, is acquired casually and almost effortlessly. For instance, in the case of the Gypsies, law may be transmitted through stories told by women or men,[220] through the relation of illustrative and entertaining gossip, and through personal observation. Similarly, when we describe someone as an "experienced lawyer," we acknowledge the wealth of legal knowl-

218. *See supra* notes 19–27 and accompanying text. Laws that are based purely on oral tradition are customarily perceived to be of an inferior nature, are occasionally ridiculed, and are not considered worthy of study. Ehrlich traces this attitude to the sixteenth century in Europe, when judges became law-trained officials of the state and were no longer required to know unwritten law. According to Ehrlich, the demise of customary law was complete by the end of the eighteenth century. EHRLICH, *supra* note 5, at 15. Since then, law based on oral tradition has been treated as a fact to be proven by the parties under stringent burdens—in other words, not as a matter of judicial notice.

219. *Id.* at 86.

220. YOORS, GYPSIES, *supra* note 42, at 142–47. Yoors explains that two forms of storytelling are known among the Lovara. *Swatura* are colorful stories based on personal or group experiences. *Paramitsha* are fairy tales. The fairy tales differ among the various Romani groups, and are sometimes influenced by stories in the respective host country. An original Romani fairy tale, contained in a German collection, reflects various implicit rules of law. The devil, disguised as a young Romani man of unknown origin, courted a young Gypsy woman. He asked her father whether he would give her to him in marriage. The father replied that it would be all right with him, if it was agreeable to her. She expressed her willingness. Ultimately, the young couple departed under some pretext without being married. Arriving at the young man's tent, the woman soon discovered that her companion was the devil. She induced him to return to her parents on a visit. While the devil was drunk in the parental tent, a priest was brought to the scene. The devil escaped a ceremony of consecration, but a week later the young woman died. ZIGEUNERMÄRCHEN 266–68, 381 n.55 (Walther Aichele & Martin Block eds., 1962).

Keeping in mind that the "young woman" in the fairy tale may have been a child, see *supra* note 101 and accompanying text, the rules of law implied by the story are:

edge that person has accumulated from sources other than written law. Much of this knowledge has been acquired over time by observation and by listening to stories told by colleagues. A person who comprehends only written law would be inadequately prepared to practice law.

The most important tenets of private law are experienced and absorbed into the individual's psyche and reservoir of knowledge. What Sigmund Freud called the superego is largely an internalized reflection, as well as a continued source, of private lawmaking.[221] Although oral legal traditions may restrict individual liberty, their coercive features are not necessarily perceived by the members of the society. Even if the society notices the coerciveness of these legal traditions, it tends to tolerate them because they present themselves in the popular mind as "the way things always were" and consequently are more readily accepted than the printed laws imposed by the state.[222]

Memory may also affect the ways in which laws are changed. In an oral system, the chiefs who are trusted for their wisdom and knowledge may influence law over time by the ways they remember it. For example, the chiefs may make imperceptible changes in those legal traditions that no longer serve useful functions or reflect notions of times long gone by. Just as Gypsies change law in this fashion,[223] much unwritten

---

(1) A marriage should be a concern of the families involved, not of the individuals.

(2) One should not marry unknown outsiders because they may turn out to be evil.

(3) Young women should not impose their will on elders.

(4) Elders should exercise control over their offspring.

(5) The sanction for violation of the rules could be death.

For a general description of the relationship among folktales, lore, and law, see HAROLD D. LASSWELL & MYRES S. McDOUGAL, JURISPRUDENCE FOR A FREE SOCIETY: STUDIES IN LAW, SCIENCE AND POLICY 353–55, 406 (1992).

221. A definition of the superego illustrates the relation between this concept and private lawmaking: "[a] Freudian term for that aspect of the psyche which has internalized parental and social prohibitions or ideals early in life and imposes them as a censor on the wishes of the ego. . . ." 17 OXFORD ENGLISH DICTIONARY 217 (2d ed. 1989). Although the relation to Gypsy law and other forms of private lawmaking is evident, the definition seems to be less applicable to state law, especially in its technical aspects. We are indebted to Nancy Scheper-Hughes, Department of Anthropology, University of California at Berkeley, for suggesting a relationship between private lawmaking and internalized standards of conscience.

222. VON SAVIGNY, *supra* note 6, at 24 ("In the earliest times to which authentic history extends, the law will be found to have already attained a fixed character, peculiar to the people, like their language, manners and constitution. . . . That which binds them into one whole is the common conviction of the people, the kindred consciousness of an inward necessity, excluding all notion of an accidental and arbitrary origin.").

223. GROPPER, *supra* note 79, at 98–100, mentions several ways in which *romaniya* (Gypsy law) changes: (1) Archaic laws such as the prohibition against living in urban apartment complexes are simply ignored. Older rules disallowed such living arrangements because of the belief that women on higher floors were a polluting presence. (2) Use of hospitals for childbirth modifies older and restrictive *marime* rules. (3) The conflicting precedents of *kris* trials are used for creative court arguments. As in our

institutional law is gradually altered by selective forgetting. Such changes are hardly noted because they come about through organic growth or evolution. If the new rules are formally articulated as changes, so that participants become fully conscious of the fact that changes are taking place, then those changes might be rejected.[224] In this respect, articulation can become a conservative force preventing innovation.

A legal system that relies solely on collective memory might not require experts in the law, because such a regime is manageable enough to be essentially self-executing. Nevertheless, individuals who know the law, or even better, who conform to it, may receive favored treatment. Among the Gypsies, for example, an individual's stature may increase to the point that the person becomes a candidate for leadership positions, such as a judge in a *kris*.[225]

Finally, although oral law exists at all levels of lawmaking, it is most effective within smaller social units: a family, a clan, or an institutional group, such as a faculty, a board of directors, a committee, or a court.[226] Although each of these

---

legal system, precedent thus becomes a safety valve that permits rapid legal change. (4) Extenuating circumstances are often invoked to adjust the law to the hardship of an individual case. One could look generally at law reform as a set of emerging competing norms that are slowly incorporated into the earlier traditional norms, sometimes replacing them.

224. Weyrauch observed a similar phenomenon in an experimental setting on the Berkeley campus. This experiment, financed by NASA, took place in the spring of 1965 and was primarily concerned with nutritional aspects of prolonged space exploration. Nine male volunteers, between twenty-one and thirty years of age, were confined under close observation for about three months. Weyrauch's task was to observe and catalog the law that the experimental group generated under strict confinement. The fundamental rules that evolved within the group included:

1. Rules are not to be articulated. In case of articulation they are to be discarded, regardless of whether such articulation was accidental or deliberate. If a substantial segment of the group has in fact talked about the rule, the necessary level of articulation is reached and its existence is acknowledged.

   A rule that has become spurious by articulation and acknowledgment can be discarded by any form of behavior designed to destroy its effectiveness, for instance by deliberate disregard in a demonstrative fashion without the normal group sanctions which otherwise would have been imposed.

2. The closer a rule comes to a taboo area, the less articulate it should be. Minor administrative matters may be articulated.

3. The stringency of a rule is determined by the level of its articulation. The more articulate it is, the less the necessity to follow it.

Weyrauch, *Basic Law, supra* note 6, at 59; *see also* WEYRAUCH, THE LAW OF A SMALL GROUP, *supra* note 6, at 40–41; Weyrauch, *Law in Isolation, supra* note 6, at 39, 41–45.

Professor Funk has commented that the rule of "nonarticulation" seems to apply to law faculties: "We do certain things in fact, though we sometimes do not want to admit it. If someone identifies and articulates what we really do, the group may change its actions. Our prior rule of behavior has changed because we cannot face its articulation." GROUP DYNAMIC LAW, *supra* note 6, at 178.

225. GROPPER, *supra* note 79, at 82–84; Lee, Kris, *supra* note 51, at 25–26.

226. *See supra* notes 22–27 and accompanying text. A collegial court, for example, would apply the formal laws governing its jurisdiction as well as the unwritten law that governs its members. In fact, the

units may have unwritten understandings, uniformity among them is not guaranteed or even a goal, which in turn may encourage dispute. Fundamentally, oral systems do not address themselves to the needs of a mass society as such, even though they satisfy the needs of the smaller units that compose a mass society. Rather, printed laws are better equipped to serve the needs of mass governance.[227]

ORAL AND PRINTED LAW CONTRASTED

Law based on printed sources contrasts dramatically with oral legal traditions. Since voluminous libraries house most of the printed sources of law, these sources can only be retrieved through catalogues, indices, and computers. Inevitably, print discourages the use of memory.[228] It also requires literacy in the traditional sense. This reliance on literacy in legal society partially explains why non-Gypsy cultures object to the alleged illiteracy of Gypsies.[229] Since literacy assists in the

---

latter may be crucial to the ultimate outcome of a particular litigation. *See, e.g.,* Murphy, *supra* note 24. For a popular account of the informal rules of the Supreme Court, see Bob Woodward & Scott Armstrong, The Brethren: Inside the Supreme Court (1979). Former Chief Justice Burger's complaints about the low "quality" of attorneys appearing before the Supreme Court may have included an objection to their ignorance about the unwritten rules and understandings of the Court. *Id.* at 379. A high-ranking German appellate judge expressed similar views:

> A selected group of specialized attorneys who constantly argue cases before us are not likely to waste our time. They know what we justices want to hear, and they bring just that. The out-of-town attorneys have no experience before a court of last resort. They talk too much.

Walter O. Weyrauch, The Personality of Lawyers 230 (1964) (footnote omitted). As in any other social setting, the Supreme Court may have factions, which develop their own legal systems. Woodward & Armstrong, *supra*, at 65–69 (describing conservative faction within Burger Court). The informal law of a faction may clash with the law of other factions and the law of the group as a whole. *See supra* note 99 (autonomous systems within autonomous systems).

227. For example, contemporary tax collection, without a code or some other printed source, would be impossible.

228. The same is likely to be true of computers. *See, e.g.,* Paul Schwartz, *Data Processing and Government Administration: The Failure of the American Legal Response to the Computer,* 43 Hastings L.J. 1321, 1355 (1992) (claiming that extensively trained professionals have been replaced by clerks who are only expected to process paper and operate machines); *see also* Moore, *supra* note 192, at 26–28 (describing conflict between oral tradition and record-keeping reform in colonial Africa).

229. *See, e.g.,* McLaughlin, *supra* note 58, at 37 (stating that "most gypsies [in America] are illiterate or, at best, semiliterate"). *But see* Hancock, *Review, supra* note 35, at 73 (noting that among Vlax men literacy is not unusual; among Bashalde and Romanichal literacy is common). The persistent emphasis on Gypsy illiteracy, *see supra* note 204, reflects a disturbing hubris. According to a U.S. Department of Education report, based on a Princeton Educational Testing Service survey, nearly half of the American adult population has a low level of literacy—lower than that which a moderately demanding job would require. But when asked whether they read well or very well, 71% of those in the bottom fifth replied "yes." Paul Gray, *Adding Up the Under-Skilled: A Survey Finds Nearly Half of U.S. Adults Lack the Literacy To Cope with Modern Life,* Time, Sept. 20, 1993, at 75.

control and governance of large masses, a person perceived to be illiterate is more suspect to the host authorities and consequently more vulnerable to persecution.[230]

Under a system of printed law, then, memorization of legal sources is practically impossible and is in fact discouraged.[231] The ability to retain knowledge of law through memory, as in an oral legal culture, fades. Eventually the doctrine of constructive notice emerges; the content of printed law is deemed to be known by all. In other words, a legal fiction compensates for the growing inability to remember and is sufficient to hold people legally responsible despite their lack of knowledge or even their capacity to know.[232] Actual knowledge of printed sources of law promulgated by the state, to the extent that it is still required or needed for purposes of legal education, admission to the bar, or administration of justice, is acquired by a process of forced memorization. This compulsory process breeds resentment and results in a reduced ability to retain the learned information.[233] It also creates a professional class of lawyers.[234]

The rules of law as represented in printed sources tend to become increasingly abstract.[235] Concrete legal stories are no longer viewed as primary sources of law, although they have to some extent survived in common law systems that rely on case collection. The more compact and abstract the printed norms, the more they lend themselves to the development of theory—a feature that is not present in private lawmaking based on oral traditions.[236] The capacity for abstract and theoretical thinking becomes a mark of intelligence, as distinguished from wisdom, in mass

---

230. People who are illiterate ordinarily cannot be naturalized as U.S. citizens. 8 U.S.C. § 1423 (1988).

231. *See, e.g.,* EHRLICH, *supra* note 5, at 458 (referring to Georg F. Puchta's statement "As the law develops, the mass of legal material increases to such an extent, and the science of law becomes so refined that a comprehensive knowledge and a scientific mastery of the law can be found only among the jurists."). Although Ehrlich refers in this context to "juristic law" as a means of articulating customary law, one may assume that at this advanced stage of development, the sources of law can no longer be found in oral tradition, but rather exist in custom that has been reduced to writing. *Id.* at 450.

232. For a discussion of fictions, see LON L. FULLER, LEGAL FICTIONS (1967); HANS VAIHINGER, THE PHILOSOPHY OF "AS IF" (Charles K. Ogden trans., 2d ed. 1935); *see also* FRANK, *supra* note 15, app. VII at 338–50 (commenting on Vaihinger's book).

233. *See* Paul T. Wangerin, *Skills Training in "Legal Analysis": A Systematic Approach,* 40 U. MIAMI L. REV. 409, 469 n.121 (1986) (noting that cramming can temporarily improve performance, but leads to decline of performance in long run).

234. TURNER, *supra* note 193, at 225–26 (discussing how differentiation of law requires professionalized lawyers and judges).

235. On abstract rules, see POSPISIL, ANTHROPOLOGY OF LAW, *supra* note 6, at 20–37. The law of the Romani people and the private laws in our society do not depend on the abstract rules described by Pospisil. They rely on legal tradition as communicated by word of mouth and observation. These forms of autonomous lawmaking continue to exist contemporaneously, usually unnoticed, with abstract rules of the law of the state. *See supra* note 30 and accompanying text.

236. EHRLICH, *supra* note 5, at 348 (describing evolution of "juristic science").

society. Tests develop to designate at an early phase potential candidates for key positions along these lines of merit.[237]

Printed law tends to be relatively static and is difficult to alter. Once law is reduced to print, one is often "stuck with it," unless an ambiguity can be found; even then change or adaptation requires special effort. The procedures for change are complex, especially in comparison to the ease with which oral law can be altered.[238] Printed law can be changed by statutory amendment, by overruling precedent, or by reinterpreting existing law to accommodate new circumstances. Some of these methods of reform may employ subterfuge.[239] Therefore, realizing these changes usually requires a conscious effort.[240] Merely forgetting or employing a qualified oral account will not suffice. Printed law of the state may also result in dead-letter law, namely, law that is no longer applied but continues to retain a nuisance value by being on the official books. Such dead laws may sometimes come to life in unpredictable ways.[241] Furthermore, as outdated laws grow unfamiliar, the populace perceives their application to be oppressive and unfair.

The jurisprudential distinction between the law-in-books and the law-in-action suggests an emphasis on printed sources in legal systems which place value on written law. Yet, even where institutions of written legal history prevail, law-in-action may shape legal practice and thereby incorporate private lawmaking into the law of the state.[242] Accordingly, the dichotomy between oral legal traditions and the written law of the state is not absolute. The actual outcomes of cases tend to be

237. Weyrauch, *Governance, supra* note 46, at 150–53; *Developments in the Law—Equal Protection*, 82 HARV. L. REV. 1065, 1166–67 (1969). For example, the notion that the capacity for abstract thinking (as opposed to other forms of intelligence) is at the core of American IQ tests has been developed in Arthur R. Jensen, *How Much Can We Boost IQ and Scholastic Achievement?*, 39 HARV. EDUC. REV. 1, 19 (1969). Jensen's article, perhaps inadvertently, exposes the cultural and ethnic biases in prevailing conceptions of intelligence. *See supra* note 46.

238. *See supra* note 223 and accompanying text (ease with which *romaniya* changes).

239. *See, e.g.*, LLEWELLYN, *supra* note 14, at 70–76, 97–105; HENRY S. MAINE, ANCIENT LAW 23–32 (Henry Holt & Co. 1906) (1861); HENRY S. MAINE, EARLY LAW AND CUSTOM 118–21 (London, John Murray 1891); JULIUS STONE, SOCIAL DIMENSIONS OF LAW AND JUSTICE 130–33 (1966).

240. This method of expressing law in a fashion that outwardly conforms to precedent but actually submits it in an altered form seems to be common in Romani legal proceedings and can also be observed in other gatherings that rely on oral tradition, such as committee and faculty meetings.

241. POSPISIL, ANTHROPOLOGY OF LAW, *supra* note 6, at 26–27. For a discussion of dead laws and how they may be reinstituted, see Robert C. Berry, *Spirits of the Past—Coping with Old Laws*, 19 U. FLA. L. REV. 24 (1966). Mashburn points out that seemingly dead rules are dangerous because they lend themselves to unpredictable and selective enforcement. Amy R. Mashburn, *Pragmatism and Paradox: Reinhold Niebuhr's Critical Social Ethic and the Regulation of Lawyers*, 6 GEO. J. LEGAL ETHICS 737, 783–84 (1993). As illustration, she refers to MODEL RULES OF PROFESSIONAL CONDUCT Rule 8.3 (1983), according to which attorneys must report the misconduct of other attorneys. This rule is essentially unenforced, but in one controversial case, an Illinois attorney was suspended from practice for violating the rule. *In re* Himmel, 533 N.E.2d 790 (Ill. 1988); Ronald D. Rotunda, *The Lawyer's Duty To Report Another Lawyer's Unethical Violations in the Wake of* Himmel, 1988 U. ILL. L. REV. 977.

242. POUND, *supra* note 18, at 19.

influenced by norms of unwritten law which are never fully articulated. These unwritten norms may prevail in clashes with the traditional printed sources of law because such norms have greater persuasiveness.[243]

This analysis demonstrates that, while there are fundamental differences between legal systems exclusively based on oral tradition, such as Gypsy law, and those based on written tradition, the law of the state is based much less on written law than is commonly assumed. In fact, the law of the state could not survive without the continued influence of orally transmitted legal traditions. Yet this influence often goes unnoticed, and the nature of law is increasingly viewed by legal scholars in terms of the written law of the state. Consequently, misunderstandings permeate every phase of law and affect legislation, judicial processes, the practice of law, and legal education. Perhaps the most significant impact of these misunderstandings can be seen in popular misconceptions of law. Law is often viewed as an oppressive force that runs counter to what is truly sound and just, but the popular conception of law usually is based only on the law of the state and those who apply it. It fails to include a broader understanding of law that also considers the effects of private lawmaking. Accordingly, those who are dissatisfied with law may not realize that some of the more oppressive elements of the law may stem from the spheres of private lawmaking.

Procedure and Substance

Unlike state law, private lawmaking does not draw a strict distinction between procedural and substantive rules. In systems of law that are based on oral tradition,

---

243. This statement may apply more to legal processes in the United States than in civil law countries that rely on essentially written procedures in the courts. *See, e.g.*, Richard C. Maxwell & Marvin G. Goldman, *Mexican Legal Education*, 16 J. LEGAL EDUC. 155, 170 n.62 (1963) (noting anomaly that Mexican lawyers, after passing oral examinations, apply written procedures in court, while American lawyers pass written tests and then use oral advocacy before judge and jury). American law relies heavily on oral skills and thereby facilitates the influx of notions based on oral tradition. In divorce cases, for example, written law may grant husband and wife equal rights to the custody of their children. In spite of this, it is difficult for a divorced husband to obtain custody of his twelve-year-old daughter. There is an unarticulated cultural norm, no matter how factually inaccurate, that a single adult male cannot be trusted in an intimate living arrangement with a young female. It would be impossible, however, to articulate this highly prejudicial concern openly in court. Lawyers instead prefer veiled references to sexual concerns by arguing that the daughter is "maturing" and needs the guidance of the mother in "hygienic matters." *See, e.g.*, Boroff v. Boroff, 250 N.W.2d 613, 617–18 (Neb. 1977) (noting that although Nebraska law provides both parents with legal right to custody of their children and twelve-year-old girl expressed preference to live with her father, trial court improperly awarded custody to mother until twelve-year-old "gets through maturity"). On the dominance of unwritten and often prejudicial private law in child custody matters, see *supra* note 17 and accompanying text.

Mashburn offers another illustration demonstrating how unwritten private law prevails over written law. Experience demonstrates that the informal private law among lawyers prevails over the official and written mandate to report on each other. Mashburn, *supra* note 241, at 783–84, 788.

procedure and substance do not serve identifiably discrete functions.[244] Nevertheless, some of the rules of oral legal systems might be described as more procedural than substantive in nature. For example, Gypsy law emphasizes that grievances are not to be resolved by violence; rather, certain procedures must be followed to obtain redress. In the case of the Vlax, a *divano* has to be called, possibly followed by a *kris*. These procedures require the resolution of several issues: who may serve as a judge (*krisnitori*); who may present evidence as a witness; who may be present at the proceedings; and what language will be used in the proceedings. Language, in particular, has consequences for substantive legal issues as well as procedural ones.

ROLE OF LANGUAGE

One may view language, which shares certain characteristics with law in general as a form of private lawmaking. For example, language is shaped by strict rules that may result in sanctions when violations occur.[245] Inappropriate or casual usage at the wrong occasion (for example, in a formal setting or examination) can permanently mar the offender's social status and professional career. In a Vlax *kris* only Romani may be spoken; those who inadvertently switch to English are shouted down and may lose some social esteem in the eyes of their peers.[246] Those speaking in a *kris* use a special oratory, comparable to the elocution of lawyers or politicians, which differs in grammar and content from ordinary speech. A Gypsy who masters this oratory gains respect and may be selected as a chief or *krisnitori*.[247]

Proper use of language, especially the skillful use of nuance and connotation, may be one vehicle for private lawmaking. Because legal allusions, implications, and inferences tend to be more effective than articulated rules,[248] it may be more important for a non-Gypsy lawyer to know what can be inferred from the law than to know what the law actually says. Interpretations of rules reach matters that are not fully articulated in the rules themselves. Thus interpretation becomes a method by which private lawmaking and the printed rules of the state are fused.[249] Most private lawmaking has low visibility, but the rules governing construction, inter-

244. Though our legal system has highly sophisticated and distinct roles for procedural and substantive rules, it is important to note that decisions based on procedure often mask substantive results. Stanley Ingber, *Procedure, Ceremony and Rhetoric: The Minimization of Ideological Conflict in Deviance Control,* 56 B.U. L. REV. 266, 270–73 (1976); Walter O. Weyrauch, *Law as Mask—Legal Ritual and Relevance,* 66 CAL. L. REV. 699, 714–26 (1978) [hereinafter Weyrauch, *Law as Mask*].

245. *See, e.g.,* Jones v. Hallahan, 501 S.W.2d 588 (Ky. Ct. App. 1973) (holding that same-sex partners are incapable of entering into marriage because dictionary definition of the word "marriage" requires union of male and female).

246. Hancock, Letter, *supra* note 151, at 4 n.44; Lee, Kris, *supra* note 51, at 28.

247. *See supra* note 144 and accompanying text; *see also* GROPPER, *supra* note 79, at 84–85.

248. *See supra* note 243 and accompanying text.

249. *See, e.g.,* United States v. Universal C.I.T. Credit Corp., 344 U.S. 218, 221 (1952) (Frankfurter, J.) ("Generalities about statutory construction help us little. They are not rules of law but merely

pretation, implication, and inference in relation to state laws are of major significance, even though they must be applied differently in each set of circumstances if
they are to be effective.

Because language remains unrecognized as a form of private lawmaking, it is
often unevenly applied, leading to seemingly inconsistent results. For instance, in
litigation under the laws of the state, a party may lose because of the blunders of
counsel who communicated the wrong inferences at the wrong time or who relied
on a technically correct legal argument without realizing that the argument also
conveyed negative implications.[250] Language thus affects the application of both
private and state law and brings about results that may be hard to remedy.

The reasons for the lack of procedural remedies may be different, though, in
private and state law. In private lawmaking, certainly in the case of Gypsy law, language and law are indistinguishable, and the ultimate outcome of a controversy
must be accepted. In proceedings under state law, language is not recognized as
falling under the traditional definitions of law, although it obviously affects outcomes. A damaging implication, even though inadvertent, creates problems on appeal, partly because the record may not reflect it and partly because the parties,
viewed as having had their day in court, are held responsible for any avoidable
mishaps. Realistically, language must be recognized as a form of private lawmaking that is necessary for the state law system.

ROLE OF LEGAL STRATEGY

The misguided notion that substantive law promulgated by the state can uniformly
and mechanically resolve disputes relegates procedural strategy to a secondary and
disparaged status. Similarly, emphasizing theory over practice often neglects the

---

axioms of experience."). Justice Holmes made the same point in Boston Sand & Gravel Co. v. United
States, 278 U.S. 41, 48 (1928); *see also* FRANK E. COOPER, LIVING THE LAW 71 (1958) ("The law in action
is principally concerned with problems of statutory interpretation and application."); GRAY, *supra* note
7, at 125 ("Nay, whoever hath an *absolute authority to interpret* any written or spoken laws, it is *he* who is truly
the *Law-giver* to all intents and purposes, and not the person who first wrote or spoke them.") (quoting
Benjamin Hoadly, Bishop of Bangor, from his sermon preached before the King in 1717). These authorities lend support to the proposition that interpretation may be a surreptitious means by which private lawmaking tends to prevail over written law. The "axioms of experience" referred to by Justices
Frankfurter and Holmes, then, are really incidents of unrecognized private lawmaking.

250. Any lawyer can attest to numerous experiences of this kind, both on the trial and appellate
level. The problem may also exist in other contexts such as negotiation. In spite of their negative impact, these occurrences ordinarily go unrecorded. Furthermore, lawyers do not view them as violations
of oral legal traditions, but as inadvertent slips or as the result of incompetence.

Gossip is one of the main enforcement mechanisms of private lawmaking in *romaniya*, as well as
within a law firm or university faculty. SUTHERLAND, *supra* note 29, at 100 (noting gossip as major form
of social control among the Roma). The absence of due process in gossip is self-evident. Yet, gossip is
a double-edged sword. It may result in severe sanctions if used unjustifiably. Tillhagen, *III, supra* note
130, at 29–30 (referring to *kris* sentences against gossiping women among Swedish Roma).

role of strategy in the application of law.[251] Strategy incorporates private lawmaking into the process of adjudication. Because strategy plays a role in the resolution of legal disputes, the more skillful advocate is likely to prevail, regardless of what the law of the state may ordain.

An essential element of strategy is the exploitation of the preconceptions of the people who are addressed, whether they are part of a court or some other decision-making body. If this were done directly, it would probably be resented or considered insulting. If, however, the advocacy remains at the level of innuendo, it confirms the preconceptions of the addressee and thus establishes sympathy for the advocate and the cause. The persuasive power of innuendo in legal argumentation may have its source in private lawmaking. The innuendos imply that the lawyer who makes them is "in the know." There is no need for the advocate to be direct because the participants are assumed to be knowledgeable anyway. Furthermore, articulation of the lawyer's reliance on private lawmaking might paradoxically result in the judge's or jury's decision to refuse to consider the informal rule.[252] The advocate's implications tend to relate to informal processes that, rather than being based on state law, reflect what law "actually means." Whether the inferences in fact do so is a matter of conjecture, but this approach tends to be persuasive. One could ask whether such strategies merely appeal to power relationships. But it is more accurate to assume that when such strategies are employed, private lawmaking (premised on communal authority as a higher form of law) is invoked.

Consequently, private lawmaking, although often neglected by legal theory and administration, actually plays a critical role in determining legal outcomes. One might argue that legal strategy, as well as emphasis on forms of private lawmaking, could detract from or damage law by propagating skills that are devious or unethical, such as winning a controversy by creating innuendos that are hard to refute and impossible to review. A response to this objection is that these strategies permeate law at all levels and cannot be eliminated. Furthermore, these strategies should be considered a generally beneficial intersection between public law and norms that are widely held but unacknowledged because they are products of private lawmaking.

Lynn LoPucki has expressed a related thought: because legal strategies have determined the outcome of cases without regard to the cases' merits, many people have concluded that the development of legal strategies is unethical, regardless of whether the "rules of the legal game" were observed. In such instances the superior strategists would be better manipulators of the system, not better thinkers.[253] LoPucki counters that the development and publication of legal strategies is highly

---

251. *See, e.g.,* I ANN F. GINGER, JURY SELECTION IN CIVIL & CRIMINAL TRIALS at ix–x (2d ed. 1984) (discussing uneasy relationship between legal theory and practice in United States).

252. *See supra* note 224.

253. LYNN M. LoPUCKI, STRATEGIES FOR CREDITORS IN BANKRUPTCY PROCEEDINGS at xxix (1st ed. 1985).

ethical. Exposing contradictions between legal theory and practice encourages and facilitates law reform. It would be unfortunate, LoPucki concludes, if those who expose the need for reform face the stigma of being labeled "unethical."[254]

Yet what LoPucki calls the "merits" of a case is an elusive concept that often cannot be determined with any degree of certainty. Such a determination, elusive as it is, comes primarily from the laws of the state rather than private law. Indeed, the strategies or rules of the legal game to which LoPucki refers are in fact an application of private lawmaking to the process of adjudication. But law reform is exclusively focused on the formal laws of the state. Law reform in that limited sense is not likely to reach private lawmaking, which, like Gypsy law, is shielded by its invisibility. But the invisible forms of private lawmaking around us are governed by identifiable patterns that can be observed and learned. To that extent, perhaps private lawmaking can be regulated somewhat. At a minimum, legal theory would no longer limit itself to analysis of an essentially closed system of law, but would become more comprehensive by acknowledging that competing private legal systems exist.

Strategy plays a role in the *kris* of the Vlax, although the Gypsies may not be conscious of a dichotomy between strategy and the merits of a case. The Gypsies use what might be called strategy in the preliminary phase of the proceedings, attempting to use the selection of the *krisnitorya* to influence the outcome. This strategy is, however, of limited effectiveness; both prospective litigants must agree on

---

254. *Id.* at xxx; *see also* ROBERT E. KEETON, TRIAL TACTICS AND METHODS at x–xi (2d ed. 1973) (observing that candid discussion increases appreciation and understanding of danger).

For an illustration of the crucial impact of strategy on litigation, see the closing argument of Pennzoil's lead trial counsel in Texaco, Inc. v. Pennzoil Co., 729 S.W.2d 768 (Tex. Ct. App. 1987), *cert. dismissed*, 485 U.S. 994 (1988), resulting in a verdict in excess of $11 billion against Texaco:

> You people here, you jury, are the conscience, not only of this community now in this hour, but of this country. What you decide is going to set the standard of morality in business in America for years to come.
>
> Now, you can turn your back on Pennzoil and say, "Okay, that's fine, we like that kind of deal. That's slick stuff. Go on out and do this kind of thing. Take the company, fire the employees, loot the pension fund. You can do a deal that's already been done."
>
> That's not going to happen.
>
> I have got a chance. Me. Juror.
>
> I can stop this. And I am going to stop it. And you might pull this on somebody else, but you are not going to run it through me and tell me to wash it for you. . . .
>
> You can send a message to corporate America, the business world. Because it's just people who make up those things. It isn't as though we are numbers and robots. We are people. And you can tell them that "you are not going to get away with this."
>
> I ask you to remember that you are in a once-in-a-lifetime situation. It won't happen again. It just won't happen. You have a chance to right a wrong, a grievous wrong, a serious wrong.

THOMAS PETZINGER, JR., OIL AND HONOR: THE TEXACO-PENNZOIL WARS 398–99 (1987); *see also* Michael Ansaldi, *Texaco, Pennzoil and the Revolt of the Masses: A Contracts Postmortem*, 27 HOUS. L. REV. 733, 836 n.396 (1990). Earlier, Pennzoil had succeeded in removing the case from the Delaware courts, which are known for their expertise in corporate law, to Texas, for a trial by jury. *Id.* at 835 and n.394. The emphasis thus shifted from application of the law of the state to private lawmaking.

the choice of judge and voluntarily consent to abide by the decision of the *kris*. If one party attempts to use strategy too forcefully, the other party may refuse to co-operate.[255] During the trial, the parties or their chosen representatives attempt to influence the resolution of the controversy by skillfully presenting the case, resort-ing to precedent and even folklore.[256] These maneuverings are not, however, fully "strategy" in the *gajikano* sense of the word, for Gypsies believe that supernatural powers, not tactics, decide the merits of a case.[257] Gypsy law traditionally places great emphasis on the oath in the examination of the parties and of witnesses, a practice that might be compared to elements in our own law with an historical ori-gin, such as the ordeal and adversarial advocacy.[258]

In the Anglo-American tradition, calling upon God as a witness while falsely swearing an oath was assumed to bring about the wrath of divine powers, regard-less of whether the perjury was ever discovered. Similarly, the ancient ordeals (e.g., gripping a heated iron without serious consequence) invoked the powers of divin-ity to furnish proof of a witness's veracity. Some of these notions have survived in contemporary proceedings under state law. The oath is still available as a method of evidence. Declining fear of divine punishment, however, has weakened the oath as a legal institution—witness the modern state's need to impose worldly penalties on perjurers. The notion has also survived that, in a competitive contest between two attorneys in the examination and cross-examination of witnesses, the truth emerges. Irreversible negative consequences of minor flaws in strategy, committed not by the parties but by their legal representatives, are considered justified and sometimes even hailed as indications that the winner had a better case. Indeed, al-though declining fear of divine punishment has weakened the significance of the oath in our own law, the oath persists as a mode of evidence. Such practices, com-mon to both Gypsy law and contemporary law of the state, attest to the underlying

255. *See, e.g.,* GROPPER, *supra* note 79, at 81–82; Lee, Kris, *supra* note 51, at 26, 29.

256. GROPPER, *supra* note 79, at 83–85; Lee, Kris, *supra* note 51, at 29; Nemeth, *Field Notes, supra* note 128, at 128–33.

257. Jeatran, Social Control, *supra* note 139, at 25 ("The *kris* has a sacred aspect which is absent in American courts. The concept of *marime* is an important part of Gypsy religious thought, and its pres-ence in the *kris* tends to blur the distinction between crime and sin. One observer has likened the *kris* to a religious cleansing, much like the (Roman Catholic) sacrament of confession."); *see also* Hancock, *World Citizens, supra* note 170 (manuscript at 5) (describing Romani belief in *kintála*, a state of spiritual "bal-ance" that includes strict adherence to Gypsy law).

258. *See, e.g.,* Helen Silving, *The Oath: I,* 68 YALE L.J. 1329 (1959); Helen Silving, *The Oath: II,* 68 YALE L.J. 1527 (1959). Descriptions of the oath in Romani procedures (Gypsy law) can be found in YOORS, GYPSIES, *supra* note 42, at 177–79; Lee, Kris, *supra* note 51, at 28–29; Tillhagen, *III, supra* note 130, at 21–24. On the ordeals, wager of law, and trial by battle, see THEODORE F.T. PLUCKNETT, A CONCISE HIS-TORY OF THE COMMON LAW 113–19 (5th ed. 1956). Similar to the old English ordeal of the "cursed morsel," *id.* at 114, Gypsy law provided for a form of ordeal, at least in Europe. In the Gypsy ceremony, a substance would be given to the plaintiff and defendant to swallow; the party who became ill would be assumed to be at fault. *See* GROPPER, *supra* note 79, at 97. For a comparison of lie detector tests, oaths, and ordeals, see *id.*

belief that powers beyond human control favor the person who is right. To the extent that the authority of the *kris* stems from a belief in divine powers, a dichotomy between strategy and merits is not really possible. The Gypsies perceive the outcome to be determined on a plane that is beyond the reach of human manipulation, and even strategy is viewed as a manifestation of a higher will.

ROLE OF SUBSTANCE

There is no clear demarcation between procedure and substance in Gypsy law.[259] Similarly, those aspects of Gypsy law that can be viewed as essentially substantive in nature cannot be subdivided into criminal law, civil law, or other branches of law. There is no need for such distinctions because Gypsy dispute resolution dispenses corrective measures against socially inappropriate or deviant behavior regardless of whether such behavior would be criminal or civil under our classification scheme; Gypsy law uniformly applies the same standards of evidence and methods of proof, without concern for the type of case.[260] By contrast, in the law of the state, the standards of evidence and proof, as well as sanctions, differ in civil and criminal proceedings because of the social opprobrium that attaches to criminal but not civil violations. This differentiation is more appropriate in non-Gypsy society, which is not as cohesive as Romani society (although divisions exist there, too). Treating all segments of the non-Gypsy society according to such a uniform standard for all infractions is not possible in a culturally diverse society.

These differences are reflected in the differing roles of substantive law. Gypsy law's emphasis on states of purity or pollution seems removed from our perceptions of the nature and function of law. The treatment of women and sexual matters by Gypsy law appears irrational and antiquated by non-Gypsy standards. But this apparent irrationality may be a clue to the effectiveness of Gypsy law. Under these orally transmitted rules, a whole culture has succeeded in protecting itself from the pervasive influences of host countries.

259. The Romani word *kris* reflects the various aspects of Gypsy law combining procedure and substance. It has been defined by Gropper as "justice" or "court trial." GROPPER, *supra* note 79, at 205. Gropper writes: "This concept is central to Gypsy culture and refers to a whole complex of ideas and behavior patterns, including the whole body of customary law, the procedures of holding a court trial, and the underlying world view and value system." *Id.*

260. *Cf. supra* note 244 and accompanying text; *see also* HOLLEMAN, *supra* note 20, at 5–9. According to Holleman, the main function of tribal procedure is to maximize rather than to restrict the scope of substantive inquiry. Although Holleman discusses tribal law within African cultures, much of his argument is applicable to *romaniya* (Gypsy law). It is also applicable to informal adjudication of private lawmaking in Western societies, as it occurs in institutional settings. Illustrations include ways in which it is traditionally decided whether an associate in a law firm should be made partner; whether in a university faculty a candidate should be granted promotion or tenure; whether and to what extent salary increases should be given; whether disciplinary measures should be initiated; and in what form they should be imposed. On the Clarence Thomas confirmation hearings' resemblance to a tribal adjudication, *see supra* note 23.

Reference to matters of an intimate and sexual nature may have a mnemonic function that should not be underestimated. In an oral legal tradition, rules must be preserved in a form that allows for easy recall, such as stories.[261] Such stories must have a content that catches the attention of the audience. Any rule that incorporates intimate matters directly or indirectly related to procreation will more likely be remembered and observed because it is concerned with the survival of the species. The rigidity of such rules and their apparent absurdity to the contemporary non-Gypsy observer erect protective hurdles against interaction with persons belonging to the surrounding cultures. This separation results in an assertively endogamous society in which the women have a special role in safeguarding cultural identity through the enforcement of substantive rules of law.[262] Indeed, law of this type plays a critical role in these respects because it cements the cultural unity of the people.

This role for law appears at first glance to be unique to the Gypsy culture, but there are parallels in the American legal system. Although American law presents itself as neutral, it still functions to cement the cultural unity of the people. As in Gypsy law, many elements of United States law represent aspirational norms that are rarely fully realized, but instead hold out a promise.[263] Since there is commonality of neither ethnic origin nor religion in the United States, law assumes a major role in expressing common hopes: the equality of all people, for example. To the extent that the law of the state relies openly on aspirational fiction, it issues demands that are justified on the basis of facts and reasoning which do not correspond to reality. Some rules of law that have been attacked for generations because of their apparent irrationality have shown an uncanny capacity to survive and persuade when argued in court.[264]

261. Such was the function of rhymes, assonance, and alliteration in early epic poems and sagas handed down orally at a time when print was not available. *See, e.g.*, Charles Collier, *Origins and Development of Medieval European Epic: The Problem of Cultural Transmission and Transformation*, 9 MEDIAEVALIA 45 (1983). On the role of story, myth, and magic in the oral tradition of the Romani people, see CLÉBERT, *supra* note 44, at 161–90; *see also* Rade Uhlik, *Serbo-Bosnian Gypsy Folk-Tales*, 38 J. GYPSY LORE SOC'Y 134 (B. Gilliat-Smith ed. and trans., 1959).

262. *See supra* notes 80–108 and accompanying text. Subordination of Gypsy women to men has been stressed in the literature; see Okely, *Gypsy Women, supra* note 62, at 58–60. Yet, "*Marime* is what a woman has—that's her power." Miller, Thesis, *supra* note 63, at 40 (quotation from Romani source). One aspect of this apparent subordination is that women have become central figures in Romani culture. It is conceivable that the concept of gender subordination derives from contemporary *gajikano* culture (our society) and provides little understanding of the status of women among Romani people. Their status is likely to be greater than perceived from the outside. *See also* CLÉBERT, *supra* note 44, at 140–41 (noting propensity of Gypsies to have cults of the female). Perhaps these factors should be considered in determining whether the treatment of Gypsy women violates international human rights standards. *See* Reisman, *Comment, supra* note 46, at 416.

263. FULLER, MORALITY, *supra* note 11, at 41–44 (aspirations of law), 104 (aspirations of constitutional law); *see also supra* note 12 (referring to theories of Grey).

264. Among such rules are the statute of frauds and the parol evidence rule. *See, e.g.*, 2 ARTHUR L. CORBIN, CORBIN ON CONTRACTS § 275, at 14 (1950) (noting statute of frauds promotes "illusion of

The parallels between Gypsy lawmaking and private lawmaking are even more apparent. Institutional ritual, especially if it appears to be irrational, can often have great staying power. Sometimes it is frozen in articulated form, such as Robert's Rules of Order or the various collections relating to social etiquette.[265] The apparent irrationality in institutional rituals may actually enhance institutional cohesion and continuity. The willingness of participants to submit themselves to the government of these private rules, especially if they are tedious, may attest to institutional loyalty. If some members attempt to deviate from the rituals, they become known as persons on whom one cannot rely, and are prevented from assuming significant responsibility. Whether their protests are justified under the traditional law of the state is not the issue. The determinative factor is whether objecting members violate the mandates of unwritten private law, a reason why private law tends to prevail when it collides with laws of the state.

The sanctions imposed on a person who has violated an unwritten code within an institution or business often cannot be ameliorated through the remedies available under the laws of the state.[266] The whistleblower, for example, may conform to a moral and legal duty to inform, but such an act invariably violates the unwritten internal law not to inform.[267] Even if the whistleblower wins in court and receives damages for wrongful discharge or reinstatement, he or she will not likely survive as a member of the group whose unwritten code has been breached. Similarly, a legislatively required loyalty oath may be constitutionally flawed. Yet if governmental employees raise this issue and withhold their signatures, they may find themselves unemployed, and even if they win in court they will rarely in fact be reinstated. More likely they will settle and voluntarily go elsewhere. In other words, the unwritten group norm which demands punishment for an employee who is disloyal to the group is likely to prevail over any remedy mandated by the state.[268]

---

certainty"); 3 *id.* § 573, at 370 (1960) (noting parol evidence rule "presents many problems" in "its practical application"). With regard to procedure, see FREDERIC W. MAITLAND, EQUITY, ALSO, THE FORMS OF ACTION AT COMMON LAW—TWO COURSES OF LECTURES 296 (1929) (common law forms of action rule us from their graves).

265. HENRY M. ROBERT, ROBERT'S RULES OF ORDER (Sarah C. Robert ed., 1990); *see also, e.g.,* JUDITH MARTIN, MISS MANNERS' GUIDE TO EXCRUCIATINGLY CORRECT BEHAVIOR (Warner Books 1983) (1982).

266. For an example of such a violation with severe consequences, see Lopucki v. Ford Motor Co., 311 N.W.2d 338 (Mich. Ct. App. 1981) (holding work-related suicide is compensable under state law).

267. *See, e.g.,* DANIEL P. WESTMAN, WHISTLEBLOWING: THE LAW OF RETALIATORY DISCHARGE (1991); *see also* MASHBURN, *supra* notes 241, at 783–84, 788 (describing how professional duty of attorneys to report unethical conduct of other attorneys violates operative rule among lawyers, "Do not report other attorneys").

In cases of this nature, as in the whistleblower situations, an attorney could commit a form of malpractice even though advice to the client was correct under the law of the state. This could happen if the attorney neglected to point out the risks of private sanctions. In other words, an attorney could be under a legal duty to know the external law of the state and, in addition, to be informed of potential risks that result from private lawmaking within the institution or business employing the client.

268. *See, e.g.,* Connell v. Higginbotham, 403 U.S. 207 (1971) (per curiam), *aff'g in part and rev'g in part* 305 F. Supp. 445 (M.D. Fla. 1969) (holding Florida statutory loyalty oath, in its unconstitutional

The illustration of the discharged government employee can be generalized. A legal provision that is void or questionable under the law of the state, if operative within an institutional context, can serve to identify those willing to raise a legal issue, thus revealing their proclivity to cause trouble. The institution can then neutralize or eliminate the individual through sanctions invoked under informal procedures. Although some institutional standards of fairness may exist, due process tends to be relatively ineffective at this level. The individual under scrutiny often must forego all legal claims under the external law of the state and embrace the demands of the internal law of the group in order to avoid some of the more dire consequences of being named a "troublemaker."

In fact, every controversy can be analyzed from this dual perspective: what the law of the state outwardly mandates and what unwritten private law internally demands. The law of the state may, on occasion, adapt itself to the demands of private lawmaking. But in most cases of direct clashes between the two, private lawmaking in one form or another will prevail.[269]

Laws of Evidence

ABSENCE OF EXCLUSIONARY RULES

Rules of evidence play a critical role in Gypsy law. They encourage a broad scope of inquiry and, contrary to non-Gypsy proceedings, are not designed to keep out information which is only remotely related to the controversy. Neither exclusionary

---

portion, cannot provide for dismissal without hearing or inquiry required by due process). After lengthy negotiations about the terms of reinstatement, a dismissed professor affected by the ruling decided to stay at his new location.

269. In clashes between *gajikano* law (the law of the state) and *romaniya* (Gypsy law), the latter is likely to prevail. *See supra* notes 168–83 and accompanying text; *see also* GROPPER, *supra* note 79, at 103–06; Tillhagen, *V, supra* note 145, at 131–33.

Similar dynamics prevail within Gypsy law. A Rom may be entitled to a legal remedy through a *kris*. However, according to competing norms of a more private nature, see *supra* note 99, a stigma attaches to one who informs on another Rom. In a case reported in YOORS, GYPSIES, *supra* note 42, at 176–79, a Gypsy woman stole some gold coins from another Gypsy woman. A *kris* was held to detect the Rom who had committed this serious offense, but she escaped detection by falsely swearing an oath as to her innocence, in spite of the curse that she might die in horrible pain. Much later, upon her deathbed, she confessed in agony to her misdeed and the coins were recovered. Nevertheless, the original victim felt guilty for having initiated the proceedings which had seemingly caused the death. In her view, this was an indirect murder. GROPPER, *supra* note 79, at 97 (reporting interview with Yoors supplementing his earlier account with additional facts).

According to a Gypsy source, the traditional Romani form of initiating a complaint by skirt-tossing as a means to contaminate the alleged offender is now discredited among American Gypsies. Attempting such an act might cause the skirt-tosser and her family to become *marime* themselves. *See* Jeatran, Social Control, *supra* note 139, at 27. This report seems to indicate that private norms of proper conduct sometimes prevail over the more archaic norms of Gypsy law, thereby bringing about change.

rules nor rules against hearsay evidence exist;[270] the parties or their spokesmen may speak freely and at length about their grievances. Similarly, the witnesses may present their testimony colorfully and expansively. In short, they may refer to past events, use exaggerations, and try to gain the favor of the judges and audience. The presentation of facts does not focus on clarifying a single issue.

To evaluate the disparity between Gypsy and *gajikane* standards of evidence, one must examine the purposes of a broad scope of inquiry. The Gypsies appear to be concerned primarily with the presentation of a complete picture of events and evidence, even at the expense of what non-Gypsies might call due process and the rights of the individual. The litigants air their grievances before representatives of a tightly knit group who will most likely be very familiar with every aspect of their lives. Audience members come from the same community as the parties, and thus follow the proceedings with an intense sense of participation and a strong desire that justice be done. This attitude may lead to spontaneous offers of testimony, as well as expressions of approval or disapproval from the audience.[271] Evidentiary relevance cannot be determined in advance, but rather gradually emerges as the discussion progresses.

While the judges have been chosen because of their personal authority,[272] they are expected to allow behavior that might be considered prejudicial or disruptive in non-Gypsy trials. Participation by the audience is expected and encouraged by custom. Members of the audience, although not formally called as witnesses, may feel justified in expressing views. Whether their contribution to the proceedings is based on personal observation or opinion does not matter. Ultimately the judge does not apply an exclusionary standard of relevance, but rather weighs the probative value of the cumulative evidence to make rulings. The extent to which the decision makers can identify with what has been said might be a significant standard in the mind of the judge as he assesses the probative weight of the evidence. Parties or witnesses will be perceived as credible if their state-

270. *See supra* notes 140–45 and accompanying text. These assertions are based on the characteristics of tribal adjudications, as developed by Holleman, *supra* note 20, at 5–9. Although Holleman was concerned with African tribal law, similar observations have been made about the *kris* of the Vlax Gypsies. *See, e.g.,* GROPPER, *supra* note 79, at 81–85; McLAUGHLIN, *supra* note 58, at 23–24; Yoors, *Lowari Law, supra* note 126, at 12–17. A scheme of cross-cultural procedural preferences has been suggested by Stephen LaTour, Pauline Houlden, Laurens Walker, and John Thibaut. The degree of disputant control over evidence presentation is a crucial factor for parties' satisfaction with the procedures followed and the outcomes thereof. Stephen LaTour et al., *Procedure: Transnational Perspectives and Preferences,* 86 YALE L.J. 258, 280–84 (1976).

271. *See, e.g.,* GROPPER, *supra* note 79, at 83 (viewing the audience as a form of "jury"); McLAUGHLIN, *supra* note 58, at 24 (noting that members of audience act as devil's advocates); Lee, Kris, *supra* note 51, at 26 (noting that members of audience may question witnesses and argue about testimony); Tillhagen, *III, supra* note 130, at 24 (noting that audience may remind court of incidents that litigants have forgotten or did not want to raise).

272. *See* GROPPER, *supra* note 79, at 82 (noting high respect for certain judges); Lee, Kris, *supra* note 51, at 25 (noting high repute and distinguished track record of judges).

ments have "the ring of truth." A person who can demonstrate in court that he or she has conformed to accepted communal standards may also be considered credible by the court.

A method of proof dependent on communal standards may at first appear prejudicial under our conceptions of legal theory. Nonetheless, it may in fact closely resemble what often transpires in our own courtrooms, especially when a jury makes the determination of fact. In a closely knit society, such as that of the Gypsies, this method of presenting and evaluating evidence may be as accurate as possible under the circumstances. The vindication of individuals' rights, as understood in a non-Gypsy context, is not of the utmost significance in a Gypsy *kris*. Instead, the reestablishment of peace in the group is the proceeding's prime objective; because all participants share essentially the same social values, the proceedings of the *kris* can easily be accepted by the entirety of the concerned population. Individuals will view themselves as members of a larger group that has been treated in accordance with the law, even if they lose the case. A feeling that justice has prevailed pervades.[273]

GETTING AT THE ROOTS OF CONTROVERSY

This account, although somewhat speculative, suggests that the basic policies governing the admission of evidence in Gypsy societies are drastically different from those of the law of the state. By extending the judicial inquiry to remote aspects of the controversy, such as matters of the distant past, the proceedings will be more likely to uncover the roots of the current trouble. As a consequence of this process, the parties feel satisfied that they had an opportunity to be fully heard.[274] A skillful judge, aided by the spokesmen of the litigants and assisted by the audience, may

273. The tradition of having a feast upon termination of the *kris* symbolizes the cathartic effect of the proceedings. Custom requires that the aggrieved parties and others involved be present. Tillhagen, *V, supra* note 145, at 127 (loser is usually host; sometimes winner pays); Yoors, *Lowari Law, supra* note 126, at 9 (stating that in spirit of reconciliation winner pays in carefree manner). Of course, if the sentence is for temporary or permanent *marime* there is no celebration. Yet if at a later time after a separate *kris* the *marime* is lifted, the rehabilitated Rom rejoins the community in a "ritual of commensality." *See* Miller, *Defilement, supra* note 62, at 52. The social life of a Gypsy centers around commensality, the spiritual and moral bond created by sharing food and drink. Miller, Thesis, *supra* note 63, at 17–19. Commensality is antithetical to rejection or pollution (which may occur by being publicly defiled by a woman tossing her skirt or by being declared *marime* in a *kris*). The resulting state of pollution means that commensality is to be withheld from the rejected person. *Id.* at 19. Consequently, any ceremonial readmission to the Romani community involves joint eating and drinking celebrations, which symbolize that the Gypsy concerned is again in good graces. *Id.* at 20–21. Reinstatement involves "a long, arduous and expensive procedure requiring frequent appeals for a new *kris* and new evidence." *Id.* at 42 n.7.

274. Similar observations have been made by Holleman, *supra* note 20, at 6, in discussing standards of pleading and proof in African tribal procedures. Since the controversy may have a long history, the parties are urged to reveal even remote aspects. Although individual redress is sought, the parties are also concerned with reestablishing their esteem in the community.

steer the parties toward a possible settlement. In such instances, the spokesmen act more as mediators than as attorneys.[275]

These types of resolutions are favored over the drastic sanction of a sentence of *marime*. The whole proceeding aims to reestablish peace between the warring parties by exposing and hopefully eradicating the source of disruption. The proceedings must also make the participants feel respect and appreciation for their leaders, their peers, the *kris*, and the law. For Gypsy societies, surrounded by a foreign and essentially hostile environment and dependent upon mutual assistance and good fellowship, such conciliatory results and evidentiary methods are vitally important. Even when sanctions such as temporary *marime* must be imposed, they are likely to be accepted because they are based on ancient custom and because there is little other choice.[276]

The exclusion of evidence in adjudications under the laws of the state rests on assumptions different from those of the *kris*.[277] In a legal culture such as that of the United States, inquiries are narrowed to lessen confusion and conflict among groups holding a diverse set of values. Procedures limit the trial to a narrow scope of inquiry, whether or not other matters appear relevant to a party. The non-Gypsy system presumes that a wide range of investigation may cause more trouble than benefits. Matters of a personal or intimate nature may not be raised if they would infringe on individual rights, even if justice in the isolated case before the court would be better served by the disclosure. A broad scope of inquiry would inevitably slow down the proceedings, and might also distract attention from the specific incidents that have triggered the controversy. Most importantly, the litigants in our culture do not have confidence that they share basic values with others who are involved in the process. To allow floods of complaints and grievances under such circumstances would serve no beneficial purpose. The narrow focus of inquiry in adjudicative proceedings[278] therefore seems to suggest that a society such as the United States has highly diverse basic values, many of which are not compatible with each other.

---

275. In matters concerning damages or payment of debts, the parties are assumed to have made their requests with an implicit understanding that bargaining may take place within certain margins. The judge is expected to become active within these boundaries. Tillhagen, *III, supra* note 130, at 25 (discussing Roma in Sweden).

276. This presentation corresponds to the aspirations of *romaniya* (Gypsy law). In reality, Romani participants may sometimes be dissatisfied with the actual or potential dispositions of a *kris* and resort to "extralegal" remedies, such as moving elsewhere. Lee, Kris, *supra* note 51, at 31–32 (describing how Canadian Rom avoided jurisdiction of *kris* by disappearing); Tillhagen, *V, supra* note 145, at 127–30 (discussing self-help); *see also* GROPPER, *supra* note 79, at 102 (stating that institution of *kris is* predicated upon "voluntary participation"); YOORS, GYPSIES, *supra* note 42, at 174 (noting that *kris* may have to resort to supernatural sanctions, such as curses, to prevent defiance).

277. For a comparison of restrictive Western standards of evidence with all-inclusive standards in African tribal law, see Holleman, *supra* note 20, at 5–9. The principles developed in that article are fully applicable to the procedure of the *kris*, as practiced by the Vlax group of the Romani people. For further details, see Johan F. Holleman, *Some Problems of Evidence in Shona Tribal Law, in* STUDIES IN AFRICAN SOCIAL ANTHROPOLOGY 75 (Meyer Fortes & Sheila Patterson eds., 1975).

278. Weyrauch, *Law as Mask, supra* note 244, at 706.

In the state law adjudication system, the losing party will likely feel that justice has not been served by the narrow inquiry, since exclusionary rules of evidence will have prevented, in the loser's view, a full presentation of the case. As a result, parties do not fully trust judges, and they suspect attorneys of being manipulators and hairsplitters.[279] In contrast, private lawmaking has more in common with tribal law and the proceedings in the *kris.* Within an institutional or otherwise private context, controversies tend to be discussed and settled without the use of exclusionary rules of evidence, and are usually not even as formal as the *kris* of the Vlax. A skillful leader in this setting will draw on communal support much as an experienced tribal chief would, rather than relying on rigid rules or running roughshod over the proceedings. This use of private lawmaking inevitably involves resort to custom. The laws of the state, with their exclusionary standards of evidence and relevance, will be invoked only when institutional resources have failed. Even in these instances, the rigidity of the laws of the state will be tempered by the customs of private lawmaking.[280]

Much unnoticed and informal lawmaking and adjudication takes place in many legal systems. The private law aspects of proceedings before the *kris* of the Vlax find their parallels in other widely disparate legal cultures. The role of the chief as judge, the participation of the audience in the proceedings, the broad scope of inquiry, and the effort to mediate and expose the roots of the controversy find surprising parallels in African tribal adjudications[281] as well as in Asian societies such as China and Japan.[282] The extraordinary efficacy of private lawmaking (which may cross the line of oppressiveness) has occasionally been exploited in state attempts to impose a particular ideology at the local level, where it can have its strongest effect. The Chinese have used private lawmaking in this way in mediations and adjudications where efforts to get "to the roots of the problem" are perceived as ideological struggles.[283] In

279. This is a perennial complaint about American law. *See, e.g.,* ALBRECHT MENDELSSOHN-BARTHOLDY, DAS IMPERIUM DES RICHTERS 151 (1908).

280. *See supra* notes 243 and 248 and accompanying text.

281. *See* Holleman, *supra* note 20, at 6–7.

282. On China, see Roger Grace, *Justice, Chinese Style,* CASE & COM., Jan.–Feb. 1970, at 50 (discussing dispute settlement in Chinese-American communities); Stanley Lubman, *Mao and Mediation: Politics and Dispute Resolution in Communist China,* 55 CAL. L. REV. 1284 (1967). On Japan, see RUDOLF B. SCHLESINGER ET AL., COMPARATIVE LAW 332–34 & n.108 (5th ed. 1988) (observing that private lawmaking still prevails in country as highly developed as Japan and even affects proceedings before ordinary courts and administrative agencies); Nobuaki Iwai, *The Judge as Mediator: The Japanese Experience,* 10 CIV. JUST. Q. 108 (1991); Joel Rosch, *Institutionalizing Mediation: The Evolution of the Civil Liberties Bureau in Japan,* 21 LAW & SOC'Y REV. 243 (1987).

283. For a detailed report by a New York state justice who attended a criminal trial in China, see Mary J. Lowe, *The Trial of Ran Kao-chien,* JURIS DR., Apr. 1978, at 12. The Chinese trial had many parallels with the *kris* of the Vlax, in particular the wide scope of what is considered relevant; the absence of evidentiary, constitutional, and procedural hurdles; the representation by nonprofessional advocates; and the participation of the audience. Ideological elements included judicial exhortations to confess. *See also* Lubman, *supra* note 282.

Cuba, similar attempts have been made to politicize and control neighborhoods.[284] But these efforts ignore the reality that private lawmaking is almost impossible to control, even in repressive societies. It takes place at all times and places; it is of ancient origin and universal application.

General Considerations

In the light of the broad definition of law articulated at the outset of this chapter,[285] several observations can be made about *romaniya*, or Gypsy law, and other forms of private lawmaking. Although the Romani people do not formally gather to pursue an objective, their need to survive as a distinct and isolated group provides them with a common purpose; Gypsy law ensures that host countries' legal systems and cultures minimally influence Gypsy life. Although *romaniya* has sacred aspects that direct Gypsies to lead their lives properly by attaining a state of purity and preventing contamination, it does not advocate proselytizing or imposing its values on·non-Gypsies. Its·main purpose is to achieve a state of balance (*kintála*) that pleases the spirits of the ancestors (*mulé*).[286] Conversion of the *gaje* would not make much sense because they and their ancestors are outside the Gypsy universe.

Dissent within the Gypsy community is possible only in a limited number of realms, such as economic matters and territorial disputes. Dissent is not permitted with regard to basic social taboos. Outside the *romaniya,* there is not much conceded lawmaking within Gypsy communities. Some forms of behavior are tolerated if they are done with discretion and not openly acknowledged. For example, young male Gypsies may gain sexual experience with non-Gypsy women, provided there is no romantic involvement.[287] Yet these matters continue to be viewed as deviant behavior and do not become part of *romaniya*.[288] They are not even viewed as custom because there is no acknowledged difference between custom and law. If com-

---

284. Jesse Berman, *The Cuban Popular Tribunals,* 69 COLUM. L. REV. 1317 (1969). *But see* Luis Sales, *The Emergence and Decline of the Cuban Popular Tribunals,* 17 LAW & SOC'Y REV. 587 (1983) (describing increased formality imposed after popular courts came under criticism): Luis Salas, *The Judicial System in Postrevolutionary Cuba,* 8 NOVA, L.J. 43 (1983) (traditional Western procedural safeguards reinstituted). Fidel Castro presumably came to perceive the Popular Tribunals as a potential threat to his regime; he could not control them to the extent he had anticipated.

285. *See supra* text accompanying note 8.

286. Hancock, *World Citizens, supra* note 170 (manuscript at 5). The conceptions of *romaniya* are of ancient Indian origin and thus not part of the Judeo-Christian tradition. Interestingly, Cover, *supra* note 6, at 11 n. 31, uses similar language in describing the Torah as one of the pillars of Judaism: "The Hebrew '*Torah*' refers both to law in the sense of a body of regulation and, by extension, to the corpus of all related normative material and to the teaching and learning of those primary and secondary sources. In this fully extended sense, the term embraces life itself, or at least the normative dimension of it. . . ."

287. Hancock, *Review, supra* note 35, at 77–78.

288. Perhaps the routine consumption of alcoholic beverages during Prohibition is comparable. Cover, *supra* note 6, at 21 n.63, calls this a "fact of life" rather than an assertion of revolutionary lawmaking power.

mon behavior creates visible problems, such as women wearing jeans instead of long skirts, a *divano* or *kris* may be called.[289]

By comparison, non-Gypsy forms of private lawmaking are equally concerned with cohesion and survival of the group, at least with regard to their own distinct characteristics, but they tend to be more vulnerable to external influences than Gypsy law. If they have aspirational functions, they are less directed toward lofty moral ideals than toward maintenance of group cohesion. Instead of an internalized demand for purity, such systems may stress unwavering group loyalty. Even mere suspicion of disloyalty may lead to severe sanctions. Adjudication is done informally and without attention to traditional standards of fairness, such as the right to be heard.[290] In the vast majority of cases, the law of the state is incapable of, perhaps not even concerned with, remedying any unfairness that may have occurred in these private lawmaking systems. Most of the oppressive aspects of private lawmaking occur outside the scope or even vision of state authorities. While some may find unsettling the idea that any small group can engage in lawmaking, such lawmaking is a manifestation of inherent human needs.[291] By imposing a yardstick for measurement of "worthiness" we also project external standards that have no more intrinsic claim for accuracy than any other standard, although the observer positioned outside of the group may strongly sympathize with such universal standards.[292]

A significant difference between Gypsy law and other forms of private lawmaking may be that the members of *gajikane* groups are also members of numerous other gatherings and participate in a wide range of social discourse. A law firm, for example, is divided into various subgroups, such as partners, executive committees, junior partners, associates, and staff members, each having its own set of legal norms and implicit threats of sanctions.[293] The members of the firm are also members of families and participants in a great number of social organizations, some of them recognized under state law, others more or less invisible. Each of these groups has its own autonomous legal system that is not necessarily compatible with the laws of the other groups or with those of the law firm. This situation

289. *See* Hancock, Letter, *supra* note 151, at 5 n.46. On the other hand, Gypsy society, just as any other society, may in fact be permeated by autonomous subsystems which sometimes deviate from binding rules of *romaniya*. Thus, a Gypsy family may relax some restrictions within the confines of the home and intimate life. *See supra* note 99.

290. *See supra* text accompanying notes 265–68.

291. Weyrauch, *Basic Law, supra* note 6, at 58.

292. Cover has maintained that the law created by the Mennonites, for purposes of constitutional meaning, assumes an equal or superior status to the law as interpreted by the Justices of the Supreme Court. Cover, *supra* note 6, at 28 (referring to Bob Jones Univ. v. United States, 461 U.S. 574 [1983]). With regard to the important problem of human rights standards raised in Reisman, *Comment, supra* note 46, at 416, see Walter O. Weyrauch, *On Definitions, Tautologies, and Ethnocentrism in Regard to Universal Human Rights, in* HUMAN RIGHTS 198, 199–200 (Ervin H. Pollack ed., 1971) (discussing difficulties in defining universal human rights).

293. Weyrauch, *Legal Profession, supra* note 22, at 480–81.

results in internal adjustments by the individual member to these multiple social institutions. The resulting accommodations, although reached individually, must have an impact on the laws of all of the groups concerned. True isolation in *gajikane* society is utopian, and the continuing adjustments that are achieved on an internal and individual level are bound to be reflected in lawmaking within each group and even externally in the laws of the state.[294] From that perspective the dichotomy between private lawmaking and the law of the state disappears, and law, even in its traditional form, can be viewed as a network of small-group interactions.

Such a view of law cannot be applicable in the same degree to the Gypsies, who by choice avoid exposure to conflicting loyalties with the outside world. Nevertheless, although they need and depend on contacts with their host countries as a source of their livelihood,[295] they do not want to be part of these societies in any sense that would involve compromise of their basic beliefs. It is *romaniya* that makes such separation possible. If there is any semblance of compromise, it may be in the Gypsies' willingness to adapt to the requirements of their surroundings, although by adapting a Gypsy risks being assimilated or losing his or her identity as a "Gypsy."[296]

This isolation of the Romani people is sustained not only by centuries of persecution, but also by their deep commitment to retain their ethnic identity. Although they live among their hosts, Romani reservations about the hosts are strong and, considering historical events, understandable. Perhaps only isolated island communities have succeeded to a greater degree than the Gypsies in maintaining their almost utopian autonomy. A rare illustration is Tristan da Cunha, a territory of the British Colony of St. Helena, midway between Africa and South America.[297] In this case, the separation is physical, with thousands of miles of ocean in every direction and only sporadic communications with the outside world.[298] The fewer than three hundred island inhabitants have developed a unique legal system recognizing no leadership of any sort and no communal decision process.[299] There is no crime or violence. The main sanction for misbehavior is teasing, a powerful de-

294. *See* Cover, *supra* note 6, at 30–33 (referring to CAROL WEISBROD, THE BOUNDARIES OF UTOPIA [1980]); Stone, *supra* note 6, at 891–92; Weyrauch, *Basic Law, supra* note 6, at 56–58.

295. OKELY, TRAVELLER, *supra* note 62, at 28–29.

296. *See supra* notes 213–17 and accompanying text.

297. For details, see generally PETER A. MUNCH, CRISIS IN UTOPIA: THE ORDEAL OF TRISTAN DA CUNHA (1971).

298. The decline of sailing ships seems to have increased the isolation for many years. The inhabitants of the islands are said to have learned about World War I only after it was almost over. Carl Mydans, *Strange Story of a Flight from Our Century: Far-Off Exiles of Tristan*, LIFE, July 12, 1963, at 72; *see also* MUNCH, *supra* note 297, at 94.

299. MUNCH, *supra* note 297, at 1–18, 74–91; Letter from Peter A. Munch, Professor of Sociology, Southern Illinois University at Carbondale, to Walter O. Weyrauch (May 5, 1977) (on file with authors) (referring to unpublished student paper about informal legal system of Tristan da Cunha: "[She] has not in my opinion recognized the full impact of the 'legal system' (if one can call it that) of anarchism in Tristan da Cunha: Looking for 'leaders' and instruments of communal 'decisions,' she did not seem to recognize that at the time she was concerned with, no instrument of communal decision existed on

terrent because the island's inhabitants have nowhere to go to escape.[300] The most serious violations are assuming a position of superiority and interfering in any way with the life of other inhabitants. The population is reserved but good-natured and cooperative toward occasional visitors.

Tristan da Cunha has no religious history. It was founded as a business partnership between the three initial settlers who were the ancestors of the present population. The partnership document, dated November 7, 1817, expressed a fundamental conception of absolute equality.[301] It provided, in part: "That in order to ensure the harmony of the Firm, No member shall assume any superiority whatever, but all [are] to be considered as equal in every respect, each performing his proportion of labour, if not prevented by sickness. . . ."[302] This was later amended by a document of December 10, 1821, signed by all male members of the community: "No person subscribing to these articles are [sic] to continue reminding particular persons of their Duty in point of Work, or otherwise, as in such Case nothing but *Disunion* will be the consequence. . . ."[303] These formal pronouncements were later transformed by custom into the utopian legal microsociety which still exists today. It seems clear that such a normative state of mind can only be achieved in situations of extreme geographical isolation. Although the Romani people may come close, none of the groups engaged in private lawmaking discussed in this essay can quite match such successful isolation.

V. CONCLUSION

The traditional view that law emanates from the state is too narrow. Numerous sources of private lawmaking, though little noticed, coexist with the law of the state.

---

the island, and anyone who would assume the role of a 'leader' would find himself without followers and would be the object of the subtle sanction of avoidance because he would have deviated from the accepted pattern of proper behavior. . . ."); *see also* Peter A. Munch, *Anarchy and* Anomie *in an Atomistic Community,* 9 MAN 243, 250–58 (1974).

300. Mydans, *supra* note 298, at 77.

301. The full text of the partnership agreement is reproduced in MUNCH, *supra* note 297, at 29–30. The original partnership document is now in the British Museum.

302. *Id.* at 29.

303. *Id.* at 37. Professor Robert M. Cover essentially described Tristan da Cunha when he theorized about an imaginary world:

In an imaginary world in which violence played no part in life, law would indeed grow exclusively from the hermeneutic impulse—the human need to create and interpret texts. Law would develop within small communities of mutually committed individuals who cared about the text, about what each made of the text, and about one another and the common life they shared. Such communities might split over major issues of interpretation, but the bonds of social life and mutual concern would permit some interpretive divergence.

Cover, *supra* note 6, at 40 (citation omitted); *see also* Stone, *supra* note 6, at 828–29 (discussing legal visions within Jewish communities).

This autonomous lawmaking takes place imperceptibly within institutions, corporations, families, and wherever else people join together to pursue common objectives. Violation of these informal legal norms, as in the case of any other infraction of law, results in sanctions applied in private adjudications. In many respects, these private legal systems have characteristics similar to those found in tribal law. They are based on highly persuasive oral traditions that easily adapt to changed conditions. Language plays an important role in these systems, not only in terms of what is articulated, but also in terms of what can be inferred and understood in any given setting. If a dispute arises, any form of evidence, including evidence regarding remote events, can be submitted to help get at the source of the particular disturbance. Due process in the American legal sense is markedly absent. Shared values and communal peace, not individual rights, are the prime interests protected.

In view of the many similarities between private lawmaking and tribal law, the legal system of the Gypsies provides a useful vehicle for developing theory. Like other forms of autonomous lawmaking, it is hardly noticed, although it competes effectively with the laws of the host culture. It assures the survival of the group by emphasizing group loyalty and relationships over the rights of individual members, and it usually prevails when it comes into open clashes with the surrounding legal system of the state.

Studying the capacity of any form of private lawmaking to prevail over or influence official state law enriches legal theory and practice. Clashes between informal institutional law and the traditional law of the state are frequent and unavoidable. Yet because participants and decision makers traditionally do not regard private law as law, such norms seldom appear openly in court. Instead, private law rules are communicated by way of appropriate hints and suggestions, and are injected into traditional state law by means of interpretation and construction. These norms influence decisions on the probative value of evidence. And what is commonly called strategy is in actuality often an application of the norms of private lawmaking. Juries are inevitably sensitized to oblique innuendo. Even judges, in their interpretation of legal materials and in their judgment of the merits of argument, will likely be swayed by skillfully placed implications. None of this process ordinarily reaches the level of consciousness. Yet advocates who are able to base their arguments on unstated innuendo are likely to have an advantage. By contrast, attorneys who base their arguments on the letter of state law may lose persuasive power.

But state law and private law commonly interact more subtly than in direct confrontation. For example, the law of the state may greatly influence the internal norms of a law firm both through direct regulation and indirectly through implicit mores which influence the interaction of members of the firm. State law also influences the law of the Gypsies, albeit to a lesser extent. Gypsies may acquiesce to some aspects of state law because of economic necessity, for example, by conforming to administrative laws on regulation of business. In addition, Gypsies may have adjusted the laws of their own legal system to the laws of their host countries, particularly if these adjustments do not clash with their values. The Romani rejection of most crimes of violence provides an example.

As this essay has demonstrated, autonomous systems also have powerful influence in shaping state law. Just as oral traditions and unarticulated cultural norms may play a great role in determining the outcome of disputes in the formal justice system of the state, values in autonomous systems may gradually shape the very substance of state law. The Gypsy system is no exception. As the state either fails to enforce its own norms or overtly acknowledges the value of norms embodied in the Romani legal system, it responds to the influence of the autonomous system.

Thus, law reveals itself as a multitude of autonomous systems operating simultaneously with the formal law of the state. Each system shapes the other systems with which it has contact. Only total isolation will prevent any legal system from being shaped by others. Indeed, some isolation is required for any autonomous system to be truly "autonomous," for any group with such a system must be insular to some extent. The degree of that insularity determines the shape and the strength of the autonomous system itself.

As far as American law is concerned, readers may find the degree of de facto autonomy given to *romaniya* and to the *kris* of the Vlax surprising. They may also find the autonomous informal adjudications in our own private lawmaking disturbing. Some may prefer to call these adjudications arbitrary and contrary to American ideals and not think that they should be part of the definition of law at all. Yet private lawmaking here and elsewhere can hardly be successfully regulated or suppressed, except perhaps by relegating it to the sphere of the unconscious. In addition, it cannot be prevented from filtering into the traditional proceedings under the law of the state. But it is not proper to view private lawmaking as a negative phenomenon. Autonomous legal systems run inextricably through state law. If our traditional legal proceedings have any effectiveness, it is because of the features of submerged private lawmaking they possess—features that respond to a desire for group cohesion and satisfy fundamental human needs. If private lawmaking were more widely recognized, much of the gap between theory and practice could be narrowed or at least more effectively explored in an analytical fashion. The theoretical structure of law could be revitalized, and perhaps the application of state-made law would even gain somewhat in popular acceptance.

THREE

Theorizing Gypsy Law

Thomas Acton, Susan Caffrey, and Gary Mundy

INTRODUCTION

The recent study of Gypsy law by Weyrauch and Bell (chap. 2 in this volume) has been widely circulated, often in second and third generation xerox copies, among European Romani intellectuals. It has also brought Romani social control mechanisms into the main-stream of legal philosophy. Weyrauch and Bell take these mechanisms as an example of autonomous lawmaking, which serves to maintain internal order and control while at the same time unifying and protecting Gypsies and Gypsy traditions against potentially hostile host societies. Their examination, however, is limited to the system built around the *kris* of the Vlach Rom, and they fail to see the relevance of other forms of Gypsy social control such as the blood feud of the Finnish Kaale Rom, which they rule out of their discussion. This limits their understandings of the possibilities within the operation of Romani law and indeed of the *kris* itself. This paper argues that in fact there is a structural inversion between *kris* systems and blood-feud systems, which shows how similar value systems can be enforced via very different forms of social control. It is suggested that the different forms of social control are appropriate to different nomadic and sedentary modes of life in different Romani groups; and that in fact, using the theories of Pashukanis, one might theorize the *kris* as an embryonic state developing a criminal law from the historically prior civil law embodied in the norms of Gypsy groups regulating conflicts through the feud system. These contrasts enable a deeper understanding of Gypsy lawmaking processes, which resolve some of the problems shared both by Weyrauch and Bell and by their critics, such as Reisman.

At first sight no two systems of social control could be more different than the systems of private vengeance found among the old nomadic Romani communities of northwestern Europe and those public tribunals (the *kris*) which regulate all civil and criminal disputes among many of the Rom of Eastern Europe, especially the great Vlach Rom *natsiya* (ethnic groups), the *Kalderari, Lovari, Churari* and *Machavaya,* both in the Romanian-speaking territories of their original settlement and in their worldwide migrations of the last two centuries. These differences in the way in which Gypsies in different groups seek justice have led both to radical misunderstandings by Gypsies of the value systems of other Gypsy groups with whom they come into contact, and to a fragmentation of ethnographic work, as sociologists and social anthropologists have described the practices of "their" group without locating them in any broader historical and structural context.

This paper will draw on the literature to present and contrast two ideal-typical models, which we will call the "feud" model and the "tribunal" model, in order to show that they are polarized variations of a common structure. In other words, there are alternative ways of expressing and embodying *Romaniya* in social action and organization, which must be seen as sociological variables. The feud model belongs to a more anarchistic and nomadic lifestyle; the tribunal model to a more settled and structured one.

Often these alternatives present themselves to the individual Romani person as moral choices which other Gypsies have just made wrongly. Thus, with respect to the difference between marriage by elopement and marriage by arrangement, what we hear in our fieldwork from the Romanichals, "Those Rom—they sell their daughters, you know," is matched from the Rom by "Those English Gypsies—they steal their wives, you know." The variant a person chooses, or with which he has been brought up, becomes a vital part of his personal identity and integrity, and is seen by him as a boundary-marker of Romani identity as such. This means that ethnographers often follow their informants in taking particular forms of Romani social organization as standard; that is to say, they treat particular values of social control variables as being invariants; such an approach was virtually elevated to the status of methodological principle by de Marne,[1] provoking a detailed critique by Acton,[2] who set out principles which enable the analysis presented here.

We wish to suggest that when the social control systems of particular Gypsy groups are considered in isolation, something of the genius of Romani culture, and its ability to preserve itself and protect its members, to adapt and contribute to social change in the world as a whole, is always going to be missed. Of course individual Gypsy groups do not fit exactly the ideal-types we will present, and may indeed be ranged somewhere between them and vary over time, changing and dividing their identities. Indeed, in some exceptional situations, such as that of the *Baro Shero* among the Polska Rom,[3] the social authority may be embodied more in the judge than the tribunal, a status which presents a standing temptation to ambitious

---

1. Philippe de Marne, "L'Organisation d'un groupe tsigane," 31 *Études Tsiganes* 25 (1985).
2. Acton, "Oppositions Théoriques entre 'tsiganologues' et distinctions entre groupes tsiganes," in Patrick Williams (ed.), *Tsiganes, Identité, Évolution* 87–97 (1989).
3. Jerzy Ficowski, *The Gypsies in Poland—Histories and Customs,* 72–73 (Eileen Healey trans. 1990).

Kalderash and Lovari *Bare* (family leaders) who are aware of it and seek to emulate it, often with the most unfortunate consequences.

The current systems, however, which help to define each group as it is here and now, are inherently likely to present themselves as conservative, perpetuating an existing social order. We hope to show that a multitude of overlapping small-scale conservatisms may in aggregate constitute a surprising global radicalism, offering to those who are politically tough more choices, and more access to the process of lawmaking and enforcing than is immediately apparent. Who would have thought even ten years ago that we would have seen a Romani women's movement begin to constitute itself in country after country[4] almost in the way that the "new Gypsy politics" constituted itself in the 1960s?

This has very broad implications for the theory of law and social control in general. Until the pioneering work of Weyrauch and Bell,[5] legal theorists largely neglected the implications of the existence of Gypsy organizations as an example of what Weyrauch and Bell call "autonomous lawmaking" taking place within the geographical boundaries of modern states. Their work has already provoked debate in legal circles: Reisman criticizes them as "historicist" for presenting Gypsy law as the "organic and inexorable" outcome of tribal tradition, and for thus treating law "as a sort of felt experience, rather than conscious choice."[6] He argues that this leads Weyrauch and Bell into an attitude of moral indifference towards various reactionary and individually oppressive particularisms of Gypsy society.

The intention of this paper is to present this legal debate within a broader Romani Studies context, and in doing so, hopefully to dissolve some of the problems as they appear in the debate between Weyrauch and Bell and Reisman. Our view is that Weyrauch and Bell's work is flawed because its whole analysis is based on only one of the polar ideal-types of Romani social control. Citing Acton,[7] they say, "Because the Romanichals, Bashalde and Sinti have quite different customs, in spite of cultural similarities, academic literature neglects them. Therefore, unavoidably, so does this essay."[8]

The trouble is that they have misread Acton's assertion that *American* literature neglects them as suggesting that the literature *in general* neglects non-Rom Gypsies.[9] Per-

4. Aziz, " 'We will not go into houses—it will turn us mad'—Sylvia Dunn, founder of the new Association of Gypsy Women, talks to Christine Aziz," *The Independent on Sunday*, 24 (June 5, 1994). Asociación de Mujeres Gitanas, "Las actividades del año 1994 ¡Y continuamos!"; *Revista Para la Promoción Social y Cultural de la Mujer Gitana* 21 (1994).

5. Weyrauch & Bell, "Autonomous Lawmaking: The Case of the Gypsies," chap. 2. in this volume.

6. Reisman, "Autonomy, Interdependence and Responsibility," 103 *Yale L. J.* 401–17 (1993) [hereinafter Reisman, *Autonomy*].

7. Acton, "Academic Success and Political Failure," 2 *Ethnic and Racial Studies* 231, 234 (1979).

8. Weyrauch & Bell, supra n. 5, at 22.

9. Id. at 22, n. 36.

haps they fail to realize that "much of the factual information"[10] they cite is from works on the Romanichals, especially those of Acton, Okely, and Trigg.[11] That they are able to do so points to a greater commonalty in the *content* of Gypsy law than they recognize, a fact acknowledged by Sutherland when she cites similarities between her cleanliness prohibition data from Rom and Okely's data from Romanichals.[12]

The authors of this paper cannot pretend to be any exception to the rule that observers can only understand—that is make sense of—the institutions of cultures strange to them by mapping them in some way onto institutions familiar to them. We hope to show, however, that deconstructing the unnecessary limitation that Weyrauch and Bell placed on their analysis will allow us a freer and more flexible mapping, which will thereby allow us a deeper understanding of Romani identity and of the nature of law and overlapping private and public jurisdictions. We hope to show that there may be values, which are embedded in culture and enforced in law, which yet can be shown to be more than cultural and more than legal, informing rather than created by culture and law.

We shall try to show that when one takes the varieties of Romani lawmaking together, one can use them to illustrate a much richer conception of the relationship between law and the state and of the way in which the state is constituted through legal developments, through the construction of society as a fictitious legal personage with obligations, interests, and rights. In this we will draw on some of the formulations of Pashukanis on the development of criminal law from civil law,[13] without, we hope, succumbing to the definitional polemics of Marxist scholasticism as to when social norms "truly" become law.

This broader view of Romani legal development, drawing explanations from real and contingent historical changes rather than "tradition" in the abstract, can, we feel, strengthen Weyrauch and Bell's underlying thesis about the importance and inevitability of autonomous lawmaking by meeting Reisman's critique of their historicism.[14] At the same time, by showing the greater range of moral debate which informs Gypsy lawmaking, we hope to defend Gypsy law itself against the charges of oppressiveness that Reisman also brings.[15]

Let us first posit our two ideal types, the "feud" system of private vengeance, and the "tribunal" system of the *kris*.

<hr/>

10. Id. at 27, n. 51.

11. Elwood B. Trigg, *Gypsy Demons and Divinities* (1973); Judith Okely, *The Traveller Gypsies* (1983); Thomas A. Acton, *Gypsy Politics and Social Change* (1974).

12. Anne Sutherland, *Gypsies, The Hidden Americans* xiii (2nd ed. 1986).

13. Evgeniy Pashukanis, *Law and Marxism* (Barbara Einhorn trans., Chris Arthur. ed. 1978, from *Allgemeine Rechtslehrs und Marxismus: Versuch einer Kritik der juristischen Grundbegriffe*, 1929) [hereinafter Pashukanis, *Law*].

14. Reisman, *Autonomy*, supra n. 6, at 403, 408.

15. Id. at 416.

PRIVATE VENGEANCE: THE FEUD SYSTEM

This system is most completely described by the one great ethnographer that Weyrauch and Bell fail to cite, Martti Grönfors,[16] who discusses the Finnish Kaale Gypsies. The rather sensational title "Blood-feuding among Finnish Gypsies" belies the content of his monograph, which shows that just as a prison sentence is still very much an exceptional sanction in modern industrial society, so actual bloodshed is the exception in a blood-feuding system; it is only necessary when, in a sense, the system fails, and social norms have not held. The system he describes is very similar to that which holds good among English Romanichals, and indeed as we proceed through our own fieldwork we come across abundant case material.[17]

In such a system individuals are responsible for asserting their own rights, and the rights of family dependents who are weaker than they are or of friends or kin who are unjustly outnumbered. To appeal to the non-Gypsy state is generally unacceptable except in certain clearly defined exceptional cases (drug-dealing is frequently one such); and there are among Romanichals and Kaale no Gypsy authorities to appeal to, either. Rather, if one is robbed, one must muster sufficient friends to recover the property oneself; physical or sexual assaults must be matched by counter-assaults leading to submission or, in extreme cases, death; unhygienic behavior matched by excluding the unhygienic person from one's personal space. Not to stand up personally for one's rights or those of a weaker dependent if one has been wronged is to be shamed, *"ladged"* in English Romani.

It might be thought that such a system might lead to continuing endemic violence; but in fact most observers agree that English Romanichal life is rather easygoing and peaceable on the whole. The reason for this, as Grönfors shows, is that although there is no policing authority in such societies, nonetheless there are socially prevalent norms, a fact which means that on the whole individuals are quite aware as to whether any particular action is right or wrong, and avoid actions which will provoke someone else to a defense of infringed rights, especially if they are anywhere in the near vicinity at the time.[18]

What happens if one does commit an action by which another perceives himself as wronged? Then the other must demand satisfaction. For example, one young Romanichal man in our fieldwork, X, bought a car from another, Y. As he was buying he

---

16. Martti Grönfors, *Blood Feuding Among Finnish Gypsies* (1977) [hereinafter Grönfors, *Blood*].

17. Grönfors, *Blood*, id., may seem to show reconciliation as being more difficult among the Kaale than we believe it to be among Romanichals; but this appearance may be a consequence of the nature of Ph.D. fieldwork, which compels the publication of data a very few years after the commencement of fieldwork, and therefore may fail to pick up on longer-term social processes such as reconciliation, especially when the achievement of reconciliation often radically affects not only the presentation of the past, but even an individual's actual recollections of the past. Leonardo Piasere, "Les amours des <<tsiganologues>>," in Patrick Williams (ed.), *Tsiganes, Identité, Évolution* at 101 shows that Romani studies, given their academic marginality, are particularly prone to the achronic biases of the transitory Ph.D.

18. Grönfors, *Blood*, supra n. 16, at 85–159.

said, "To save me taking the carpets up, tell me the floor is sound." Y told him it was. When X took the car back to his own encampment he found that the floor was actually almost rusted through. He took the car back to Y and demanded his money back.

Y at this point was faced with a choice of actions. He could well have tried to appeal to the very strong Romani ideal that a buyer must take responsibility for his own actions (the principle of *caveat emptor*). Had the fieldworker (Acton) brought the car back, he probably would have been met with the taunt "Go and deal with the children!"—in other words, an assertion that he ought to have been ashamed to admit having been worsted in a deal, something very shaming (a *"bori ladge-up"*) to any adult. X asserted, however, that it was not a question of his having failed to check, in which case he never would have dreamt of complaining, but that Y had told him a specific lie direct, which he regarded as theft ("You *chored* my bit of vongar"). If Y did not refund the money, he would "beat it out of him."

As it happened X was out on bail for attempted murder on charges relating to the discharge of a firearm on a London caravan site. Y in fact almost immediately accepted that he had gone beyond hard dealing into actual lying (*"penning hokkapens"*) and refunded the money. Y then had to accept and live with the shame of having backed down, which he dealt with by keeping out of X's way for some time to come. And that was the end of the matter.

Why did Y not gather his own friends to resist X's demand? For a balance of two reasons. First, X's reputation as someone who would not back down meant "it wasn't worth the aggravation, mate." But second comes a fact which Y left unstated, that in fact most of Y's friends would have felt very ambivalent about his calling upon their loyalty to back him up in what was, after all, a *hokkapen*. And X would then have had little trouble in mustering his friends, and the trouble could have spread endlessly.

When someone comes to realize they have offended in a way that cannot be sustained by public opinion, it is up to them to keep out of the way of those who have a justifiable grievance against them. One of our Romanichal friends had to stay away from Epsom for years on end after an argument about a bet on a game of pitch and toss. In somewhat the same way as God used to defend the right in medieval trial by combat, because the wrong would be unmanned by their realization that God was not on their side, so among the Kaale and the Romanichals justice generally prevails because those who are in the wrong come to know they are so and act appropriately by physically avoiding those they have wronged until some reconciliation is arranged. The characteristic social control mechanism in this system is therefore enforced avoidance; violence and killing are rare occasional ultimate sanctions needed to keep the whole system in being.

Such an account matches the classic Marxist position of Pashukanis that "the origin of criminal law is associated with the custom of blood vengeance,"[19] even

19. Pashukanis, *Law*, supra n. 13, at 168.

though he extracts from Kovalevsky a rather over-lurid picture in which "[e]very offense, even that perpetrated in revenge, forms grounds for a new blood vengeance . . . often to the point of total annihilation of the warring clans."[20] In fact, far more characteristic of the stable system of private vengeance among Romanichals and Kaale is the picture Pashukanis presents of the decay of the practice of feuding: "Vengeance first begins to be regulated by custom and becomes transformed into retribution according to the rule of the *jus talionis*: 'an eye for an eye and a tooth for a tooth,' at the time when, apart from revenge, the system of composition or of expiatory payment, is adopted."[21]

Where Pashukanis, however, presents theoretical speculations about systems far removed from his actual experience, Grönfors gives us abundant rich details from painstaking and empathetic field work. The private quarrels of the Kaale are far harder to document than the public disputes of the Rom in the *kris;* Grönfors takes us to the heart of such personal emotions and actions to give us one really good ethnography of a vengeance system to stand alongside the many studies of the *kris.*[22] He shows us that what at first might seem random and bloodthirsty is in fact a courtly and institutionalized system for minimizing violence and maximizing individual freedom by making each individual responsible, to the extent of his ability, for the freedom of all.

Such a conflict resolution system is consonant with the marital, economic, and political systems of the Romanichals and Kaale. Both groups practice marriage by elopement. Marriage marks the point when individuals take responsibility for their own lives. It is a shame for parents publicly even to consider the possibility of their children forming sexual relationships (though of course there are private discourses where that is not so). The man and woman who wish to take each other have to do just that—and then a well-documented game-like practice of formal reconciliation with the parents, similar to reconciliation after other offenses, has to take place.[23] The new nuclear family then becomes a political unit with its own sovereignty. Even the nuclear family of one's parents is in the end no more than an ally. The nuclear family is also the independent economic unit—perhaps cooperating with others, but never forming the *"kumpania"* which marks economic organization among the Rom.

It will be obvious that pursuing a commercial nomadic lifestyle obviously facilitates such a system. Both avoidance and elopement are easier if one was planning on making a move anyway.

20. M. Kovalevsky, *Modern Custom and Ancient Law of Russia* (D. Nutt, trans. 1891, from *Sovremenny Obychay I Drevny Zakon* 1886).

21. Pashukanis, *Law*, supra n. 13, at 168.

22. Grönfors, *Blood*, supra n. 16.

23. Judith Okely, *The Traveller-Gypsies* 154 (1983); Thomas Acton, *Gypsies* 23 (1981); Salo, "The Gypsy Niche in North America," in Aparna Rao (ed.), *The Other Nomads* 91 (1987).

THE TRIBUNAL SYSTEM: THE *KRIS*

By contrast with the relatively inaccessible practices of private vengeance, the public proceedings of the *kris* have been well documented in a literature which Weyrauch and Bell describe in some detail.[24]

The *kris* is a public assembly held by many groups of Rom, and in particular those Rom whom the Gypsylorists call Vlach and the *Khorakhane* call Gajikane,[25] and who refer to themselves as the four natsiya of the *Kalderash, Lovari, Churari* and *Machavaya*. Either it can be held to hear and resolve an accusation by one person or group of persons against another, or it can be held without there being a specific plaintiff or defendant to resolve some general issue of public policy which might become a cause of conflict, such as the allocation of business territories, or degree of reward permitted to those who assisted Romani holocaust survivors in making successful claims for individual war reparations. These assemblies are presided over by a small number of judges (*krisnitoria*) who possess no formal qualifications, but are agreed and invited by the parties to the *kris*, some leaning to the plaintiff, some to the defendant, with an impartial president. These judges, however, do not deliver judgment as such, but rather preside until the assembly reaches a consensus, with all the adult men present able to speak and be heard until the issue is exhausted. Sometimes women are excluded; but varying degrees of female participation are sometimes found. Often the ethnographic reports present such female participation as wholly exceptional; but in a system which is not based on written rules, to define female participation as *a priori* exceptional is just to beg the question about how far the *kris* system *has* to reinforce patriarchal authority. The *kris* can bring women in if it wishes, because the *kris* makes its own rules—but only by unanimity. The system promotes oratorical ability, and ability to speak in this mode in Vlach Romanes is the major criterion for admission to and participation in the *kris*. (Perhaps this may explain why, in the West, where there is intermarriage between Vlach Rom and Khorakhane Rom, it is the Khorakhane rather than the Vlach Rom who become bi-dialectal.)

---

24. Weyrauch & Bell, supra n. 5, at 42, n. 128.

25. The problem of terminology arises from Vlach Roma's tendency to use the word "Rom" to describe both themselves and the broader category of Gypsies who call themselves "Rom" but are not seen as "our Rom" by most of the Kalderash, Lovari, Machavaya, and Churari. "Vlach" is a convenient label attached by non-Gypsy experts referring to the Romanian influence common to the dialect of these four groups; Romanes *vlaxikane* is a modern back calque from this. *Gajikane* is used by many of the Muslim (*Khorakhane*) Roma of the Balkans to describe the Orthodox Vlach Roma, with the implication that any form of Christianity carries with it a certain de-Gypsification; but in the Balkans time has often robbed this terminology of its offensiveness, so that, in context, "*Me sim gajikano Rom*" can mean simply "I am not a Muslim." In the United States, however, those who are *gajikane Rom* in the Balkans use the term to mean non-Gypsy, or to stigmatize non-Rom groups such as the Romanichals, as de-Gypsified.

The *kris* system regulates both marital and economic affairs. Both Vlach and Korakhane Rom have arranged marriages, in which the father of the groom pays a bride-price to the father of the bride. Subsequent marital discord may thus easily lead to a *kris* about repayment of this bride-price. The extended family has an authority which it lacks among the Romanichals, and the Rom work together in *kumpanias*, which bring together several families and which will make use of the *kris* system to assure their area of operation.

To draw out the contrast between the tribunal system and the feud system, let us just try to imagine what would have happened to our friends X and Y had they been young Rom instead of young Romanichals.

In the first place, they probably would have been part of the same *kumpania*, so the question of buying or selling the car would not have arisen; it probably would have belonged to a father or an uncle, and the question of who would use it would have been decided in the way that the use of goods within a household is usually negotiated (e.g., how do we decide who gets to sit in the seat with the best view of the television screen? At home this is decided by age/gender power in negotiation, in contrast to a seat at the cinema, where the quality of one's seat is dependent on how much one pays.)

Suppose, however, X and Y were acquaintances from different *kumpanias*, and X did persist in an accusation of theft against Y. In such a case his correct course of conduct would be the very opposite of what we recorded above. To make a threat of personal violence would be, so far from a vindication of personal honor, as serious and dangerous an offense as the original alleged theft. If the matter was not resolved by mediation by relatives, then X's senior relatives should say "*Ame mangas kris*" (which means both "We demand justice" and "We ask for the holding of a *kris*"). At such a *kris*, Y's action would be treated first of all as an offense against the community, to be admonished or punished by some measure ranging from bearing the expenses of the assembly to some degree of exclusion, and only secondarily as an occasion for the making of restitution to X.

Pashukanis's conception of the relation between civil law and criminal law may illuminate this contrast. Pashukanis's general thesis is that law is formed and progresses as a reflection of the advance of commodity exchange relations.[26] It might be thought that the *kris* presents a counter-example to this general account of legal development, because in the *kris* system (which, at least in contrast with the feud system, is an example of public law) there is a larger area of daily life in which goods are not commodified compared with the private vengeance system. We shall argue, however, that in fact the form of *kris* emerges (as Weyrauch and Bell suggest)[27] as a form of lawmaking which is private compared with that of the overall non-Gypsy state. We shall further suggest that it does so because of the commodity values that have been established in its general social environment.

---

26. Pashukanis, *Law*, supra n. 13, at 109–33.
27. Weyrauch & Bell, supra n. 5, at 48.

Arthur sums up Pashukanis's distinctive position against other Marxist legal theorists in the 1920s as pointing out that not only civil law but also "public law relations, e.g., criminal law, are an extension of forms generated by relationships between commodity owners."[28] This must be seen within the general concept (which Pashukanis shared with most of his contemporaries) of the historical progress of legal relations developing, as Maine phrased it, "from status to contract."[29] Human groups were seen as having originally socially constructed conceptions of right and wrong as personal obligations which individuals feel and expect to and from each other within the group. This is civil law, constructing individual subjects (through the development of commodity relations, say Marxists) as bearers of legal claims. Only when the community itself is actualized as the state, as a "fictitious bearer of right" against whom the individual can offend as well as against another individual, do we have criminals and criminal law. Finally we may expect the collective institutions which enforce criminal law also to seek the monopoly of enforcing civil law, to outlaw private vengeance.

Among the Romanichals and the Kaale we find only civil law, not criminal law, and the ultimate sanction against its breach is private vengeance, the feud, although the power of morality (or shared concepts of shame) and public opinion is such that generally in feuds, fortune favors the righteous. These groups, therefore, although individualistic and even anarchistic in contrast to the Kalderash and Lovari (whose collectively regulated society possesses in the *kris* an embryonic form of the state, a "fictitious bearer of right"), nonetheless have an articulated social morality. We thus see here a structural inversion: remarkably similar conceptions of morality, property, cleanliness, and honor are enforced in totally different ways.

POSTULATING A HISTORICAL RELATIONSHIP BETWEEN THE FEUD AND THE *KRIS*?

For most of the Vlach Rom who come to any understanding of Romanichal or similar social control systems, their perception of its historical relation to their own *kris* system is very simple: they see these "other" Gypsies as having "lost" the *kris*. Those North American anthropologists who have taken Vlach Rom Gypsies as their major or only informants have tended to follow the ethnocentric views of these informants.[30] The *kris* has been seen as a primitive, authentic, and essential form

---

28. Arthur, "Editor's Introduction," in Pashukanis, *Law*, supra n. 13, at 15.

29. Sir Henry S. Maine, *Ancient Law* 141 (1905, originally 1861). The quotation is the last sentence of chapter 5.

30. Rena C. Gropper, *Gypsies in the City* 13 (1975); Anne Sutherland, *Gypsies—The Hidden Americans* 16–18 (2nd ed. 1986, originally 1975), but note an apology for earlier ethnocentrism at xv; Werner Cohn, *The Gypsies* 17, 24–26 (1973).

of Romani culture, if not, indeed, a survival of something like the Indian pan-chayat system.

Acton, however, argued that it is in fact far more plausible to see the theoretical relationship which we have drawn from Pashukanis as also a historical relationship. The Vlach Rom are so called because of the influence of Romanian on their Ro-mani dialects. They were among those Gypsies who were (for periods probably varying between the different *natsiva*) enslaved or who continued in slave status under the Romanian neo-feudalism which developed from the sixteenth century onwards.[31] The distinctive character of Romanian neo-feudalism has been bril-liantly dissected by the father of Romanian social science, Henri Stahl, who used an exemplary mixture of anthropological fieldwork on surviving non-feudalized village assemblies and local archival research on feudalized villages to analyze the transition to neo-feudalism. The account given of the manners of village assem-blies is startlingly reminiscent of the way in which the *kris* operates among the Vlach Rom today.[32]

We can hypothesize that among enslaved communities it is not so easy to prac-tice avoidance mechanisms as among the free commercial-nomadic Romanichals and Kaale. It is necessary for the slave communities to present a common front to their masters to try to avoid the extremes of extraction of surplus value. What could be more natural than that they should use the political forms available to them, which made sense in terms of the rural Romanian polity of the day, even if the pur-pose and content of those political forms was derived from Romani and not Ro-manian culture? Perhaps, as noted above, relations of exchange between individual Rom of some goods move from commodity exchange to domestic negotiation; but that is within the context of chattel slavery, where they themselves, their actual phys-ical bodies, have become commodities which can be sold in the market place. If some man wishes to find a wife for himself or his son, and the woman desired be-longs to another master, then his own master must actually purchase the woman for him. The payment of the bride-price between Vlach Rom co-parents-in-law (*xhanamiki*) today might thus perhaps be seen as a definitive statement that slavery no longer exists—the Rom own themselves (but in a way in which Romanichals are not owned at all).

We must be careful, however, not to overstate the historical case for the priority of one or another system. Sixteenth century European sources may be seen as sug-gesting the existence of an internal justice mechanism amongst the earliest Romani visitors to Western Europe; but the repeated attempts of Scottish Gypsy leaders at that time to get the Scottish state involved in their quarrels suggests that, if they

---

31. Acton, "Rom Migrations and the end of Slavery," 3 *Journal of the Gypsy Lore Society*, Series 5, 77–89; Gheorghe, "Origin of Roma's Slavery in the Romanian Principalities," 7 *Roma, Journal of the In-dian Institute of Romani Studies* at 12–27 (1983); Panaitescu, "The Gypsies in Moldavia and Wallachia," 20 *Journal of the Gypsy Lore Society, Series III*, 58–72 (1941); Ian F. Hancock, *The Pariah Syndrome* 14–29 (1987).

32. Henri H. Stahl, *Traditional Romanian Village Communities* (1980).

had a tribunal system, it cannot have been exactly the same as the modern *kris*.[33] Functional needs within different sections of the Romani diaspora, and historical catastrophes breaking up established symbioses, may have shifted social practices in both directions between tribunal and feud systems more than once.

Nonetheless, we may see the form of the Vlach Rom *kris* over the past century as determined by the way in which commodity relationships developed within and around chattel slavery as an adjunct to Romanian neo-feudalism. It has to consider the interests of the Romani community as though they were those of a fictitious bearer of the kind of rights and obligations already defined in looser and less structured forms of Romani social life. In contrast, however, the feud system is appropriate and functional for many groups of free commercial-nomadic Gypsies.

Both of these systems are the products of history; but this does not mean their present ephemeral forms are set in tablets of stone, or that they are inherently conservative or reactionary, as Reisman suggests of the *kris*.[34] In fact the kind of criticisms which Reisman makes of conservative American Rom uses of the operation of Vlach Rom law may also be found among European Rom. One English Kalderash Baro specifically told Acton that he had settled in England because he felt American Rom were trivializing the *kris,* following recondite matters of gender pollution while ignoring important issues such as a young person getting involved in drug dealing.[35]

Pentecostal Rom in New York and some other cities have specifically rejected the *kris* as an institution in conflict with the Christian gospel, an attitude which contrasts markedly with the attitude of many European Pentecostal Rom. In Western Europe sometimes the *krisnitoria* have been specifically balanced between Pentecostals, Catholics, and Orthodox; we are even aware of one case where a *kris* was threatened in a dispute over bible translation between Pentecostal Rom. To a sociologist, rebels and dissidents and subordinates, whether male or female, must be seen as much authentically members of their own cultural groups as conservatives and patriarchs. All cultures are arenas of conflict, and all present possibilities of reconciliation; all law and polity is the object of struggle. Romani law and polities give us living examples of a theoretical variety we can barely find elsewhere. In the end we may have to acknowledge that we can trace a master value-system in Romani cultures, a system building on notions of propriety and honor, which, as Pan-Romani politics and a Romani intelligentsia have developed, can be recognized as intersubjective realities between Gypsies from different groups, despite their own prejudices, insults, or even legal prescriptions to the contrary. Although relations

33. Sir Angus Fraser, *The Gypsies* 119 (1992). We are grateful to Fraser for his criticisms of overstated historical arguments in an earlier version of this essay.

34. Reisman, *Autonomy,* supra n. 6, at 416.

35. Acton, "The Functions of the Avoidance of moxadi kovels Amongst Gypsies in South Essex," 50 *Journal of the Gypsy Lore Society, Series III,* at 117 (1971).

with the state are beyond the scope of this essay,[36] there is a standpoint from which Gypsies in general may expect *Gaje* to acknowledge that they have been treated wrongly. Perhaps, in fact, as so often when looking at Gypsy history, we have to acknowledge that fundamental questions of right and wrong may be something more than local etiquette.

36. Perhaps the best starting point for the study of the exercise of social control by the state over the Gypsies is Martti Grönfors, *Ethnic Minorities and Deviance: The Relationship Between Finnish Gypsies and the Police* (1979).

FOUR

Informal Systems of Justice: The Formation of Law within Gypsy Communities

Susan Caffrey and Gary Mundy

INTRODUCTION

Recent criminological theory has laid increasing stress upon the importance of informal controls in cooperation with state agencies in the prevention of crime and the apprehension of those who have offended. Gypsies and other ethnic minority groups are often represented as having a lifestyle which is built upon criminality, the areas where they live being seen as supportive of a criminal way of life.[1] We wish to show that these so-called crimogenic communities have their own system of law which could be seen to have something to offer to the host society. By looking at Gypsy communities, who already manage conflict and justice without recourse to the formal systems of justice, we propose to see how informal controls work, and under which conditions they successfully operate. Attention will be given to the problems of assuming that similar informal controls can be developed within modern urban societies.

Recent years have seen an increase in concerns both over the level of crime and over the ability of "legitimate" state agencies to control crime effectively. These concerns have manifested themselves politically in a number of reforms of the criminal justice system which have had the prime objective of making governments appear to do something about a problem which is "out of control."[2]

It might be said that there currently exists an acknowledged discrepancy between the ability of state agencies to be effective in controlling and preventing crime and their position as the sole legitimate agent in the carrying out of this task.

---

1. For a discussion of 'social dangerousness' as a category applied to Gypsies, see Tamar Pitch, *Limited Responsibilities: Social Movements and Criminal Justice* 23 (1995).

2. For an overview of the persistence of rising crime rates in Britain and the United States see J. Young, J. Lea & R. Kinsey, *Losing the Fight Against Crime* (1986).

Recent developments in criminological theory, specifically that which has emerged under the name of "left realism,"[3] have increasingly pointed to the fundamental role of the public, and the informal controls which it can assert both in the reduction of crime and in the recognition of offenders. In the light of such developments, it is useful to look at specific social groups who do operate such systems within, yet independent of, the system of justice and social control of the society in which they reside. Gypsy communities, both in Britain and elsewhere, are an example of such a group and as such can be used as a means of investigating exactly how communities which have minimal or, in some cases, no formal institutions for the control of their members manage to maintain order and deal with offenders amongst themselves.

Weyrauch and Bell[4] have used material gained from anthropological studies of Gypsies, mainly in North American society, to demonstrate an example of what they refer to as "autonomous lawmaking." In this sense Weyrauch and Bell recognize that, although Gypsies have to work within the institutions of the host society in which they reside, they nonetheless have developed amongst themselves a system of regulation and justice which, for the most part, enables them to avoid any recourse to the institutions of that society.

CHANGES IN SYSTEMS OF CONTROL

Cohen's[5] theoretical and chronological approach to penal institutions in Western societies contrasts the way in which industrial society organizes control with the manner in which social control was organized in pre- and early industrial Europe and America. This account portrays the history of penal institutions as a steady development from minimal state intervention to a "widening of the net," in which increasing numbers of individuals come into contact with state run, formal institutions of social control. The types of controls which Cohen identifies as prevalent prior to this development (minimal use of the criminal law, informal over formal methods of control, punishment within as opposed to outside of the community, more decentralized process of criminalization) can be seen as bearing a similarity to the way in which control and order today is maintained amongst Gypsy communities within host society systems.

Both Cohen's work and that of realist criminologists point to the decline of informal methods of social control within modern industrial society and the desirability and potential effectiveness in controlling crime that a building up of such informal controls might have. It is within this context that the anthropological stud-

---

3. For a contextualization of the emergence of 'left realist' criminology, see Young, "Incessant Chatter: Recent Paradigms in Criminology," in *The Oxford Hand-book of Criminology* (M. Maguire, R. Morgan & R. Reiner eds., 1994).

4. Weyrauch & Bell, "Autonomous Lawmaking: The Case of the 'Gypsies'," chap. 2 in this volume.

5. S. Cohen, *Visions of Social Control* (1985).

ies of Gropper[6] and Grönfors[7] of Gypsy communities in the United States and Finland, as well as work on Gypsies in other countries,[8] particularly the Romanichals who constitute the majority of the Gypsies within England, can be used to look at how such controls work in practice, and what they might offer to the formal systems of control which operate within the host society. The information gained from Gypsy communities might also be seen as indicating the necessary conditions for such controls to work effectively. With regard to this last point, it can be argued that by looking at Gypsy communities and the way in which their system of control operates under specific social conditions, the uses and limitations of approaches to crime which stress the importance of the development of informal "community" controls can be assessed in terms of wider social structures and their systems of control.

Braithwaite[9] uses an example of the type of society in which informal controls provide the primary means of social control. Braithwaite argues that the small scale "village" society, the object of much anthropological research, is one in which order is maintained not so much through the threat of punishment as through the social shame which is delivered upon offenders. Braithwaite argues that this is a much more effective manner by which to ensure that regulation into social norms is maintained, as it is a system in which control is very difficult to avoid. This might be seen as providing a more constant process of socialization into group values for the younger members of the society.

Grönfors' study of the Kaale Gypsies in Finland highlights the way norms and values of the community are transmitted to the young through the use of particular stories which show how certain forms of behavior are unacceptable to members of that society. Laws, in this instance, can be seen as internalized by felt experience rather than conscious choice. It is this kind of socialization process which results in individuals being much more closely regulated by the laws of the society in which they live.

In contrast to this, host societies are ones in which the socialization process encompasses a plurality of values, although the state does try to enforce a dominant set of values. The aversion which the parents of Gypsy children are often said to have towards sending their children to state schools can be better understood in the context of a community which is trying to preserve a distinct way of life, one which is free of the kinds of conflicting values which such an education might give them. Gypsy communities can be seen as strikingly similar to those small scale societies in which minimal or no formal controls exist. These societies do not have

---

6. R. Gropper, *Gypsies in the City, Culture Patterns and Survival* (1975).

7. Martti Grönfors, *Blood Feuding Amongst the Finnish Gypsies* (1977).

8. The similarities between the avoidance systems used by the Kaale in Finland and the Romanichals in England are discussed in Acton, Caffrey, & Mundy, "Theorizing Gypsy Law," chap. 3 in this volume.

9. J. Braithwaite, *Crime, Shame and Reintegration* (1989).

the bureaucratic apparatus of the state, although the *kris,* or tribunal system of justice, can be seen as prefiguring a state form.

The differences between Gropper's study of the *kris* system used by the Vlach Rom living in the United States and Grönfors's study of the "blood-feuding" system used by the Kaale gypsies living in Finland highlight the methods by which Gypsy communities display a large degree of variation in the way social control is managed. In this sense it would be wrong to refer to Gypsies as a homogenous group, or, to repeat a mistake commonly made by those studying Gypsies, to take one particular Gypsy group as representative of "the" way of "real" Gypsies.[10]

Although almost all Gypsy groups can be characterized as having a system of justice which is autonomous within the system of the host society, the ways these systems work display very marked differences. The two ideal-typical systems represented here are not the only systems of social control which can be found amongst Gypsy communities. However, the *kris* and blood-feuding systems can be seen as highlighting important differences in terms of law enforcement.

THE *KRIS* AND THE BLOOD-FEUD: DIFFERENCES AND SIMILARITIES

The *kris* is basically a meeting of group members in which a specific conflict relating to inter-group relations, mainly between families, is discussed and some resolution of this dispute is reached. It should be said, though, that this does not encompass all of the reasons for which a *kris* can be called. For example, the *kris* has been called to discuss how Gypsies should approach governments with regards to claiming reparation payments for the families of those killed in Nazi Germany. The *kris* is also called when there is a dispute between different Gypsy groups. In this sense the *kris* can be seen as creating international law amongst distinct Gypsy communities.

This system, portrayed by Gropper in her study of Vlach Rom groups in the United States,[11] is one which displays a large difference compared to that used by the Kaale in Grönfors' study. Whereas the *kris,* which stands between members of the community as a mediating and decision-making body and has been compared to the court system of host societies, might be thought of as an embryonic form of state apparatus,[12] groups such as the Kaale do not have anything resembling a state even in this minimal form. Disputes amongst the Kaale are not resolved through individuals taking their case to a specialized third party who is external to the dispute, or through calling a meeting to decide how an offense should be treated. Instead of such an institution, each member of the Kaale community is responsible for taking action against any individual who has offended against them.

10. For a discussion of the politics of Gypsy identity, see Thomas Acton, *Gypsy Politics and Social Change* (1974).

11. The Vlach Rom are also the subject of Weyrauch & Bell's essay, supra n. 4.

12. Acton, Caffrey, & Mundy, see supra n. 8.

A further distinction can be made between those groups which have the *kris* and those which have the blood-feuding system in terms of their use of experts in the process of administering justice. Whereas neither have the highly professionalized system of host societies, they do display a variation in the extent to which there is a division of labor with regards to the resolving of disputes. The *krisnitorya*[13] chair the *kris* and have the most influence over its decisions. It is made up of members of the community who have shown themselves to have good skills in conflict resolution and a particularly good knowledge of the principles upon which the Rom should act.

The studies of Gropper and Weyrauch and Bell both indicate that certain conventions function to make particular individuals more likely to be chosen as a *krisnitori* (singular of *krisnitorya*). The Rom language is always used, and oratory skills are most effective when contributing to a case. Also, Gropper points out that although there is no formal exclusion of women from the *kris,* their contribution is substantially less than that of their male counterparts and they are never chosen to act as a *krisnitori.*

Although the law does not constitute a specialized sphere of knowledge in this instance (unlike within the host society, in which there is a large gap between a layperson's knowledge of a moral code i.e., having a good sense of fairness, and his being seen as being able to be active in the judicial process), it can nonetheless be said that knowledge of the law alone does not make a member likely to be chosen as a *krisnitori.* To some extent there is a parallel between this situation and that which exists within host societies in so far as knowledge of societal values alone does not make one a legitimate practitioner of the law. In other respects, however, there are limits on the extent to which this comparison between the *kris* and the courts of the host society can be made. For example, it would be wrong to see the *krisnitorya* as "judges" in the same way as these function within the host society. The krisnitori do not issue law by decree, but rather they put forward suggestions as to what might be a satisfactory way of resolving a conflict (indeed, this ability to suggest satisfactory outcomes is a large factor in deciding who gets to be a *krisnitori*).

Also contrary to the host society court, the *kris* cannot be dissolved successfully until a consensus has been reached by all parties involved as to what the outcome should be. This can be in direct contrast with courts in the host society in which decisions do not have consensus as a principle of their operation. Grönfors's study of the Kaale demonstrates there is not even this minimal division of labor between who can and who cannot hold legitimate positions of authority with regards to decision making. The process through which individuals are revealed to be guilty or liable to make reparations is one which does not directly involve the use of any specialized third party at all, but rather makes the individual and his or her kin

---

13. For a full discussion of the role of *krisnitorya* see Gropper, supra n. 6, at 83: Weyrauch & Bell, supra n. 4, at 43–44.

responsible for the enforcement of a decision, a decision which they themselves have made.

This, however, does not result in a merely arbitrary law or justice being enacted, but rather in a degree of consistency maintained through the shared nature of values and ideas of shame held by the community concerned. Grönfors[14] points to the way in which particular actions amongst the Kaale are likely to bring shame upon those who perform them. Kaale will incur shame if they do not go to the aid of one of their kin, regardless of whether they are in the right or not.

The obligatory defense of one's own kin can be seen as an important controlling mechanism for preventing potentially offensive behavior. Members of the Kaale community have a vested interest in not offending, as such behavior is likely to bring shame upon their kin as well as upon themselves. Grönfors points to the way in which avoidance goes beyond the individuals involved in the initial dispute, but is a much more general pattern in which contact between the kin groups of those involved in the dispute is avoided, Grönfors[15] shows that Kaale who meet for the first time are often reluctant to reveal their family ties until each is sure that the other is not anyone from a kin group whom one's own kin is avoiding. Even when the dispute is not between two specific individuals, Grönfors[16] shows that conflict can result from their discovering one another's kin links. Grönfors also shows, however, that this threat of shame which comes from involving one's kin in defending a dishonorable act means that conflict can be minimized. A potential offender will be more likely to retract from a situation which will cause shame to his or her kin.

LOCATION OF PUNISHMENT

Stan Cohen[17] has pointed to the way in which the place of control has shifted from the communities themselves to specialized institutions which remove individuals from them. Although of different Gypsy groups, Gropper's study and that of Grönfors both display the importance of the community in implementing punishments itself. Weyrauch and Bell, who take at least part of their information from studies done on the same group as Gropper's, also identify one of the main functions of Gypsy systems of justice as avoiding contact with the institutions of the host society.[18]

For the Vlach Rom who use the *kris* system, the community is involved both in the decision-making process and in the carrying out of any sanctions which it imposes. For example, in the case of a person declared *marime* or *moxadi*,[19] it is the

---

14. Grönfors, supra n. 7, at 108–16.

15. Id. at 121–22.

16. Id. at 122.

17. Cohen, supra n. 5.

18. Weyrauch & Bell, supra n. 4, at 27–28.

19. *Moxadi* is the specific term used by the Romanichal Gypsies in England, but is a universal concept within Gypsy communities, *marime* being the term used by the Vlach Rom. It has generally been translated as meaning "polluted" or "corrupt." See J. Okely, *The Traveller Gypsies* (1983); Acton, "The

community as a whole that must avoid contact with the offender and thus isolate him from his previous ties.

For the Kaale, the community is not represented in any specific form, as in the way that the *kris* represents the Vlach Rom community, but individuals and their kin are responsible for making offenders realize their offense and for enforcing the idea of shame upon the offenders which makes them back down and move away from the community. To emphasize the extent to which these communities are committed to the idea that it is they who are responsible for punishing their members, Grönfors[20] points to incidents amongst the Kaale in which members of the community have tried to punish offenders even when they are being dealt with by the authorities of the host society.

Cohen also points to the shift from public, "spectacular" forms of punishment to those which take place in seclusion. With regards to Gypsy groups; it can be seen that punishment falls into the former category; there exist no specific locations where punishment is dealt out, but rather it occurs for all in society to see. Grönfors' study of the blood feud underlines the central position of institutionalized avoidance in the justice system of the Kaale (the Romanichals can also be included in this), as they do not have the *kris* system. This entails the guilty party voluntarily moving away from the group in which they have been living in order to avoid those against whom an offense has been committed. This contrasts with the system in host countries in which punishment and control is operated externally by specialized institutions (police, prisons, etc.) and largely removed from community involvement.

As Grönfors[21] comments, avoidance can be seen as the way in which the Kaale "plead guilty" to an offense and take on the responsibility of the punishment. Unlike the systems which operate in host countries, the system relies upon a recognition of guilt and an acceptance of the punishment by the offenders themselves. In contrast, although the formal Criminal Justice System may wish to operate with a system which ensures that those who have committed an offense accept their punishment, there are a number of reasons why this does not happen. For a punishment to be acceptable it has to be seen and felt to be a just one. This situation is less likely to arise where certain communities become selected out by the criminal justice system as crimogenic and thus as in need of harsher policing, stiffer penalties, etc. The likelihood that these punishments will be seen as just is diminished.

These communities are often seen as crimogenic because their values do not adhere to the values of the wider society. Studies such as the Islington Crime Survey,[22] however, show that contrary to the representation which has been made of these

---

Functions of the Avoidance of Moxadi Kovels (amongst Gypsies in South East Essex)," in 50 *The Journal of the Gypsy Lore Society* (3–4 July 1971); Miller, "American Rom and the Ideology of Defilement," in *Gypsies, Tinkers and Other Travellers* (F. Rehfisch ed., 1975); Gropper, see supra n. 6.

20. Grönfors, supra n. 7, at 91.
21. Id. at 94.
22. B. Maclean, T. Jones & J. Young, *The Islington Crime Survey* (1986).

communities, they are not ones which have a radically different set of values or an opposition to the principle of policing. Policing becomes problematic only when it is seen as focusing on particular offenses and particular types of offenders. When this occurs, the result is that many of those who perceive their treatment as unfair are subsequently less likely to use this system when they know of an offense which has occurred, thus allowing offenders to avoid punishment and denying justice to those who have been wronged. Amongst Gypsy communities, however, anybody can call a *kris* and anybody can start a feud, in contrast to the host society, in which it is up to the discretion of state representatives to embark upon a criminal prosecution. This in itself is a problem to certain communities when one considers that offenses such as racial crimes do not have a specific category in the criminal law.

FORMS OF THE LAW

With regard to the actual type of law which is used against individuals, Cohen points to the way in which pre-industrial societies were ones in which the use of civil law was much more prevalent than the use of criminal law. Pashukanis[23] has emphasised the way in which the increased use of the criminal law is a process which is related to the extension of centralized states which, as representatives of society, formulated laws which were ostensibly for the protection of society as opposed to merely dealing with relations between individuals. Marxist positions, like that of Pashukanis's, however, would not see the criminal law in this manner. Laws which relate to the rights of private property, etc., are not seen as protecting all members of society in an equal fashion. Pashukanis provides a critique of the bourgeois notion of "equal right before the law." This notion, in practice, is undermined by the material differences between members of society, which operate to make the law unequally protective.

Whilst bourgeois law might be seen as addressing the rights of individuals, Gypsy law can be seen as primarily concerned with the collective rights of the Gypsy community. Although it is only amongst those groups which have the *kris* that offenses are materialized as a specific offense against the community (the *kris* could be seen as Pashukanis's "fictitious bearer of right"[24]), Grönfors's study of the Kaale shows that even where no such institution exists and where individual rights appear to be the only ones which are enforced, the fact that these require backing from one's own kin and other members of the group in general indicates that a measure of collective protection operates. This applies even where these offenses are not represented as "communal" offenses.

How else does one explain why certain offenses incite more collective anger than others? As Grönfors argues in his study, the collective values can be seen at work in the way in which offenses against certain members of the community, particu-

---

23. E. Pashukanis, *Law and Marxism. A General Theory* (1978).
24. Id. at 168.

larly children and the elderly, invoke much stronger feelings than others and are thus more likely to gain the support of the group against those who have offended. One might see this as contradicting the way in which Pashukanis has portrayed the feud as a system which does not have a concept of an "offense against society." Grönfors's examples indicate that although the Kaale do not represent their community in the form of a "fictitious bearer of right," it cannot be assumed that individual rights, as opposed to collective rights, are the only ones which are instrumental in structuring the feuding process.

This being said, however, certain other distinctions can be made between the form of authority employed by the Kaale and that employed within host societies for which Pashukanis's arguments can be employed. For example, Pashukanis sees the fundamental characteristic of "bourgeois legality" as the concept of "equal right" before the law. However, Grönfors's study suggests that amongst the Kaale no such notion of "equal right" can be seen to exist. The rights which one has are very much determined by one's social position within the Kaale community. Indeed, one can initially say that one has to be a Kaale in order to be afforded any "rights" at all. As Grönfors[25] points out, it would appear that the elderly command greater respect and thus greater "rights" to protection against certain types of behavior than younger members of the community. Also, at the other end of the age scale, Grönfors notes that the very young are likewise protected from acts of violence.

It is difficult to see in operation here the idea that all members of the community are "the same" when it comes to judging the way in which the Kaale behave towards each other. Therefore, right is not related to any notion of a universal right, but is related to one's needs. Thus we have the right to be unequal.[26] In contrast, although all members of the host society are able, in principle, to use the justice system, some people might feel they are unable to achieve justice because their cases are not treated so as to take into account relevant differences. If one takes the offense of racial attacks, for example, it is categorized along with other crimes against the person when it is in fact exclusively directed at specific groups within society.

PROFESSIONAL DOMINANCE, PUNISHMENT, AND THE RIGHT TO CONTROL

Cohen points to the way in which, within Western societies, professional dominance has grown over the past two centuries with regard to the punishing of offenders. This process is inextricably linked with the advancement of the state in

---

25. Grönfors, supra n. 7, at 109.

26. This idea of the right to be unequal is illustrated in Marx's "Critique of the Gotha Programme," in *Karl Marx: Selected Writings* 569 (D. McLellan ed., 1977), in which Marx argues that for "rights" to be equal in their effects they would have to be unequal in their application.

the criminal justice system. With regard to Gypsy groups, it appears that such intrusions are not operated by Gypsy groups themselves in the process of administering justice. Individuals are not "professionally" assessed with regard to what punishment and treatment is appropriate.

In contrast to what Foucault[27] has referred to as the constant search for knowledge of the individual offender, the main concern of Gypsy justice is with the correction of the act and not with the correction of the offender. As far as we know, no study mentions Gypsies ever attempting to understand or express an offense in terms of the pathology of the actor. Issues of whether to punish or "cure" do not arise because the offenders are always treated as knowing what they are doing. This is not to say that mitigating circumstances do not play a part in determining how offenses will be dealt with, but rather that these circumstances are external to the offender and are usually used to imply that the individual is not liable for the offense.

However, the degree to which such circumstances can be seen as excusing offenders of the offense varies according to whether the tribunal or blood-feuding system operates. The Vlach Rom who have the *kris*, for example, seem more sensitive to ideas of circumstance when deciding how a case should be settled. The Kaale, on the other hand, do not place so much emphasis upon the facts surrounding an offense. This appears especially true in more serious offenses such as murder. Grönfors gives the example of the Kaale who say of an accidental killing, "even in a case like this the Kaale avoids, even if it were an accident."[28] Grönfors sees this as an indication of the fact that even when a killing is accidental (in one case it was a gun which went off unplanned), the desire for revenge and the shame felt by the person who fired the gun is so strong that avoidance remains the only way to avoid further bloodshed.

The situation in which controls are exclusively in the hands of the community concerned can be contrasted with the host society in which social control is limited to professionals. Communities have become increasingly denied the right to administer informal controls. This can be seen as undermining the process of socializing their members into appropriate forms of behavior. The professionalization of control leads to a situation where people's beliefs about what constitutes appropriate behavior in the process of socialization can be very different. Professional approaches to control and socialization are ones which, by their very status as professional, imply that the knowledge employed is superior to that of the layperson. As a result of this, the understanding of a situation among professionals and ordinary members of a community are likely to be very different.

---

27. See M. Foucault, *Discipline and Punish* (1979) for an account of the relationship between criminal justice and the production of psychiatric knowledge.

28. Grönfors, supra n. 7, at 120.

Specialization and professionalization in this sense, and in the sense understood by Bourdieu,[29] are as much linguistic and symbolic as they are distinct practices. Within Gypsy groups the prime function is to unite a specific Gypsy community and give it a shared set of meanings and definitions for specific situations. For example, the rules which specify a person or situation as being *marime* or *moxadi* are ones which provide Rom with a more or less common universe of explanation. Where disagreements do occur, they are, nonetheless, ones which members of the community themselves can negotiate with. In the host society, by contrast, explanations of bad behavior by a child, for example, become translated into professionalized terms such as "hyper-activity," with which the layperson is denied this process of negotiation.[30]

Moreover, it is more often than not the case that these definitions are not ones openly shared or made understandable to those who are outside of the profession, for it is the very fact of mystification which maintains one group's prioritized status over another.[31] This can be seen to work against the establishment of more informal controls within the host society. This is because those with the appropriate skills are not seen as capable of exercising those controls. The agents of formal social control frequently do not trust those who could operate these informal controls, because they live in areas which have been labelled as crimogenic.

This, in turn, leads to local inhabitants' not being able to enforce those controls which they believe to be important, and subsequently to diminishing the types of controls which might be more effective in ensuring that regulations are complied with. Informal controls by ordinary members of society are ones which are difficult to avoid due to the fact that they are more or less ever-present. When the enforcing of controls is left to a selected few who cannot always be present in the way that ordinary members of society are, then controls are not enforced as regularly as they might be, thus allowing acts to go unapprehended and unpunished and encouraging the idea that detection is something which can be avoided.

REALIST CRIMINOLOGY AND THE PROBLEM OF "COMMUNITY"

Recent developments in criminology have moved away both from "left radicalism," which has been seen as denying the problem of crime, and also from "social positivism," which was seen as taking criminality uncritically and locating "solutions" to crime solely in the improvement of social conditions, e.g., family and locality.

---

29. Pierre Bourdieu, in *Language and Symbolic Power* (1988), argues that language is a primary means through which social hierarchies are communicated.

30. See Box, "Where Have All the Naughty Children Gone?," in *Permissiveness and Social Control* (National Deviancy Conference ed., 1980), for a discussion of the issues around the professionalization of lay knowledge.

31. Bourdieu, supra n. 29.

Contrary to such one-sided approaches to crime, "realist" criminology, as exemplified by the work of Lea and Young,[32] posits a "multiple approach" to tackling the problem of crime, by both "taking crime seriously,"[33] that is, recognizing its debilitating affects on its victims and society in general, and at the same time not accepting uncritically the entire process of criminalization and policing.

This criticism is largely aimed at the way centralized states criminalize many acts which communities might themselves not consider to be a problem, or conversely, not criminalize certain behaviors which the community feels to be important. Gypsy communities have no formal agent to set the agenda regarding which offenses are a priority and which are not. As a result, there is a much closer fit between the priorities of the community and the kinds of cases it deals with. Moreover, the *kris* system treats each case as unique, that is, as an opportunity for making law as opposed to merely dispensing it. By contrast, the formal system within the host society is not amenable to the prioritizing of laws which reflect the needs of the local inhabitants. However, a point which needs to be addressed is whether the potential exists for the development of the type of communities which would be necessary if more informal mechanisms of control were to be successfully implemented.

There are economic and societal forces operating against the maintenance of shared values, and consequently, against the development of effective informal systems of social control. These are, at the economic level, the globalization of the economy and the demise of traditional industries, and at the societal level, the gentrification of property and the presence of racial tension. These factors can produce a situation whereby a sense of belonging which arises from shared values is less probable.

Dick Hobbs, in his study of working class communities of the East End of London, demonstrates the way in which property development in and around the Docklands area has undermined the sense of solidarity and control over the area which its inhabitants once had.[34] The London Docklands Development Corporation (L.D.D.C.) was set up to bypass local government authority, effectively removing any control from these communities over what was built and who moved in. There is, then, a contradiction between those areas of the state which have set up quangos like the L.D.D.C., which bypass local controls, and those which have of late been emphasizing the potential for community control over local institutions. Furthermore, the ideas of "community" upon which such policies are predicated have little resemblance to reality. As Lacey and Frazer have argued, the appeal to community might best be seen in terms of the fear which its actual disappearance has

---

32. John Lea & Jock Young, *What is to be Done About Law and Order?* (1984).

33. See Young, "Thinking Seriously About Crime," in *Crime and Society* (M. Fitzgerald et al., eds., 1980) for an overview of the realist position that crime needs to be approached as a 'real' social problem. This is contrasted with social constructionist or 'moral panic' accounts.

34. Dick Hobbs, *Doing the Business* 217–27 (1988).

generated about maintaining social order. The "rhetorical device" of community stands in for its actual existence.[35]

Despite the problematic nature of establishing communities in modern industrial societies, one can point to a number of benefits which have been posited as coming from a return to traditional forms of informal involvement in the process of control. Firstly, as both Lea and Young and Cohen[36] point out, community initiatives can often enhance the quality of life without necessarily having any great influence on the actual amount of crime recorded.

One of the possible reasons for this is that under conditions in which there is greater community involvement more people might well be encouraged to come forward when a crime has been committed. It can be argued that the ability to do something about crime, and the enhanced sense of a shared set of values, make individuals more likely to be more responsive when it comes to the reporting of crimes. As victimization studies like the Islington Crime Survey indicate, when there is a high degree of correlation between the ideas which social members have about what is wrong, then the more likely it is that these crimes will be reported. Following Durkheim, it can be argued that when a community becomes more cohesive it is likely to be more sensitive to undesirable behavior and more likely to act upon it.

One of the fundamental challenges which crime presents to communities is the fear of its occurrence. This fear can be seen to work against the establishment of informal controls as it becomes the case that individuals try to avoid using the streets after dark, etc. It is the overcoming of this fear which can lead to a situation in which informal controls are increased, people begin to feel more at ease using their area at night, and it becomes more difficult for certain offenders to go undetected.

Community involvement in this sense can be seen as beneficial even where crime itself is not actually reduced in any significant way. The benefit of informal control is that it acts to empower communities and to give people a sense of having some control over local events, thereby creating a situation in which informal controls become more effective. As Cohen argues, community empowerment can revitalize an area, even if its short-term effect on the actual crime rate is negligible.[37]

Formal legal systems can be seen as having gradually eroded the ability of citizens to act in any way but a preventative one (more locks on doors and windows, complex alarm systems, etc.). In fact, the so-called "administrative criminology" would argue that the only way forward to reduce crime is to install preventative measures, both social and physical.[38] Thus this removes from the local community the power to develop their own controls. Gypsy control methods, on the other hand,

35. N. Lacey & E. Frazer, *The Politics of Community* 135–41 (1993).

36. Cohen, supra n. 5, at 263; Lea & Young, supra n. 32.

37. Cohen, supra n. 5, at 263.

38. See J.Q. Wilson, *Thinking About Crime* (1983) for an example of the theoretical position of 'administrative criminology'.

are ones in which the opposite is true; the community is fully involved in the identifying of offenders and the administering of justice.

The individuals within Gypsy society are not, then, powerless to act when an offense has been committed, but can enforce controls themselves. This contrasts with our criminal justice system in which state agencies are responsible for selecting out specific individuals for punishment and removing those individuals from the areas where they live. Not only does this not involve the community, but as Young has pointed out, it also has little effect on the actual crime rate, whereas informal controls can be effective in reducing crime. Lea and Young have given the example of how informal networks can reduce crime through the willingness of communities to give information to the police regarding offenders. The success or failure of much formal policing can be seen to rest upon these informal networks and the manner in which they relay information to the policing agencies.[39]

Contrary to the position that the withdrawal of formal controls would result in disorder, Grönfors's example of the blood feud shows that such a system does not result in an arbitrary or anarchistic deliverance of sanctions between individuals, but rather that the principle of "moral right," which is central to the blood-feuding process, serves to create a system of law which is able to maintain order.

One can also speculate as to how certain actions might appear to potential offenders under a system of more informal controls. At present, offenders often see crimes such as vandalism, criminal damage, and burglary less in terms of the harm that they do to individual members of society and more as acts of revenge against the state. This belief is further enhanced by the removal of offenders from their immediate neighborhood by an anonymous state criminal justice system involved in their conviction and punishment. Thus it is the anonymous state that offenders are confronted by, rather than their own immediate neighbourhood. One could argue that this process will be further exacerbated by the few detention centers for the persistent young offender. This is again highlighted by comparison to the way in which Gypsy groups maintain control and order. The way avoidance amongst the Kaale operates indicates that informal controls ensure that the offender does fully realise the way in which the crime has offended the community.

This is a situation which has, on occasions, been acknowledged by the police force of the host society. Sylvia Dunn, secretary of the first National Association of Gypsy Women, asserted at a recent conference on Romani law[40] that police would bring errant boys to Uriah Burton, the Romani owner of a site. As long as the parents of the boys would agree to the punishment that the site owner decided for them, the police would not prosecute. Dunn said, "He had a trotting track and used to make them run on it twice a day a number of lengths and he would run alongside them. It was not hard, but after an exercise like that they soon learnt their lesson the hard way."

39. Lea & Young, supra n. 32, at 188–97.
40. Acton, Caffrey, and Mundy, supra n. 8.

There are, however, limitations to the generation of such informal controls. One that has already been discussed is the ability for there to be cohesive communities in the context of a changing and fluid industrial society. The other limitation arises from the potential for injustice within this type of community. Weyrauch and Bell's[41] work argued that Gypsy criminal law was instrumental in protecting that society against "outsiders" and in protecting Gypsy values and practices. It can be expected, then, that communities, if given the power to act autonomously in maintaining controls, will also have controls the aim of which is the protection of values, etc., that the community feels are vital to its continuation and protection against the host society.

There are other limitations to the effectiveness and fairness of informal systems such as those found amongst Gypsy communities. As Reisman[42] argues in his reply to Weyrauch and Bell's article, Gypsy laws can often be repressive and unfair (especially to women) but are justified under the condition that they "protect" Gypsies from a potentially hostile host society by preserving cultural traditions. Given this, one might ask what the potential effects might be on those who are seen by communities as posing a threat to community values. The potential for injustice against ethnic minority groups in certain inner city areas, for example, is easy to imagine, but the problem not only applies to ethnic minorities. It is one which can be extended to other marginal groups, for example, those whose sexual orientation conflicts with that of the local community. Lacey and Frazer,[43] in their critique of "communitarianism," have also argued against communal values as a source of progressive politics, or at least against the assumption that they would be. As they point out, focusing upon the importance of community values in shaping policy often can involve taking these values uncritically.

For all the failings of a centralized criminal justice system in its appropriation of power and control from communities, it can be seen that any extensive decentralization and "democratization" of controls might pose a threat to the liberal values which the current centralized system protects, i.e., the tolerance of difference within society. Even advocates of informal controls like Lea and Young recognize the fact that in societies which are divided by class, gender, ethnicity, etc., state control can serve as a progressive force. This being said, Pashukanis indicates that the formal legal system itself, with its notion of "equal right," does not fully protect the values which it represents itself as having. Whilst all individuals are formally "free" to use the law, material inequality means that formal legal systems, and the ability to get justice from them, is more open to some than others.[44] This should not be forgotten when one is weighing up what has been lost and gained by such a system.

41. Weyrauch & Bell, supra n. 4.
42. Reisman, "Autonomy, Interdependence, and Responsibility," 103 *Yale L. J.* 401 (1993).
43. Lacey & Frazer, supra n. 35, at 130–62.
44. Pashukanis, supra n. 24.

The problem, then, appears as one of using traditional mechanisms effectively in empowering members to exert control over their area, but at the same time preventing the systematic victimization of certain members of these communities. The example of Gypsy groups suggests that a lack of formal controls does not mean that groups fall into disorder and anarchy. On the contrary, Grönfors's work describes a community in which order is successfully maintained whilst allowing maximum freedom to individuals. However, there is a problem with the way informal controls can be potentially oppressive to marginal groups within society.

This is related to the further problem of whether the potential for community involvement on any large scale exists under social and economic conditions that work against the maintenance of shared values on a level which would allow all individuals within communities to feel that they were fairly dealt with. It can be asked, then, To what extent does social inequality prevent the types of communities in which effective informal controls might be successfully operated, and to what extent can more informal systems operate under such conditions?

FIVE

Gypsy Law and Jewish Law

Calum Carmichael

The essay on Gypsy law by Walter Weyrauch and Maureen Bell is a pioneering attempt to describe the role of law among the Roma (Gypsies).[1] Because there is no written law, Weyrauch and Bell are not in a position to give an account of the development of Romani law over its approximately one-thousand-year history. This lack is in striking contrast to Jewish law. Although there are eras when we know little or nothing about Jewish law, we can nonetheless give an account of its development over a very long period of time.

JEWISH LAW

Jewish law has existed for about three thousand years and is observed in some parts of the world today. It is virtually impossible to say much about its historical beginnings. There is a sense in which many rules (prohibiting murder, stealing, e.g.) in every culture are without origin. The laws of the Bible share features with legal material familiar from other cultures in the ancient Near East. The question of how to evaluate the overlap is much debated and no convincing link has emerged. Hammurabi's code existed well into the first millennium. It constituted an academic body of law and the biblical lawgivers may have shared its intellectual stance by setting out theoretical constructions focused on topics of their own concern (the release of debts every seven years, returning land to its original possessors every forty-nine years).[2]

---

1. Weyrauch & Bell, "Autonomous Lawmaking: The Case of the 'Gypsies'," chap. 2 in this volume.
2. All groups tend to paint ideal pictures of themselves. Social anthropologists report that native informants, describing what goes on in their societies, set out normative ideals as if they are describing how things actually are. See Bronislaus Malinowski, *The Sexual Life of Savages in North Western Melanesia*

A marked feature of biblical laws (the Book of the Covenant in Exodus 21:2–23:19, the laws in Deuteronomy 12–26, and the many rules in the Books of Numbers and Leviticus) is that they are attributed to Moses. Only exceptionally does God communicate rules directly (to Noah and his sons in Genesis 9, and in the Decalogue in Exodus 19 and Deuteronomy 5).

In his laws, Moses takes up problems in his own time (his people's oppression in Egypt), problems that existed among his ancestors (Abraham's marriage to his half-sister Sarah), and problems long after he lived (the appointment of a king in Israel). The purveyors of this legal material seem to be engaged in a process which occurs in the life of most nations, namely, they invent their own legal traditions. A negative consequence is that it is exceedingly difficult to work out the early history of a nation's law.

Biblical law is unique in that different bodies of legal material are incorporated at different points in a narrative history up to the point at which Moses is about to die and the people of Israel are about to enter the land of Canaan. The unknown scribes responsible for this merging of law and narrative adopted a convention common in the ancient world. They made of Moses a legendary figure who judged past developments in his nation's history as recorded in Genesis-Deuteronomy and anticipated future ones as recorded in Joshua-2 Kings. The literary traditions in these books of the Bible thus contain the same issues taken up in the laws. When we work out the links between the laws and the issues in the individual narratives, we can account, with remarkable precision, for the substance of the laws, the language of their formulations, and the often bewildering sequence in which they are set out (in the Decalogue, a rule about murder comes after a rule about honor to parents with its promise of living long upon the land [Hebrew = ground], because the focus is Cain's murder of Abel and its consequence that he was no longer allowed to till the ground).[3]

Under the leadership of Ezra and Nehemiah, the Israelites completed their return from exile in Babylonia in the fifth century B.C.E. The Torah (the first five books of Moses) was made the sacred constitution of the returned community and it inspired harsh reforms. Although not originally having legislative authority, the rules in the Torah came to be treated in later books of the Bible as if they had. This development brings to a conclusion what we know about ancient Jewish (biblical) law.

The next major body of law is the Talmud. As well as representing an advanced stage of legal development, it shows that Jewish law was a system in movement,

---

503–72 (1953). In her account of Gypsy society, Patti J. Jeatran states that "the behaviors described [in her paper] may be largely ideal and should in no way be construed as representative of the reality of daily life for any single individual, much less an entire group of people." See "Disputing and Social Control Among American Gypsies," (Nov. 14, 1990, unpublished paper, University of Illinois, Department of Criminal Justice), 3. Similar considerations should always be kept in mind when looking at biblical and later Jewish legal material.

3. See Calum Carmichael, *The Spirit of Biblical Law* 92–96 (1996).

undergoing great changes between 100 B.C.E. and 500 C.E. (negligence added to dishonesty as a standard for contractual liability, Scriptural precepts took precedence over examples as authoritative in legal exegesis). The Talmud contains material from the first pre-Christian century but its main body of law begins in the second century C.E. There are two Talmuds, the Jerusalem or Palestinian (about 425 C.E.) and the Babylonian (about 475 C.E.).

Each Talmud consists of commentary, the Gemara, on the Mishnah and Tosephta. The Mishnah is a codification of Jewish law written in Hebrew at the end of the second century C.E. by Rabbi Judah the Prince. The Tosephta consists of additions to the Mishnah by Rabbi Judah's pupil, Hiyya bar Abba. The dominant feature of the Mishnah is its focus on juristic constructions coming from the Tannaites, the Rabbis who lived between 50 B.C.E. and 200 C.E. The Gemara represents the views of the Amoraites, the Rabbis who lived between 200 and 500 C.E. Written mostly in vernacular Aramaic and embracing all facets of life, the Talmud consists of often unresolved legal and non-legal arguments. Its discursive, educational thrust is unmistakable.

The Talmud reveals that much of Jewish law developed independently of what is found in the biblical sources. From the second century B.C.E. the Pharisees, an educated class much committed to the study of law and religion, were particularly prominent in this development. It is their traditions which are preserved in the Talmud. The Sadducees, a class representative of old, land-owning families, opposed Pharisaic positions. Their complaints that the Pharisees disregarded Scriptural precepts prompted Hillel (first century B.C.E.) to make full use of Hellenistic rules of interpretation to "prove" that Pharisaic lawmaking was indeed derivable from Scriptural laws. Rabbi Ishmael (second century C.E.) used thirteen hermeneutic norms (*mid-doth* [Hebrew], *mekilata* [Aramaic], *kanones* [Greek]) to derive laws from biblical rules. Rabbi Eliezer ben Gelili later listed some thirty-two norms for interpreting all biblical texts. It is this complex process of interpretation that accounts for the difficulty often experienced in following the logic of Talmudic ratiocination. Beliefs and institutions contrary or new to what Scripture contained are based on it nonetheless (belief in resurrection, proselyte baptism, modes of capital punishment, monetary damages in place of retaliation).

The Aprocrypha, the translations of the Bible into Greek (the Septuagint) and Aramaic (the Targums), and the documents from a Jewish military settlement under the Persians in Egypt (the laws of the Elephantine papyri, fifth century B.C.E.), from Qumran (the Dead Sea Scrolls), and from Jewish Christian circles (the New Testament) all contribute to our understanding of ancient Jewish law between the biblical period and the Talmudic. Commentaries on Scripture by Philo of Alexandria in Egypt (20 B.C.E. to 40 C.E.) and by second century C.E. Rabbis on legal and other material in the Book of Exodus (the Mekhilta) likewise provide important insights. The Apocrypha, unreliable for Jewish law as a whole, may reflect regional usage. The Elephantine papyri reveal a tendency to incorporate facets of foreign law. The vocabulary of the Septuagint suggests a greater awareness of legal concepts than hitherto. Philo's allegorisation of biblical law combines refined legal analysis with wide-ranging intellectual pursuits. The Dead Sea Scrolls convey the narrow but lively interests of sectarian groups, and the Judaism of the New Testament is indispensable in plotting the history of concepts and conventions that show up in the Talmud. Noticeable in all of these sources is how the ancient law is constantly being modernized. Narrowly focused rules are generalized. Antiquated institutions are brought up to date; for example, Hillel's *Prosbul* neutralized the rule in Deuteronomy 15:1–11 requiring the release of debts every seven years by enabling a loan to be enforced even after the Seventh Year (*Mishnah Shebiith* 10:3f., *Mishnah Gittin* 4:3). Later, around 1000 C.E., Rabbi Gershom of Mayence prohibited polygamy.

Codifications extracting and elaborating the legal constructions, ethical demands, and wise sayings of the Bible continued being written throughout the Middle Ages: the Halakoth Gedoloth (by Simon Kayyara, ninth century), Rif (Isaac Alphasi's Halakoth of the eleventh century), Mishneh Torah (by Maimonides, eleventh century), Turim (by Jacob ben Asher around 1300 C.E.), and the Shulhan Arukh (by Joseph Caro, sixteenth century) with its popular abridged sequel, the Qiṣṣur (by Solomon Ganzfried, 1864). There are also later sectarian developments: the Karaite Book of Precepts (by Benjamin ben Moses Nahawendi of the ninth century) and Mantle of Elijah (by Elijah ben Moses Bashyatchi and Caleb Alfendolopo of the fifteenth).

Commentaries on the later codes of law are much larger in size than the codes themselves. Preeminent among them is Rashi's (Rabbi Solomon ben Isaac's) commentary on the Gemara, written in the eleventh century, and printed in the margin of the standard editions of the Gemara.

Monographs on particular topics of the law are not found before the Middle Ages. In the first half of the tenth century, Saadya Gaon produced some dozen in Arabic, of which the Book of Inheritances survives. A major source of written law is the *responsa* literature, the replies of scholars to questions submitted to them. Only after the completion of the Talmud did they come to be written down. To this day they provide a source of judgments and advice on everyday problems.[4]

GYPSY LAW AND JEWISH LAW

Only in a tangential way is it possible to make some observations that might prove illuminating when comparing and contrasting the laws of the Roma and those of the Jews. The comparisons that immediately come to mind, notions of cleanness and uncleanness attaching to food and to women, are less striking than one might imagine. For one thing, in regard to Jewish dietary laws we are in the dark as to their origin and it is likely that their significance for Jewish life varied over time; for example, they probably became of much greater significance after the destruction

---

4. For particular aspects of the above summary, see Carmichael, supra n. 3. I am indebted to David Daube for permitting me to use unpublished material of his.

of the Temple in 70 C.E.[5] For another, the terms "clean" and "unclean" can be misleading and conceal complicated notions concerning life and death which attach to blood and to food, and also concerning reverential attitudes to women, which come into play in all cultures.[6]

The Human Body and the Law

Walter Weyrauch emphasizes that the concept of purity among the Gypsies involves a profound interaction between the purity of the human body and ethical purity in the sense of the person's observing proper rules of conduct: "The legal significance of the human body, rather than of abstract concepts, seems also to be a distinctive feature [of Gypsy law]."[7] Terms for defilement express breaches of the social rules. Carol Miller cites the examples of the irregular unions of a godparent to a godchild and a Gypsy to a non-Gypsy. The former defiles because "ritually disparate marriage abrogates the responsibilities associated with placement in the age-sex-status respect system," and the latter because "the risk of venereal disease is reason enough to *marimé* [to defile] those having intimacies with *gadžé* [non-Gypsies]."[8] The union between a Gypsy and a non-Gypsy provides a specific example where a matter to do with the human body, venereal disease, carries over into a rule.

One can observe similar links between bodily matters and social rules in the history of Jewish law. The Hebrew term *niddah*, "impurity," commonly used of menstrual blood in the book of Leviticus, is surprisingly used metaphorically of the forbidden union between a man and his brother's wife in Leviticus 20:21. The sobriquet is used of no other prohibited union. The use of the term to depict this particular union is owing to the fact that the lawgiver focused on the biblical example of the

---

5. What triggered their formulation (not their origin) was the response to the idiosyncratic situation in Joseph's Egypt when Joseph, in the role of vizier, could not eat with his brothers because the Egyptian rules about food prohibited him from doing so (Genesis 43:32). See Calum Carmichael, *Law, Legend, and Incest in the Bible: Leviticus 18–20*, chap. 7 (1997).

6. On menstruation as embodying powerful notions of life and death, see Buckley & Gottlieb, "A Critical Appraisal of Theories of Menstrual Symbolism," in *Blood Magic: The Anthropology of Menstruation* 26 (Thomas Buckley & Alma Gottlieb, eds. 1988). For these notions about life and death in the biblical rules about menstruation, see Jacob Milgrom, *Leviticus 1–16*, at 767, 768, 934, AB (1991), and in the biblical rules about food, see Carmichael, "On Separating Life and Death: An Explanation of Some Biblical Laws," 1–7 *Harvard Theological Review* 69 (1976). There is some basis in real life for the view that Gypsy women command more respect than the men. "Women are regarded as cleaner [than the men] in a moral sense, as well as the ritual sense. Their relationships with the *gadžé* [non-Gypsies] are circumscribed and restricted by women's greater obligations to the dictates of virtuous behaviors, especially as these affect the family unit"; Carol J. Miller, "Mačwaya Gypsy *Marimé*," 38 (unpublished thesis, University of Washington, 1968).

7. Weyrauch, "Oral Legal Traditions of Gypsies and Some American Equivalents," chap. 11 in this volume, at 246.

8. Miller, supra n. 6, at 20, 24.

union between Onan and his brother's wife, Tamar, in Genesis 38. An exceptional feature is Onan's ejaculating outside her. The Priestly lawgiver viewed the expulsion and destruction of Onan's life-giving fluid as similar to a woman's loss of menstrual blood. Leviticus 15 sets down together the topic of impurity which is caused by male and female discharges. The loss of semen and vaginal blood was similarly regarded because each embodied the polarity of life and death.[9] The biblical lawgiver's linking of the incest rule forbidding a sexual relationship with a brother's wife and Onan's act is most illuminating because it is the only example we have of a lawgiver's linking bodily impurity and the apparently unrelated impurity of a particular form of human conduct.[10]

The Hebrew term *niddah*, "impurity," is close in meaning to the sense of the Romani term *marimé*, which is variously translated as "impure, shameful," "defiled," "polluted," or "unnatural."[11] Gypsies distinguish between a notion of the clean and the dirty which is based on sensory perception (*mulali*) and a notion that has a mystical content (*marimé*) which derives from religious belief.[12] There is, however, a likely overlap between the two notions. In biblical law, one sometimes finds a focus on the blemish left by wrongdoing, rather than on the wrongdoing itself. Where a murder has occurred and it is not known who has committed the offense, a ceremony of expiation is required not by way of addressing the guilt of the offender but by way of removing the blemish from the land caused by the dead body on it (Deuteronomy 21:1–9). Both sensory perception and mystical belief about the land play a role.

A later illustration in Jewish circles of the linking of literal and metaphorical uncleanness is the riddling injunction by Jesus: "There is nothing outside a man which by going into him can defile him; but the things which come out of a man are what defile him" (Mark 7:15; Matthew 15:11).[13] Like Rabbi Johanan ben Zaccai, in an example cited below, Jesus rejects the notion of mechanical defilement. One's moral attitude is paramount in determining who is clean and who is unclean.[14] Among the Roma, the notions of purity (*vujo*) and impurity (*marimé*), far

---

9. This polarity plays a major role in biblical law, just as mutually exclusive categories play a similar role in Gypsy thinking; for example, elaborate funeral feasts express a need to keep the dead from impacting on the living. See Carmichael, supra n. 3, at 126–41; Elwood B. Trigg, *Gypsy, Demons and Divinities: The Magic and Religion of the Gypsies* 126–57 (1973); Jeatran, supra n. 2, at 14. For discussion of the rule in Leviticus 20:21 about the impurity of a marriage between a man and his brother's wife, see Carmichael, supra n. 5, at Chapter 7.

10. On the complex relationship between unclean things or acts and socially disruptive acts among the Gypsies, theft, for example, see Trigg, supra n. 9, at 54–56.

11. See Jeatran, supra n. 2, at 14.

12. Miller, supra n. 6, at 15.

13. The injunction is riddling because there is full acceptance of the dietary rules by Jesus and the community he addresses. They were eventually rejected by the Church, which used his pronouncement in support of their position. See Vincent Taylor, *The Gospel According to St. Mark* 342 (1952) (if Jesus spoke clearly in the matter, it is difficult to account for the early disputes in the Church about observing the dietary rules).

14. See David Daube's discussion, *The New Testament and Rabbinic Judaism* 142, 143 (1956).

from having just physical application, represent aspirations to *kintala*, to physical and moral "wholesomeness." A similar sentiment about the rejection of bodily impurity is conceivable among the Roma should a claim be made that bodily purity is the sole aim of all their rules. Interestingly, the head and the mouth are thought of as the purest parts of the body. The fact that children are not subject to the rules about bodily impurity is further indication that such impurity is not perceived in mechanical fashion.[15]

Responses to Outsiders

As a consequence of living amidst foreign cultures, both groups have turned to their respective legal traditions to deepen their sense of identity. Adherence to their laws enhanced the self-identity of the Vlax group of Roma when they experienced serfdom for some five hundred years in Wallachia and Moldavia.[16] The laws in the Bible are probably geared to the need of the Jews living in Babylonia after 586 B.C.E. to secure an identity there.[17] An analysis of the language of the Greek translation of the Bible (the Septuagint, third century B.C.E.) suggests that Hellenistic Jews became more alert to the role of law in sustaining their own cultural identity. The term "sin" in the Hebrew Bible becomes reduced to *adikia*, *anomia* (injustice, lawlessness) in the Septuagint. The Greek word *nomos*, "law," translates the Hebrew term *torah*, which means instruction in precepts but also the interpretation of history and knowledge about God. Hebrew for the word "law" is *miṣvah*, or *ḥoq miśpat*. For the later Rabbis, not living in the diaspora but still living in their homeland, *torah* continues to mean the whole of the Pentateuch, not just *nomos*.

The attitudes of different groups to the larger society in which they function can produce quite different stances. Gypsies and Jews, but not Christians (with exceptions), are intent on preserving their ethnic identity in whatever society they are living. Consequently, their stance can be markedly different from the Christian one. Gypsies do not go in for proselytizing, and missionary activity by Jews over the centuries is minor compared to the efforts of Christians. Christians had to be much more conscious of what they believed in and were more given to doctrinal statements than Jews. The nonexistence or lack of proselytizing activity on the part of Gypsies and Jews is one reason why it is much more difficult for outsiders to comprehend their ways and beliefs. It is largely the explanation why outsiders view both Gypsies and Jews as adhering to rules that appear to be mindlessly given over to the minutiae of daily life. For example, items to be washed by the Gypsies "are sorted not by color but by the degree of defilement and the extent to which their

15. See Jeatran, supra n. 2, at 15, 18.
16. See Weyrauch & Bell, "Autonomous Lawmaking," supra n. 1, at 23.
17. For an illustration, see the following discussion about the rules forbidding certain mixtures in Deuteronomy 22:9–11 and Leviticus 19:19.

purity needs to be preserved";[18] or blessings by an orthodox Jew are given "when he gets up in the morning, before and after meals, on drinking a glass of water, on smelling an odorous plant, on seeing a beautiful tree or animal, on seeing a deformed person, after relieving nature . . . on going to bed and so on."[19] There is a failure on the part of the outsider to understand that profound beliefs underlie the observance of such rules. For the Gypsy, the natural order of the cosmos has to be maintained and consequently anything perceived to be unnatural in daily life, such as the defilement that comes from items of clothing, must be avoided. For the orthodox Jew, the higher ideals of his religious faith are so securely anchored that the forms of his religious practice are all that are necessary.

Unlike Christians, for example, the way in which Gypsies choose not to reveal themselves to outsiders is in fact what is noteworthy. It is commonly reported that a Gypsy, when granting an interview to a non-Gypsy, uses the occasion to disseminate wrong information about Gypsy culture.[20] Gypsy names and rituals lose their magical effectiveness if uttered to non-Gypsies.[21] There are in fact prohibitions against members of the Roma informing outsiders about their laws.[22] A comparable Jewish stance is found in those Talmudic discussions in which an outsider approaches a Rabbi and asks a question about the strange practices of the Jews, for example, the pagan who asked Rabbi Johanan ben Zaccai (first century C.E.) about the purification of a person who has had contact with a corpse (*Numbers Rabba* 19:2, *Pesiqta de-Rab Kahana* 40a f). The pagan saw the practice as sheer sorcery. The Rabbi responded by drawing attention to a comparable pagan practice for dealing with a demented person. In other words, there was no attempt to enlighten the pagan about the Jewish practice. The intention rather was to push him away. After he left, the Rabbi's disciples expressed dissatisfaction with their master's response ("Rabbi, him you pushed away with a fragile reed"). The Rabbi then expounded the "true" reason for the Jewish practice. The ritual for purification (by means of water containing the ashes of a red heifer) was one of those statutes to be accepted as the will of God for which no rational basis could be discerned.[23]

Rules often serve not just to cement an attachment to one's group but to promote a sense of superiority to the outsider. Commenting on this aspect of Gypsy culture, P.A. Jeatran states that "individuals who wish to retain the perceived superiority conveyed by membership in the secret group will not risk rejection and the subsequent loss of status by breaking its rules."[24] In Jewish tradition the rules of the Mishnah, which come from the Pharisees, reveal an intense insider/outsider

18. Jeatran, supra n. 2, at 16.

19. Daube, "Two Jewish Prayers," 6 *Rechtshistorisches Journal* 195 (1987).

20. Jeatran, supra n. 2, at 1.

21. Martin Block, *Gypsies* 13 (1939).

22. See Jean-Paul Clébert, *The Gypsies* 132 (1963).

23. For this example and the prevalence in Rabbinic circles from the first century onwards of an uncommunicative stance in dealing with outsiders, see Daube, supra n. 14, at 141–50.

24. Jeatran, supra n. 2, at 12.

consciousness. The rules typically use the participle in their formulations: "In the month of Ab, one is reducing joy" (*Mishnah Taanith* 4:6); "One is not selling pagans bears or lions or anything dangerous" (*Mishnah Abodah Zarah* 1:7). These participles of the correct practice, which simply record observations, have nonetheless directive force. As David Daube has so well shown, they are the rules of a group claiming superior status: "What endows the factual description of a custom with regulatory effect is the addressee's desire to belong to the nobility singled out by this bearing."[25]

Avoidance of Enlightenment

On occasion both Jews and Gypsies will avoid enlightenment even among themselves about their own laws, customs, and lore.[26] For the Gypsies this is especially true for matters affecting bodily functions. Rules relating to purity and pollution are adhered to but not talked about.[27] To be sure, the role of euphemisms in every society reveals similar traits, as does the role of the self-understood, that is, certain matters are so firmly grounded that there is no need or wish to talk about them. However, in that Gypsy law is so dominated by notions of bodily purity the avoidance of instruction about it seems surprising. Walter Weyrauch reports how one Romani informant who read his manuscript on Gypsy law stated that no Gypsy could in strictness read the part about the legal significance of intimate personal matters "without the risk of being polluted by the mere act of reading."[28] A possibly similar attitude in Jewish tradition is the notion that disturbing portions of Scripture, for example, King David's adultery with Bathsheba (2 Sam 11:2–17), might be read (in Hebrew) but not interpreted (into Aramaic for the unlearned who did not know Hebrew, *Mishnah Megillah* 4:10); or, the more complicated notion, that all of Scripture, or the Song of Songs and Ecclesiastes, or only the Song of Songs "renders the hands unclean" (*Mishnah Yadaim* 3:5).[29]

---

25. See David Daube, *Ancient Jewish Law* 82 (1981).

26. David Daube told me that his mother belonged to a *hevra qadishah* in both Freiburg and London. She visited the sick and the dying, and spent time with the dead. No non-Jew could come near the dead or dying. The rule was that no report of anything they said or did when they were dying would be reported beyond this circle. Daube never learnt anything about any of the many people she had dealt with in these circumstances. He had never enquired into the rules that prevailed in such an entity, which was only to be found among the very Orthodox. Literary convention in Babylonian, Egyptian, and Israelite antiquity had a dying man's words (Jacob's in Genesis 49 and Moses' in Deuteronomy 33, for example) made public because they were regarded as possessing supreme worth.

27. "Gender and ethnic limitations of *romaniya* are meant to prevent free communication of intimate matters among Gypsies and from Gypsies to the outside," Weyrauch, supra n. 7, at 256.

28. See Weyrauch, supra n. 7, at 254.

29. G. F. Moore, *Judaism in the First Centuries of the Christian Era* (1966), vol. 3, 66 n. 9, expresses difficulty about working out the origin and significance of the rule that contact with Scripture makes the hands unclean. Herbert Danby, *The Mishnah* 626 n.4 (1933), thinks that because the Scriptural scrolls were stored with the produce for the Heave-offering they attracted mice and hence caused contamination. This may have to do again with an interesting interplay between physical and spiritual uncleanness.

Sometimes Jewish authorities do not inform members of the community who fail to observe certain strict rules (abstention from meat and wine, for example) that their non-observance is wrong. The justification for this stance is that a Jew who does not know what he is doing is wrong ought not to be told because "it is better the Israelites should transgress in ignorance than wilfully" (*Babylonian Baba Bathra* 60b; *Tosephta Sotah* 15:10).[30]

Common Claims

Both Gypsies and Jews have in common a trait that many other groups share. They invent myths about the uniqueness of their origins by way of proclaiming their identity to both insiders and outsiders.[31] The story of the Exodus plays this role in Jewish tradition as does the attribution of almost all the laws to Moses.[32]

Both groups view the decisions of their courts to be influenced by supernatural guidance. "Gypsies believe that supernatural powers, not tactics, decide the merits of a case, for example, the *kris* of the Vlax Rom."[33] Examples in biblical tradition are the use of Urim and Thummim (possibly dice that functioned as oracles) in cases where the earthly authorities could not decide, and the claim that the decisions of the central tribunal are under divine direction (Deuteronomy 17:8–13). In the Talmud judges are allied with God (*Babylonian Sanhedrin* 6b).

For the Gypsies moral behavior determines the content of the law. Biblical law reveals the same stance. The codes of law in the Bible bring together both ethical and legal matters without any indication on the part of the compilers that they should be kept separate. For the Rabbis the Torah is the supreme law— even God himself is bound by it—and it "stands for the highest conception of

30. See *Collected Works of David Daube, Talmudic Law* 8 (Calum Carmichael ed. 1992). The problem the authorities faced was that of defiance. On the problem among the Roma, see Weyrauch & Bell at 48.

31. "Myths surrounding the Gypsies and their origins might have been a matter of faith, or perhaps were devised to mislead non-Gypsies, and thus to support their own cultural insularity." See Weyrauch & Bell, supra n. 1, at 28. The Vlax Rom assert that their *kris* system of public assemblies to resolve disputes and formulate policies is an authentic, ancient form of Romani culture which may even go back to the Indian *panchajat* system. In fact, the origin of the *kris* system appears to be in the Romanian village assemblies of the sixteenth century at the time when the Vlax Rom became enslaved in Romanian neo-feudal society. See Acton, Caffrey & Mundy, "Theorizing Gypsy Law," chap. 3 in this volume at 98–99.

32. A version of the Exodus story is one of the legends the Gypsies tell about their origins; Trigg, supra n. 9, at 19, 20. On the invention or reinvention of a nation's legal system in particular, see for seventeenth-century England, J.G.A. Pocock, *The Ancient Constitution and the Feudal Law* (1957); for Scotland, MacQueen, "*Regiam Majestatem*, Scots Law and National Identity," 74 *Scottish Historical Review* 1–20 (1995); for ancient Athens, Cohen, "Greek Law: Problems and Methods," 106 *Zeitschrift der Savigny-Stiftung für Rechtsgeschichte* 101 (1989); also, on more general aspects, *The Invention of Tradition* (Eric Hobsbawm & Terence Ranger, eds. 1983).

33. See Weyrauch & Bell, supra n. 1, at 73 n. 257 (quoting other authorities). On the quite different system of social control among the English Romanichals and the Finnish Kaale Rom, see Acton, Caffrey & Mundy, supra n. 31.

fundamental goodness, for that basic morality which is a prerequisite of civilisation."[34]

In both cultures claims based on a purist view of behavior clash with claims coming from a pragmatic one. Although regarded as deviant behavior and not tolerated by *romaniya*—the term that like the Hebrew term *torah* denotes the sum of religion, tradition, and law—young male Gypsies may gain sexual experience with non-Gypsy women so long as discretion is shown.[35] In Jewish tradition one can find the decidedly non-purist view that a leader who cannot control his passions may engage with a prostitute so long as the community is kept in the dark.[36] In both biblical and later Jewish sources there are many examples of rules which, on account of expediency or because of the need to compromise with ineradicable human sinfulness, incorporate commands or permissions that the ideal order of things would not tolerate.[37]

Role of Deception

Jewish authorities over the centuries have worked out rules to cope with the problem of oppression experienced in their communities. In those extreme situations when a heathen power demands that a member of the Jewish community be handed over to be put to death and failure to do so entails the extermination of the entire community, Jewish law goes in for a distinction. If the person is unnamed, there must be resistance and a facing up to the dire consequences. If he is named, the community may hand him over. Indications are that originally the position was that no member, named or unnamed, should be handed over. The distinction probably came into being after the defeat of Bar Kochba's rebellion in 135 C.E. when the Roman government began a systematic persecution of the Jews in Palestine.

If the demand by a hostile group is for a Jewish woman to be defiled, or otherwise all the women will be defiled, the Mishnah is uncompromisingly opposed to handing her over (*Mishnah Terumoth* 8:12). Later the Jerusalem Talmud introduced a concession. If the entire company of women is under threat, two kinds of women may be surrendered, (Jewish) slave-women and a woman known for her immoral behavior (*Jerusalem Terumoth* 46b). Later again, in the Middle Ages, Jewish scholars did introduce the distinction prevailing in regard to handing over

---

34. C.G. Montefiore & H. Loewe, *A Rabbinic Anthology* 171, 683 n. 70 (1938).

35. See Miller, supra n. 6, at 26, 40 (up to a point sexual experience with non-Gypsy women is tolerated for young male Gypsies, who generally enjoy more freedom and authority to do as they please).

36. *Babylonian Moed Qatan* 17a, *Kiddushin* 40a. For a discussion of purism versus pragmatism in Philo, New Testament, and *Talmudic* sources, see Daube, "Neglected Nuances of Exposition in Luke-Acts," 25 *Principat* 2329–56 (1985).

37. See Carmichael, "A Common Element in Five Supposedly Disparate Laws," 29 *Vetus Testamentum* 129–42 (1979); Daube, supra n. 30, at 1–13. For a philosophical critique of actions that are basically wrong but are nonetheless required by the law, see Hans Kelsen, *General Theory of Law and State* 21 (1945).

a person for killing. There could be a handing over of a named woman but not of an unnamed one.[38]

Gypsies go in for concealment of their identity in order to avoid bad treatment at the hands of the host culture. Certain Jewish rules reveal the longstanding view that it is permissible to deny one's Jewishness in order to avoid persecution. Certain distinctions, however, are brought to bear. Denying that one is Jewish in a private setting is less reprehensible than in a public one, and to give an evasive answer to a hostile interrogator is preferable to an outright lie.[39]

Each group resorts to deception in the face of hostility from the *gaje* (non-Gypsies) to the Gypsies and from *goyim* (Gentiles) to the Jews. "The evasionary strategies of Gypsies toward non-Gypsies are ingenious."[40] The Mishnah explicitly requires that Jews mislead murderers, robbers, and excise-gatherers (*Mishnah Nedarim* 3:4, cp. *Tosephta Nedarim* 2:2). Recognizing that compromise is necessary in dealing with the government, the Gemara drops the reference to publicans, but its stance is probably that deception is still in order (*Babylonian Nedarim* 28a).

An incident in the third century C.E. furnishes a good example in Jewish history where, despite a harmonious relationship with the Gentiles, deception (in the form of a dodge) is still necessary to safeguard Jewish religious sensibility. Opposition to all forms of idolatry required Jews to be extra-sensitive so as not to encourage it on the part of pagans. On pagan festival days when thanksgiving to idols was part of the celebrations, a Jew in dealing with pagans might not even accept a gift, never mind lend money or give a gift. On one occasion when Rabbi Judah II was sent a gold piece by a pagan, a colleague (Resh Laqish, a former gladiator and prize fighter) instructed him to take it from the pagan's messenger but, standing beside a well, to drop the coin into it as if by accident (*Mishnah Abodah Zarah* 1:1; *Babylonian Abodah Zarah* 6b). The messenger would report that the gift was accepted but, because of its loss, his master was not likely to give thanks to his god for the transaction.[41]

Oddness of Rules

Rules that have the appearance of being irrational, antiquated, and mysterious—such as the Gypsy laws relating to states of purity and pollution[42]—turn out on closer inspection to serve the community's need to preserve its sense of identity. In

38. On both problems, the surrender of a man to be killed and the surrender of a woman to be defiled, see Daube, supra n. 30, at 63–135.

39. See Daube, supra n. 30, at 45–62.

40. See Weyrauch & Bell, at 25 n. 45. On the complex relationship between secrecy and persecution, see Jeatran, supra n. 2, at 11 (secrecy can be both the result of persecution and a pre-determined mode of operating in order to anticipate and cope with it).

41. See David Daube, *Appeasement or Resistance and Other Essays on New Testament Judaism* 49, 50 (1987).

42. See Weyrauch & Bell at 74. Acton, Caffrey, and Mundy tell of an English Kaldarash Baro who complained about "recondite matters of gender pollution" which interfered with the capacity of the *kris* of the American Rom to attend to important practical issues. See supra n. 31, at 99.

Jewish law no rules better illustrate the focus on preservation of identity than those about forbidden mixtures in the books of Leviticus and Deuteronomy: "Your cattle you shall not breed with two kinds. Your field you shall not sow with two kinds of seed. And a garment of two kinds, *shatnez*, shall not come upon you" (Leviticus 19:19); "You shall not sow your vineyard with two kinds of seed: lest the whole yield be rendered taboo: the seed which you have sown and the produce of the vineyard. You shall not plough with an ox and an ass together. You shall not put on *shatnez*, wool and linen together" (Deuteronomy 22:9–11).

Far from coming from an ancient epoch when apotropaic customs existed which are no longer understood by modern inquirers,[43] these rules are clever, cryptic, proverb-like judgments by later lawgivers on the conduct of Israel's ancestors who compromised their ethnic identity.[44] The patriarch Judah, eponymous ancestor of the Jews, marries a Canaanite woman, produces by her three sons who are consequently half-Israelite and half-Canaanite. He also has two sons by the Canaanite cult prostitute, his own daughter-in-law, Tamar. The reason why he has children by Tamar is that she, changing out of her widow's garments and disguising herself as an attractively dressed harlot, seduces him on his way to a sheepshearing festival. She becomes pregnant on the occasion (Genesis 38). Judah's involvement with Canaanite women has its precedent when the Canaanite Shechem seduces Dinah, the daughter of Jacob, and seeks to marry her. He "treats her as a harlot" according to her brothers, Simeon and Levi (Genesis 34:31). As for Joseph in Egypt, he is subjected to sexual harassment from an Egyptian's wife (Genesis 39). He survives the negative consequences from that incident but ends up marrying the daughter of an Egyptian priest. It is the pharaoh who gives Joseph his wife, at the same time arraying Joseph in a special linen garment to mark his elevated position in Egyptian society (Genesis 41:42). Previously, his father's gift of a garment marked him as the favored son in his family (Genesis 37:3). His brothers in Egypt also receive a mark of distinction in line with their talents as cattlemen. The pharaoh invites them to become keepers of his royal herds (Genesis 47:6).

43. See Martin Noth, *Das dritte Buch Moses: Leviticus* 123 (1962); G. von Rad, *Das fünfts Buch Mose: Deuteronomium* 101 (1964).

44. The use of stories to convey or formulate rules is an area of research well worth pursuing. I contend that the formulation of biblical rules comes from the lawgivers' use of the legal and ethical issues contained in biblical narratives; see, for example, Carmichael, supra n. 3. For the role of biblical stories in the development of Canon law, see Helmholz, "The Bible in the Service of the Canon Law," 70 *Chi.-Kent L. Rev.* 1557–81 (1995). The Dinka tribe of the southern Sudan transmits its laws through folktales; see Reisman, "Autonomy, Interdependence, and Responsibility," 103 *Yale L.J.* 406 n. 12 (1993), and the literature cited. Jan Yoors, *Gypsies* 142–47 (1967), discusses the importance of storytelling among the Gypsies for the communication of rules. In response to Yoors' observations Weyrauch and Bell draw attention to the phenomenon in contemporary legal culture in the United States, for example, the role of circulating stories that proves crucial in imparting unwritten rules that make for an "experienced lawyer" (Weyrauch & Bell supra n. 1, at 62–63).

Each of the interactions with foreigners in these Genesis narratives inspired rules which gave symbolic expression to the issue of ethnic identity. Both the Deuteronomic and Levitical lawgivers were intensely interested in matters of identity.[45] The rule against sowing a vineyard with *two* different kinds of seed took up Judah's attempt to propagate his father's line with half-Israelite, half-Canaanite seed. The comparable rule in Leviticus 19:19 about not sowing a field with *two* different kinds of seed focused on Jacob's choosing to incorporate into his (Israel's) family Joseph's half-Israelite, half-Egyptian sons, Ephraim and Manasseh, by his Egyptian wife. In the rule about the vineyard there is a threat of a penalty. The resulting produce may be rendered holy, that is, removed from ordinary existence. There is no comparable threat in the rule about the field. The narrative event that inspires the threat of the penalty in the Deuteronomic rule is when two of Judah's sons are indeed stricken from existence by divine intervention (Genesis 38:7, 10). Nothing comparable happens to Joseph's sons.

The rule against an ox and an ass plowing together took up both Judah's marriage to a Canaanite woman and Dinah's seduction by a Canaanite (Genesis 34, 38). The rule was formulated in line with the Dinah incident because the lawgiver always turned to the earliest example of a problem in Israelite tradition. Thus the son of the Ass, Hamor (Hebrew for ass), "plows" sexually the daughter of the Ox, Jacob/Israel, who refers in Genesis 49:5–7 to his own group as an ox precisely in reference to this incident. The rule against plowing with an ox and an ass together referred to the human interaction in the story because the lawgiver used the animal imagery in it. The comparable prohibition in Leviticus 19:19 about not breeding with two different kinds of cattle took up from that aspect of the Joseph story when the brothers, having cattle of their own, are invited to oversee the Egyptian cattle. To pursue such a vocation entails for these sons of Israel the cultivation of Egyptian ways. The rule serves as a warning about the loss of one's identity in a foreign land.

The rule in Deuteronomy 22:11 against putting on *shatnez*, wool and linen together, commented negatively on Judah's involvement with the foreign prostitute Tamar. Harlots are typically dressed in alluring linen garments. Tamar changes from her widow's garments into, we can infer, such linen array when she waylays Judah—on route to shear his sheep and gather wool. The foreign term *shatnez* is a synecdoche in this context: the linen garment of the prostitute is the part of her that defines the whole person. When Judah "put on" *shatnez*, the alluringly dressed prostitute and the wool and linen symbolically come together. The comparable rule in Leviticus 19:19 focused on Joseph's loss of identity. His linen garment marking him as an Egyptian of high status conflicts with his previous identity, when as a son of his father, Israel, he wears a special garment.[46] The Levitical rule, prohibiting a

---

45. See Carmichael, supra n. 3, at 49–61.

46. For an illuminating discussion of the role of clothes in the Joseph story, see Matthews, "The Anthropology of Clothing in the Joseph Narrative," 65 *Journal for the Study of the Old Testament* 25–36 (1995).

garment of two kinds coming upon an Israelite and differing in formulation from the Deuteronomic rule, warns the Israelites to avoid dual identity. The prophet Zephaniah predicts dire punishment for those in Judah of high status who dress in foreign attire (Zephaniah 1:8): "The garments they [the upper class] wear reveal the nature of their ideal. They do not hesitate to surrender their distinctive national characteristics in their desire to make themselves and the nation one with the neighbouring peoples."[47] Living in the midst of the host Babylonian culture, the Israelites would have read the rules about forbidden mixtures as a warning against similar pitfalls in coping with the influences and temptations of their surroundings.

Penalties

In the matters of curses and rituals of disgrace Gypsy law and Jewish law prove mutually illuminating. On initial reflection the role of the curse as a sanction in such biblical rules as Deuteronomy 27:15–26 appears to be a less than effective way to deal with the problems the rules took up. The curse is used because of the problem of detection. The rules focused on offenses committed in secret (setting up a graven image in a secret place), or by the powerful against the weak (removal of a neighbor's landmark), or in a devious manner (misleading a blind person), or in the family (a son's intercourse with a father's wife). Earthly means of administering justice are by and large not available for such offenses and the curse as an appeal to the offender's conscience seems to be a second best attempt to deal with the offenses.

The role of the curse in Gypsy practice, however, may indicate that the curse is a much more effective sanction than appears on first reflection. The conferring of *marimé*, of rendering a person unclean by the woman's act of lifting or tossing the skirt, is fundamentally a curse and proves remarkably effective because it inflicts social death on the person. Equally effective in preventing defiance of a decision by a *kris*, the Vlax court of law, is its resort to supernatural sanctions in the form of curses.[48]

A shame-cultural aspect of a biblical law serves to illuminate the most powerful sanction in the Gypsy arsenal, the penalty of *marimé*.[49] In this volume (p. 246),

---

47. G.G.V. Stonehouse, *Zephaniah and Nahum* 36 (1929), "Double allegiance is the root evil here"; so C.L. Taylor, noting particularly Zeph 1:5, in *Zephaniah* 1015, 1016 (1956). On the question of whether or not Romani women could wear jeans, see Weyrauch & Bell, supra n. 1, at 46, n. 151.

48. See Yoors, supra n. 44, at 174. On other aspects of curses, see Watson, "Oaths, Curses, Ordeals and Trials of Animals," *Edinburgh Law Review* 2 (1997). I am indebted to Alan Watson for helpful comments on my paper.

49. Capital punishment among the Roma is rare because, just as murder is a *marime* act, so similar contamination awaits the judicial executioner. Underlying the thinking is the view that the unnatural taking of life upsets the harmony of the universe; see Jeatran, supra n. 2, at 24. Similar thinking underlies the famous formulation in Genesis 9:6, "Whoever sheds the blood of man, by man shall his blood be shed for God made man in his own image." The rule is given after the chaos of the flood when a

Walter Weyrauch states that "as far as Gypsy women are concerned menstruation is given special significance, in accordance with contemporary Indian customs, thus giving them [the women] symbolic power over others, including men, for example, by tossing their skirt. Yet the genital aspect should not be overemphasized. A woman may throw her shoe at another person with the same polluting effect." A good deal more can be said about the symbolic gestures cited in this statement. A particular biblical rule in Deuteronomy 25:5–10 and the story of Ruth are relevant.

The only rule in the Bible where public disgrace is the penalty is the shaming of a man who, under an obligation to re-establish a childless dead brother's estate, refuses to give conception to his widow (Deuteronomy 25:5–10). Before the public authorities the widow removes the offender's shoe and spits in his face. Ever after his name is known as "The House of the Unshoed One." Almost all interpreters think that the significance of this penalty has to be worked out in reference to a ritual found in the book of Ruth. On closer inspection of both passages, however, the differences are more significant than the similarities, and we are left with the task of explaining precisely the point of the punishment in the Deuteronomic law.

In Ruth the issue is also one that involves the denial of a child to a widow by a kinsman. However, what comes up first is not, as in the law, any complaint by the woman Ruth before the public authorities that this (unnamed) kinsman is denying her conception, but the issue as to whether or not he is willing to redeem the parcel of land that belongs to the family of Ruth's dead husband. A less close kinsman, Boaz, in a scene the night before on his threshing floor, has already responded positively to Ruth's request to act as redeemer. He informs the nearer kinsman as to his prior obligation and tells him that if he is unwilling to take it on, he, Boaz, will do so. The man says he will redeem the land. Boaz then informs him that in doing so he is also obliged to take Ruth as a wife and raise up a child to his dead relative. The man responds negatively and calls off the entire transaction. It is at this point the author of Ruth explains to the reader the procedure by which in former times in Israel one person transferred to another the right to redeem land. The person holding the right took off his shoe and gave it to the new redeemer (Ruth 4:7). The kinsman so proceeds and Boaz then takes on the duty of buying the land and taking Ruth as his wife.[50]

---

state of rest prevails and certain fundamental distinctions have to be made and preserved. One such distinction is that between humankind and animals. Because of this a man can kill an animal and such killing is non-hostile in character. No such distinction exists, however, between one person and another and it is consequently wrong to kill a fellow human being. Such a hostile killing requires the murderer's own death at the hands of a judicial executioner. For the latter's act to be non-hostile, however, he has to bear the image of God so that an appropriate distinction prevails between himself and the murderer. Only by acting in God's place does the executioner preserve the difference in status necessary for the orderly functioning of the world. See Carmichael, "A Time for War and a Time for Peace: The Influence of the Distinction upon some Legal and Literary Material," 25 *Journal of Jewish Studies* 62, 63 (1974).

50. In the absence of written documents, the kind of ceremony described for the transfer of a right to acquire an immoveable object such as a piece of land is quite intelligible. Instead of the new holder

The symbolism of the ceremony in the book of Ruth is quite different in significance from the woman's removal of the man's shoe to express his unwillingness to give her conception. For one thing, the verbs used in each ceremony to describe the removal of the shoe are different (*shalap* in Ruth, *ḥalats* in the law). For another, the purpose of the woman's removal of the man's shoe in the law is to disgrace him before his compatriots, whereas no such disgrace attaches to the handing over of the shoe from one redeemer to another. Another line of enquiry is necessary to explain the woman's dishonoring action with the man's shoe.

It is crucial to note that the woman is shaming the man and, because he refuses to raise up a child to his dead brother, his denial of sexual intercourse is the central issue. Significantly, the verb *halats* (to remove) has sexual overtones because a related word signifies a man's loins in the sense of the place of his virility. Indeed, it is the hidden language about sexual activity that explains everything about the woman's gesture. What she does brings out matters of universal significance and is relevant to a Gypsy woman's use of her shoe to shame a man.

Consider first one of the symbolic meanings attributed to shoes. In contemporary African-American circles an expression for sexual intercourse is "to knock boots." Whatever the origins of this particular expression, the notion of a shoe as symbolising a woman's genitals is found at all times and places. Here are some other examples.

A Bedouin divorce ceremony has the man say, "She was my slipper; I have cast her off."[51] Among the Manchus a bride gives gifts of shoes to her husband's brothers because as the younger brothers they will have the right of sexual congress with her. The shoes are decorated with the *lien hua*, in common speech the vulgar term for the female genitals.[52] In nursery rhymes—often not originally composed for children—there are the following two examples: "Cock a doodle doo!/My dame has lost her shoe/My master's lost his fiddlestick/And knows not what to do," and "There was an old woman who lived in a shoe/She had so many children she didn't know what to do." The slipper in the tale of Cinderella has similar symbolic meaning.[53] Advice to a bridegroom in Germany is, "Man muss nicht die Füsse in fremde Schuhe stecken" (he is not to go around sticking his feet into other shoes; compare also the attachment of shoes or boots to the bridal car).[54]

---

of the right having to walk round the land before witnesses to indicate that he has acquired the right, he instead acquires from the transferor the latter's shoe by way of symbolising such an acquisition. Compare in the promise to Amenophis III, "You will be king of Egypt and ruler of the desert. All lands are under your surveillance, the boundaries lie united under your sandals," W. Helck, *Urkunden der 18. Dynastie* (1961), cited by Claus Westermann, *Genesis 1–11*, at 159 (1986).

51. See W. Robertson Smith, *Kinship and Marriage in Early Arabia* 105 (1903); G.W. Freytag, *Lexicon arabico-latinum* (1837) lists "*coniunx viri*" (wife of the husband) as one of the meanings of *na'l*, "shoe."

52. See R.D. Jamieson, *Three Lectures on Chinese Folklors* 75 (1932).

53. See Bruno Bettelheim, *The Uses of Enchantment* 264–77 (1976).

54. Feet (or foot) also have the transferred sense of male (or female) genitals, for example, in the French expression, "prendre son pied." In biblical literature, see Exodus 4:25; Deuteronomy 28:57; 2 Samuel 11:8, 11; 2 Kings 18:27; Isaiah 36:12 (urine is "water of the feet"); Issiah 7:20; Ezekiel 16:25. Note

In order to shame the man for an action he refuses to engage in, the woman in the law likens him to the proverbial example of such a refusal, Onan's seeming action in Genesis 38. Onan takes his brother's widow, Tamar, but to avoid giving her a child he withdraws from intercourse and ejaculates outside her. The removal of the shoe from the man's foot indicates withdrawal from intercourse and the spitting the ejaculation of seed.[55] Again there are many parallels to this shaming of a person by likening him (or her) to a proverbial example in legend or history, for example, a Peeping Tom (from the story of Lady Godiva), a Jezebel (a loose woman among African Americans), and a Lolita. In Hebrew the name Onan mockingly means "The Virile One."

The term "skirt" also comes to stand for a woman in most cultures. In the Koran wives are "raiment for you and ye are raiment for them" (Q.2:187). In the Bible, in the story of Ruth, she pays Boaz a nocturnal visit, waits until he is drunk, uncovers his feet, and lies down beside him on his threshing floor. When Boaz wakes up and finds the woman at his feet, she asks him to spread his garment over her (Ruth 3:9). She is suggesting that, taking off his garment, he put a new one on, namely, herself as a wife. The symbolic meaning is well illustrated in Ezekiel 16:8, "Now when I [God] passed by thee [Jerusalem], and looked upon thee, behold, thy time was the time of love; and I spread my skirt over thee," and in Deuteronomy 23:1, "A man shall not take his father's wife, nor uncover his father's skirt." Ruth's action of uncovering Boaz's feet is similarly with a view to offering herself—sexually—as his new shoes. In other words, "skirt" and "shoes" have similar symbolic sexual significance in this section of Ruth.

In Gypsy culture it would appear that we have the following development. The actual exposure of a woman's genitals by lifting her skirt in order to shame a man has sometimes been replaced by throwing a piece of cloth torn from her underskirt or by throwing a shoe. The action with the piece of cloth or the shoe communicates in a transferred way that disgrace and sexual impurity have been inflicted on the person. We are observing another example of a shift from a direct literal action that conveys symbolical meaning to a figurative one that conveys the same meaning. When Walter Weyrauch states that "the genital aspect should not be overemphasized. A woman may throw her shoe at another person with the same polluting effect," it is important to stress what precisely the shoe communicates.

There is evidence that the traditional use of the woman's skirt is becoming discredited among Gypsies. The reverse effect may be accomplished, the woman (and

---

Jeremiah 2:25, "Keep thy feet from going unshod and thy throat from thirst" (Israel as a lusty female animal that gives herself to any partner).

55. The Talmud (e.g., *Babylonian Niddah* 16b) uses the term "spittle" for semen. In the Egyptian creation myth Atum generated the cosmic pair Shu and Tefnut by masturbation, but in a variant tradition it is by spitting. The expression "spitting image" (better: "spitten image," where spitten is the old past participle) may refer to the father's "spitting" that results in a son so resembling him.

her family) becoming the recipients of the intended state of impurity (*marimé*).[56] It is interesting to note that the ceremony of *ḥalitsah* (withdrawal of the shoe) in Jewish law has undergone a similar development. In post-biblical times it disappeared as a means of disgracing a man for failure to perform his duty to his dead brother and became instead a means of freeing the widow from the bond of levirate marriage. In both the Gypsy and Jewish developments we have the common phenomenon of the desexing of ancient customs.[57]

Why should one compare Gypsy law and Jewish law? Both peoples throughout history have been outsiders in cultures not their own. There have arisen notable similarities in some of the rules that regulate the inner workings of each community. Many of the footnotes to Weyrauch and Bell's "Autonomous Lawmaking," in which there is reference to Jewish experience, invite an examination of how at various periods of history the Roma and the Jews accommodate themselves to different host cultures. In this century the genocidal terror visited upon both peoples has sharpened our awareness of each of them—so much so, in fact, that controversy has been generated about the desirability of a comparative study of each people's experience of the Holocaust.[58]

In this essay, I have focused more on aspects of Jewish law than on Gypsy—aspects which show up in an interesting light because of the stimulus provided by Weyrauch and Bell's description of Gypsy law. Aside from the fact that my own area of expertise is Jewish law, there is the undoubted fact that because of the nature of the sources we are in a position to know a great deal more about Jewish law than about Gypsy. Consequently, because the outside world's knowledge of Gypsy law is at a beginning stage and because there is often tantalizing overlap in aspects of the legal culture of each, developments in Jewish tradition may provide suggestive avenues of research for the study of Gypsy law.

A compelling reason to study both Jewish and Gypsy legal cultures is that their very foreignness opens up to us features of our own legal culture which are often hidden from us. At a time when law schools are open to a more humanistic study

56. See Jeatran, supra n. 2, at 27, 32, cited in Weyrauch & Bell at 77 n. 269 (who add, "private norms of proper conduct sometimes prevail over the more archaic norms of Gypsy law, thereby bringing about change").

57. Circumcision in Hebrew antiquity is another example. At some point in time there was a change from carrying it out at the age of puberty, around twelve or thirteen (Ishmael, for example [Genesis 17:25], the time for sexual initiation, to having it done eight days after birth (Isaac, for example [Genesis 21:4]). In Hebrew the term for a bridegroom, *hatan*, "one who undergoes circumcision," preserves the ancient sexual significance of the rite of circumcision. Contemporary Chinese marriage practice provides another example of the desexing of an ancient custom. Whereas among the Manchus a bride used to present a pair of shoes before marriage to her prospective husband and each of his brothers, who had the right of physical access to her, nowadays it is the groom who gives shoes to his future wife's younger brothers. If originating as an imitation of the male rite, female circumcision has taken the desexing of an ancient custom to an extreme degree.

58. See Hancock, "Responses to the *Porrajmos:* The Romani Holocaust," in *Is the Holocaust Unique: Perspectives on Comparative Genocide* 39–64 (Alan S. Rosenbaum, ed. 1996).

of law, the ancient character of Jewish law or the seemingly strange character of Gypsy law invites the recognition that what happened two thousand years ago can tell us a great deal about what happens today, and that the more one scratches the surface of the seemingly strange the more one realizes that profound matters of universal significance emerge.

SIX

Juridical Autonomy among Fifteenth and Sixteenth Century Gypsies

Angus Fraser

One of the most intriguing aspects of Gypsy history is the apparent manner of their arrival in western Christendom in the early fifteenth century. For a time, they can be seen to be behaving in a fashion that, for them, was unprecedented. They moved around conspicuously, seeming almost to court attention. Some of them evidently bore safe-conducts from up high, fostering a story of their being penitents who were undertaking a seven-year pilgrimage to expiate a period of apostasy. Pretended pilgrims, like the *coquillards* of France, were no novelty in the Middle Ages, but they did not usually travel in family groups under leaders with impressive titles, as these new arrivals did. I have sought elsewhere to set out the general pattern of Gypsies' history through the centuries.[1] My present purpose is to gather in whatever can be gleaned from chronicles and archives about one particular feature of the status accorded to them when they spread out from the Balkans and central Europe—and that is the extensive recognition that administration of justice among them was largely an internal matter.

The earliest report is furnished by a north German chronicler. Hermann Cornerus found room in his world history, *Chronica novella,* to record a singular event of which he may well have been an eyewitness. Referring to the closing months of 1417, he described the progress of a party of Gypsies through northern German territories. Among much else, he wrote: "They also had chiefs among them, that is a duke [*ducem*] and a count [*comitem*], who administered justice over them and whose orders they obeyed. . . . They also carried letters of recommendation [*litteras promotorias*] from princes and especially from Sigismund, King of the Romans, according to which they were to be admitted and kindly treated by states, princes, fortified places, towns, bishops and prelates to whom they

---

1. *The Gypsies,* first published in 1992 in Blackwell's *The Peoples of Europe* series (2nd ed., 1995).

turned."[2] Sigismund had been king of Hungary since 1387 and emperor of Germany ("King of the Romans") since 1411. He would also become king of Bohemia in 1419, and of Lombardy in 1431. If one takes Cornerus's wording at its face value, the question of internal justice did not arise directly from Sigismund's letter; but it may be prudent to keep an open mind on that.

Much the same story was inserted by a certain Rufus into his Lübeck chronicle, written in Low German.[3] So similar was his account that he must have had sight of Cornerus's text, even though it was as yet unpublished. The sentence of particular interest here may be rendered as: "They had chiefs among them, that is a count and a duke, by whom they were judged when they committed a misdeed." A good deal later, Sebastian Münster described how some Gypsies had shown him a copy of a letter obtained from Sigismund at Lindau, on Lake Constance. This is generally taken to have been a copy (preserved for over a century, in that case) of the letter referred to by Cornerus, for Sigismund's presence at Constance during much of 1417–18 ties in very well with the reference to Lindau. Münster said nothing of internal justice. According to him the letter

> told how their ancestors in Lesser Egypt [*in minori Aegypto*] had formerly abandoned for some years the Christian religion and turned to the error of the pagans and that, after their repentance, a penance had been imposed upon them that, for as many years, some members of their families should wander about the world and expiate in exile the guilt of their sin.[4]

Another German chronicle, this time anonymous and relating to Augsburg, also placed the arrival of Gypsies in Germany in late 1417. Remarkably, it claimed that they "had letters, by which they might steal from anyone who gave them no alms."[5] Four and a half years pass before the next reference to special judicial status. In May 1422 some Gypsies were lodged in the marketplace at Tournai in the Low Countries. "These Egyptians," says the unnamed chronicler, "had a king and lords whom they obeyed, and had privileges, so that none could punish them save themselves."[6] Better still, in the *Diarium sexennale* of Andreas, a priest of Ratisbon (now

2. Hermann Cornerus, *Chronica novella usque ad annum 1435* in Johannes Georgius Eccard (ed.), *Corpus historicum medii ævi* (1723), 2:1225. Cornerus's text is reproduced in Reimer Gronemeyer, *Zigeuner im Spiegel früher Chroniken und Abhandlungen* 15 (1987). This compendium of early chronicles and treatises is hereafter cited as "Gronemeyer."

3. Rufus, *Lübeck Chronike* in F.H. Grautoff (ed.), *Die lübeckischen Chroniken in niederdeutscher Sprache*, 2 vols. (1830), 2:496; relevant extract in F. Dyrlund, *Tatere og Natmandsfolk* 360 (1872).

4. Sebastian Muenster, *Cosmographia universalis* (1550), 6:267–8; Latin text in D.M.M. Bartlett, "Münster's *Cosmographia universalis,*" *Journal of the Gypsy Lore Society* [hereafter *JGLS*] (Third Series), 31 (1952); 83–90 (from Basel edn. of 1559); German text in Gronemeyer, 34–35 (from German edn. of 1628).

5. *Chroniken der deutschen, Städte* (1895), 4:119; relevant extract in Winstedt, "Some Records of the Gypsies in Germany," *JGLS* (Third Series), 11 (1932): 97–111.

6. J.J. de Smet (ed.), *Recueil des chroniques de Flandre* (1856), 3:372; Bataillard, "Immigration of the Gypsies into Western Europe in the Fifteenth Century," *JGLS* (Old Series), 1 (1889):324–45.

Regensburg) in Bavaria, we are given the text of yet another imperial missive; for not only did Andreas note the arrival of some thirty Gypsies at Regensburg in 1424, he also transcribed the contents of a letter that they held from Emperor Sigismund. It is worth translating this important document in its entirety.

> Sigismund, by the grace of God King of the Romans and Emperor, and King of Hungary, Bohemia, Dalmatia, Croatia, etc. To all our faithful nobles, soldiers, chate-lains, officials, vassals, free cities, market towns and their judges, appointed and ex-isting in our rule and under our dominion:—greeting with love. Our faithful Ladis-laus voivode of the Gypsies [*waynoda Ciganorum*] and others pertaining to him came in person into our presence, and tendered their very humble supplications to us, here in Zips [*in sepus*] before us, with entreaty of supplications and prayers that we might accede to them in our abundant grace. In consequence we, being persuaded by their supplication, have thought proper to grant them this liberty: therefore at whatever time the said voivode Ladislaus and his people shall come into our said domains, be it cities or market towns, from that time we strictly entrust and order to your present fidelities that you should without any hindrance or trouble support and sustain the said voivode Ladislaus and the Cigani who are subject to him, and indeed that you shall please to preserve them from any impediments or vexations. If however any trouble or disorder should occur among them, from whomever it may arise, then nei-ther you nor any other of you, but the same voivode Ladislaus, should have the power of judging and acquitting [*judicandi & liberandi . . . facultatem*]. We command, how-ever, that this [letter], after it has been read, be always returned to him who presents it. Given at Zips, on the Lord's day before the feast of St. George the Martyr, in the year of our Lord 1423 and, of our reigns, the 36th in Hungary, the 12th as King of the Romans, and the 3rd in Bohemia.[7]

The feast of St. George falls on 23 April, and in 1423 the Sunday before that was 18 April.

One oddity in Andreas's transcript is the form of the Latin word used for "voivode." *Waynoda* is spelt with an *n* on each of its four appearances in the text printed in the *Diarium sexennale,* and also in the manuscript of the diary in the Bavar-ian State Library in Munich. The normal form in Hungarian documents of the time is *wayvoda,* generally written *wayuoda,* in accordance with the practice of using the *u* form to represent *v.* Since *u* and *n* were easy to confuse in the old, angular script, it may well be that Andreas, a Bavarian priest unlikely to have much famil-iarity with voivodes, made a copying error. As regards the text he was transcribing, the place and date—Zips, 18 April 1423—are reassuring. Sigismund was at Leutschau (now Levoča) from 4 to 9 April 1423, negotiating with the Polish king and celebrating Easter; on 15 April he was at Bartfeld (Bardejov); from 27 April to 5 May he was in Kaschau (Košice); and thereafter gradually proceeded to Buda.[8]

7. Andreas Ratisponensis Presbyter, *Diarium sexennale* in Andreas Felix Oefelius (ed.), *Rerum boicarum scriptores,* 2 vols. (1763), 1:21; Gronemeyer, 18, 22, 23.

8. Joseph Aschbach, *Geschichte Kaiser Sigmund's,* 4 vols. (1838–43), 3:179, 447.

Zips was the German name for a region in the northern part of the Hungarian kingdom that is now in eastern Slovakia and has the name Spiš. It is mountainous terrain, with many medieval castles. The biggest of these, Spiš Castle, near the town of Spišské Podhradie, was used by Sigismund as a residence on royal tours.[9] Levoča is only about ten miles to the west, Bardejov thirty miles to the north-east, and Košice the same distance to the south-east, so the dating of the document tallies comfortably with the known movements of the peripatetic emperor. So far as I am aware, there is no extant archival record. One writer has remarked that "the copy [of the letter] is kept to this day" in the castle, but that apparently refers to a modern printing of Andreas's transcript placed there for display purposes.[10] It is curious that the letter should have given no explanation of why Ladislaus and his company merited such favorable treatment, but there appear to be no grounds for regarding it as a fabrication.

What is clear enough is that, once in Gypsy hands, the documents from Sigismund were accepted by others to whom they were presented, including princes and their chanceries. References to letters of protection for Gypsies began to proliferate, whether in the name of the emperor or lesser potentates, or (a new development after 1422) in the name of the Pope. Only a few of these further records make specific mention of Gypsy legal autonomy, but there is enough to indicate that it was more than a localized or fleeting phenomenon. It had apparently spread as far as Lithuania and taken root there some little time before 1501, when Alexander, King of Poland and Grand Duke of Lithuania, is said to have confirmed at Vilnius the privileges of Wasil, voivode of the *Cyhany*, giving him the right to judge disputes among his Gypsy subjects.[11]

As Sigismund's letters, or copies of them, circulated more widely, they became encrusted with novel interpretations or misinterpretations. An anonymous chronicle in Italian, narrating the arrival of a cohort of Gypsies under Duke Andrea at Bologna on 18 July 1422, stated that "they had a decree of the King of Hungary who was emperor, by virtue of which they could thieve during those seven years [of their pilgrimage], wherever they might go, and that they could not be subjected to justice."[12] This is in line with the Tournai report of two months before and the Augsburg chronicle for 1417. It is, however, beyond belief that Sigismund would have decreed any such thing. Were those Gypsies really managing to persuade municipal officers that they had an imperial licence to steal; or were the chroniclers retailing a garbled story?

9. Bart McDowell, *Gypsies: Wanderers of the World* 83–84 (1970) (photo, 86).

10. Davidová, "The Gypsies of Czechoslovakia," *JGLS* (Third Series), 49 (1970):84–97.

11. Polish version of charter of 25 May 1501 in Jerzy Ficowski, *Cyganie na polskich drogach* 18–19 (1985), from T. Narbutt, *Rys historyczny ludu cygańskiego*, 170–2 (1830). The authenticity of the document has evidently been questioned in Lech Mróz, "Suplement do pocztu królów i starszych cygańskich w Polsce," *Etnografia Polska* 32 (1988):309–10; but I have not seen this article.

12. Ludovico Antonio Muratori (ed.), *Rerum italicarum scriptores: Raccolta degli storici italiani*, revised edn. (1939), 18:568–9; Gronemeyer, 55.

A further text with similar implications, written after a century of deterioration in public attitudes towards Gypsies, is more dubious still. A German translation of the *Annales boiorum* of Aventinus (Johann Thurmair), under the year 1439, declared: "with us, thieving and robbing are forbidden on pain of hanging or beheading; for them [Gypsies] it is allowed."[13] The original Latin version, however, had simply said that misguided citizens "think it wicked to harm them, and suffer them everywhere to lurk about, steal, and cheat with impunity," in phraseology which implied public apathy rather than official tolerance.[14]

There is no need to be suspicious of another form of elaboration that appeared a few decades later, for it is confirmed in archives. A series of royal safe-conducts issued to Gypsy chiefs during the reign of John II of Navarre and Aragon, in the period 1460–76, included wordy endorsement of some of the leaders' powers to administer justice within their companies. After struggling with the chancellery's convoluted Latin, others may have been left in some uncertainty as to the precise delimitation of Duke Paulo of Little Egypt's jurisdiction, set out in a safe-conduct of 1471, but they would have had little doubt that, throughout the royal possessions, he could order Gypsy miscreants to be seized and punished, including detaining them in chains and fetters.[15] And as the very next sentence enjoined them to afford the duke every assistance, they were perhaps hesitant, in dealing with particular cases, to quibble about whether he was exceeding his mandate, although much of the emphasis was on dealing with internal strife. Count Juan of Little Egypt, we learn from a safe-conduct drawn up at Logroño in 1476, even stood in need of protection from attacks by three rival counts.[16] In Italy around the same time, the possibility of Gypsies falling out among themselves was viewed with enough concern to warrant urging officials to strive mightily to restore harmony if any discord arose in the companies of Count Michael (1470s) or Count Joannes (1485), to whom safe-conducts were issued by Marco Pio, lord of Carpi in the Duchy of Modena.[17] The second of these, however, was careful to exclude from its coverage any damage caused to the lord's subjects or to his own possessions and properties.

Scotland affords an even closer parallel to Aragon in provision of official support for a Gypsy leader confronted with faction-feuding. On 15 February 1540, James V signed a writ of the Scottish Privy Council conferring considerable priv-

13. Johannes Aventinus, *Bayerische Chronik*, ed. Nikolaus Cisner 523 (1566); Gronemeyer, 29.

14. Johannes Aventinus, *Annales Boiorum* (1554), 6:826–27, written about 1522; Gronemeyer, 28.

15. The relevant sentence is: "Et quoniam interdum evenit per homines Egiptii de comitava dicti spectabilis ducis, in eundem ducem vicio inobedientie senales delinquint seu inter eos dimicant et contendant crimina et excessus comitendo, ut igitur dicti Egipcii, ita delinquences aliqua civili pena plectentur, damus et elargimur facultatem eidem duci per universam dicionem nostram dictos Egipcios ita delinquentes, dimicantes et contendantes captosque ad merita ipsius ducis carceri mancipandi servandos dicto carceri ad ipsius ducis voluntatem eosque verbo et civiliter corrigere catenis et compedibus detinere."

16. López de Meneses, "Los gitanos llegan a Aragón," *Pomezia*, 4 (Jan.–Feb. 1969): 242–5.

17. Full Latin texts in A.G. Spinelli, "Gli Zingari nel Modenese," *JGLS* (New Series), 3 (1909):42–57.

ileges on John Faw, "lord and erle of Litill Egypt." It referred back to letters previously issued under the Great Seal, which had instructed all those in authority in the kingdom to assist Faw "in execution of justice upoun his cumpany and folkis conforme to the lawis of Egipt" and in punishing all those who rebelled against him. It went on to forbid any succour for a splinter-group led by Sebastian Lalow, who had already deserted Faw's company after buying official documents to release him from his obligations, on the strength of "sinister and wrang informatioun, fals relatioun and circumventioun of us." Showing little confidence in the integrity of the state apparatus, King James told officials to disregard "ony oure writingis sinisterly purchest, or to be purchest be the said Sebastiane," and went on to command them to give John Faw the run of their prisons, stocks, fetters, and all other means necessary for bringing the offenders to heel. These prescriptions were renewed a few months later (though in the name of John Faw's son), and then again in 1553 during the regency that followed the succession of Queen Mary.[18]

In both England and Scotland, there is some slight evidence that homicide among Gypsies, if it came before an ordinary court, was for a time regarded as something to be treated differently from a similar crime among the general run of citizens. In June 1537, Paul Fa or Faa, a Gypsy, received a royal pardon for the murder of "an Egyptian called Sacole Femine within this realm." He and his troop were, however, banished from England.[19] In Scotland, two "respites" granted under the Privy Seal in 1553 and 1554 gave immunity to Andrew Faw, "capitane of the Egiptianis," and a number of his associates for the "slauchter" of Niniane Smaill. In this instance it is not clear whether the victim, who worked for a smith, was a Gypsy. And when, in August 1612, certain Gypsies were found guilty before the Sheriff Court of Scalloway in the Shetland Isles for the murder of one of their number, the defence advocate pleaded "that it was not usual to take cognisance of murder among the Egyptians."[20] This was a curious remark to make only three years after the Scottish Parliament had passed an "Act anent the Egiptians" that made it lawful to condemn and execute them on proof solely "that they ar callit, knawin, repute and haldin Egiptianis." Gone for good, so far as the legislators were concerned, was any suggestion that Gypsies were to be recognized as forming a separate community, subject to their own laws and justice, although for long afterwards, well into the eighteenth century, bloody conflicts between rival Gypsy clans were regarded with some indifference by other inhabitants of Scotland.

It is fruitless, however, to look for consistency towards Gypsies in those days. Divergent approaches might be adopted at the same time in different parts of one country, or a single authority might show bewildering changes of direction. In Scotland, between the writs of 1540 and 1553, already mentioned, there intervened a contrary Order in Council of 1541 revoking all letters of protection and other priv-

18. David MacRitchie, *Scottish Gypsies under the Stewarts* 37–44 (1894).
19. Winstedt, "Early British Gypsies," *JGLS* (New Series), 7 (1913–14):5–37.
20. MacRitchie, *Scottish Gypsies*, 44, 53.

ileges, and banning Gypsies from the kingdom within thirty days, on pain of death. In France, in May 1544, five years after a decree in which Francis I also banished Gypsies, he took under his protection Antoine Moreul, "his well-loved captain of Little Egypt," and ordered that Moreul and his company be allowed free passage on their pilgrimages. At the same time he formally recognized the captain's disciplinary powers, and stipulated that, if any Gypsies rebelled against their leader, he was empowered to carry out condign punishment. Henry II of France, in his turn, was equally obliging to Count Palque of Little Egypt in 1553, "notwithstanding whatever banishments may have been ordered in regard to people of the said [Gypsy] nation." The count was declared to be under royal protection and given "recognition of justice" over his company. However, when one of his lieutenants went travelling independently to Grenoble, equipped with a notarized copy of this safe-conduct, the royal procurator general persuaded the local *Parlement* to take no account of it, because of the corrupt, fortune-telling ways of the beneficiaries.[21]

Having now exhausted all known sources with a bearing on the original measure of autonomy and its direct descendance, it remains to record a few anecdotes that smack more of the folktale than of biography or history. In the latter part of the sixteenth century, according to Tallemant des Réaux, "a famous captain of Gypsies," Jean-Charles by name, devised a stratagem for robbing the wealthy priest of a village in the south of France. His company pretended that they had condemned one of their number to be hanged for theft. On the gallows, at a place outside the village, the condemned man asked for a confessor, and the curé was sent for. During his absence, a party of Gypsy women raided his house without fear of disturbance, and when they were safely back at the scaffold, the condemned man cried out that he wished to appeal to the king of Little Egypt. "Ah! the traitor!" exclaimed the captain, "I was afraid he would appeal." He at once gave order to pack bags, and the Gypsies were a long way off before the curé got home.[22] Tallemant des Réaux wrote his *Historiettes* in the 1650s. A few decades before, Agrippa d'Aubigné told much the same story, but gave the Gypsy's name as Charles-Antoine.[23] Squarely in the realm of fiction was J.J. Christoffel von Grimmelshausen's novel *Courasche*, which appeared in 1670. The main episode in its concluding chapter concerned a spurious trial and death sentence by a Gypsy chief on one of his band for shooting a hen. Once the villagers had thronged into the wood where the hanging was to be carried out, the Gypsy women plundered their houses, while the chieftain graciously acceded to the villagers' pleas for mercy over such a small offense.[24] I propose to leave such stories out of the reckoning as having flimsy evidential value.

21. François de Vaux de Foletier, *Les Tsiganes dans l'ancienne France* 55–57 (1961) (on the basis of documents in the archives of Seine-et-Oise and l'Isère).

22. Gédéon Tallemant des Réaux, *Les Historiettes de Tallemant des Réaux*, 9 vols. (1854–60), 7:485–6.

23. Agrippa d'Aubigné, *Les aventures du Baron de Faeneste*, ed. Prosper Mérimée 131–37 (1855).

24. [Hans Jacob Christoph von Grimmelshausen], *Trutz Simplex: oder . . . Lebensbeschreibung der Ertzbetrügerin und Landstörtzerin Courasche* (Utopia [Nürnberg]: Felix Stratiot [J.J. Felsegkkerr], n.d. [1670]).

Before looking at the other sources in the round, it is appropriate to underline two points. The first is that the texts cited above represent only a small proportion of the references to Gypsy safe-conducts, the majority of which were silent on the question of justice. The second is that, in concentrating on a single aspect of the Gypsies' legal status, the exposition up to now has made little of the fact that, more typically, special treatment for Gypsies was not long in taking on the sense given to *Sonderbehandlung* in the Third Reich. The pattern was set in the closing decades of the fifteenth century, when the Swiss Confederation, the Duchy of Milan, the Diet of the Holy Roman Empire, and the Catholic Kings of Spain all embarked on series of anti-Gypsy enactments. Other countries followed suit, until any letters of protection that had lingered on lost their efficacy or were expressly rescinded. Had the laws which sprang up all been enforced uncompromisingly, even for a few months, Gypsies would have been eradicated from most of Christian Europe well before the middle of the sixteenth century. That black chapter is beyond the scope of the present paper.[25]

Returning instead to the documentary material that *has* been summarized here, one can discern two distinct classes. First, there are the chroniclers, often writing some considerable time after the event. They tend to be vague, perhaps doing little more than repeating or building on what they had learned from others (not excluding Gypsies), but reflecting attitudes prevalent at the time of writing. It is principally in this category—Cornerus, Rufus, Aventinus, and the anonymous chroniclers of Augsburg, Tournai and Bologna—that the impression emerges of a jurisdiction covering all manner of offences, whether inside or outside the Gypsy community. Then we have the remaining, more verifiable group where we can examine the actual texts of safe-conducts or reports based on a sight of them. In these cases (apart from Münster, who does not raise the judicial issue at all), the emphasis is increasingly on solving internal disputes and maintaining discipline within the company. This line of evolution descends from Emperor Sigismund in Hungary to John II of Aragon, Marco Pio of Carpi, King Alexander of Poland and Lithuania, James V of Scotland, and Francis I and Henry II of France. Although it is legitimate to attach these rulers' names to the safe-conducts, as the documents themselves did, it is advisable to bear in mind also that letters of protection were the medieval forerunners of the later passport, and doubtless were often obtained by application to some official, perhaps accompanied by a payment for his trouble (or even "sinisterly purchest," as the Scottish writ of 1540 put it). It is particularly interesting that, whereas the general run of safe-conducts for Gypsies tended to follow a fairly stereotyped pattern—with set-piece references to a pilgrimage and exhortations to let them pass unhindered and afford them shelter, perhaps for a given number of days—in this more limited range the successive monarchs and lords, some at least of whom can be taken to have played a personal role, appear to have been less concerned with following routine precedent. In Aragon, the king was bent

---

25. For one account, see Fraser, *The Gypsies,* chaps. 5 and 6.

on guarding against strife among several named Gypsy leaders, as well as dealing with discipline more generally. In Carpi, the lord urged his officials to mediate if discord broke out. James V of Scotland became embroiled in putting down a feud between John Faw and Sebastian Lalow, while Francis I in France was at pains to stress Moreul's penal powers in dealing with rebellion within his company.

This leads on to the question of what may have prompted the granting of a measure of juridical independence in the first instance. I do not disguise the element of speculation involved in trying to find an answer. Assuming, as I have done, that the letters issued by the Emperor Sigismund were genuine, one has to look for a setting in which it would be credible that he should have granted important legal privileges to Ladislaus, voivode of the Gypsies. Sigismund may have neglected the numerous pressing problems of his Hungarian kingdom through his preoccupation with imperial and Bohemian affairs, for the more titles he acquired the less effective he became; but he was no fool. And any human beings armed with a special immunity of this kind might, unless they consistently matched up to canonization standards, be tempted to exploit it.

It has been suggested that the "dukes" and "counts," so often reported to be at the head of companies of Gypsies after the incursions of 1417—finely dressed, well-mounted, and lodged like men of some quality—were simply playing a part. With the passage of time, this must indeed have happened. But it would make the terms of Sigismund's safe-conduct more understandable if he had been bestowing it on someone who had already acted in a position of trust and shown that he could exercise juridical powers responsibly.

In the European countries where Gypsies were dwelling long before some started on a westward migration, the authorities sought to ensure that they were firmly affiliated into the socioeconomic hierarchy. In Wallachia and Moldavia this would develop into outright chattel slavery. More generally, rulers and law-givers were appointed over them, and it was to them that Gypsies paid their taxes. Corfu provides the best documented illustration of how this process was institutionalized. We begin to hear of a Gypsy settlement on Corfu in the second half of the fourteenth century, before the island fell into Venetian hands in 1386, and by that time their annual dues were sufficient to form an independent fief, the *feudum acinganorum*. The feudal system continued to provide the framework for Venice's rule in Corfu. A Venetian decree of 1470, conferring the fief of the Gypsies on Michael de Hugot, indicated that the baron of the fief had wide jurisdiction not only over the Gypsies settled in Corfu but also over those living in the Venetian possession on the Epirote coast.[26] The feudal lord had the right to bring any of them to trial and to punish them in all matters of civil or criminal law, with the sole exception of homicide. These were privileges denied to other feudal barons. The *feudum acinganorum*, including the judicial powers, survived in Corfu right down to the early nineteenth century.

---

26. Full Latin text in Adriano Colocci, *Gli Zingari* 37–39 (1889); and in Soulis, "The Gypsies in the Byzantine Empire and the Balkans in the Late Middle Ages," *Dumbarton Oaks Papers* 15 (1961):164–65.

Further north in the Balkans and in Hungary, the situation is less firmly attested. But over a large tract of eastern Europe, the continuance of the Gypsies became a matter of self-interest for some important personages. By the sixteenth century the custom was well established in Hungary, as in Poland and Lithuania, for a chief of the Gypsies to be chosen by the authorities from the ranks of the nobility. Eventually, indeed, several voivodes were appointed (four for Hungary, two for Transylvania). They had the right to mete out punishments and the profitable duty of levying the taxes from Gypsies. Confusingly, there were also lesser chiefs who used the title of voivode, drawn from the Gypsies themselves, and they too acquired some delegated powers.[27] Just when the state system began is far from clear. And so far as Ladislaus is concerned, all we know of him is what is said in Sigismund's letter of 1423, for he is never heard of again. But several inferences can be drawn from the letter. The personal name he bore was current chiefly in Poland (Władysław), Hungary (László/Ulászló) and also Wallachia, while his title of *wayvoda Ciganorum* appears to indicate that some form of external government by voivode may already have been in place. In referring to him as "our faithful Ladislaus," his safe-conduct was in effect saying that he was a true subject of Sigismund. His connection with Hungary must have been of some duration.

The Hungarian domains over which Sigismund ruled extended far beyond the boundaries of modern Hungary, taking in large tracts of territory now constituting Transylvania, Slovakia, the Austrian Burgenland, Croatia, and the Vojvodina; and this realm lay increasingly under the long shadow of the Ottoman expansion. After the dismal failure of Sigismund's crusade against the Turks, ending in crushing defeat at Nicopolis in 1396, many southern Slav princes and nobles found refuge in Hungary, frequently with a band of retainers. Timur's attack on the Turkish rear gave Europe some respite, but once the advance was resumed in 1416 the Ottoman raiders plundered Transylvania and the southern areas of Hungary year after year.[28]

Barons of Gypsy fiefs and the like probably stood to lose a good deal more than their subjects from Turkish incursions, and the impetus for organizing exploratory expeditions elsewhere may in the first instance have come from them. Certainly, the inexorable advance of the Ottomans into Europe created a sense of impending doom and in the end set some of the nobles, together with numbers of the priests and people, fleeing in search of a safe haven and, eventually, wandering west and looking for charity. Municipal accounts show that some of them travelled in companies under leaders with titles like the Gypsies', and were treated like them.[29]

27. Cf. Johann Heinrich Schwicker, *Die Zigeuner in Ungarn und Siebenbürgen* 45–48 (1883); Heinrich von Wlislocki, *Vom wandernden Zigeunervolke* 36–37, 55–60, 78–82 (1890); Winstedt, "Some Transylvanian Gypsy Documents of the Sixteenth Century," *JGLS* (Third Series), 20 (1941), 49–58.

28. Édouard Sayous, *Histoire générale des Hongrois*, 2 vols. (1876), 1:392; Ervin Pamlényi (ed.): *A History of Hungary* 88 (1975).

29. Cf. Winstedt, "Gypsies at Bruges," *JGLS* (Third Series) 15 (1936):126–34.

If there were early Gypsy groups headed by displaced leaders of this kind, it would make more sense of the emperor's readiness to favor them with the exceptional status we have seen. It would also have meant, of course, that leaders from such a background were obliged quickly to move their role away from the well-defined standing they had enjoyed within a structured hierarchy. Now, with the help only of whatever leverage could be derived from the backing of a remote emperor, they were having to negotiate benefits from those in power in western societies, and thus supplement the living that the group's members were able to make from activities like horse-trading, metal-working, entertaining, healing and fortune-telling.

Even if such considerations explain Sigismund's motivation, they cannot account for the stress on regulation of disputes in a succession of safe-conducts delivered to Gypsy leaders of later generations. Inevitably, as time went on, the leader's role would be assumed by others who had never known any different system, but sought to perpetuate such benefits as a safe-conduct offered and were probably not too fussy about adjusting their own names to match that of the beneficiary originally specified. Violent conflicts within or between Gypsy bands do not appear to have been a problem in preserving public law and order, and, in so far as there were any, it is possible that no one cared very much, so long as the mayhem was confined to Gypsies. But it is entirely conceivable that, after the earliest period of reconnoitering western Europe, tensions did begin to arise between rival groups of Gypsies. Recurrent visits to one locality were bound, sooner or later, to erode any readiness on the part of the *gajé* to give alms or make donations of food and drink, and would risk saturating the market for the kind of services offered by itinerant traders. It would be a natural development for attempts to be made to stake claims to particular territories, or for ambitious Gypsies within a group to seek to build up a following of their own. In such cases, a Gypsy leader, negotiating for the issue of a safe conduct, might well want to buttress his internal supremacy and strengthen his hand against rivals outside his company, by persuading the *gajo* to add something on the subject of discipline. But whatever the historical and socioeconomic roots of these Gypsies' juridical status, recognition of it would wither away once the external support mechanisms lost their special virtue through political change.

The Scottish story of John Faw and Sebastian Lalow is open to a different construction. They may genuinely have been feuding. On the other hand, the suspicion has been expressed before now that their dissension was a device for being allowed to stay in the country, in the face of impatience to bring about their departure. According to the writ of February 1540, John Faw was obliged to reunite his entire company before he could go back to Little Egypt, and the writ's stress on the need for masters of ships to assist in "furing of thame furth of oure realme" might indicate some eagerness to see that happen. The Scottish Act promulgated by the Lords of Council and Session in the following year pointed out, with a note of exasperation, that Faw and Lalow had still not compounded their differences, but had agreed to go home and have the matter settled "before the duke of Egipt." Abruptly, they were given thirty days to get out, "under the pane of deid." That did not work, and the writ of 1553 went back to the original position; since John Faw was "oblist to bring hame with him all thame of his cumpany that ar on lyve and ane testimoniall of thame that ar deid," he was to receive all official support necessary to reassert his authority over the rebels, thus putting him in a position to leave Scotland.

The biggest gap of all in the documentary material is the lack of any indication of how the internal processes of justice that were used actually operated in practice during the early period of Gypsy migrations in western Europe, when we appear to be observing fairly cohesive and far-ranging bands. The chroniclers were concerned with little beyond the basic fact of Gypsies' physical existence, except when it was a question of religious observance or conventional morality. Whatever juridical practices Gypsies brought with them no doubt had to evolve in the new environments, but there was little incentive to go over to the law of the *gajé*, whose systems were based on alien concepts. State law was bound up with the norms underlying a sedentary society in which masterless men with no fixed domicile were at odds with the established order. The pervasive canon law, often holding exclusive jurisdiction or overlapping with that of the state in controlling human behavior, looked upon fortune-telling as sorcery and penalized marriage outside the Church or any other laxity in following the Church's precepts. And mercantile law, notably the monopolistic regulations of the guilds, left small place for itinerant purveyors of services and crafts.

Given the dearth of evidence, it is impossible to say how far the social control mechanisms of the Gypsy newcomers may have resembled those in force today. There are no grounds for unequivocal assertions one way or the other, and it seems unprofitable to attempt to fill the void with unsupported speculation. I would say only that it is difficult to see how those mechanisms could have been based on the tribunal pattern made so familiar by studies of Vlach Gypsy groups, even though some writers have drawn parallels between the *kris* and tribal councils in India, treating the former as a cultural inheritance from an original homeland, rather than as a system that grew out of Balkan practices.

SEVEN

Institutional Non-Marriage in the Finnish Roma Community and Its Relationship to Rom Traditional Law

Martti Grönfors

INTRODUCTION

I studied the Finnish Roma society as a participant observer in 1976–78; the total time spent in the field was about eighteen months. Since that time I have moved to other things, but have maintained contact with my closest informants and friends and also have periodically returned to this topic with updated articles.[1] The participation was truly anthropological in that I lived, worked, and travelled with them as far as an outsider can do.

The Finnish Roma differ markedly from the Roma in other parts of the world because they do not really use the Romani language as a means of everyday communication. The language which they use, although related to Romani, is no longer understood by any other than the Finnish Roma. It is rather restricted in terms of its vocabulary and range of topics. Culturally, at least as far as can be assessed from my reading, the Finnish Roma, mainly because of their isolation from the rest of Europe's Roma for four centuries and also because of their extremely marginalized position in Finnish society, have preserved some of the general customs of the Roma in a "pure," archaic form. One such area is the general system of hygiene, the system of ritual observances connected to cleanliness[2] and pollution. I shall refer to some of those kinds of customs in this essay, insofar as these are related to the in-

---

1. However, I shall be using the past tense mostly when I refer to my ethnographic data, as the details are from close to twenty years ago. I know that many details stand also today, but I have not conducted any systematic fieldwork since the late 1970s.

2. I prefer the term "cleanliness" to other words used in this connection, like "purity," because it is a faithful translation of their own usage and also because in many instances the physical cleanliness and ritual purity are the same in everyday life. The term "cleanliness" is broader and covers both. For the Finnish Roma, if something is ritually unclean it is also then practically unclean. If something is ritually unclean, it cannot be cleansed at all by any means, whereas if something is ritually pure but practically

stitution of non-marriage. The place of the traditional legal system, the basis of which is interkin blood feuding, is another area where the cultural and social autonomy of the Roma is evident. I will connect in this article the operation of institutional non-marriage first and foremost to their indigenous legal institutions. On the basis of my fieldwork, several publications were prepared. In addition to those in English,[3] there is also a book in Finnish on Roma culture and social institutions[4] and a textbook on qualitative research methods[5] in which the experiences gathered in the field were used as a basis for more general analysis of intensive fieldwork. "Behind the scenes" I have also prepared over the years numerous statements to authorities when cultural knowledge has been important for making decisions on Roma matters. But I still do not consider myself primarily a Roma researcher; most of my production over the years has consisted of material on other minorities and issues not directly connected to the Finnish Roma. However, fieldwork of such intensity and length as was the case here had to leave a permanent mark. One would not survive in that difficult field without being able to comprehend the most important aspects of that culture.

This essay is based on my analyzed field notes, most of which have not been published anywhere before. In order to leave the reader with as clear an impression as possible of the operation of the unique system of non-marriage among the Finnish Roma, I shall leave the comparative references to a minimum. This is basically a descriptive essay in which the analytical comments and connections between the various concepts are primarily drawn from my own field experience. The validity of this essay, therefore, is not so much in the interpretation, but rather in the logical rendering of various field experiences, which—when looked at from the point of view of the Finnish Roma—form an intelligible account of the institution

---

unclean it can be cleaned, for example, by washing in the normal manner. If, for example, a coffee cup (inherently clean, i.e., ritually pure) enters a ritually unclean surface it cannot be cleaned by any means.

3. Martti Grönfors, *Blood Feuding Among Finnish Gypsies*, Research Reports, No. 213, Department of Sociology, University of Helsinki (1977) (hereafter referred to as *Blood Feuding*). Grönfors, "Ethnic Minorities and Deviance: The Relationship Between Finnish Gypsies and the Police," Sociology of Law Series, No. 1, University of Helsinki (1979). Grönfors, "Control of Ethnic Minorities: Finnish Gypsies and the Police," in 7 *Scandinavian Studies in Criminology* 147–56 (1979). Grönfors, "Police Perception of Social Problems and Clients: the Case of the Gypsies in Finland," in *International Journal of the Sociology of Law* 345–59 (1981) (reprinted in *International Reader on World's Gypsies*). Grönfors, "From Scientific Social Science to Responsible Research: the Lesson from the Finnish Gypsies," 25 *Acta Sociologica* 249–57 (1982). Grönfors, "Gypsies as a Visible Minority in Finland: The Proactive Policing of an Ethnic Minority," in Alfred Pletsch (ed.), *Ethnicity in Canada—International Examples and Perspectives* (KANADA PROJECT III), Marburger Geographische Schriften, Heft 96, at 246–55 (1985). Grönfors, "Social Control and Law in the Finnish Gypsy Community: Blood Feuding as a System of Justice," 24 *Journal of Legal Pluralism and Unofficial Law* 101–25 (1986). Grönfors, "Finnish Rom: a Forgotten Cultural Group," in Pentikäinen and Hiltunen (eds.), *Cultural Minorities in Finland: An Overview Towards Cultural Policy*, Publications of the Finnish National Commission for Unesco No. 66, at 147–60 (1995).

4. Martti Grönfors, *Suomen Mustalaiskansa* (1981).

5. Martti Grönfors, *Kvalitatiiviset Kenttätyömenetelmät* (1982).

of non-marriage, in the context of their unique history and social world they have inhabited for over four hundred years.[6]

BRIEF HISTORY OF THE FINNISH ROMA

The earliest ancestors of today's estimated six to seven thousand Roma in Finland arrived in the middle of the sixteenth century, mainly from the West, via Sweden. They were the descendants of the Romani-speaking people who left northern India about one thousand years ago. Long isolation in Finland without any known contact with the rest of the world's Roma people has meant that, in their oral tradition, all information about their earlier alliances has been lost. Finland at that time was a part of the Swedish Empire, and the special laws concerning the Roma were the same as in Sweden. The laws aimed variously at expulsion, assimilation, and control. When Finland became a Grand Duchy of the Russian Empire in 1809, the emphasis of special laws was on assimilation and control aiming at the sedentarization of the Roma. The effect of these laws was quite minimal, as they lived in the eastern and northern areas of the country, which at the time were the most sparsely populated and where enforcement of laws was difficult.

Special state committees on Roma affairs reported in 1900 and 1955, but the effect of their recommendations, which favored assimilation, was negligible. The Roma lifestyle and culture changed drastically only from the 1960s onward, when the Roma—alongside rural Finns—began to move to the cities. In 1967 the Roma organized themselves into a pressure group known as the Finnish Gypsy Association (now called the Roma Association). The association was effective in getting some important laws into the statute books, such as the law prohibiting discrimination on the basis of racial or ethnic origin (1970) and the law aimed at improving their housing conditions (1975). At the everday level, blatant prejudices and neglect are still factors in the life of the Roma.

At the state level there is a permanent Commission on Roma Affairs which operates under the Ministry of Social Welfare and Health. Its purpose is to follow the

---

6. Here I differ sharply from the approach of Thomas Acton, a notable British authority on the Roma who was much quoted in my previous works. He used his fieldwork to aid his analysis of comparative, general material on the Roma (Thomas Acton, *Gypsy Politics and Social Change* 2–5 [1974]). Intensive fieldwork was primarily used to gain an understanding of the Finnish Roma culture, social institutions, and everyday life as well as the emotive levels of feelings around kinship and other issues. This "exhaustive" method meant that I learned the logic of their lives as far as is possible for an outsider and to the extent that I could move with ease in their complex society, (and still can twenty years later). Literary references were used in my texts primarily to compare the life of the Finnish Roma with the Roma elsewhere. I feel that both approaches are valid; Acton's can be used to make generalizations and mine to understand Finnish Roma. I wholeheartedly agree with his statement as it is accurate in my own case that "I cannot pretend to be neutral . . . I am attracted by the values of family solidarity, economic independence and opposition to territorial state authorities and their boundaries, which run as recurring themes through Romani culture." (id. at 4).

development of Roma social welfare and make suggestions for its improvements. In addition, the commission sees its task as guaranteeing the rights of the Roma minority, especially in safeguarding the Roma language and culture. Those officially stated aims take a rather hollow sound when recently, in 1996, the Finnish General Secretary of the Commission was reappointed for another five years, in spite of the fact that for the first time a well-qualified Roma lawyer was also an applicant. It almost stands as symbolic of the way in which Roma affairs have been handled in Finland. A theologian who has little experience with the Roma culture and no experience with the language is preferred by the state to a Roma lawyer who has publicly stated that he would take a more affirmative stand in his fight for Roma causes.

In the past twenty to thirty years the Roma culture has changed rapidly. Now, most of them live in cities and most of those living in cities live in the large southern cities. The traditional Roma culture is rather difficult to uphold in city conditions. The communities are divided either by the availability of suitable housing or by deliberate local-authority decisions.[7] Many important Roma traditions and customs depend on close contact between significant people, especially kin members. In a society where the two most important criteria for authority are age and gender, and where elders and men are most respected, changing this system can have enormous consequences on traditional social control. In recent years Roma social problems have taken a decisive turn for the worse. Alcoholism, violence, and general criminality is thought by close observers of the Roma community to be on the increase, and new problems, such as dealing in and using drugs, have entered the scene. On the positive side it can be said that increasing numbers of Roma complete high school and enter universities, but in the context of the traditional Roma culture these factors could at times also be seen as negative by the more traditional Roma. The traditional Roma culture and the educated Finnish culture stand in opposition to one another on many significant issues. However, from that educated population must ultimately come the defenders of the Roma culture and human rights, as has amply been demonstrated by the "Sabmi" ("Lapps"), the arctic indigenous minority in Finland.

CULTURE AND SOCIAL ORGANIZATION OF FINNISH ROMA

The culture and social organization of the Finnish Roma seem to be a mixture of the culture and organization of various Roma groups found all over the world. Unlike most other Roma groups, the Finnish Roma lack any central organ for decision-making in important matters. Even the geographically closest Roma group to the Finnish Roma, the traditional Swedish "tattare," has a general judicial organ

---

7. Much of the Roma housing is welfare housing by local authorities. Authorities, therefore, are in a good position to manipulate the numbers and the kind of Roma they allow to be housed in their areas.

called "*kris*" for issues comparable to civil and criminal law.[8] No present-day Finnish Roma can remember a *kris* ever having operated among the Roma in Finland, and no documentary evidence about it exists. One could speculate that the absence of this form of authority is due to the fact that Roma of different tribal backgrounds and different arrival times could not agree on the establishment of such an organ, and that the main "judicial" power was claimed by the kin groups themselves, who acted as relatively autonomous legal units.

Finnish Roma society was, and still is, fragmented into roughly politically equal units of kin groups, and care was taken to preserve this political equality. There were a number of ways in which attempts were made to protect this feature. The traditional geographical areas, from which the families were supposed to get their livelihood from the sedentary folk, were informally divided by the Roma into non-overlapping units. Breaches of these informal agreements were met occasionally with physical hostility. In pursuit of their economic activities, each family was to be left to conduct its affairs without interference from other groups. Trading and other economic relationships were proper only between the Roma and non-Roma, not between different Roma groups. The rationale was that trading created an unequal relationship between the buyer and the seller, the latter exploiting the former by making a profit; hence the prohibition. The code of behavior required the wealthier groups to aid those in need, which meant that an effective system of equalizing wealth operated within the community. No individual group was able to exert any undue power over other groups through grossly superior wealth.

Prohibition on credit between the Roma acted in the same way. Whatever exchanged hands between different groups had to be considered a non-recoverable gift. A creditor-debtor relationship would have formed an unacceptable relationship of inequality. Similarly the traditions prohibited one Rom from working for another as an employee. That also would have created a relationship of inequality. If they worked together, they worked as equal partners. Basic for an understanding of Roma social organization and the important aspects of its culture is the understanding of collectivity, especially that between kin members. The place of the individual was important only as far as it related to his or her position as a member of the group. The status was largely ascribed, the men and older people being at the pinnacle of power and influence.

As there was no formal or even semi-established system operating between the different groups which had the task of mediating, negotiating, arbitrating, or judging intergroup conflicts,[9] the issues of social control between the groups were

---

8. Carl-Herman Tillhagen, *Zigenarna i Sverige* (1965).

9. Of course informal discussions occurred, sometimes even mediators were used to convey offers and counteroffers, especially in matters which were not particularly serious; but in the end, the success of those was entirely dependent on the skill of the mediators and goodwill of the parties involved, and it took place in an "ad hoc" fashion.

handled by rumor and gossip,[10] occasionally through duelling by the direct participants in the dispute. The most serious intergroup conflict, created by intentional or sometimes by unintentional killing or serious wounding with intent to kill, called for blood feuding.[11] As there was little chance of regular negotiative procedure in cases of disputes between the groups, physical violence remained the only effective means of handling intergroup conflicts. There is much evidence that physical violence has been extensively resorted to over time. Although in the majority of cases the form of combat was in the nature of duelling, governed by numerous regulations as to the form of the fight, the arms allowed, and the style of fighting—all of which were designed to *prevent* fatal injuries—fatalities frequently were the result of those fights. When a death occurred, the private issue, that between the direct disputants, changed to a public matter, an issue which involved the direct participants' kin groups, and blood feuding between the involved kin groups was called for.

BLOOD FEUDING AS AN INSTRUMENT OF LAW[12]

Blood feuding, as the ultimate internal organ of social control among the Finnish Roma, was the main institution of internal justice, more specifically an alternative system of justice to that of state justice. Looked at from the traditional Roma point of view, they lived like a state within the state, where ideally all their internal matters were handled within the Roma community without resort to the Finnish state legal institutions. This was true even in serious cases of killings, although in practice those invariably also came to the notice of the Finnish authorities, who dealt with them by way of the Finnish laws.[13] The "jurisdiction" within which blood

10. In an article in Finnish, "Huhut, juorut ja sosiaalinen kontrolli" ("Rumor, gossip and social control"), I have analyzed the use of rumor in social control in the Finnish Roma community. I analyzed different types of rumors created by a "scandal" in the community and discovered that rumors which were effective in social control required two major qualifications: they needed to be on truly important matters of concern for the whole community, and also they needed to be formulated in such a manner that the truth could not easily be verified. (This article appears in *Vapaus, Veljeys and Vallankäyttö* 89–110 [Pekka Kosonen & Anneli Levo-Kivirikko, eds. 1989]).

11. I had prepared a monograph on blood feuding as my first published work on the Finnish Roma. The publishing of that work, although it was done in full cooperation, created a complex and at times dangerous situation within the Roma community where the lives of my closest associates and myself were threatened. The situation illustrates the problems of the participant-observer. The close relationship between the researcher and the subjects is such that the subjects feel that it is completely "safe" to give information, but only realize afterwards that information given is actually published. And all that even when the researcher acted and explained many times his character as a researcher. I have analyzed this experience in an article, "From Scientific Social Science to Responsible Research," in 25 *Acta Sociologica* 249–57 (1982).

12. See *Blood Feuding;* see also Grönfors, "Finnish Gypsy Blood Feuding," 24 *Journal of Legal Pluralism and Unofficial Law* 101–24 (1986).

13. Over the years I have occasionally been called upon to act as an expert witness in courts, usually by the defense lawyer of a Rom who stood trial for a killing. I have always refused on two main

feuding operated consisted of the Finnish Roma community. Under no circumstances could it involve non-Roma Finns, not even the non-Roma spouses of the Roma. The children from such liaisons would be affected, though. From the Roma point of view the actions by the Finnish state authorities were irrelevant, and there was no way in which state intervention could be substituted for the operation of blood feuding.[14] The sentences handed out by the Finnish courts carried little or no stigma in the Roma community, thereby providing further support for the autonomy of the Roma legal institutions.

Feuding has been defined as "relations of mutual animosity among intimate groups in which a resort to violence is anticipated on both sides."[15] Blood feuding assumes that the relevant groups are composed of kin—"blood-relatives." In my view feuding is a condition, an atmosphere of mutual hostility from which an action may or may not follow. Intergroup killing is sufficient to create such an atmosphere, sometimes even serious intentional bodily harm. The feuding is evident in the hostile relations that the parties have and that may never lead to a counter-killing. It is crucial to understanding the nature of blood feuding that it could lead to violence and other killings.

The feuding of the Rom, like feuding elsewhere, was governed by conventions that the parties accepted and by the fact that the offense was against the whole group and not only against the individual member. It is clear from a comparative analysis of societies practicing blood feuding that it is only practiced between people who are in a reciprocal relationship to each other, and thus fall under the same "jurisdiction." Blood feuding is a very drastic way of handling internal disputes and therefore, as Gluckman argues, it is necessary to resort to drastic measures in cases of serious breaches between people who are mutually dependent on each other. Such sanctions are not necessary against people with whom the group does not maintain intimate relationships and on whom it does not depend for its survival.[16] In Finnish Roma feuding, the responsibility for revenge for the killed or wounded relative rested upon the kin. Outsiders could not participate in the feuding activities. The revenge could in principle be directed at any kin member. However, in practice the risk was reduced in cases of more distant relatives, women,

---

grounds: (a) I feel that, for a sociologist and anthropologist who is dealing with generalities or ideal types, it is not appropriate to deduce from those to concrete cases; and (b) I maintain that there is a serious risk of having a verdict of premeditated murder returned if cultural factors and blood feuding are indicated in the court. That would be the only way in which the modern state court can behave, if it behaves logically, as there is no provision for alternative cultural explanations, at least at the formal, procedural level.

14. The state authorities are often, though, called to protect those who might otherwise be a target of feuding action, to safeguard a route of escape. Also, the prison authorities attempt to place the two opposing parties in a feud in different prisons, because they fear disturbances if they were together.

15. Lasswell, "Feud," in *6 Encyclopedia of the Social Sciences* 220–21 (1931).

16. Max Gluckman, *Custom and Conflict in Africa 3*, 14–19 (1970).

children and old people. A revenge act could be launched in principle by anyone in the offended group, but in practice similar qualifications applied.

While duelling was a highly stylized form of settling disputes, the same could not be said about Roma blood feuding. In principle anything was allowed in blood feuding. Unlike in many other feuding societies, successful revenge did not stop hostilities, only the roles of the revenger and the revenged changed. Also, in Finnish Roma society there was no way in which the blood feuding could be brought to a halt by negotiation or compensatory action. The fact that "anything goes" in revenge fights could be taken as an indication that feuding was an extralegal measure, indicative of social disorder rather than order. To view feuding this way, however, would be to misunderstand its nature. Together with the attitude that "anything goes" was a concurrent inhibitive regulative force of avoidance behavior. So while the whole offended group acted ritually in a manner suggesting that imminent revenge was to follow, at the same time it followed the cultural norm of refraining from revenge by practicing substitutive avoidance of the other group and its individual members. Similarly the group who was the target of a blood-feuding action was likewise required to observe strict avoidance. The hostilities were continued at the level of ill talk and other non-direct action, but the two groups remained enemies.[17] Through feuding, the offended group had a chance to show its willingness to defend its members against other groups; or even more strongly, through feuding the idea of collectivity, solidarity, and kin-based loyalty was strengthened, as was the concept of kin-based political autonomy. It is this aspect which makes blood feuding an instrument of order rather than disorder.

As the Finnish Roma did not have any intergroup political unit or organ, much depended on the kin-based group. In addition to any economic, social, and emotional security, the kin-based group also was the sole guarantor of physical safety for its members. It is in this light that the institution of Finnish Roma's non-marriage should be examined.

MARRIAGE AS A GLOBAL INSTITUTION

In anthropological literature, marriage in its variety of forms is considered an institution that is truly global. The fact that the Finnish Roma do not seem to have that institution in its usual form does not necessarily counteract that claim. To the contrary, the various arrangements, prohibitions, and taboos which surrounded

---

17. This state of affairs continued as long as the descendants of the two parties could remember the circumstances and the participants and as long as the two groups remained distinct entities. In the bilineal Finnish Roma society, the liaisons formed between the groups over time meant that there was mixing and merging of kin-based groups. This happened even though the members of the feuding groups were not supposed to form marriage-like liaisons. Over the generations, the borders of groups were sufficiently blurred at the edges that it became unclear who was on which side of the feuding. But it usually took decades and several generations of Roma for this to happen.

Finnish Roma sexuality, liaison-forming, reproduction, and other such matters could also be taken as an acknowledgement of marriage as an institution that at the same time should be given no place in the Finnish Roma society. Its potential for making connections between kin-groups, for creating loyalties and conflicting loyalties, and for posing a danger to kin-based solidarity can also be said to acknowledge the institution while disregarding it nevertheless. Briefly, some of the general anthropological and sociological assumptions about marriage (often linked to family) are thought to involve issues such as a common residence, economic cooperation, and the reproduction, nurturing and socializing of children. More specifically, two areas come to mind when marriage as a social institution is examined. Marriage is an institution where legitimate sexuality takes place and is a source for legitimate offspring. I shall look at these aspects in relation to the Finnish Roma.

PUBERTY, COURTSHIP, AND AFFAIRS OUTSIDE ROMA COMMUNITY

To be a child in the Roma community was also the time to be as free as imaginable. Many of the complex pollution regulations did not apply before reaching puberty.[18] The older generations of the household attempted to prolong childhood for as long as possible; the recognition of the children's approaching sexual maturity was postponed as far as it could be done. In many societies elaborate rituals recognize sexual maturity. The divider between childhood and adulthood in the

---

18. A useful summary of Roma pollution, purity and impurity, can be found in Weyrauch & Bell, "Autonomous Lawmaking: The Case of the 'Gypsies'," chap. 2 in this volume. Much of what is summarized there is also true in the case of the Finnish Roma. However, there are certain important differences as well: unlike the Roma elsewhere, no specific taboos attached to menstruation; the whole issue was taboo in that it simply could not be referred to at all. Drawing attention to menstruation by having a specific taboo relating to it was not possible. Sexual activity, conception, and child birth, as well as marriage and parenthood, were all taboo. Menstruation in itself as a sign of fertility (also taboo) was taboo. The same applied to female genitalia, which were considered taboo in other Roma communities. In the Finnish Roma community, genitalia, male or female, were also in themselves taboo. The practice of "skirt-tossing" (defiling men by a female's exposing her genitals to him) did not exist among the Finnish Rom (curiously it existed in the old Finnish country traditions!). Sexual organs as organs of reproduction had a potent shame attached to them and any act, reference, or verbal expression relating to them was taboo. Another difference from the account given by Weyrauch and Bell in relation to pollution taboos and sexuality concerns the prohibition of women from being physically above men. The explanation given was that such a position would bring a woman's genital area (unclean) into proximity to a man's upper body and facial area (clean) and thus pollute the man. Yes, the women could not be above men among the Finnish Roma, but the same applied to younger men as well: they too, could not be above older men. And similar prohibitions applied among the women themselves: younger women could not be physically above older women. As there was an extreme denial of sexuality, then, it appears that sexual taboos were extended to males as well. So, in addition to the prohibitions applying between the sexes, they also applied between the generations and between members of the same gender. For example, the toilet in the traditional Finnish Rom house or flat was only for the use of the oldest male member, who is the purest. The remaining members of the group had to find other means.

life of a Finnish Rom female child was putting on the full Roma skirt.[19] From that moment onward the full taboo system started operating and she was guarded against clandestine suitors. At the same time, parent-child avoidance related to the incest taboo started operating. From the moment when the girl declared her adulthood by her dress her father could never again be alone with her. Similarly, when a boy reached his late teens and considered himself to be a young adult, and showed it not only by adult male dress but also by expected "manly" behavior, he and his mother could never be alone together again.

When youngsters fell in love they could not show it in any way lest the movements of the girl would be watched even more tightly. The only way in which the young could get together was elopement. The usual case was for them to agree to the time and place where they could meet, and after meeting to attempt to go as far as they could, often hundreds of kilometers away, without anybody's knowledge. Once their escape was discovered a search was on, often by the girl's brothers and male cousins, and if they were discovered she was brought home. Traditionally the young tried to remain in hiding for at least two years, by which time a

---

19. The Finnish female Roma costume is most elaborate. A picture of a Finnish Rom woman can be found on the cover of Judith Okely, *Own and Other Culture* (1996), a book that features one of my key informants. She met the author in London in the late 1970s. The full-length skirt is made of heavy black velvet, and can weigh many kilos. The upper body is covered with a lacy blouse which covers the arms. Usually the skirt is covered with a full-length apron, which protects the expensive skirt from actual dirt, but also protects the outside world, and especially men and old people, from potential pollution from the skirt (cf. Weyrauch & Bell, at 37). The young girl herself had to make preparations for obtaining and getting dressed in the full Roma woman's attire without as much as a hint to the older women, including her own mother and older sister, all of whom would have tried to prevent any "such nonsense" while knowing full well that this was the way they did it in their time. One day she just appeared in the attire and received the ritual scoldings from the older women in the family. She was supposed to wear the attire from then on; there was no return to the European-style clothing. From that moment on she was watched more closely, and also from that day on the full female hygiene regulations applied to her. But it was similar for boys. Although the Roma men's attire was not so markedly different from the Finnish men's clothes, there were differences. Certain garments were favored (dark straight trousers, not jeans; never just the shirt; jacket often made of leather; short back-and-side haircut; dark shoes or long boots). A teenage boy started little by little to use a more "manly" outfit until in his late teens his attire resembled that of the full-grown man. While the woman's garment was supposed to hide her feminine characteristics (often succeeding in exaggerating them!), the same applied with some reservation to males. Showing his body hair (including a beard) was not appropriate for men; they were not allowed, for example, to roll up their shirt sleeves. The shirt, which formed the first layer to cover the naked skin, was also a shameful garment and had to be covered either by a cardigan or a vest; and neither gender could appear in shorts or equivalents or ever be anything but fully dressed in front of the older generation of men and women. The tabooed garments (such as bras, men's shirts, and underclothes) could not be referred to in speech either and the Finnish Roma had an elaborate system of expressions which substituted for taboo words. The washing and drying of clothes was a major hassle, as the clothes of different categories of people could not be washed at the same time. So the clothes of each generation and gender were washed separately. In addition "clean" things (like table cloths and face towels) could not be washed with "dirty" things (like clothes). Similarly, all these categories needed to be kept separate in drying, and in addition no "shameful" garment could be visible on the washing line.

child would be conceived and about one year old, before reunification with the families was attempted. Unlike in other societies which practice elopement, the suspicion of defilement was not adequate grounds for allowing them to be together. As there was no accepted way of getting married, virginity as such was not something to be guarded in these situations. It was the girl's becoming a "wife," with the implication that she and the man slept together, that mattered. And as there was no accepted way of forming liaisons, her chances of finding another partner were not lessened by the event. Only repeated abscondings with the same man could convince the family that it was useless to try to keep them separate, and a slow process of acceptance of the liaison would start. Although they were eventually admitted into the families again, the rules of decency demanded that they should not "advertise" their union. However, even then, the only acceptable partner was a person from another kin group. No matter how distantly related the parties were, liaisons within the kin group would have been considered incestuous. In that way the Finnish Roma can be said to be exogamous.

The secrecy needed in courting Roma girls was not necessary when a Rom man wanted to seek liaisons with non-Rom women. At some level, when looked at from the point of view of Roma society, the relationship between a Rom man and a non-Rom woman could be compared to that of a relationship between a man and a prostitute. Liaisons with non-Roma women could be boasted about and referred to rather openly even in generationally mixed company, when the usual prohibitions were their most potent. Relationships with non-Roma women were sought, valued, and seen as one of the privileges of men. Even when a Rom man and a non-Rom woman formed a reasonably permanent and long-term relationship, this custom did not change much.[20] He could not refer to her by name, nor could she ever visit his home and family. If the family had to make references to her, they never mentioned her name, but called her "*rakli*," which is a Roma term used to refer to all young non-Roma women.

Children from such unions create a curious situation. In principle, any child fathered by a Rom man was part of his family. In Finnish Roma society full siblings, for example, are those children who are fathered by the same man, even when born to different mothers, whereas children born to the same woman but fathered by different men are only half-siblings. In mixed liaisons, especially if the liaison was only temporary, the man's family often attempted to persuade the mother to give

---

20. There were exceptions to this, however. Some non-Roma women have been brought into the fold of the Roma kin group, but these seem to be reasonably rare instances. In these cases, although they may have learned to observe Roma customs, it was traditionally not considered suitable if such women wore Roma skirts or in other ways attempted to appear Roma-like. However, if a Rom woman had a relationship with or even married a non-Rom man, the union was accepted, but I know of no instance where the non-Rom man would have moved to live within the Roma community. The Roma women usually moved out and lived in a non-Roma fashion, except when they had dealings with other Roma.

up her child, as the family desired to bring up all the children of their men regardless who their mother was. Many different tactics were recorded as having been used to try to get the mother to part with her child. For example, Roma families even employed the common negative stereotypes of themselves in those efforts, by pointing out to the mother consequences for her and her child of her community finding out that she had borne a child fathered by a Rom man. In a climate of extreme prejudice against the Roma, this could be one effective appeal. It was usually the man's mother, if she was still alive and healthy enough to look after the baby, who played the prime role in this. However, it was not entirely unheard of for the man's companion-in-life[21] to attempt to get the custody of the child.[22]

The extreme avoidance of anything sexual, the elaborate arrangements to ignore the institution of marriage, and the seeming openness about the exploits of Roma men with non-Roma women seem somewhat contradictory customs. However, as the only significant community for the Roma was the Roma community, influences from outsiders were of little consequence. As I will later attempt to show in more detail, the threat to kin-based solidarity came from within the Rom-community, not from the outside. Also, as the Finnish Roma considered the non-Roma to have no power to pollute the Roma or anything belonging exclusively to that community,[23] there was no need to fear contamination from the outside by these liaisons either. Therefore they could "afford" to be less concerned about sexuality and related issues which were outside their own community.

PREGNANCY, CHILDBIRTH, AND BEING A MOTHER

When a Rom woman became pregnant, the event received no public attention. No special arrangements or taboos were connected to pregnancy. In fact, since the entire matter was not acknowledged, special taboos would have drawn attention to

21. It is very hard to name the "spouse" in the Finnish Roma unions. Among themselves they avoid all references to the union. When they form permanent liaisons, the Finnish expression used occasionally by the Roma is to "join together" and "be together." For each other they use first names or nicknames and, as the community knows who is "together" with whom, there is no real need to name the participants in the relationship by any special name.

22. These efforts could have been behind the popular and age-old stereotype that the Roma steal children. Perhaps they sometimes resorted to these kinds of tactics in cases when the mother was not willing to part with the child. Also, as was the case here in Finland, sometimes those children brought into the fold of the Rom family were strikingly different in looks, for example having straw-blond hair instead of the jet-black hair of most of the Roma.

23. Here again, the Finnish Roma seem to differ from some other Roma groups, as summarized by Weyrauch and Bell (at 37–39). The rules of cleanliness, hygiene, purity and impurity in the end apply only in Roma contexts and only the Roma can pollute Roma things. A non-Roma who is visiting Roma homes can pollute, but not because of his or her person, but because of behavior which is ignorant of Roma customs, like putting a clean dish on a "dirty" surface and thus making it permanently unclean. Non-Roma homes and other things in it are considered neutral until they are moved into Roma settings and become regularly used there.

an event not acknowledged institutionally. The abundant female clothing offered good protection for much of the pregnancy. In former times, when the Roma were still a travelling folk,[24] it was common for a pregnant woman to leave her group before her time was due, together with the father of the child. When her time came, an attempt was made to secure a Finnish farmer's sauna (bathhouse) or some other neutral place for the delivery.

When maternity hospitals became more common and within reach of poor people, they were quickly used by Roma women, although the women usually did their utmost not to place themselves in hospitals or other institutions where they would be entirely at the mercy of non-Roma. The maternity hospital effectively removed the Roma women from their community for the birth. At maternity hospitals, only women younger than the mother herself were allowed to visit her. Even an older sister could not see her there. Men, including the father of the child, could never have visited her. Childbirth was attempted to be kept as much a non-event as possible, and all overt references to pregnancy and childbirth were forbidden. When references could not be avoided, for example for practical reasons, it was done in whispers and with considerable shame. Euphemisms were also employed to avoid mentioning these tabooed topics.

The ignoring of the child and of its relationship to the mother continued at least until the child was able to walk. Then the child was no longer an infant needing breast feeding but a person with whom people were able to communicate directly without the intermediate of the mother. If it were possible, the mother and the father set off on their own to travel the countryside, avoiding other travelling Roma at least for a year after the birth of their child. When the child was a toddler, they made a slow and gradual return to the Roma community.[25]

This return happened, for example, in the following way: The parents of the new born child arrived at the house or at the camp site of either set of families. The woman with her toddler stayed in the cart or sledge while the father of the infant approached the family. If the family occupied a house, he went inside, exchanged greetings, and sat down as if he had never been away. No reference was made to the woman outside or to the new child, and no inquiries were made as to where they had spent all these months, what the name of the child was and where the child and its mother were at that particular moment. The man was treated with

24. The travelling of the Finnish Roma differed markedly from the travelling of other Roma. The so-called wagon culture never seemed to have existed in Finland. The travelling, mainly around the more sparsely populated countryside, depended on the goodwill of the sedentary peasant or farming folk, who provided temporary housing—often just for a night or two—to the Roma travelling on horse drawn carts in the summer or sledges in the winter. Often the same houses were visited from one year to the next and trading, fortune-telling, and other typical Roma activities were entered into with the settled people.

25. These days it is a symbolic gesture when the mother stays away from her family and that of her male companion for a mere few weeks, but the birth is still charged with considerable shame and covered with a veil of silence.

considerable indifference. At the same time, the man was expected to show shame by appearing as inconspicuous as possible, not to initiate discussion, to answer only in monosyllables when asked something, and generally to keep his eyes downcast. This was an acknowledgement that he had done something shameful by producing a child, and he had to make his shame public. Meanwhile, the young women of the house snuck out to meet the woman and the child. They tried to coax her to come inside, but she was ashamed and reluctant to do that. Finally, one of the young women would pick up the child and go inside, leaving the mother behind. The child was taken into a room where no older people were present, and if the child had to pass by older people, they totally ignored it.

Eventually, with her head lowered and without greeting anybody, the mother scuttled into the house and ran into a room where no older people were present. While the younger women fussed over the child, the older generation entirely ignored child and mother. The father had to appear in public as if he had nothing to do with the baby or its mother. No inquiries as to the health or even gender could be made. The mother stayed out of the view of the older generation for days, even weeks, and only slowly would start participating in the everyday life of the family. Her relationship to her child remained a potent source of shame, and even a light-hearted reference linking the mother and child would send her out of the room for hours.[26]

The child was quickly assimilated into the general run of the household, and although the older generation generally ignored the child when either of the parents was in the room, considerable fuss was made over the baby when the parents were away. The younger generation, on the other hand, attended to the child's needs and paid constant attention to this new arrival in the family. In this way, the child soon learned to widen his or her ideas of the immediate kin.

In Finnish Roma society, children made especially little distinction between their natural mother and their mother's sisters or father's sisters. All children in the household, who were brought up together, were considered "brothers" and "sisters." When a child grew up, he or she would spend considerable amounts of time with any of the "aunts." A child could claim an instant membership in any of the aunts' households all through life. If the child was male, he could ask for anything that he could demand of his natural mother from all his aunts as well. The affection and care given to him by his mother's and father's sisters were little different from that of the affection and care given by his natural mother. If the child was female, her aunts could demand from her all the services which could be demanded by her nat-

---

26. The Finnish Roma have an institutional way of showing appropriate shame. If they are in the company of people to whom the taboos apply, any reference to a taboo topic sends the younger generation out of the room, and women cover their heads with aprons, and men put hands over their eyes. This is sometimes used to reinforce normative behavior when the older people teasingly and purposefully refer to taboo topics and, at the same time, expect the younger ones to show the appropriate shame. In this way, younger people let the older generations know that they know the culture and appropriate behavior.

ural mother. Even when one lived with Roma families, as I did, it still was sometimes quite difficult to assess the biological relationship between the intimate kin.
The behavior in terms of rights and obligations was not different between the children and their natural parents and between the children and their parents' siblings,
nor was it different among the children from various sets of parents who were
closely related to each other.

KINSHIP TERMINOLOGY

The non-acknowledgment of the physical relationship and the institution of marriage is shown also in the kinship terminology. The status of an attached woman was
in no way different from that of an unattached female and there were no outward
signs referring to their different situations. No special terms were applied to attached
women. She could not be called the equivalent of "Mrs.," nor could she be referred
to as somebody's wife. If it was necessary to link her to her man, then she may have
been called his "woman." In the Finnish language, which is the language of most
Roma in Finland,[27] there is a marked difference between the two words "woman"
and "wife," especially when used by the Roma. Calling somebody a "wife" meant an
acknowledged affinal relationship between the man and the woman. Such relationships not being possible in Roma society, the use of the term "wife" was taboo. If the
term "so and so's woman" was used, that showed that they habitually travelled or
stayed together, at least for the time being. Little expectation attached to the use of
the term and little implication that they would always stay together. The term meaning somebody's "woman" gave no special status to the woman referred to, except as
far as it acknowledged the authority of the man over that particular woman. Similarly, a man could not be called a "husband" but could be referred to, when such an
acknowledgment of a relationship could not be avoided, as somebody's "man," which
meant that he was a person whom a woman had travelled with in earlier times or
lived with now. The man and woman living together never referred to each other as
"my woman" or "my man," but only by first names or nicknames.

As far as the children were concerned, they were not allowed to call their natural parents (or anyone else either) by the terms "mother" and "father." The children referred to their parents simply by their first names. The only exception to
this rule was when the children were themselves parents. Then they could refer to
their aged natural parents as "mother" or "father," when the terms had somewhat
lost their meaning as the sexual triangle mother-father-child, at least to the extent
that it could be overlooked. Then the terms took a special affective, endearing
meaning, as the respect for the older-generation kin, and especially for parents, parents' siblings, and grandparents, was high.

27. Finland is a bilingual country (Finnish and Swedish). In areas where only Swedish is spoken
there are a few Roma families whose language is Swedish. The returned migrant families from Sweden, especially the younger generation, can use Swedish as their everyday language.

SPECIAL TABOOS RELATING TO SEXUALITY AND MARRIAGE

If a non-Rom asked a Rom woman about the number of children she might have, the answer "none" could contradict other evidence. Only an outsider would address the Finnish Roma with such a question; the Roma themselves would know the inappropriateness of the inquiry. As there was no arena for legitimate sexual relationships within the Finnish Roma society, anything that referred to sex became taboo.[28] To have children was breaking the taboo, and therefore it was good behavior not to draw attention to them or to attach them to particular parents.

Similarly, to inquire about the age of a child was not appropriate, because an answer would have referred to an event not legitimate in the Finnish Roma society. As age is determined from birth, and as birth is something against the norms of Roma society, giving the age would acknowledge the breach of these norms. This law was particularly strong in regard to the child's natural parents, who would have been implicated as the "culprits" of such a breach. Thus, birthdays of children were not traditionally celebrated. Only when the person grew older and when the "distasteful" event was far enough in the past could the Roma celebrate birthdays. The fortieth birthday was usually the first one celebrated in Finnish Roma society.

The norms regulating the public behavior of the couple were strict, and all were aimed at publicly telling people that the two concerned persons in no way belonged to each other. A couple could not sit publicly side by side, nor appear in photographs together. There could be no inference that they were actually sleeping together which meant that, if there was no room in the house for the exclusive use of the couple, the woman had to stay up until everybody else in the room had gone to sleep. Only then could she join her man in bed under the cover of darkness. In the morning, she had to make sure to be up before anybody else and be fully dressed before the others woke up. The couple could not touch in public or show affection in any way in front of other people, especially in the presence of the older generation. In brief, the norms of the Finnish Roma society demanded the couple to act in an exaggerated way to demonstrate that they had no intimate relationship between them.[29]

---

28. The terms which are considered sexual in the Finnish Roma society would not at first glance appear so in the Finnish society. I was once in a Rom household and the radio was on. They announced in the middle of the day a program which had the word "family planning" in it. The elder went immediately to the radio to turn it off and said in a loud voice, "what rubbish do they broadcast these days," and the younger ones flew out of the room. In fact, any word which could be traced to sexuality becomes a taboo word.

29. An anecdote from my fieldwork illustrates the strictness of these rules. I was in the field together with my wife, staying at a Rom house. I got up before my wife and came to the kitchen for breakfast. In the kitchen was a Rom woman, with whom I was chatting while I was having my breakfast. She was sitting by the wall on a chair, while I was sitting alone on a long bench by the table. My wife came into the kitchen to have her breakfast and, as soon as she appeared in the room, the Rom woman stood up

In spite of these strong taboos against forming legitimate marriage-type relationships, some Roma are and have been married officially, the union being solemnized by the church or through a civil ceremony. However, being officially married carried no status within the Roma community, and it was a matter which usually was not mentioned, and if mentioned it was stated with some shame or apology. Of the official marriages which I knew to exist among my Roma informants, all had been contracted because of some practical reasons, usually relating to real or imagined privileges married couples could have under Finnish laws. A number of them had married during the last war for the sole purpose of being able to qualify for a special leave for married men from the front. Similarly, many marriages were entered into when the spouse had been in prison in order to gain easier access to the jail or in order to qualify for a leave for married inmates from the prison. Some marriages were also entered into during compulsory military service, as only the married wife could claim a living allowance intended for married couples. More recently, mainly since my fieldwork, there has been a strong revivalist religious movement among the Roma in Finland. Because the congregation looks down on de facto relations, many Roma have married because of the pressure put on them by their parishes and parishioners. But even in those cases the official marriage does not change the general idea of non-marriage with its special norms and taboos outlined here.

STATUS OF A "SPOUSE"

As the legitimacy of marriage was not acknowledged, both parties in a liaison remained members of their own kin groups. There was no way in which the Finnish Roma society could acknowledge affinal relationships. This could make the life of a "spouse" difficult on occasion. If a woman was living with her man's kin, she had nobody readily at hand in crisis situations, for example, when her man mistreated her. In the household of her man she was usually the only non-kin female, which sometimes meant that she was also under the control of his female relations who could order her about a great deal.

The man who was living with the woman's relatives could find himself in a vulnerable situation also. He had to watch his step as far as his woman was concerned, because she could always call upon her male relatives for support. He also had to make sure that he got along well with her male relatives, who could view him as a

---

from her chair and hastily came to sit next to me. What she was doing was acting out her role as a Rom woman. One of her main tasks was to prevent any social disgrace by resorting to diversionary tactics, and to do this without anybody really noticing that such action took place. By moving next to me at the table, she effectively prevented my wife from committing a social disgrace. She thought, probably with some validity, that my non-Rom wife probably would not know about the prohibition that prevented couples sitting together. Rather than finding out if my wife knew about such a custom or not, she short-circuited a potential embarrassment by moving to sit next to me.

threat to the internal cohesion of the family and as a "seducer" of one of the women in the family. There seemed to be no particular prerequisite in terms of patrilocality or matrilocality, although it was natural that a man would prefer to have his woman living with his family. It was not uncommon, though, to find a man living with her family.

In a situation of blood feuding, the responsibility under the feuding system was not extended to people beyond the consanguine kin (the so-called blood-relatives). This could have meant, for example, that although the man may have had to be on his guard in terms of a blood-feuding relationship that his family had with another family, his woman did not have to face this kind of threat at all. She could even continue to associate with her man's enemies in a blood-feuding situation. Similarly, if she had a blood-feuding relationship with another family, her man was unaffected by this relationship. Should it have happened that the couple's respective families got into a blood-feuding relationship with each other, then Finnish Roma norms required the couple to separate immediately. The behavior expected in blood feuding was such that there was no way in which the couple could have continued to live together under such circumstances, no matter how they felt toward each other privately. Liaisons between men and women could never be acceptable if there was an existing blood-feuding relationship between their respective families.

At the everyday level, emotional and social responsibilities between the couple and between the couple and others were similar to responsibilities generally among people of their age and gender. The woman accorded deference to her man, and he had authority over her in a similar fashion to the authority he had over equivalent-age female kin, in addition to having—naturally—the publicly-ignored sexual rights. In situations of severe crisis, his sisters assumed the prime responsibility. In economic respects the woman was expected to carry the main responsibility, and the care of the children's emotional and material needs was almost exclusively a female responsibility.

SEPARATION[30]

As no importance was attached to officially or unofficially "married" people, separation in Roma society was also somewhat of a non-event and relatively frequent and untraumatic. A separated woman was always welcomed back by her people, and a woman was sometimes actively encouraged to leave her man, especially if the man was not considered to be worthy of her or was mistreating her. The cir-

---

30. Compare with Weyrauch and Bell, supra n. 18, at 36–37, which with only certain reservation applies to the Finnish Rom. "Virginity" and "infidelity" are separate issues among the Finnish Roma. If there is no legitimate area for sexual activity then "virginity" as such is of little consequence. Infidelity of an attached woman could have brought severe punishment, but after death or separation it had little significance.

cumstances leading to the separation were irrelevant, her home was always with her own family and kin. Being separated was also of little hindrance to either party forming new couple-relationships. As none of the subsequent relationships had any status in Roma society, any earlier relationships were also institutionally irrelevant. Similarly, as the Roma women's virginity was not a prerequisite for finding a man, her chances for finding a new man after the separation were not lessened by the fact that she no longer was a virgin.

DISCUSSION

In order to understand the Finnish Roma community and its institution of non-marriage, the severely stigmatized position that they have held over the centuries in Finnish society has to be taken into consideration. However, that is the experience of the Roma in other parts of the world as well. The Roma have experienced extermination, fear, and hatred of enormous proportions in their history. Thus they have no reason to trust the institutions of the established society. Security can only be found within their own society. This security requires a certain level of order within the Roma society; in fact it requires a fairly high level of order and an organized system of authority. What the Finnish Roma have in common with the rest of the Roma is a system of hygiene and a system of ritualized ways of dividing their world into pure and impure, clean and dirty, moral and immoral, legitimate and illegitimate and, consequently, allowed and non-allowed. To understand the logic of these is to understand Roma society and law.

Persons who break the rules of appropriate conduct in many Roma groups, especially those which have the indigenous legal system of the *kris*,[31] are deemed to be impure and polluted, often for a specific period of time. Among the Finnish Roma community, pollution and the condition of impurity rest on the authority of the men and the elders. Ultimately this authority structure applies only within the individual kin group, all groups forming parallel and independent systems. Because authority is vested in kin, there is little need to have specific "sentences," such as specific times during which the person is "*marime*." An offense is committed against one's kin and therefore could be considered a "private matter," handled informally the way each family sees fit. The matters which are handled by the kin groups themselves are theoretically connected to breaking the fundamental moral codes of pure and impure, clean and dirty. If the offending has happened in a situation involving a member of another family, the family of the offender would have to be notified and the punishment to be meted out by his or her family upon whom shame was brought.

The worth of the kin group in the Roma community depends on the respect it commands from other kin groups, and shameful conduct by members of the kin

---

31. See, for example, Weyrauch and Bell, at 29–48, for the condition of impurity, or "marime," and the operation of *kris*.

can reduce the honor of the family. The reciprocal honor of the kin group in the eyes of the other kin groups is very important among the Finnish Roma, and therefore it is an effective means to deal with the more common, non-serious breaches of conduct. The individual members of kin groups are well aware that they are expected to bring honor to their kin group. In the end, the only true way of doing that is to follow the rules of cleanliness, which include appropriate behavior towards those in authority, the men and the old people.

Another level in dealing with offenses, especially earlier when the Finnish Roma still were primarily engaged in traditional occupations,[32] was ritualized duelling between the men of the different kin groups. As referred to earlier, this related to matters between the direct participants in the dispute and could be considered private rather than public. The duelling was connected with the honor of the family and of the individual man. Issues such as economic rights, disputes about women, and challenges to the honor of the family and to one's manhood were some of the typical issues which were settled by duelling. If a man was challenged, it was dishonorable not to accept the challenge. If he refused, a man would have been considered a coward, and he would have brought shame over his entire kin group. If it was an armed fight, the arms allowed were such that they posed no immediate danger of death.[33] The way of fighting and aftercare was also regulated. The winner had to make sure that the loser's wounds were attended to and in general take care of him in such a way that he would not die from his injury. Killing the opponent was not the aim, winning the fight was. By winning, the person's honor was restored. This restoration required a fair fight, and in a fair fight nobody lost his life. The loser, if he had put up a good fight, did not lose much of his honor either. He lost the dispute, but not his honor. It was also required that he be a good loser. If he was hurt he had to submit himself to the care of the winner and his kin, and consider the case under dispute closed forever.

Blood feuding is the way in which the Finnish Roma deal with—not settle—the most serious offending that may occur in that community, the killing or sometimes grievous bodily injury caused by the intent to kill. Killings and injuries form the only matters which can be called "public" issues concerning the entire community. The aim of blood feuding is not to bring peace, as is the case in many other bloodfeuding societies, but it is more to show strength by the kin group. It attempts to

---

32. The most valued traditional occupation for men was horse trading, although men also engaged in other kinds of trading and in curing domestic animals, repairing copper pots, and sharpening knives and other implements. The most valued occupation for females was fortune-telling, but also selling of handiwork and other smaller items. Some elements of those have remained until today, like training and trading in race horses and cars (although this is considered inferior to trading in horses), selling watches and other small items for men, and fortune-telling and selling of handiwork for women. But according to social welfare records, the most important means of livelihood is in the form of various public help they receive under the welfare system of the Finnish state and that of the local municipalities.

33. Therefore firearms were not allowed to be used in the fighting. The most common arms were knives (which were wielded in a way to effect cuts rather than fatal stabs) sticks, and chains.

declare publicly that, although the group has suffered a loss, it can still defend its members. Blood feuding is also connected to the honor and shame of the kin groups. Showing readiness for feuding is honorable, and to shy away from it is dishonorable and could be a fatal show of weakness. As said earlier, blood feuding is kin-based in such a way that it concerns only consanguine kin.[34] As blood feuding is a truly serious matter in the Finnish Roma community, a calamity of huge proportions, to survive it intact requires an absolute loyalty from the kin members.

It is here where the possible explanation for the absence of marriage as an institution rests. In the Finnish Roma community so much is laid on the shoulders of the kin-based groups that it cannot afford any competing or conflicting loyalties. As the finally accepted partner in a couple-relationship has to come from another kin group, there is a danger that in a crisis situation the demands of the kin group and those of the person who comes from another kin group might conflict. By giving no status to such relationships, there is a clear message that first and foremost the loyalties must lie with one's own kin group. By not giving any place for marriage or any affinal relationships which might result from marriage relationships, the lines of loyalty are always well drawn.[35]

Other cultural choices could have been available to resolve this issue of absolute kin-based loyalty. Instead of defining acceptable partners exogamously,[36] a similar end result with respect to absolute kin-based loyalty could have been achieved by endogamous marriage arrangements, a situation where the spouses would have also been consanguine relatives and with no problems of conflicting loyalties. Therefore, it is not surprising that some Roma groups might engage and value endogamous marriages.[37] But as the rule of exogamy is paramount among the Finnish Roma, and as they lack any central office to deal with serious disputes, the demands of kin-based loyalty make it logical that the Finnish Roma ignore the institution of marriage altogether.

34. As affinal kin members are not possible in the Finnish Roma community, all kin relationships are consanguine, biologically-based kin relations.

35. One notable exception is the children born out of this relationship. In the bilineal society of the Finnish Roma the children are members of both kin groups, mother's and father's. Should the parents get into opposite sides of a blood feuding, the children's position is unclear as they are related to both warring parties. The blood-feuding relationship therefore does not extend to them, as they are at the same time friends and enemies of the same person. When they grow older, the children may choose on whose side their loyalties lie, and especially the men in such situations frequently did this, but still they avoided getting into open conflicts with either side.

36. A cultural marriage regulation stipulating that the partners must come from different groups, in this case that the only finally acceptable partners must be from different kin groups.

37. Although the evidence is not conclusive, there are reports from England and Wales of cross-cousin marriages (see Judith Okely, *The Traveller Gypsies* 156–57 [1983], and Anne Sutherland, *Gypsies: the Hidden Americans* 143–44 [1975].

EIGHT

A Glossary of Romani Terms

Ian Hancock

The following is a glossary of words occurring in the essays in this volume, plus a number of others directly or indirectly relevant to the topics dealt with. Where they represent usage in different dialects, this has been indicated.

Romani orthography, and indeed the Romani language itself, is only now in the process of being standardized. The spelling used here has been regularized according to the system outlined in Ian F. Hancock, *A Handbook of Vlax Romani* (Slavica Publishers, Columbia, Ohio, 1995). Briefly, the letters and letter combinations have the following values in Kalderash Vlax: [j] is like English "y," [c] like "ts," [š] like "sh," [č] and [tj] both like "ch," [ž] like "s" in "pleasure," [dž] like [ž] with the tongue curled back, [čh] like [š] with the tongue curled back, [dj] like English "j," [r] a flapped or trilled "r" as in Scottish English, [rr] a throat "r" as in French, [x] like "ch" in German "Achtung." [v] sounds like "w" for many speakers. The stress-bearing vowel is marked with a grave accent.

[Throughout this volume no effort has been made to standardize the spelling of Romani words. Thus, variations in spelling occasionally occur, depending on the preferences of the individual contributors. Ed.]

Abjàv	"wedding," pl. **abjavà**. Also **bjav**.
Amìra	Oath taken at the beginning of a **kris;** var. of **amràn**.
Amràn, Armàn	"curse," pl. **armàja, amrìja**.
Anàv gadžikanò	Non-Romani name for use in dealings with the outside world. This may be an arbitrary choice, or may be an anglicizing (hispanicizing, etc.) of the Romani name; thus *o Stanko le Mičosko* might call himself "Stan Mitchell" in English. An

individual may have several **anavà gadžikanè,** as well as a nickname (used only within the community).

Anàv rromanò   Romani name. Amongst the **Vlax,** *q.v,* this consists of a given name, plus a patronymic, plus a matronymic, plus the name of the clan affiliation; thus *o Stànko le Mičosko la Gežàko ànda le Papinèšti vìca* translates as "Stanko, son of Mičo, son of Geža, of the Papinešti clan." In ordinary discourse, only the given name and the patronymic are used.

Angloromani   Variety of restructured Romani spoken by Romanichals in Britain, North America, Australia, and elsewhere, consisting of Romani words in an English-language grammatical structure. Called **pogadi jib** or **rumnis** by its speakers. Like **Sìnti,** *q.v,* also a northern dialect.

Anglo-Romany   The inflected dialect of Romani spoken in England until the turn of the present century and in the United States until the 1950s.

Ansurimè   "married," of a man. **Vlax** only.

Arxentìnurja   **Vlax** in North America whose ancestors migrated via Argentina.

Bàjo   "trouble."

Bajur, bajour   Misspellings and mispronunciations of **bužò,** *q.v.,* popularized by a 1950s Broadway stage production.

Bangjaràv   "I accuse." Also **rrestisàvav, purriv.**

Bankožiro   Holder of the community funds. Also **bankàri. Vlax.**

Barò   *See* **Rrom barò.**

Bashaldò   Name of a Romani group originating in Hungary, *lit.* "musician." Pl. **Bašaldè.**

Baulo   Angloromani word meaning "pig"; slang for "policeman." Pronounced *bàwlo.* **Balò** in Common Romani.

Baxt   "luck, fortune, fate"; also **surručimòs.**

Bèda   "trouble, problems."

Bedàko   "troublemaker, troublesome." Pl. **bedàča.**

Beng	"devil."
Bèshiben	Word used in Northern Romani dialects, equivalent to **kris;** *lit.* "sitting."
Bezèx	"sin, gross wrongdoing."
Bibàxt	"misfortune."
Bibìo	Term of direct address to female elder (< **bibì,** "aunt").
Bikinimàski hertìja	"contract for sale (document)."
Bipatjivalò	"dishonorable, dishonorable man." Pronounced **bipakivalò** in Russian Kalderash Vlax.
Biprindžaripè	"neglect, ignoring."
Blakbolimè	"shunned by the community" (< Eng. "blackball(ed)").
Blokimè	"shunned by the community" (< Eng. "block(ed)").
Bolimè	"shunned by the community" (< Eng. "(black)ball(ed)").
Bolimòs	"baptism."
Borì	"daughter-in-law; new bride."
Bori ladge-up	Angloromani phrase meaning "disgrace"; in common Romani, **barò ladžàv.** *See* **ladž, ladžajmòs.**
Butjàki hertìja	"contract for work (document)."
Bužò	"a pouch." This is used in a confidence trick, also called **bužo,** involving the exchanging of money for cut-up paper. Pl. **bužurja.**
Čačimòs	"the truth."
Čapladò	"mentally impaired, mentally impaired male."
Cepenimòs	"deadlock, stalemate," at a **kris.**
Cèrxa	Among **Lovàra,** the name used for clan; the equivalent of **vìca,** literally "tent." *See also* **šàtra.**
Čhaj	"umarried Romani female" (as opposed to **raklì,** *q.v.*). A female is referred to as **čhaj** whatever her age if she is unmarried. A 25-year-old woman (in non-Romani terms) is still a **čhaj,** while a married girl of twelve has become a **Rromnì.**
Čhavò	"unmarried Romani male" (as opposed to **raklò,** *q.v.*).

Čhej	**Vlax** dialectal variant of **čhaj.**
Čhinèl (e) kris	"sentence, condemn."
Chor	"to steal" (Angloromani).
Choring	"stealing" (Angloromani).
Choring mush	"thief" (Angloromani).
Chovihàni	"a witch," Angloromani dialect. *See* **čoxani.**
Činasàra	The eve before a **slàva,** Kalderaš Vlax dialect.
Činavàs	"we agree upon, decide"; also "we make an offer."
Činavipè	"agreement, negotiation, decision, an offer."
Civilians	A term sometimes applied by American Vlax when speaking English to the non-Romani population.
Čor	"thief."
Čoràv	"I steal."
Čoxanì	"a witch," **Vlax** dialect. Also pron. **čoxajì.**
Čuràri	"member of a **nàcija** of **Rrom,**" *q.q.v.,* pl. **Čuràra.**
Dadèski dej	"paternal grandmother."
Dàki dej	"maternal grandmother."
Dàrro	"dowry, given at Vlax wedding."
Das	A non-Romani person, in some southern European dialects of Romani; fem. **dasnì.**
Del	"God." Also **Devèl.**
Den kris	"they are holding a **kris** (*q.v.*)," "they are bringing judgment."
Devèl	var. of **Del,** *q.v.*
Dìdikai, Dìdikoi	Impolite term used by Romanichals for individual having just one Romani parent.
Diklò	"scarf," worn at the neck or on the head; distributed at an **abjav.** Pl. **diklè.** Also **diklorrò.**
Dinò Devlèstar	"mentally deficient male," *lit.* "God-given." Fem. **dinì-Devlèstar.**
Divàno	"conversation, discussion, advice session," preferred to a **kris** as a means of settling a dispute. *Maj fedèr te huladjòn sar amalà and'ekh divàno, de sar dušmàja and'ekh kris:* "It is better to part as friends from a divano, than as enemies from a *kris.*"
Divinìv	"I advise, I discuss."

Dji, odjì, gi Life force, "soul."

Domba Name applied by academics to the pre-exodus population(s) in India who came to constitute the Romani people.

Doš "guilt, fault."

Došalò "guilty."

Drab "potion, medicine, drug."

Drabaràv "I apply medicine, I heal." Also, "I divine, I heal spiritually."

Drabarni "female diviner." Commonly called in English a "reader," "adviser," or "fortune-teller." *See* **gičisvàra.**

Drabèngro "physician, pharmacist," in northern Romani dialects.

Dukàto American Vlax word for "lawyer," also **avdukàto.** From var. European forms such as **advokat,** with metathesis. Pl. **dukàturja.**

Dukker "predict the future," Angloromani form of Common Romani **durikeràv,** *q.v.*

Dukkering "divining, predicting the future" (Angloromani).

Durikeràv "I predict the future" (from reading palms, tea leaves, coffee grounds, etc.).

Durjardò Banished from the community. *Lit.* "sent afar."

Džukìv "I confront."

Familìja, familja "extended family."

Farmečìv "I curse, put a spell on." **Vlax** Romani.

Gadžì "adult female non-Romani person," pl. **gadžja.**

Gadžìkanì baxt "bad luck," *lit.* "non-Romani luck."

Gadžikanò "non-Romani," adjectival form of **gadžò.**

Gadžikanò dukàto "a non-Romani lawyer."

Gadžò "adult male non-Romani person," pl. **gadžè.**

Gàlbeno "gold coin" (*lit.* "yellow"); *see* **Gàlbi.**

Gàlbi Plural of **Gàlbeno,** gold coins traditionally worn as a necklace or as buttons and as a form of personal wealth (there being no access to banks, they were available for paying/bribing officials).

Gaver "policeman" (Angloromani). Also **gav-mush, musker.**

Gèro

A non-Romani person in Angloromani (var. **gèra; gorò** in other dialects).

Gičisvàra

"woman who claims to predict the future." **Vlax** Romani. For some speakers there is a distinction between a **gičisvàra** and a **drabarnì**, the former being a hustler, the latter being more "professional" and proud of her skills. From a Romanian word meaning "guess."

Glàba

"a fine." Paid, though not exclusively, as the result of a decision made by the **krisnitòrja**.

Glabìv

"I fine."

Gomì

A non-Romani person, in some southern European Romani dialects.

Gonimè

"banished, driven out of the community." This does not necessarily have to be because the offender is ritually polluted. *See* **marimè**.

Gonimòs

"expulsion from the community."

Grèkurja

Vlax in America whose ancestors migrated via Greece.

Gypsy

Common English word for person of Romani descent, derived from Renaissance English *'gypcian,* i.e., "Egyptian," it being supposed that Egypt was the country of origin of the Roma. The term is intensely disliked by some Roma, and tolerated by others. The persistence of its use in English lies in the fact that there is no single Romani equivalent which is agreed upon by all Romani groups (see **Rrom**). The policy of most Romani organizations is to use their self-ascripted ethnonym (**Sìnti, Rròma, Kààle,** etc.) and to avoid the use of all externally-created labels ("Gypsy," "Gitano," "Tigan," etc.). One suggestion has been to employ the adjectival form **Romani,** plural **Romanies,** as a general noun, an alternative already in use in the British media. If the word "Gypsy" is used in English, it should be written with a proper noun's initial capital letter.

Hokano baro

"technique of extorting money from a victim by deceit," *lit.* "big lie." A nonce term coined by George Borrow and supposedly of Spanish

Romani origin (see **Lavo-lil,** below); the correct Angloromani for this is "**bori hokaben**" or variants (see **penning hokabens**).

Inkàlka "trespassing."

Inkalkìv "I am trespassing."

Jàdo "world outside of the Romani environment."

Jakhalò "the evil eye," although this word may also mean "attractive."

Jenisch A population of mixed origins inhabiting Germany, Switzerland, Belgium, the Netherlands and eastern France. Probably originally consisting of displaced citizens of Hanseatic Germany, and later joined by Roma, Jews, and others, today they constitute a distinct ethnic population with its own speech and family names. Also spelled **Yéniche.**

Kàko Term of direct address to respected male elder (< **kak,** "uncle"). Also **Nàno.**

Kalderàš Name applied to several **Vlax**-speaking Romani groups and their dialects. The term was originally occupational, meaning "coppersmith." Eastern and Western Kalderaš populations (in, e.g., Russia and Serbia) differ considerably in speech and custom. Pl. **Kalderàša.**

Kapàra "wedding gift."

Ketrìnca apron worn over traditional skirt, symbolizing modesty.

Kidimòs "meeting." Also **kidinimòs.**

Kinimàski hertìja "contract for a sale (document)."

Kintàla "spiritual balance, harmony." The Romani world view is a bipolar one, the universe falling naturally into pairs, though not all of them the antithesis of the other: Rrom–gadžo, clean–defiled, God–the devil, male–female, luck–misfortune, upper body–lower body, sexual being–non-sexual being (see **phurimòs**), and so on. Balance is upset by not observing the appropriate behavior. Also **kintàri, kintuimòs, kuntàla.**

Kintàrì var. or **kintàla,** *q.v.,* also **kuntàri.**

Kir(i)vì "godmother."

Kir(i)vò "godfather."

Kris, krìsi

The primary meaning of this word is "law" or "judgment"; thus **e Devlèski kris,** "God's law," or **e manušèski kris,** "the law of man." But it is most familiarly associated by Romanologists with the tribunal or hearing which is part of the internal legal system amongst Vlax Rroma. For some people, **kris** is used to refer only to Romani law, while **zakòno,** *q.v.,* is used to refer to non-Romani law. The word is from the Greek κρίσις. It may be a retention of the Indian *nasab* or *panchayat,* modified by a similar social structure found among Balkan villagers. **Krìsi** in Polish and Russian Vlax. There are similar judiciary councils of elders among other Romani groups, though not referred to by this name.

Kris bandjì

A **kris** resulting in a negative decision by the **kris-nitorja.**

Kris čačì

A **kris** resulting in a positive decision by the **kris-nitorja.**

Kris Rromanì

The tribunal or hearing which is part of the internal legal system amongst Rroma.

Krisàki čhib

Oratorical style of speaking Romani; heard at **krisà** but also at weddings, funerals, and other formal occasions. It is not appropriate for younger people to use this register.

Krisàki putjèrja

Power of the Romani tribunal.

Krisàko

"legal."

Krisàko kher

"courthouse." Usually in a non-Romani context.

Krisàlo raj

"judge."

Krisimè

"judged, sentenced."

Krisisardilèm

"I was sentenced, I was condemned." Also **krisisàjlem.**

Krisìv

"I sentence, I judge, I condemn."

Krisnitòri

"judge at a **kris.**" Also **kriznitòri, krisitòri.**

Kukaštàra

"lavatory," an impolite word. **Thòjla** in American Vlax (< "toilet").

Kumpànja

A work alliance, of colleagues, family members, or members of unrelated Romani groups, which may either last for just one job or be of more or less permanent duration. Also pron. **kumpanìja.**

Kununìl

"he performs marriage." **Vlax.**

Kununimè	"married." **Vlax.**
Kununimòs	"wedding ceremony." **Vlax.**
Kununisàvel	"he gets married." **Vlax.**
Kùrva	"immoral woman; adulterous wife." **Vlax** word. Also **xàndra, lubnì, lugnì, bèštija.**
Kurvàri	A man who solicits the company of immoral women; a whoremonger.
Kutàri	"What's-his-name, so-and-so," applied to a male.
Kutàrka	"What's-her-name, so-and-so," applied to a female.
Ladž	"Shame, disgrace, immodesty, immorality."
Ladžajmòs	"Shame, disgrace, immodesty, immorality" (**Vlax** dialect).
Ladžàv	"Shame, disgrace, immodesty, immorality" (**Vlax** dialect).
Lavo-lil	The name of a book on the dialect of the **Romanichals,** *q.v.,* by nineteenth-century British writer George Borrow, *lit.* "word-book." Despite its many errors, it has been the most widely consulted work on the Romani language, even though it is of minimal value for the understanding of any other dialect, especially **Vlax,** *q.v.*
Lìra	Fifty dollars. **Pandž lìri** = $250.
Lovàri	A **nàcija,** *q.v.,* of the **Rrom,** *q.v.,* pl. **Lovàra.**
Lovè	"money," a plural noun.
Lubnì	The same as **kùrva,** *q.v.*
Mačvànka	A **Mačvàno** woman, pl. **Mačvànči.**
Mačvàno	One of the Vlax-speaking **nàciji,** *q.v.,* originating in the region of *Mačva* in eastern Serbia (although one suggested etymology is < Serbian *mač,* "sword"). Well represented in Australia and the Americas, but not in Europe itself. Pl. **Mačvàja.**
Magerdipè	Ritual pollution, defilement. Word used in Central Romani dialects and in Polish and Russian Vlax.
Magerdò	Ritually polluted or defiled. Word used in Central Romani dialects and in Polish and Russian Vlax.
Mahàla	"district, neighborhood, Gypsy quarter." Mačvano word (see also **pòga**).

Makhardò — Ritually polluted or defiled, *lit.* "smeared," a reference to menstrual blood.

Mamì — kinship term, "grandmother."

Manger — "lawyer." Scottish Romani word (rhymes with "hanger").

Mangimòs — "begging." **Vlax.**

Manùš — A Romani population mainly inhabiting France, and closely related to the **Sìnti** and (historically) the **Romanichals.** *Lit.* "men."

Marimè — **Vlax** term meaning ritually defiled or polluted, from the Greek meaning "to make dirty." Unlike **pokelimè,** this has the additional meaning of "banished from the community because of defilement." Not the same as **gonimè,** *q.v.* Var. **maxrimè, marimè.**

Màrtja — "spirit of death."

Màrturo — a "witness," Kalderaš Vlax dialect.

Melalò — "dirty," also "shameful."

Meljardò — "made dirty."

Meretimè — "married," of a woman. **Vlax** only.

Mòkadi — Angloromani form of **makhadò,** *q.v.*

Mong — "beg," in Angloromani.

Mulò — "dead"; "the dead"; "spirits of the dead." Pl. **mulè.** The **mulè** remain in the vicinity of the family and keep watch over the activities of family members. They cause **prikàza,** *q.v.,* a signal that an individual has upset the balance required by **rromanìja,** *q.v.*

Musker — "policeman." Angloromani.

Nàcija — One of the divisions of the Romani population calling itself **Rrom,** *q.v.,* all of which speak dialects of Vlax Romani and descend from the slaveholding principalities of Wallachia and Moldavia. They include the **Kalderàša,** the **Lovàra,** the **Mačvàja,** and the **Čuràra,** among others. For some speakers, this word is used to mean these divisions themselves.

Nahija — The geographical area of jurisdiction associated with the **šàto,** *q.v.* Mačvano Vlax word.

Našalàs	"we abduct," also **našadaràs.** Sometimes the **borì,** *q.v.,* will be "kidnapped" by members of the groom's family. Variation of **Našàv.**
Našàv	"we flee." Sometimes a betrothed couple will "flee" from their families and consummate the union before the **abjàv,** thereby reducing the **dàrro,** *q.v.* (done as an economy measure).
Našipè, našimòs	"elopement."
Njàko, nijàko	A mattock, double-headed (axe and hammer), **barò's** symbol of authority.
Njàmo	"relative," pl. **njàmurja.** Vlax Romani.
Òfisa	"fortune-telling parlor." American Vlax (< Eng. "office").
Pal	Angloromani form of Common Romani **phral** meaning "brother." This has entered colloquial English, meaning "friend."
Pàle čìdo	Sìnti Romani equivalent of **magerdò,** *q.v., lit.* "put back." Also **čìdo pàle.**
Paramìča	"story," pl. **paramìči.**
Parrujmòs	"a barter, an exchange."
Parruvàv	"I trade, barter."
Pàrtija	"Share, portion of earnings," pl. **pèrci. Vlax** dialect.
Patjìv	"honor, respect, esteem." Kalderash var. = **pa(j)kìv.**
Patjivalò	"honorable." **Kalderash** var. = **pakivalò.**
Pato	"bed," a **Vlax** word adopted from Romanian. Use of this word is considered indelicate in mixed company, the euphemism **than** (*lit.* "place") being preferred.
Patrìn	"leaf," pl. **patri(n)ja.** Also "page" and "trail sign(s)." In Angloromani, **pàteran.**
Pečàta	"brooch, badge," formerly worn on the breast by the **Rrom Baro** to indicate his status.
Pekàla	"impurity," var. of **pekelimòs.**
Penning hokabens	"lying, telling lies," Angloromani.
Phandadò[1]	"arrested, jailed."
Phandadò[2]	"off limits, spoken-for," of a town "owned" by a family or **vica,** *q.v.*

Phurì	"a female elder."
Phurì daj	"grandmother," Northern Romani. Equiv. to **mami** in Vlax Romani.
Phurimòs	"age." A distinction is made between children and post-climacteric adults (both outside of child-producing age), on the one hand, and persons in their young and middle adult years, who are able to reproduce and who have a "sexual" identity, on the other. The judgment of an older person (e.g., at a **kris**) is considered to be more balanced because it is less subjective and emotional than that of a younger adult.
Phurò	"a male elder."
Phurò them	"old country." American Rroma more commonly refer to any country in Europe, and to Europe generally, as the **themà,** "countries."
Pirrimòs	"gossip, slander; informing (to police)."
Pirrìv	"I inform (police)." Also **pupuìv.**
Počitajimòs	"dignity, esteem."
Počitajimòs rromanò	"high esteem within the Romani community." *See also* **rrùndo.**
Podàrka	"gift, present."
Pòdja[1]	"slip, underskirt," *cf.* **telunì rròtja.**
Pòdja[2]	"menstruation."
Pòga	"district, neighborhood, area of jurisdiction."
Pokàla	"sentence" (decided upon by the **krisnitòrja**).
Pokelimè	"defiled, impure." Also **pekelimè.**
Pokelimè and'o muj	"foul-mouthed."
Pokelimòs	"defilement, impurity." Also **pekelimè.**
Pomàna	"a wake." Pl. **pomèni.**
Pomenjàke càlja	Clothing worn by the one representing the deceased at a **pomàna,** *q.v.*
Porradì	"deflowered." *See* **Porradì bešèl.**
Porradì bešèl	She is sitting immodestly with the legs apart," *lit.* "spread apart" (applied to females).
Porrajmòs	The Romani Holocaust (1933–1945), also **Barò Porrajmòs,** *lit.* "the great devouring, raping (of the Romani people)." *See also* **Uštavipè.**
Potjinàv	"I pay." Kalderash var. **pokinàv.**

Potjinimòs   "payment." Pronounced **pokinimòs** in Kalderash Vlax Romani.

Pràzniko   "a religious festival or feast."

Prikàza   "retribution"; misfortune or accident as a result of upsetting the balance of **kintàla,** *q.v.,* through not observing right conduct (see **vòrta Rromani fòrma**). Sometimes translated as "bad luck."

Primàko, premàko   Male equivalent of a **bori,** *q.v.,* son-in-law obliged to join wife's family, usually for economic reasons. This status is a shameful one.

Public   In American Vlax English, this applies only to the Vlax population at large, not to the non-Romani population.

Pupuimòs   "gossip, slander; informing (to police)."

Pupuìv   "I inform (police)." Also **pirrìv.**

Raklì   "non-Romani girl," as opposed to a **čhej/čhaj.**

Raklò   "non-Romani boy," as opposed to a **čhavo.**

Ròma   A word being increasingly (and inaccurately) used in English as a singular or plural noun, or even as an adjective, to mean "Gypsy"; thus "he is a Roma," "Roma language." In Romani itself, **Rromà** is a plural subject-case, masculine noun only.

Romanès   Sometimes used to refer to the **Romani** language. *See* **Rromanès.**

Ròmani   The English adjective (sometimes spelled **Romany**) for "Gypsy"; thus "the Romani people," "the Romani language." The word is also used by itself to refer to the language (*see also* **Romanes**), and sometimes as a noun to mean a Romani person ("they are Romanies").

Ròmanichal   Name of a division of the Romani migration which entered France and then Britain. British Romanichals have migrated to all parts of the English-speaking world. In France, spelled **romanitchel.**

Romer'd   Angloromani word meaning "married." **Romerdò** in other non-Vlax dialects. *See* **ansurimè, kununimè, meretimè.**

Rràjo   "heaven."

Rràso	Vlax word meaning "race," sometimes applied to distinguish Romani populations (as a **Rràso**) from other non-Romani **rràsurja** (pl.).
Rrestisàvav	"I accuse," also **bang jaràv, purrìv.**
Rrobìja	"jail." American Vlax. Original European Vlax meaning was "slavery."
Rròbo	"prisoner." American Vlax. Original European Vlax meaning was "slave."
Rrom	"person of Romani descent." However, because of their isolation, the Romani populations who were held in slavery for between five and six centuries in Romania have come to regard themselves alone as being the "real" **Rrom,** distinct from other non-Rrom Gypsy populations such as the **Sìnti** or the **Bašaldè.** Nevertheless, all non-Rrom populations refer to their culture and language as **Romani,** and use the word **Rom** (rather than the specifically Vlax **Rrom**) to mean either "Gypsy" or "husband." Pl. either **Rrom** or **Rromà.**
Rrom amerikàča	Roma from the United States.
Rromanì butjì	Romani matters, typical Romani affairs.
Rrom barò	The leader of a Romani community.
Rrom kanadàča	Roma from Canada.
Rrom krisàko	Experienced older Rom with a reputation for fairness in serving as a **krisnitòri,** *q.v.* Pl. **Rrom(à) krisànge.**
Rrom krisòngo	A **Rrom** who attends **krisà** as a **krisnitòri,** reputed for his fairness and whose participation is frequently sought.
Rrom mesik(an)àča	Mexican Vlax Rom (pl.).
Rrom themènge	Rroma from Europe.
Rromàle čhavàle	Term of address to a group, *lit.* "married men, unmarried men."
Rromanè čhavorrè	"Romani boys," label of emphatic affirmation (because of the intentional tautology).
Rromanès	The adverb derived from **Rromanì,** meaning "Gypsily, in the Romani way." In Romani this grammatical form is used when referring to the

language; thus **vrakeràv Rromanès,** "I speak in the Romani way," i.e., "I speak Romani." Using this adverbial form in English as though it were a noun is incorrect.

Rromanestàn
The notional homeland of the Romani people.

Rromanì
The singular subject-case adjective derived from **Rrom.** Its use (as **Romanì**) for the name of the language in English derives from its function as a feminine singular adjective in **Rromanì čhib,** "Romani language."

Rromanì fòrma
"correct behavior, behavior according to **Rromanija.**"

Rromanìja
"Romani culture, behavior, and values"; "Romani-ness." Any behavior likely to defile or pollute, and therefore disturb **kintàla** and bring **prikàza** and **bibàxt,** is **gadžikanìja,** or "non-Romani ways." The form is Vlax (**-ija** < Romanian); in other dialects it is **Romanipè(n).**

Rromnì
"married Romani female."

Rrùndo
"rank, status." **Dav tut and'o rrùndo,** "I hold you in esteem."

Rupunì rovlì
Clan leader's baton; *lit.* "silver rod." **Vlax.**

Šàto
In American Vlax, a local leader or representative (< Eng. "(big)shot"). The wife of such an individual is a **šatàjka.**

Šàtra
"clan, vica." Term used among Polish and Russian Vlax speakers; *lit.* "awning, tent, canopy." *Cf.* **cèrxa.**

Selìja
"bridal veil," also **vàla.**

Sèmno
Same as **rupunì rovlì,** *q.v., lit.* "symbol, sign." Vlax romani.

Šerèngro
"head man, leader," in Northern Romani dialects.

Šerèskro
"head man, leader," in Northern Romani dialects.

Šerò Rrom
"head man, leader." Common term in European Romani; usually **šato** in North America. Also **šorò Rrom.**

Sìnto
Member of a division of the Romani migration which moved into northern Europe, pl. **Sìnti.** Today, **Sìnti** are found from France to Russia, and as far south as Austria and northern Italy. They

	are particularly associated with Germany, and suffered the greatest losses there in the Holocaust. Also **Cìnto**.
Slàva	Amongst **Vlax** Rroma, a saint's day feast, such as St. George, St. Anne, etc.
Solàx	"an oath." **Vov del solàx**, "he takes an oath."
Stàgo	"wedding staff."
Stàriben	"jail," Angloromani dialect. Also **Stìrapen**.
Stràža	"Banishment." **Vlax** dialect.
Stražimè	Banished from the community. **Vlax** dialect.
Šùniben	"a hearing." Northern dialects.
Surručimòs	"intent."
Surručìv	"I intend (to do something)."
Svatàš	"spokesman, speaker."
Svàto	"word."
Svedòko	"a witness," **Mačvàno Vlax** dialect. Also **svidètelo**.
Svidetìv	"I bear witness" at a **kris**.
Tektèri	"detective." American Vlax word.
Tekterìca	"female detective." American Vlax word.
Teljàri	"dollar." **Glàbi, dàrrurja** (*q.v.*), etc., are paid in dollars counted in lìri (*see* **lìra**).
Telunì rròtja	"slip, petticoat." This garment is "unclean" and can be used to disgrace and defile a man if it is brought into contact with his head. Also **teluvì rròtja, telalujì rròtja**. *Cf.* **pòdja**.
Than	Euphemism for "bed." *Lit.* "place."
Tharajimòs	"deception."
Tharàv	"I mislead."
Ţigan	Romanian word for **Rrom**, considered extremely derogatory. Pl. **Ţigani**.
Tomùja	"incense (frankincense)," used for purifying premises.
Traš'd	"afraid," in Angloromani (Common Romani **trašanò**).
Trušùl	"cross."
Turvinipè	"advice." Also **sovèto, divinimòs**.
Uštavipè	A word for the Holocaust, *lit.* "upheaval."

Vàla	"bridal veil," also **selìja.**
Vèčera	"eve before a **slàva,**" Mačvano Vlax dialect. See **činasàra.**
Velinimòs	"slander."
Velinìv	"I slander."
Vìca	"clan," among some **Vlax**-speaking groups. A **vìca** may descend from a common ancestor, or from a common occupational group during slavery, or it may have separated from another **vìca** which had grown too big. From a Slavic word meaning "vine" or "offshoot." Pl. **vìci.** *See also* **cèxra.**
Vlax	Designation of a division of the Romani population which traces its ancestry in Europe to the former slaveholding principalities of Wallachia (hence **Vlax**) and Moldavia, now Romania. Also written **Vlach,** although this spelling can also refer to a separate and unrelated population of indigenous Romanian origin. *See* **Rrom.**
Vòrta Rromanì fòrma	The correct observance of Romani behavior and ritual necessary to maintain spiritual cleanliness and balance and to avoid **marimos.** *Lit.* "right Romani way."
Vortàko	"male partner; work partner," pl. **vortàča.**
Vozdèla	"trust."
Vudžilè	"being in debt." **Me dav lèske vudžilè,** "I make him a loan"; **me lem vudžilè,** "I borrowed." Also **udžilè.**
Vudžilimòs	"a loan; a debt."
Vužjardò	"(declared) clean," at a **kris,** after earlier having being declared **marimè.**
Vužò	"clean," both physically and/or spiritually.
Xalò	A non-Romani person, in Sìnti and other Northern European dialects of Romani.
Xanamìk	What each spouse's parent is to the other (of the same gender); in some dialects, brother- or sister-in-law. Pl. **xanamikà.**
Xoraxanò	"Muslim (especially a Balkan Turk); member of an Islamic Romani population." Pl. **xoraxanè.**
Xoxajimòs	"a lie."

Xoxajipè	"a lie; deceit." Also **xoxajimòs.**
Xoxamnì solàx	"a false oath."
Xoxamnò	"a liar."
Yéniche	The French spelling of **Jenisch,** *q.v.*
Zakòno	"law," sometimes non-Romani law in particular, as opposed to **kris.** Pl. **zakòja** or **zakònurja.**
Žandàri	"policeman." Vlax Romani. Pl. **žandàrja.**

NINE

The Rom-Vlach Gypsies
and the *Kris-Romani*

Ronald Lee

INTRODUCTION: LEADERSHIP AMONG THE ROM-VLACH GYPSIES

Before discussing the *kris-Romani*, or "Gypsy Court," it may be useful to describe the leadership structure among the large group of Rom in Canada and the United States who have been defined as the Rom-Vlach Gypsies.[1] Many Gypsiologists and writers who have written about this group have borrowed from previous sources and, in my opinion, have failed to clarify the exact nature of leadership among them. In some ways, they have created a new set of stereotypes to replace those they have attempted to demolish—for example, the semi-mythological "Gypsy Chieftain" or "tribal leader" has now been redefined as the "big man," or *baro*. Some of these modern "big men" have even been cast as all-powerful urban-gangster types in the image of the typical Hollywood godfather.[2] The term *baro* is

The opinions expressed in this article are the author's own and do not reflect the official policy of the Romani Union. As a Canadian Rom of British descent he respects the anonymity of living Roma. Those named herein are deceased, or referred to in other published sources in connection with information that itself is already public. The spelling of Romani words is his own. For equivalent spellings see Hancock, "Glossary of Romani Terms," chap. 8 in this volume.

1. The Rom-Vlach Gypsies are a widespread group of interrelated clans and families who exist in Romania, and by emigration in Western Europe and elsewhere, including in North and South America. Their Romani dialects contain a large battery of athematic items or loan words taken from the Rumanian, in contrast to the non-Vlach Romani dialects, whose speakers have borrowed words from other languages. The ancestors of the present-day Rom-Vlach were held as slaves in the former slaveholding principalities of Wallachia (hence *Vlach*, from *Vlachiya/Vlaxiya*). The term *Rom-Vlach* is used by Gypsiologists and others who study the Rom and is not a term used by the Gypsies themselves. In Romani linguistics, it is a convenient term to categorize the Romani dialects spoken by this particular group.

2. Peter Maas, *King of the Gypsies* (1975). The slant of this book, based on dubious source material, presents a picture of an urban-gangster type (at 4ff) not in keeping with the image of its subject, "King" Tene Bimbo, held by the Rom themselves. I met him a few times in Montreal and found him an affable man, with many friends among his contemporaries who admired and respected him. The film, itself only loosely based on the book, is Hollywood fiction bearing little reality to the man and his milieu.

of Indic origin (Hindi: *bara*) and appears in the Romani expression, *O Rom O Baro*, contracted to *O Baro Rom* and finally to *O Baro*. Basically this means "the important Gypsy," since the adjective *baro* means not only big but also important, significant, mighty, and powerful. "Big man" is an anthropological term often used to define the leader of a primitive group that lacks any organization beyond the extended family or clan level. Today, the word *baro* is being replaced among Canadian and American Rom-Vlach groups by the term *shato*, a contraction of *O Baro Shato*, the bigshot. Again, these *baré* (pl.) and *shaturia* (pl.) have been erroneously defined as the only form of leaders among these groups.

The reality is that the leadership among the Rom-Vlach can be divided between the *shaturia*, whose leadership extends to the territorial/economic areas of Rom-Vlach society, and the patriarchs or *puré* (elders, from *puró*, elder). The latter's area of influence centers around the spiritual, traditional, and religious areas as well as around the *kris-Romani*, or assembly of Rom elders convened to administer justice under the *Romaniya* (laws of the Rom). A *shato*, however, can resort to the *kris-Romani* to enforce Romani law in territorial disputes. Like any other Rom, he must do this within the framework of Romani law (*Romano Zakono*). Even a *shato* can be accused of a defiling offense and forced to defend himself before the assembly of judges.

Among the Canadian and American Rom-Vlach, the *shaturia* are not elected or appointed by the state, as among some non-Vlach Gypsy groups such as the *Polska* Rom (Polish Gypsies),[3] but are self-selected from within the group. There is, however, a tendency for them to be dynastic. The son of a *shato*, not necessarily the eldest, often will try to assume his father's role after the latter's retirement or death. One reason for this practice is that the son may have been trained or groomed for the role by his father. Another reason might be that the family wishes to retain its hold on the territory and on its status among other Gypsy families. To cement the power in his own immediate family, a *shato* often will marry off his sons and daughters into families of other *shaturia* in different cities or in different territories within the same megalopolis (e.g., New York or Los Angeles). These in-law families can be counted on for support when the time comes for the son to assume his father's role. All Rom families practice clan alliance through marriage in order to gain allies and to have the right to work in the territories controlled by their in-laws, in reciprocal arrangements.

Among the Rom in Montreal, for example, the leadership has run from the grandfather (first generation Canadian-Rom) to his third son and then to the third

---

3. Jerzy Ficowski, *The Gypsies in Poland* (1990). In the eighteenth century, "Gypsy Kings" in Poland were appointed by the rulers. Later, after 1918, the Polish Gypsies themselves chose one of their own leaders. *Kalderash* (Rom-Vlach) kings in Poland in this century seem to have appointed themselves. Many from the Kwiek family succeeded one another and some tried to extend their control over the long-established indigenous Polish Gypsy groups (the non-Rom Vlach), who naturally resented this (id. at 54ff). Lately, the rulership of the Polish non-Rom Vlach Gypsies also has tended to become dynastic (id. at 62f).

son's eldest son, who is the current *shato*. Sometimes leadership will run in the same family but not through lineal descent; a brother or cousin might assume the role of a deceased *shato*. While the role of a *shato* basically is to defend the territory of his *kumpaniya* (territorial group) from other Rom, he also helps those in the *kumpaniya* obtain justice from non-Gypsy courts and assists in other ways wherever influence and connections can be useful. He also is eligible to sit as a judge on the *kris-Romani* if so requested and approved, but there he has no more power or influence than any other Rom. A *shato* is not necessarily a *Rom-krisungo*—a man well-versed in the workings of the *kris*—nor a *krizinitori* (judge), though occasionally an elderly *shato* might attain that status.

The *shato* is the temporal leader of an economic unit usually referred to as a *kumpaniya*, a group of Rom living in a territorial area which they claim collectively as their exclusive working domain for the Gypsy economic strategies they practice. Such activities may include fortune-telling done by the women and the trades worked by the men, such as dealing in used cars and trailers, automobile body work and the servicing of restaurant kitchens. Other strategies followed by individual members of the local *kumpaniya*, such as dealing in jewelry or real estate, are not considered territorial. Not all families living in a large or numerous *kumpaniya* are necessarily related, but they must all be Rom-Vlach. Gypsies of other groups who are not Rom-Vlach do not constitute a threat, and are allowed to live in the territory and follow any work strategy they wish as long as it does not bring the attention of the law enforcement agencies onto all the Gypsies living in the territory. The *shato* would have no control over non-Vlach Gypsies but he could pinpoint them to his contacts on the local police force and explain that his people are not engaged in these activities.

An understanding of a typical *shato* and his area of influence might be offered through the example of a *shato* in Montreal in the early 1980s. He lived there with his family/clan members, composed of his married sons and their families, married daughters and their families, some of his brothers, their wives and children, and a few Rom-Vlach families either distantly related by blood or by marriage, including even a small group of immigrant *Lovara* families originally from Yugoslavia. Such general descriptions of any *kumpaniya* are useful only at the time given. Conditions will change, some families will leave, others will arrive, fortune-telling by-laws could alter, an economic slump could depress one of the major work strategies, or any one of a wide variety of unforeseen factors could have a demographic impact on any existing *kumpaniya*, including the demise of the current *shato*.

By the end of the 1980s, the Montreal *shato* did pass away and his son, who assumed his role, then closed the town to all outsiders who were not directly related to him, except for a few whose track record showed them to be unlikely to create problems. This decision was the indirect result of the actions of the "Gypsy Squad," a special police unit of Gypsy hunters formed to crack down on "Gypsy crime and Gypsy-type crime" (sic) in Toronto, formed along the lines of similar squads in the United States. This new "Gypsy Squad" began harassing Rom-Vlach Gypsies in Toronto, and some families decided to move to Montreal, where there was then no such squad. Since the families who wanted to relocate were naturally those most likely to attract the attention of the Toronto "Gypsy Squad," the Montreal *shato* became apprehensive and visualized possible negative ramifications resulting in a police crackdown on all Gypsies in Montreal. To protect his *kumpaniya*, he placed Montreal off-limits, or *pandadó* (closed), to all Rom-Vlach newcomers in general, so as not to alienate any particular family from elsewhere. Efforts by other Rom-Vlach family heads who wanted to relocate to Montreal had to be made cautiously through their non-Gypsy attorneys, who would contact the attorney representing the Montreal *shato*. If these feelers were favorably received, those interested in relocating were then invited to discuss the matter at a *diwano* (informal meeting).

Basically, the Montreal *shato* did not want any Rom-Vlach families moving into his territory (*naihiya*) who might try to work *buzho*, or witchcraft swindles, which would then have an adverse effect on the women of his *kumpaniya* who were operating the traditional and honest reader-adviser parlors. The usual reaction from City Hall when some Rom-Vlach families are working *buzhuria* (plural of *buzho*, a bundle) is to run all the Gypsies out of town and rescind all licensing of reader-adviser parlors, thus punishing the innocent along with the guilty. A "closed town" indicates to Rom outsiders that the local *shato* has an understanding with the local law-enforcement officials that he will not allow his own women to work these swindles. Because many cities in both Canada and the United States are "closed," there is a floating population of Rom-Vlach families who have committed such swindles and created problems in the past. They are unwelcome in most towns and they, in turn, sometimes try to overthrow a weak *shato* and take over his town.

In the mid-1980s there was a lucrative reader-adviser business in Los Angeles. When one swindling family did manage to set up shop and pull off a *buzho*, the late John Merino, the local *shato* of the area (*kumpaniya*) in question, had the money refunded and promptly evicted the interlopers. In the case of Montreal, the crackdown in Toronto also drove some immigrant Gypsy families to Montreal who were not Rom-Vlach and who were allegedly involved in petty crime such as shoplifting, since no one had been charged or convicted among those who came to Montreal. There was little the Montreal *shato* could do, except to inform his police contacts that these were not his people nor under his influence. These families did not engage in *buzho* but in petty crime such as shoplifting, according to police spokespeople who were quoted in the local press.

Part of the local *shato's* role is to serve as a "fixer" or adviser between families in his *kumpaniya* and non-Gypsy agencies with which they are unfamiliar. He can often help them obtain a driver's license, birth certificate, or related document, and help them find suitable housing or a reliable non-Gypsy attorney. To facilitate this and for his own needs, he goes out of his way to cultivate friendships with important non-Gypsies, such as social workers, detectives, attorneys, private investigators, journalists, members of the clergy, businessmen, and others. Sometimes these special non-Gypsies are asked to become godparents of the *shato's* children or of children in the family-clan network of the *shato*. This is a purely symbolic gesture because there are always genuine Rom *kirivé* (godparents). *Shaturia* such as these learned how to put into practice the old Romani saying, *Rom le Romensa tai Gazho le Gazhensa*—to be a Rom among other Rom and a non-Gypsy among non-Gypsies.

Another function of a *shato* is to collect the *kidemos* (voluntary financial contribution). If a Rom family in his *kumpaniya* falls on hard times, he will go to each family in turn and ask the family head to donate some cash to help the family out. The money collected is then given to the needy family and does not have to be repaid. The family in question is never told who contributed, how much was contributed, or who did not contribute.

How an individual *shato* administers his territory varies according to the personality of the individual. Some *shaturia* are remembered with affection, others amass enemies and inherit a bad reputation. Most are somewhere in between these two poles, but regardless, according to Rom belief, animosity is supposed to end with death: *Mek les Le Devlesa*—Leave him to God to be judged.

In his description of the *Polska* Rom (Polish Gypsies), Ficowski described the elected *Shero Rom.*[4] At one time, this "head Gypsy" was elected in Poland; and the term *shero* (head) can be found in many Romani dialects from different groups, as in Welsh Romani *shereskero,* in Anglo-Romani *sherengero,* and in various *Sinti* dialects, all with the meaning of "head man" or "leader." In many ways, these men served the same function as the modern *shato* among the Canadian and American Rom-Vlach. Another term used by Ficowski was *baro shero,*[5] which he seemed to believe was synonymous with the term *shero Rom.* Actually, *baro shero* means an ostentatious person, show-off, or "swelled-headed person." It is used in this sense by both the Rom-Vlach and by non-Vlach Gypsies such as the Hungarian *Romungere* and others. It is not a valid term to describe leadership among the Rom of any group.[6] Ficowski also states that the *shero Rom* had jurisdiction over pollution offenses;[7] how-

---

4. Id. at 56.

5. Id. at 56. From Ficowski's text, one might speculate that the original *Shero Rom* was a genuine elected or appointed leader of the Polish Gypsies and that the later term, *Baro Shero,* was more of an expression of ridicule and grudging acceptance of a self-imposed leader who flaunted his "authority" by ostentatious behavior. This is certainly the meaning of *Baro Shero* today among Gypsies of many groups.

6. There is a widely held belief among many Gypsiologists that a Rom who is physically big (tall or overly corpulent) has more of a chance of achieving leadership as the "big man" simply because of his impressive size or the fact that he might have a large head. It is true that Rom in general are impressed by corpulent people. They have retained the old European fallacy that only the affluent can afford enough food to become corpulent, and must therefore, be successful, while thin people are not astute enough to be able to afford enough food to become overweight. However, not all *shaturia* are tall or corpulent.

There are even a few examples of Rom-Vlach women who have assumed the leadership of the local *kumpaniya* after the demise of their husbands, though typically they had adult sons to help them.

7. Id. For the right of the Polish Gypsy *Shero Rom* to judge offenders against the Romani pollution laws, see id. at 66-7. Among the present-day Rom-Vlach, the *kris-Romani* would have this function through the appointed judge and his panel of peers.

ever, this is not the case with the Canadian or American *shato*. These offenses are dealt with by the *kris-Romani*.

Terms like *shato* and *baro* are used internally by the Rom-Vlach. When such a leader presents himself to the outside world, he generally uses a term of leadership he feels will have some impact on those it is intended to impress. Historically, we read of Gypsy "counts," "dukes," "earls," and of course "kings." "Gypsy king" is a term that has been hacked to death by cub journalists who often get sent out in the rain to cover the funeral of a Gypsy *shato*. Somehow the term fits nicely into the journalistic Gypsy mythology, along with horse-drawn caravans, dancing bears, tambourine-playing Gypsy temptresses, knife duels over the clan virgins in the moonlight etched by the flickering flames of the tribal campfire, and other storybook fiction. I have on file a plethora of clippings from a wide variety of publications, in many languages, dating back over a long period of time, reporting the deaths, marriages, and coronations of enough Gypsy kings and queens to populate the largest *kumpaniya* in the modern American megalopolis. As Russel Demitro, a former Montreal *shato* once told me wryly: *Sa krayla sam kana meras*—"We're all kings when we die." Out of respect, the family of a decreased *shato* will usually tell the press that their "king" has died. Some *shaturia,* however, take themselves a little too seriously and will sometimes even have gold crowns made for themselves and their "queens" by custom jewelers. They will wear these crowns at Rom gatherings and flaunt the image of the *baro shero* (show-off) to the press, as the reporters devour this ethnic romanticism for the benefit of their readers. It goes without saying that such crowns have no impact on the Rom, who simply regard the *shato* as an eccentric.

At least two Canadian Gypsy leaders sported such crowns in the 1970s. The late *shato* of Montreal and his wife each owned one, as did Reszo Dudas in Toronto. In the United States, there have been many Gypsy kings in the past, but one colorful *shato* has remolded his image to something more suitable for a republic. He has presented himself as Senator James Marks II (there is no first) in Spokane, Washington. When interviewed by the press, instead of a crown, he usually wears a hand-crafted cowboy stetson and the entire J.R. Ewing outfit, complete with snakeskin Tony-Lama boots.

The *shaturia,* however, are not the cornerstones upon which Rom society is built. Just as the death of a stallion does not mean the end of a herd of wild horses, so the death of a *shato* never implies the demoralization and destruction of those under his influence. There are always others who will gladly assume the role. The modern American and Canadian *shato* is probably the result of urbanization of the Rom-Vlach, where urban territory has assumed a much greater importance compared to the administration of a nomadic group. Closer contact with non-Gypsies has resulted in the need for a local spokesman who can represent the *kumpaniya* to the outside authorities on a daily basis. In large urban centers such as Los Angeles, New York, or Chicago, there are many Rom-Vlach territorial divisions, each with its own *kumpaniya* and *shato*. We may thus accept that the modern *shato* is more the product of the urbanized Rom-Vlach culture than a remainder of the type of leadership that existed in Europe, rural America, and Canada when the Rom-Vlach were more nomadic.

Spiritual Leadership

The other level of leadership among the Rom-Vlach that has not yet received much attention from Gypsiologists or has been confused erroneously with the role of the *shaturia* is that of the patriarchs. This group of men, called *puré* (elders), are the custodians of the Rom laws and traditions. To the Rom, age implies wisdom. Thus, the patriarchs are the spiritual heads of large, multi-generational, extended families. They serve also as *krizinitoria* (judges) on the *kris-Romani*. While it is true that any Rom can serve as a judge on the *kris,* those who are eagerly sought after are the *Rom-krisunge,* men well versed in the workings of the court and of legal precedent. The patriarchs, by virtue of their age and experience, are storehouses of knowledge. This knowledge is vitally important in the administration of the *kris,* since nothing is written down. Also, since the *puré* are older men who have passed through their "wild youth," they are less inclined to be impulsive, overly judgmental, or vindictive.

Though somewhat conservative in their outlook, *puré,* by virtue of their life experience, attained a degree of spirituality, wisdom, and impartiality. They might be considered the equivalent of sachems or medicine men among the American Indian cultures, while the *shaturia* could be compared to the hunting chiefs or war chiefs. I prefer the term "patriarchs" for these spiritual elders, but among the Rom-Vlach they are addressed as *Kako Kutari* (Uncle So-and-So).[8] Their female counterparts are addressed as *Bibío Kutarka* (Auntie So-and-So). Uncle in the vocative is *Kako* and Auntie is *Bibío;* the person's name is then added to this, usually also in the vocative inflexion. Thus, Uncle Steve would be *Kako* Stevane or Auntie Mary would be *Bibío* Maro (vocatives of Stevo and Mara). The "aunties" serve to counsel younger women of the group and to instruct them in the female lore of the Rom, which is taboo for the males of the group. They are also the source of the semi-mythological *Phuri Dai* (Old Mother), so beloved of romantic writers and armchair Gypsiologists.[9] These also have their equivalents among some native cultures in Canada, where the Tribal Mother or Clan Mother serves a similar function.

8. The term *kak* or 'uncle' is used in this way by other cultures. The 'uncle' in question need not be related by blood or marriage. He is simply a patriarch among the Rom-Vlach who is a spiritual figure in the community. The word *kako* is the vocative inflection of the nominative *kak* and is used in direct address. The 'auntie' or *bibi* is the female counterpart of *kak.*

9. The *phuri dai,* or "old mother," is not an expression employed by Rom-Vlach speakers. It has its origin mainly in a plethora of novels about Gypsies and in nonfiction of dubious authenticity. See Jean-Paul Clébert, *The Gypsies* 162 (1967). Clébert's reference is to *Sinti* Gypsies, who are not a Rom-Vlach group, and even among this group the term is not in widespread use to denote the role attributed to the *phuri dai* by the author. Each Gypsy group must be treated separately since customs and beliefs held by

The patriarchs are also well versed in family and clan history. They can delve back through their own lifetimes and recall much of what they were told by their parents and grandparents. Rom history only extends as far as these patriarchs, collectively, can remember. Anything before that is lost in the night of time. Patriarchs are also the only source of family genealogy for their own and related families. Any *shato* who lives long enough will eventually attain the status of a patriarch by virtue of his age and position in society.

The patriarchs also perform ceremonies and fulfill functions among the Rom that the *shaturia* do not. If a Rom believes the house he has just moved into is *bibaxtaló* (bringing ill-fortune) he will ask a patriarch from his family to purify it. The elder will do this by passing through each room with a tray containing burning *tomuya*, the special Greek incense that the Rom-Vlach use for ceremonies in Canada. He will also recite a prayer to Sainte Anne or some other patron saint asking this religious figure to drive out the evil and restore the host's *baxt* (good karma). The patriarchs marry Rom under the old ceremony of bread, salt, and wine. They officiate at the feasts of the dead (*pomani*), at which they first purify the feast table by passing around it with a tray of burning incense and then recite the benediction and invoke the presence of the ancestral dead to partake of the feast and perform other spiritual tasks. At this ceremony, they also purify the clothes to be worn by the person representing the deceased (*pomenake tsalia*) by the use of burning incense and by saying a prayer. In these and similar ceremonies, the patriarchs are actually performing religious rites usually allocated to priests, witchdoctors, or medicine men in other societies.

Since the Rom follow what can best be described as a folk religion with a veneer of Christianity, the patriarchs are the de facto religious leaders of the Rom community. The belief system of the Rom, from the concept of purity and defilement to the belief in *baxt* (good karma), personal respect (*pakiv*), dignity in the community (*potchitayimos Romano*), shame (*lazhav*), and the *Romaniya* are all aspects of an ancient folk religion originating from pre-Christian sources, mostly in India. The veneer of Christianity grafted onto this basic core, such as the *slavi* (feasts honoring a saint), pilgrimages such as to Sainte Anne in Canada, the use of the clergy and churches for baptisms and funerals, and other visibly Christian elements are simply the overtones of a host-culture religion accommodated into this pre-Christian Rom folk religion, much like voodoo of the former African slaves in the West Indies is a mixture of an original African religion and an overlay of host-culture Christianity.

The fundamental belief in *baxt*, usually translated as "luck" by non-Gypsy writers, is a far cry from the Las Vegas gambler who wanders into a strip casino with a rabbit's foot in his pocket. To the Rom, luck does not happen haphazardly. It

---

one group are not necessarily applicable to other groups of Gypsies. The equivalents of the Rom-Vlach *kak* and *bibi* exist in most other Gypsy groups but the names vary along with the functions.

must be earned through following the *Romaniya* and by not antagonizing the ancestral spirits (*mulé*), which would cause them to send a *prekaza* (jinx) resulting in *bi-baxt* (bad karma). The Rom who receives such a jinx must then ask a female deity (sainte) to intercede on his behalf by throwing a *slava* (feast) in her honor. This shaktism comes from India, as does the code of purity and defilement, the Rom caste system, and the belief in God (*Del* or *Devel*) as an abstract, undefined entity.

These aspects of the Rom beliefs can be interpreted only by the patriarchs, who also are the "holy men" who administer the ceremonies connected with them. Since they are also the judges of the *kris-Romani*, the patriarchs, again, are best suited to understand and administrate these religious beliefs at the *kris*. Finally, once a man has passed sixty among the Rom, he is considered to have attained what they call "sainthood," since he is no longer supposed to be or assumed to be sexually active. In essence, as in Hinduism, he has passed from the realm of the physical and the carnal into the realm of the spiritual and the meditative.

The role of matriarchs among the younger *Romnyá* (wives) is equally important. It is to the matriarchs that the younger women go to seek advice, to interpret dreams and omens, and to learn about the intricacies of the "secret mysteries" concerning the women's role in the code of ritual purity and defilement. Most Rom men are unaware of many of these, and simply for a man to ask women about them or to discuss them in public could result in his being declared *pukelimé ando mui* (dirty in the mouth), resulting in social avoidance by his peers. These older women also have a vast store of life experience that they can draw from. They also fulfill a religious role in their community.

Fortune-telling, or what today is called "reading," is also a part of the Rom folk religion. It is connected not only with predicting the future for money (a work strategy), but also with herbal lore and white magic. The term *drabarimos*, used by the Rom-Vlach today for "fortune-telling," best explains this. The root is *drab* (drug, medicament, from Sanskrit *dravya*) and originally the term *drabarimos* encompassed the use of herbs and drugs in healing and magic. As late as the 1960s some Canadian Rom-Vlach matriarchs were reputed to be able to lay curses and to work *farmichi* (magic, again related to drugs and herbs through Greek and connected with English "pharmacy"). In nomadic days, these older women were able to use herbal remedies to induce labor, cure ailments, and provide other "medical services" for the women of the group as midwives and folk gynecologists. Like their male counterparts, a woman who passes through her menopause among the Rom becomes sanctified (*swunsomé*), since she is no longer able to bear children and thus no longer able to defile men. She then becomes a spiritual "auntie."

The male elders then become *krizinitoria* (plural of *krizinitori*, judge) and form the nucleus of available patriarchs from which the younger Rom can choose the *krizinitori o Baró* (supreme judge) they want to represent them at the *kris*. He will then suggest a small body of his peers as co-judges and advisers. Age, however, is not the sole criterion. Some relatively young men who have gained a widespread reputation as *Rom-krisunge* (experts in Rom law) can also be asked to serve as judges because of their past experience in *krisake shinemata* (rendering of verdicts in the *kris*).

Social Organization and Rom Identity

The primary identity of any member of the Rom-Vlach group is the family. The individual Rom-Vlach Gypsy then belongs to an extended *familiya*, which along with other numerous families forms a *vitsa* (clan), and a large number of *vitsi* (plural of *vitsa*) form a *natsiya* or nation. To put it simply, if a man's name in English is Frank Demitro, his English family name will be Demitro. He might then belong to the clan of *Mineshti*, which is his *vitsa* stemming from his father's clan. All the other *Kalderash* clans belong to the *Kalderash natsiya*, or nation. There has been much confusion among non-Gypsy authorities relating to this family-clan-nation identity. Some have denied the existence of the nations and called the *Kalderash* group a *vitsa* (clan). In the Rom reality, there are four major nations—the *Kalderash* (coppersmiths), *Lovara* (horse traders), *Machvaya* (disputable etymology), and *Churara* (sievemakers). Other Rom-Vlach groups such as the *Karpati* of Hungary are not well represented in Canada and the United States.

Gypsies not of the Rom-Vlach nations, even if they speak inflected dialects of Romani which are more or less intelligible with the Rom-Vlach, are not considered to be a part of the clan-nation grouping and thus not *Rom Amarendar* (our kind of Gypsies). The other Gypsy groups respond by claiming that the Rom-Vlach of the Gypsy nations are not the same kind of Rom as they are. One genuine Rom-Vlach nation that has been slandered by non-Gypsy writers, beginning with Jan Yoors, is the *Churara*, whom he labelled the "knifers" or "murderers."[10] The etymology is *churo*, meaning a sieve, and thus *Churara* are known as "Sieve Makers." *Kalderash* comes from Rumanian *Kalderari* (Tinker), while *Lovara* stems from the Hungarian word *lò* and means Horse Traders. The origin of the term *Machvaya* has been debated. Modern Gypsiologists think it comes from *Machva*, claimed to be a region in Serbia from where they migrated to Canada and the U.S. It is more likely to stem from Serbian *mač* (sword) and thus mean "Sword Makers" or "Weapon

---

10. Jan Yoors, *The Gypsies* (1967). For Yoor's erroneous etymology of *Tshurara* (Leg. *Churari*) see at 128, where he theorizes that the origin or root of the word is *tshuri* (knife) and thus might mean the "knifers" or "murderers". Many later writers picked this up and perpetuated the myth, which is widely held among Gypsiologists. According to the grammatical rules of Rom-Vlach Romani, the root element of *churi* would give *churiash*, which is an actual word in the language meaning "knife-grinder." I have heard Rom-Vlach using the term *churiash* to mean "slasher" or "stabber" in the term *O Jack O Churiash* when they were discussing a movie they had seen on TV about Jack the Ripper. The word *churo* (sieve) on the other hand, takes the affix-*ari*, thus giving *Churari*, which means a Maker of Sieves. This is the explanation given by the *Churari* themselves when asked. See also the article by Derek Tipler in 48 *Journal of the Gypsy Lore Society*, parts 1–2, at 30 (1969), where he describes a *Churara* clan in Italy and correctly defines the origin of the term as "Sieve Makers."

Makers." This was a trade followed by Rom-Vlach Gypsies in the Balkans during and after the Turkish rule.[11]

The *vitsa* names are often patronymic, recalling some distant and usually forgotten ancestor of the group, such as the *Grofeshti* (from Grofo) or the *Zurkeshti* (from Zurka). The two main Canadian Rom-Vlach clans, both *kalderash*, are the *Mineshti* and the *Papineshti*. Both are hotly disputed as to their etymology, even by patriarchs of the groups concerned.[12] It is doubtful if anyone has been able to compile a list of all the Rom-Vlach clans in the United States, Canada, and elsewhere. Some clans have become so large that they have split off into new *vitsi*.[13] This process is continuing.

The Rom-Vlach person has no surname in Romani. If a man was christened *Babi* (Bob), for example, in order to identify himself to others of the group, he would use his own Christian name combined with the genitive inflection of his father's Christian name. Thus, if Bob's father was called *Stevo* (Steve), he would identify himself as *O Babi le Stevosko* (Bob, the son of Steve, literally Steve's Bob).[14] If this still wouldn't suffice, he could then add the Christian name of his paternal grandfather whose name (say) was *Zurka* (*O Babi le Stevosko, le Zurkasko*). To Rom from distant clans who were ñot familiar with his group, he could then add *anda'l Mineshti* (of the Mineshti clan). Since the alien host culture always demands that ethnic and linguistic minority-group members have a conventional surname that can be spelled and pronounced by bureaucrats, *Babi* will then provide them with a *nav-Gazhikanès* (non-Gypsy name) such as Bob Wilson. This non-Gypsy name is simply a rendering unto Caesar and has no significance whatsoever among the Rom. It can be discarded and replaced, and in fact, it is

---

11. It is my personal belief, after having discussed this with Rom-Vlach elders, that the true origin of *Machvaya* can be found in Serbian *mač* which means "Sword" and, by extension, "edged weapons." *Machvaya* would thus mean "Sword Makers." This was a trade followed by Rom-Vlach in the Balkans and no other existing group has this trade definition.

12. *Papineshti* seems to be fairly straightforward in its meaning of "Goose or Geese people." The most likely explanation seems to be that the clan collected goose feathers from farmers, which they either used to make feather-stuffed eiderdowns by themselves or sold to non-Gypsy factories who made bedding. The 1967 film, *Skupliaée Perja* (I Even Met Happy Gypsies), by Alexander Perović, shows Rom doing this in the Balkans in the 1960s.

Mineshti, on the other hand, seems more obscure. One story claims there was an old Gypsy woman in Serbia (*sic*) who had a large pig called Mina who used to carry her small children when the family traveled. Another story says the woman was called Mina and her children are *Mineshti*. Still another claims that the ancestor of the group was a beggar who used to call out to people to give him a *mina*, which was supposed to be a coin according to the narrators. Most likely the name is patronymic and derives from an ancestor called Mina. Modern members of the group like to claim *Mineshti* stands for "The Mean People" and thereby implies that they are people not to be trifled with.

13. The term *vitsa* is *Kalderash* only and stems from a Slavic term meaning "a tendril," "branch," "offshoot." Other groups employ different terms to define the clan, such as *Lovara tsera*, meaning "tent."

14. When two Rom-Vlach men meet for the first time, the host will ask the newcomer: *Kasko san tu?*—"Whose son are you?"

usually one of many names (aliases) that the Rom provide to Caesar or use for business purposes.[15]

Like most other Rom-Vlach Gypsies, *Babi* will have a nickname such as *Rikono* (Puppy) or *Tanko* (Tank, because of his corpulence). This could have been given to him at birth or later in childhood. Canadian Rom-Vlach men had nicknames in both English and Romani, such as Hemstitch (because the bearer always used to wear hemstitched suits), Cowboy (because he always wore cowboy hats), *Niurtso* (Sandpiper in Romani), and Chicoutimi (because he was born there).

If *Babi's* sister was called *Mara* (Mary), she would take the name of her father until she married, then switch to the genitive inflection of her husband's Christian name. Her nickname could be *Lulugi* (Flower) or *Papusha* (Dolly). These nicknames are never given to the host culture unless they become part of the non-Gypsy name provided for Caesar. Besides their genuine Romani Christian name and their Romani nickname, most Rom-Vlach women also have a number of professional names in their reader-adviser business. These change as the trade dictates.[16]

A new clan could be formed (as many are) quite easily. Let's say an immigrant Rom-Vlach man arrived today in the U.S. and married an American-born Rom-Vlach woman from a clan called *Bareshti (sic)*. He and his bride would eventually produce a large number of sons and daughters, who would then produce a large number of grandchildren. If this immigrant Rom's name was *Duyo* and he had no established relatives (clan members) in the United States or Canada, his descendants could then assume the clan name of *Duyeshti*. Their only claim to American Rom-Vlach status would be through Duyo's American-born wife and her clan (*Bareshti*). *Duyo* would most likely marry off his sons and daughters to families connected to the clan alliance structure of the *Bareshti*. The two clans would become allied while *Duyo* would have created a new *vitsa* (clan).

This clan alliance structure also plays an important role in the *kris-Romani*, since the accused will usually try to have a judge appointed who is connected to his clan alliance and not to that of the plaintiff, who in his turn will try to do the same.

---

15. Many Canadian and American Rom-Vlach men who work at a variety of trades employ different last names for each trade, or sometimes employ a reversal of the non-Gypsy name. In a hypothetical example, Michael John might be a name used for dealing in used automobiles, while John Michaels the name used for selling jewelry. When a phone call comes in, the person answering or the man himself will know immediately which business this refers to. He can then assume the role necessary for the type of business at hand. Thus, the same Rom may deal in used cars, wholesale jewelry, repair hydraulic equipment, and sandblast industrial buildings. He will then have four non-Gypsy names and four separate business cards. This is similar to a corporation which may deal through subsidiaries in real estate, investment, insurance, and consultation. The Rom simply do it in a more primitive way.

16. Women who work as reader-advisers change their names to suit their clients. In a heavily ethnic, religious neighborhood where the clients are likely to be Roman Catholic and Hispanic, the woman will choose a name like Sister Maria or Sister Fatima. If the neighborhood is more avant-garde she might use the psychic approach and call herself Crystal Astra, and if the town happens to be in the Deep South, she might call herself Dixie Belle.

Sometimes these clan alliances can be distant. For example, the late Waso Russel Demitro, the former *baro* and patriarch of the Demitro family in Canada, was a *Kalderash*, but distantly related to the Adams family of the *Machvaya* through his wife Rosie Lee-Adams, who was a sister of the late Big George Adams, the Los Angeles *baró*. Now, Russel's grandchildren have almost lost contact with the Adams family in California but continue to claim kinship with related *Machvaya* families living in British Columbia in the Vancouver area.

In Canada and the United States, the term *Kalderash* appears to be an umbrella term used to define what were originally many different groups of Rom-Vlach who migrated from Europe a few generations ago. These original groups can still be identified by their former host-country definitions, such as *Rusuria* (Russian Rom), *Serbiyaya* (Serbian Rom), *Moldovaya* (Moldavian Rom), *Gerkuria* (Greek Rom), and *Vlaxuria* (Rumanian Rom). After the emancipation of the Gypsy slaves in Rumania (1864), groups of Rom-Vlach went to different countries (they appeared in Poland in 1865)[17] and eventually, from there they migrated to the United States and Canada. Related Rom-Vlach groups were already living in countries bordering Rumania before 1864 (Besserabia and Hungary), and some of these groups migrated from there. Because they all spoke mutually intelligible dialects of Romani and followed the same basic customs, these groups merged in the United States, resulting in a levelling of dialects into what are now identified as *Kalderash* or *Machvaya*. Now, after living close to a hundred years in the United States and Canada, these original groups have become *Rom-Amerikacha* (American Rom) and *Rom Kanadacha* (Canadian Rom).

Unfortunately, these former host-country definitions and the clan-nation classifications have confused non-Gypsy writers from journalists to Gypsiologists, resulting in some meaningless and even ludicrous breakdowns of the types and groups of Gypsies in the United States and Canada, with "tribes" of Russian Gypsies, Greek Gypsies, *Kalderash* Gypsies, *Mineshti* Gypsies, Hungarian Gypsies, Coppersmith Gypsies, etc. Tribe, in its anthropological definition, is not a term that can be applied to any Gypsy group. Now new groups of Gypsies, both Rom-Vlach and non-Vlach, are appearing in both Canada and the United States to complicate further the breakdown of groups resulting from the collapse of communism, ethnic cleansing, and the rise of anti-Gypsyism in Eastern Europe and the Balkans. This has been paralleled by neo-fascism in Central and Western Europe, spearheaded by skinheads and other dangerous elements who have appeared out of the woodwork.

Rom Xoraxai (Muslim Gypsies) from the former Yugoslavia have now become established in New York and elsewhere in the United States, and other groups, such

---

17. Ficowski, supra n. 3. See photos 7–10. The Rom-Vlach *Kalderash* in these photos are wearing their Rumanian costumes, which would indicate they arrived in Poland about one year after the emancipation of 1864. They may also have been freed earlier in the 1850s, but in any event they show what ex-Rumanian *Kalderash* slaves looked like when they arrived in Poland.

as the *Lovara* (Rom-Vlach), have arrived in considerable numbers. Non-Vlach Gypsies such as the *Polska* Rom (Polish Gypsies), *Shiftari* (Bulgarian Gypsies), and *Romungere* (from the former Republic of Czechoslovakia) have also arrived in growing numbers. The United States has seen an "invasion" of Rom-Vlach Gypsies from Mexico and Central and South America who are descended from the same original stock as the American and Canadian Rom-Vlach groups. They arrived around the turn of the last century but have been living in Latin America since then. When I was visiting Los Angeles in 1993, a young American *Machvano* Rom youth was shot to death by an immigrant Mexican Rom youth in the washroom of a rented hall while attending a *Machvano* wedding. The Mexican Rom youth had been pestering or flirting with the sister of the victim in the hall and the matter of *pakiv* (respect) had resulted in a violent argument.

Among American or Canadian Rom youths, this encounter would have resulted in fisticuffs, not gunplay, and the *Machvaya* Rom were apprehensive about the *Meksikaya* (Mexican Rom) and their renowned propensity for using firearms to settle disputes.[18] America has once again become the "Promised Land" for Gypsy refugees and asylum seekers, fleeing xenophobic persecution in Europe and economic problems in Latin America. It might be wondered what impact these new groups will have on the long-established American Rom-Vlach, who have for so many generations had the exclusive territorial possession of the United States. Certainly this new wave of immigration will present future Gypsiologists with a much wider area of fieldwork among the new groups now that they have practically exhausted the potential of the long-established, homegrown American Rom-Vlach Gypsies. It might also be significant to see if these new groups will accommodate themselves to the existing *kris-Romani* of the American and Canadian Rom-Vlach, and if the existing *kris* structure will be able to exert any influence over them. Much will depend on to what degree they intermarry with the existing American Rom-Vlach and the resulting clan alliances.

The Kris-Romani *and the Marimé Code*

Compared to what it was, say even thirty years ago in Canada, the *kris-Romani* is not what it used to be in terms of its ability to administer problems that arise in the Rom-Vlach community. American Rom *shaturia* such as the late Lazo Megel

18. In Mexico, the *kris-Romani* broke down and failed to deal with a situation that resulted in violence and the deaths of some Rom who were shot to death by Rom enemies and by hired *pistoleros*. Accounts vary as to the reasons behind the vendetta, but territorial claims seem to have been at the root. In the end, the *Hulupeshti*, or "Killer Wolves," were driven out of Mexico and then resettled themselves in South America. Since then (the late 1940s) there has been peace in Mexico, but the Mexican Rom keep firearms in their homes just in case the "Killer Wolves" might return some day. This is an example of what can happen when the *kris* cannot keep a lid on an explosive situation. An account of this vendetta can be found in the article by Frédéric and Anne Max, "The Gypsies of Honduras," 48 *Journal of Gypsy Lore Society* 10–14 (1969).

(Alexandria Beach), the late John Tene (Boston), and the late John Merino (Los Angeles) have also claimed that it is not as effective in the United States as it once was. However, it still exists and its effectiveness varies from one area to another depending on the number and ages of the Rom living in certain regions plus other factors. The *Machvaya* in California are reputed by many *Kalderash* Rom to be stricter in their adherence to the *kris* than other Rom-Vlach communities in the United States. In Canada, the *kris* still functions, but the younger generation does not hold it in as much esteem as their parents did. There is more of a tendency to resort to non-Gypsy courts and lawyers during squabbles among the younger Rom, especially in the area of elopement. But as always, the *kris* is the only resort where a pollution offense is involved since only the *kris* can reinstate a Rom accused of being defiled or polluted by a *marimé* (defiling) agent or action. Normally, unless a defiling or pollution offense is the issue, the Rom will try to settle their disputes in a *diwano* (informal meeting), and thus avoid having to go through the financial and emotional cost of a *kris*.

A *diwano* is usually held at the home of a third party unrelated to either the plaintiff or the accused. Local patriarchs will be invited to attend and offer their advice. Actually, this is a form of "mini-*kris*," since the patriarchs (who are entitled to sit as judges) will hear both sides of the story, question witnesses, and arrive at what they feel is a just solution. At a formal *kris*, this is what would happen anyway, except that in a *diwano* the elders can only offer their advice and urge the two sides to accept their solution. Rom who wish to move into the territory or an existing *kumpaniya* will also ask for a *diwano*, where they will try to negotiate this entry to the satisfaction of the established *kumpaniya*. In this type of meeting, the local *shato* would also attend since the issue concerns territory. Most *kris* cases are preceded by a *diwano* (unless they involve pollution offenses) and it is usually only when the two sides in the dispute cannot reach an agreement that a *kris* ensues. The *diwano*, unlike the *kris*, is also a feature of other Rom justice systems. It might be tempting to assume that the *diwano* (from Persian *diwan*, council of state) is older than the *kris* itself because some non-Vlach groups, like the *Sinti* (Western European Gypsy groups whose non-Vlach dialects are influenced by German loan words) and the British *Romanitchels*, have rough equivalents of the *diwano*. The formal *kris*, on the other hand, is said by those who have researched it to have its origin in the justice system employed by Rumanian villagers, even though in function it resembles the Indian *panchayat*.[19]

19. The origin of the term *kris* is found in Greek even though the concept seems to be related to the Indian *panchayat*. Among non-Vlach Gypsy groups, there is or was an assembly resembling the *diwano* of the present-day Rom-Vlach where matters were discussed, and in which the elders of the group played an important role in offering advice. But, as with the Rom-Vlach today, most Gypsy groups employ the equivalent of shunning or banishment when an individual Rom is guilty of a polluting offense or fails to live up to the standards set by the group. This can range from social avoidance to actual ostracism depending on the group and the offense. Among the Czechoslovak Gypsies, historically, a person accused of being *magiardo* was ostracized. In England, the term was *mokado* among the *Romanitchels*; among the modern *Sinti*, the term is *pale-chedo*, or "put back, put down."

Since the *kris* is rooted in the Rom folk religion, the code of personal behavior, Rom customs and laws, and the concept of ritual pollution, it is difficult to explain to outsiders not familiar with these aspects of Rom culture. To a modern Canadian suburbanite, the concept of being defiled if a woman strikes him over the face with her skirt would probably seem ludicrous since he probably uses her castoff underwear to clean his car. The same man would see nothing wrong with changing the baby's diapers on the kitchen table or feeding the family dog from plates used by the family. To a Rom, all of these acts would result in serious breaches of the *Romaniya* or code of laws of the Rom. The difference between the non-Gypsy concept of cleanliness and visible dirt, on the one hand, and Gypsy purity and invisible pollution, on the other, is difficult to explain to outsiders other than those who have similar customs (Jews, Hindus, Muslims, etc.).

The *marimé* code (*Romaniya*) is a complicated system of taboos concerning areas of pollution and defilement. It also embraces a Gypsy's personal behavior towards his fellows, and its rules have been outlined by some researchers who have studied it.[20] Basically, there are certain polluting agents by which a Rom can be defiled. He can then spread this pollution to other Gypsies with whom he comes into close contact (just eating in their home is enough) unless he is formally absolved of the pollution by the *kris*. Today, these issues take up far less time in the *kris* than issues concerning the elopement of young couples and the payment of the bridal dowry (*daró*), territorial disputes, and other economic squabbles.

Because of constant "skirt tossing" (defilement of men by women), the *kris* in the 1970s gradually adopted a ruling, which spread all over Canada and the U.S., that any Rom who accused another of being polluted was to be considered polluted himself until the matter was resolved. Prior to this ruling, pollution offenses were common complications in issues where pollution was not the original offense. For example, if a young woman eloped with a man whom her parents didn't deem to be a suitable match, a squabble would erupt between the two families involved. The families might then agree to a *diwano* to discuss the matter and, upon leaving, the father of the young man might be "assaulted" by the mother of the woman. The mother might be waiting outside to strike him on the face with her *teluvi rokyá* (underskirt), thus defiling him and forcing him to go to the *kris* to be absolved of pollution. This type of "skirt tossing" was also used in revenge situations to get

---

Irish Travelers, or "Tinkers," who are not ethnic Rom, settled their differences in a fight or "punch-up" in which justice was obtained through either physical violence or the threat of this. This type of vendetta has spread to English travelers in Britain, although it is not originally a Romani custom. Spanish Gypsies often settle "matters of family honor" through a ritual knife fight in which the first cut to an opponent is usually sufficient to settle the matter.

20. Many books and articles deal with the subject of the *marimé* code or include it in a general survey of the Gypsies. One of the best articles is by Rena Cotten, "Sex Dichotomy Among the American Kalderash Gypsies," 30 *Journal of Gypsy Lore Society* 16–25 (1951). See also Rena C. Gropper, *Gypsies in the City* (1975), under the appropriate sections.

back at somebody in the community. This type of offense is now rare, although it is claimed to be more common among the *Machvaya* in California than among the *Kalderash*.

The *marimé* code also governs the type of work Rom-Vlach men are allowed to perform. There is an often-told story among the Canadian and American Rom-Vlach, which is probably partly apocryphal, about the *Rom Kulalé*, or Honey-Dipper Gypsies. They were reputed to have been a Rom-Vlach family in the United States who earned a living by emptying cesspools with tanker trucks. Because of this polluting occupation, the Rom claim, the entire family was declared *marimé* and outlawed forever—or for a very long time, depending on the individual narrator. Each family group will name another family as the "culprits," and I have even heard the same story from members of groups who, named as offenders by other Rom, will in turn point to another group! Plumbing is a trade forbidden to Rom-Vlach men. Even Gypsy doctors come under criticism. I have mentioned to Canadian Rom that there are Rom doctors in Europe who speak Romani and who are active in Rom civil rights organizations. The consensus is that if they are brain surgeons, that is acceptable, but not if they are gynecologists or proctologists. Any income connected with garbage is forbidden, from contracting the removal of industrial or municipal refuse to working as janitors or cleaners. Undertaking is another taboo profession. Thus, even Rom who deal in used vehicles will handle neither a hearse nor, especially, a refuse truck or sewage tanker.

A Rom's sex life also comes under scrutiny. The *kuntari* (balance) is for a man to be married and be the father of children. The Gypsy woman should be married and a mother. Celibate adults are frowned upon, as are women who do not bear children—both are seen as out of balance. Homosexuality is also taboo. At the pilgrimage to Sainte Anne de Beaupré in the late 1980s, I saw two gay Rom feasting at a small table on the church camping ground. They were shunned and avoided by all the other Rom pilgrims, who told me they were *pampuritsi* (gays) from the United States. They had a few non-Gypsy guests at their table and seemed oblivious to the other Rom. Gays and lesbians among the Rom conform to the norms demanded by the group. They marry and put up the front of a heterosexual existence to remain in the Rom community or they leave and live in the non-Gypsy world. There is another story, probably partly apocryphal, of a particular family in an American city who had a female member of the family nicknamed *Metchka* (she-bear); she was reputed to be a lesbian and brought *lazhav* (shame) on the family until she was accidently burned to death in a fire she started by falling asleep with a lit cigarette in her hand.

Individuals guilty or suspected of sexual abuse or incest are also ostracized. Cases of this type seldom appear before the *kris* since the *lazhav* (shame) is so great that the family in question usually deals with it internally by banishing the guilty party themselves. A few such people exist peripherally at the rim of Rom society, but they are avoided by the community at large. There have been cases where a father-in-law will try to seduce the *bori* (bride) who has married his son, usually because he is a widower or divorced. This then becomes a matter for the *kris* because of the shame attached which rebounds onto the father of the bride.

While the Rom accept the dangers of drug abuse and forbid the use of illegal drugs, they generally do not consider alcoholism to be a problem. This results in situations where alcoholic Rom get into fights and other situations at group gatherings where acts are committed or words said which lead to problems that must be settled at the *kris*. If the guilty party committed the offense during a blackout, he then cannot remember what offense he committed or is accused of committing. His defense is then to admit his guilt and say *Lya ma e rakiya*—"The whiskey took me." This will be acceptable as a defense since the Rom believe that visible or invisible forces can act on their own to influence actions of people. The action is not described in the passive, as it is in English. For example, if a Rom falls into the river and drowns, they will say: *Mudardya les o pani*—"The water killed him." If he is accidently electrocuted, *Mudardya les o ilektriko*—"The electricity killed him." Thus a Rom does not get drunk; the whiskey takes control of him and compels him to commit some act he would not commit if he were sober.

Thus, the force, not the subject, is guilty. This can be seen in the following: If a Rom is killed in an automobile accident but the vehicle is still in good shape, it will immediately be sold to a non-Gypsy. The car, in the eyes of the Rom, has become a *mudarimasko mobili* (killer car) and has become *bi-baxtaló* (a bringer of bad karma). It was thus not the Rom's careless driving or the fact that he had been drinking before the accident that caused the accident, but the car which has killed him. This is taken into account at the *kris* when it is pertinent to the trial. For example, if a Rom lends his car to another and this Rom is killed or injured in an accident while driving the car, no blame will fall on the Rom who loaned him the vehicle. However, if the car in question had been in an accident, repaired, and then loaned to another Rom, it would be considered a *bi-baxtaló* (unlucky) car and the blame could be attributed to the Rom who owned it and then loaned it to the Rom who became the accident victim.

The Rom household comes under separate rules of the *marimé* code. Male and female clothing must be washed separately and items worn above the waist must be separated from those worn below the waist. Clothing such as women's gold lamé party dresses worn at festive occasions are sent to the dry cleaners. Dishes must also be washed in special dishpans kept for this purpose. Modern Rom often use a dishwasher for family dishes. Some dishes are kept for Rom guests and others for non-Gypsies who may be invited to eat in the home, such as detectives, landlords, employees, and babysitters. Rom guests must never be served food or drink in cracked or chipped dishes—this is seen as a mark of disrespect and a polite way of saying the guest is not welcome. Rom-Vlach families will often install new toilets and sinks in a home they intend to rent for some time and the location of all water pipes must be protected from pollution. Fire, on the other hand, is a cleansing agent and whenever possible *marimé* items are burned.

In mixed company, certain topics of conversation are taboo, such as terms describing the genitals, body waste, toilets, underwear, and, of course, a person's sex

life. There are technically no swear words in Romani, as in English, or socially unacceptable words like the Anglo-Saxon "four-letter words." Thus, Rom cannot
swear as in English, but even the use of clinical and medical terms for below-the-
waist body parts is forbidden, except among members of the nuclear family. Insults yelled during arguments are usually connected with copulation, defecation,
or sex organs, for example, *Xiná ma an kyo mui*—"I defecate in your mouth." If said
in mixed company at a festive gathering, this could be considered a *pukelimé* (disgraceful) offense, but not an issue for the *kris*.

In mixed company, if a guest wishes to find out where the washroom is, he will
ask another Rom something to the effect of: *Kai pravaren tume le grasten?*—"Where
do you feed the horses?"—which in a Rom camp in the nomadic days implied the
"washroom." A woman will simply ask another woman: *Kai zhan le ranyá?*—"Where
do the ladies go?" The word *kukashtara* (toilet) is a no-no in polite conversation. Blas-
phemy is also taboo in mixed company. The Rom believe that to insult a deity brings
disharmony or *bi-baxt* (bad karma). Thus, if two Rom were to get into a violent argument or a fist fight at a feast held in honor of Sainte Anne, the host would feel
that his table was polluted and the sainte insulted. If he then experienced a string
of bad luck, he could bring the offenders before the *kris* and ask for restitution for
their having disrupted the balance by insulting the sainte at his *slava*. The Rom believe that a Gypsy must live according to *Devleske zakonuria* (Divine laws) and that
good karma (*baxt*) comes from abiding by these laws (the *Romaniya*). If a Rom experiences a series of misfortunes, he will assume one of two things, that he has inadvertently broken one of these cosmic rules of balance and has attracted a *prekaza*
(jinx), or that he is the victim of a jinx caused by somebody else.

To rectify this, he will try to change the course of his karma by giving a feast to
Sainte Anne, who is the arch female religious figure. She embodies the element of
the matriarch or "auntie," being the grandmother of Christ. If there is sickness, either personal or of a close relative in the family, the Rom will make the pilgrimage
to Sainte Anne de Beaupré in Quebec. There he will throw a lavish feast for his fellow Rom while the women of the family will offer flowers and rice cakes to the sainte.

Rom are very careful not to anger the ancestral (or recent) dead of their family,
whom they believe can exact retribution in the form of a jinx. I once attended a
funeral feast of a Canadian Rom to whom I was not related. After the feast, a group
of us, then young men, went to the home of one of the group who was the nephew
of the deceased. There we ate and drank the food and beverages we had brought
back from the feast and jammed together, since most of us were amateur musi-
cians. During the jam, the large window of the nephew's rented flat fell inward,
shattering into tiny fragments. A few minutes later, the son of the deceased Rom
walked in through the unlocked front door. It is a custom among the Rom-Vlach
that no member of the family of a deceased Rom should play music, sing, dance,
or show any kind of merriment during a *pomana* (duration of the mourning period).
The young nephew of the deceased was so unnerved by the broken window and

the appearance of the son that he later attributed a string of misfortune he underwent to his breaking of this law. He was sure that he had attracted a *prekaza* (jinx) from the deceased. This happened during the 1960s when even we young Canadian Gypsies were somewhat affected by the hippie movement, but this event convinced the nephew of the dead Rom that the *Romaniya* should be taken seriously. He was considered *pukelimé* (disgraced) for quite some time by the other members of his family until his luck finally changed for the better and they assumed that the deceased had been placated.

The *marimé* code has many gray areas and only the patriarchs can really define which offense is *marimé* and which is simply *pukelimé*.[21] Often, the *kris* must be convened simply to define the status of new offenses or even of existing offenses because of changes in the Rom environment, technology, influence from the surrounding host culture, and other factors. Squabbles over territory can also result in pollution offenses which are often obtuse. In one instance, a family opened a reader-adviser parlor (*ofisa*) close to another. Since the exact distance between parlors was not rigidly defined in this particular territory (London), the established family tried to get interlopers to move through a *diwano*, but to no avail. They then paid some non-Gypsy youths to break into the parlor of the interlopers (which was a room in their flat) while they were all attending a feast to smear excrement all over the walls. This effectively rendered not only the parlor but the entire flat *marimé* to the present occupants and to all other Rom tenants thereafter. This was important because the flat was one of many in London which were part of the Gypsy housing network, administered by a slumlord who catered to Gypsies and other marginals who had difficulty renting from British housing agents or landlords.

The injured party in this case sued the established family for loss of income and belongings since everything inside the flat was now *marimé*. Eventually they were awarded a decent amount by the offenders after a heated *kris*. The offenders had prejudiced their case in the eyes of the local Rom community by polluting and rendering untenable a prime location for a parlor in London, where such prime properties were difficult to find.

---

21. The terms *marimé* and *pukelimé* are related but not synonymous. Substances that can defile a person are *marimé* and a person so defiled can spread this pollution to others. Generally speaking, such a person is *pukelimé*. On the other hand, a Rom who is guilty of disgraceful social conduct having nothing to do with the issue of pollution can also be declared *pukelimé*, for example, a man who exposes himself in public, uses foul language in front of a woman, or who simply fails to show proper respect to his fellows. Slanderers are also considered to be *pukelimé ando mui* or defiled in the mouth (a matter for the *kris*), as are those who spread harmful gossip. A Rom sentenced for contempt of court after a *kris* trial is *pukelimé* for the duration of his sentence and will be ostracized. Not all the Rom-Vlach groups use these terms in the same way. My definitions are those of the Canadian *Kalderash*. Both of these terms are now being replaced by modernisms which are explained ably by Dr. Ian Hancock in his article (See chap. 8).

A woman who has been wronged by a Rom, other than a man in her immediate family, can also bring this man to the *kris* through skirt tossing. This creates a *marimé* issue whereby her male relatives can bring up the real issue, which could be a slander, sexual impropriety, or some other breach of Rom law. As already mentioned, this type of skirt tossing has declined but it still remains the woman's right. Certain animals are considered *marimé* by the Rom—mainly those which can lick their own private parts, such as dogs and cats. Horses are not considered *marimé*, but there is still a defecation problem with any animal. Rom also consider non-Gypsies in general to be *marimé*. This only becomes an issue when the *Gazhé* are admitted into a Rom environment or when the Rom are forced into a non-Gypsy environment, as in a jail or detention center, a hospital or an airline flight. Here, food, toilets, washbasins, everything will be potentially polluting.

At home, a Rom will not touch food before washing his hands and must wash hands after using the washroom, touching his shoes, or handling any potentially defiling item, such as a dog. Here the Rom divide what a Rom must do (like putting on his shoes) which, while defiling, is necessary, and what he should not do (like smoking a cigarette which fell onto the floor). A Rom must also wash his hands and rinse his mouth immediately on waking and before speaking to any member of the household. Sleep is an area between life and death and potentially polluting. The mere touching of a doorknob can be polluting if the Rom does not wash his hands afterwards. Rom who are seen to break these rules in public are soon branded *pukelimé* and, while this is not a *marimé* offense, they will be socially ostracized, not invited as guests, served cracked dishes, and otherwise made to feel unwelcome until they alter their habits in public. The rules for women are even stricter than those for men since menstruating women are always polluting agents.[22]

Rom do not sit in the bathtub. They shower standing up so that the water flows from the head down. If no shower is available, they will stand in the tub and pour warm water from the head downwards (or have someone acceptable do this for them). Ultra-traditional Rom will not even sit on a toilet seat but squat over it. Nobody must go to the bathroom while people are eating a meal and, whenever possible, Rom try to relocate the toilet as far away from the eating area as possible. In warm countries, the outhouse is preferred.

There are also strict rules concerning sexual matters among the Rom. Virtually anything beyond the "missionary position" and genital intercourse is taboo. Any Rom who even alludes to oral intercourse or sodomy, or talks about the "kinky" aspects of his sex life, will be considered to be *pukelimé ando mui* (dirty in the mouth) and condemned. Lovemaking must take place in the dark and without audible sounds of lust if there are other family members within hearing distance (which

---

22. Menstruating women are excluded from serving food and from performing other tasks which can pollute guests. Menstrual blood is a polluting agent and must be avoided according to the Rom-Vlach. Customs vary from one Rom-Vlach clan to another, and some are more strict than others, but all consider the menstruating woman as taboo.

there usually are). Menstruation and childbirth are governed by taboos and rules, as is death. If a Gypsy dies in a rented home or caravan the family must move out since it is now untenable. Even if they own the house, Rom law says they should vacate the premises since it has now become *bi-baxtalo* (a carrier of bad karma). This is not strictly followed by many modern Rom.

Rom in Canada and the United States have adopted the conspicuous consumption of the non-Gypsy society around them. At group gatherings they appear well-dressed in expensive clothing, and their home furnishings, vehicles, and jewelry reflect this fad.[23] In some European countries, Rom tend to appear ragged and destitute among the *Gazhé* for fear of being robbed by lawless elements or of arousing envy among the badly-dressed, poor people among whom they live. This precaution is no longer needed in Canada and the United States. Here, Rom will look down on other Rom who do not dress to keep up with the Joneses or drive impressive vehicles.

This brief description of the *Romaniya* (Romani laws), combined with the supernatural and spiritual belief of the Rom, might serve to show that the *Romaniya* is actually the basis of a folk religion when seen in its totality, a factor little understood by non-Rom researchers.[24] It is really only by living among the Rom as part of the community on a long-term basis that one becomes aware of the *Romaniya* and its importance in everyday life. The existence of the Rom folk religion is only now surfacing, thanks mainly to Indian writers who have compared the customs of the present day Rom with those of certain Indian religions. The benediction recited by the patriarchs on solemn occasions, such as at the table of the dead, is one prime example. It sounds as follows: *Kama. Shona tai Devla—ashun man!*, or "Sun, Moon and God—hear me!"

23. In Canada and the United States, Rom-Vlach women no longer wear their expensive necklaces of *galbi* or gold coins in public since some were assaulted and robbed by muggers. They also seldom wear them in their parlors, unless men are present. Too many have been robbed by thieves posing as clients. In London, in the 1960s and early 1970s, many Rom-Vlach women kept large dogs nearby to deter clients from robbing or sexually assaulting them. In Canada and the United States, Rom-Vlach homes have also been burglarized and their valuables have been stolen.

24. The underlying folk religion of the Rom-Vlach has been little understood by researchers and has been misunderstood even by the Rom themselves. University-educated "Gypsylorists" and others doing fieldwork should learn Romani and then question their informants in their own language, rather than quote their replies in the substandard English vernacular common to those not formally educated, including the Rom.

Indian scholars see the Hindu roots of the Rom folklore, roots unnoticed by academics trained in the Judeo-Christian concept of religion. Experts have erroneously written that Romani has no future tense and thus that Rom have no concept or concern over the future. They have also written that Rom have no words for "duty," "possession," or "obligation," (again all erroneous), and even that they have no religion of their own and thus no concept of God. "God" in Romani is *Del or Devel* from Sanskrit *deva* (divinity), and it is an abstract concept quite familiar in Hinduism. The folk religion or *Romaniya* is the unwritten Bible, while the patriarchs are the spiritual heads of the community. The definitive work on the Gypsies still remains to be written.

Here we have a remembrance of the Rajput belief that the *kshatriya* tribes or clans were descended from the sun and the moon, while the concept of "God" or a divinity (Sanskrit *deva*) is seen in the abstract to be interpreted in many ways. Sainte Anne de Beaupré is simply a focal point where the present day Rom are able to worship the matriarchal deity; and if we compare the ceremonies with those performed in France at the shrine of Sainte Sara (called *Sara e Kali* in Romani), we become aware that the worship of Kali/Durga/Sara has been transferred to a Christian figure (Sainte Anne) and, in France, to a non-existent "sainte" called Sara, who is actually part of the Kali/Durga/Sara worship among certain groups in India.[25] It is thus ignorance of Indian religions among Western scholars which has resulted in the fallacy that the Rom have "no religion," when Indian scholars can clearly see the survivals of Hinduism among the modern Gypsies. The Rom have no churches and no Holy Book; as they say: *Amari Bukfa nai ramomé*—"Our Bible is unwritten." It has simply been preserved in the *Romaniya*.

The Rom have preserved and modified the Indian caste system, seeing themselves as being of caste (*wuzhó*), other types of Gypsies as being of lower caste, and the *Gazhé* as casteless or untouchables.[26] Just as in India a person does not fall from a higher caste to a lower caste, the Rom who loses caste becomes an outcast if he or she breaks one of the caste rules and must be reinstated by means of purification through the *kris*. Again, we even see the Laws of Manu operating among the Rom, where the occupations followed by the clan or group rate its members at a higher or lower status in the eyes of their fellows. *Kalderash* who pride themselves as metalworkers and skilled craftsmen look down on musician Gypsies or scrap collectors, and the *Machvaya* consider themselves to be superior to the *Kalderash*. Other groups of Rom who do not follow the same caste rules of the Rom-Vlach are seen as belonging to a lower caste (*Pol-*

---

25. For an excellent discussion of the religious connection between the Rom-Vlach and other Gypsy groups and Hinduism, see the article by W.R. Rishi, "St. Sarah (Goddess Durga/Kali), in *Roma*, No. 25, (July 1986), at 4–8. This gives the connection between the Rom worship of female "saints" and the original Indian shaktism of the Durga/Kali/Sara worship which has survived among the Rom.

26. The word *Gadjo/Gazho* is generally defined as "non-Gypsy" by Gypsyologists and others who have written about the Rom. The origin of the word can be found in Sanskrit *garhya* (domestic) through Pracrit *gajjha*. Recent theories have connected the term to Muhammad Ghazi, the eleventh-century invader and plunderer of northern India, who smashed the power of the Rajput Confederacy. The theory goes that the ancestors of the Rom who feared and hated Ghazi fled India but evermore remembered his name in the words *Gazho-Gazo-Gazi*, which they applied to oppressors and enemies. The change from *Ghazi* to *Gadjo-Gazho* is hard to explain. If, as the latest studies are revealing, the Rom are connected to the Rajputs, the original Sanskrit-derived word would have been *gadjo*, which probably meant a member of the camp-follower class, of lower caste than the Rajput kshatriya. Once the Rajput kshatriya and their camp followers left India, the various elements fused into one people with a common language and religion, and outsiders were seen as casteless. The group may then have called themselves Rom and all outsiders would have become *Gadje* or casteless people, potential polluters of the Rom and socially distinct. These outsiders were then probably paid to do the menial and polluting tasks the Rom considered defiling. Even today, Rom-Vlach families in Canada and the United States pay derelicts to clean their homes and do other chores the Rom are not allowed to do under the *Romaniya*.

ska Rom, for example, or *Sinti*), while they in turn have their own hierarchy of caste structure. To live with honor and respect among his own people, a Rom-Vlach must have *pakiv* (respect) and be considered to be *pakivaló* (respectable). If he loses this, in the eyes of his peers, and becomes *bi-pakivako* (man without honor) he must for his own sake and that of his family be reinstated; otherwise he becomes a casteless outlaw from Rom society. Thus, the *potchitayimos Romanó* (Romani respect) is the cement which holds the Rom society together and through which the *kris-Romani* is able to function.

THE *KRIS-ROMANI*

The *kris-Romani* exists to deal with specific breaches of Rom law that arise in a given Rom-Vlach community and to act as the only body capable of defining or redefining Romani law. At its basic level, it is an ad-hoc body of elders who can be convened to deal with a specific local problem. It has no jurisdiction over crimes against the state, which are handled by the regular criminal courts (Rom charged with murder, armed robbery, assault against a non-Gypsy, parking violations, swindling of non-Gypsies, etc.). The individual Rom, however if found guilty by the *kris-Gazhikani* (non-Gypsy criminal court) of a serious charge such as manslaughter, murder, rape, or some other crime against people will be censured by his own people. Such serious crimes among Rom-Vlach, however, are very rare. They are in general a peaceful, non-violent people. Whatever physical violence they do commit is usually abuse and other family violence. These are handled by the *kris* when necessary. I personally know of a few "bad eggs" among the Canadian Rom-Vlach, young men who were arrested and incarcerated for robbery. These were almost always men who were the result of mixed marriages with non-Rom mothers who had been brought up with a foot in both cultures. In other cases, the offender had been brought up by non-Gypsy foster parents.

Contrary to what has been written in novels and alleged by writers,[27] the *kris* does not have the power to sentence a person to death or to order physical mutilations as punishment for adultery. No Canadian or American Rom-Vlach elder I have questioned about this has ever heard of any such punishments, nor have the French-based *Kalderash* with whom I was closely associated in the latter 1950s and the 1960s. They actually found the concept ludicrous. The vast majority of the cases handled by the *kris* are of a mundane, petty nature. The basic areas of jurisdiction can be summarized as follows, bearing in mind that the legal system of the Rom is highly complex and that no written lawbooks exist to which judges can refer. Decisions are rendered according to legal precedent whenever possible, as interpreted by the head judge and his advisory body.

(1) Allegations of pollution and defilement where a person so defiled threatens to spread this pollution to the community as a whole, unless he is formally absolved

27. For example, Clébert, supra n. 9, at 166–67.

and reinstated. The prime example of this is the "skirt tossing" which has now become rare because of the ruling brought in the 1970s already mentioned. In some cases, a Gypsy home may be declared to be defiled because the head of the family was reported to have repaired his own toilet fixtures. Men accused of working with contaminated substances can also be forced to defend themselves under this breach of Rom law.

(2) Problems among the community members which can set two or more families at loggerheads. The trouble could expand and involve an ever-growing number of people, divided by family and clan alliance. Since this could result in a vendetta, it is vital that the problem be dealt with. Typical of this was a case which occurred in Montreal in the 1970s. A teenager eloped with the daughter of the brother of the *shato* in Ottawa while visiting the city. He was from Montreal and a nephew of the Montreal *shato*. The question of the elopement was settled at a *diwano* where the young man's father agreed to return the woman to her father and pay damages, since she had already been promised to another man from an American Rom-Vlach family. At the Easter feast, a few months later, the woman's father and mother came to Montreal to celebrate at the home of a relative. The young man who had eloped with their daughter also attended with an uncle (a brother of the *shato*). At the feast, after everybody had been drinking, the young man got into a savage argument with the father of the girl. As harsh words were yelled back and forth, the mother of the woman collapsed and the Rom thought she had suffered a heart attack. Her husband rushed her to the hospital where the doctors examined her, gave her a tranquilizer, and released her. As the father and mother of the young woman emerged from the hospital, they were assaulted by the suitor, a few of his teenage friends, and his uncle. After a fistfight, the father of the girl was admitted to the hospital where he remained for a few days under observation, with his wife and an ever-growing number of relatives who arrived from all over Canada at his bedside.

Here was a serious situation in the making, a possible blood feud between the Montreal and the Ottawa Rom divided by family/clan alliances. Thankfully the young man's father had a family marriage alliance with relatives of the father of the woman, and they were able to step in and mediate. A formal apology was made to the father of the woman, and he was financially compensated. A few years later, both participants were happily married to others, with children of their own, and I saw the young man and his uncle (the attackers) sitting with the father of the woman at another feast with all animosity forgotten. In this case, the *kris* was avoided by prompt action of intelligent elders who suggested the solution to the parties concerned.

Other cases of this type include wife beating or other forms of spousal abuse, adultery with a Rom-Vlach woman, the contraction of venereal disease by a Rom whose wife will then leave him and have her father accuse him of a *marimé* offense, the breakup of a recent marriage where the repayment of the bridal price is disputed, and related issues. Adultery with a woman of the group is a major crime since both would be married to somebody else. Affairs with non-Gypsy women are not an issue for the *kris* unless the philanderer contracts a sexual disease. A man's wife could leave him over this, however, and her father could then demand recompense. Rom-Vlach men who frequent professional women are considered to be *kurvaria* (rakes), and it is not socially acceptable but not really an issue for the *kris*. The man would, however, be considered *pukelimé* (guilty of disgraceful social behavior). Rom who contract AIDS or venereal disease are ostracized until they die (in the case of AIDS) or until they are cured. Their homes will be considered to be off-limits. One Canadian Rom family has been so ostracized because of herpes and forced to live in isolation from the rest of the community. Drug addiction has also now become a problem among some younger Rom, and this can be grounds for divorce and the repayment of the bridal dowry.

Allocation of guilt is another serious issue. This can be best explained by the example of the "killer car" already given. One Rom either does something or is responsible for something which causes death, injury, or financial loss to another Rom. Another financial issue may arise from partnerships. Two or more Rom-Vlach men who work together can often get into arguments over the sharing of profits or one partner will accuse the other of not sharing equally. One partner may have gone and obtained the work, but might have been sick on the day the other did the job. He will then demand his share of the profit. If refused, he will ask for a *kris*. Repayment of personal loans can also be an issue for the *kris*, along with money won by a Rom while gambling with other Rom if the losers refuse to pay.

(3) Territorial disputes arising primarily when the invasion of a territory is claimed either by a single family (working territory) or by the local *kumpaniya* as a whole (town or section of a city). There are two basic areas involved here according to the late Lazo Megel (Alexandria Beach) and other Rom *shaturia* in the United States and from my own knowledge in Canada. One is the establishing of a fortune-telling parlor in an area claimed by an established family as their working territory, and the other is the undercutting of prices by a Rom for a job or contract at a business establishment which is the exclusive territory of another Rom. Let's say Rom A has approached a non-Rom and obtained the contract to do a certain job for a certain price. Rom B, knowing about this, goes there and offers to do the same job for a lower price, which he then does and receives payment. Rom A finds out about this and demands that Rom B pay him half of what the profit would have been if he had had the job himself at the higher payment rate he had initially arranged with the non-Gypsy. If Rom B refuses or haggles, then this becomes a matter for the *kris*, if it cannot be resolved at a *diwano*.

This same rule extends to the used-car business. It is illegal under Rom law for a Rom to go to a dealer who is the source of vehicles for another Rom. The free-for-all car auctions, on the other hand, are open to all Rom along with anyone else who attends, as are vehicles advertised in the local newspapers. When I worked as a travelling *Kalderash* with my partner Vanya Kwiek in the 1960s, we did tinning, retinning, and repairing of mixing bowls, vats, and steam-jacket boilers, along with the servicing and cleaning of restaurant kitchens. Our string of bakeries, factories, and restaurants was our exclusive domain and other Rom were not allowed to undercut our prices or to work for these contracted places without paying both of us a full share as partners. Admittedly, there was only one other *Kalderash* group doing this work in eastern Canada at the time and the rule was respected. Canadian-born Rom had by then long forgotten the plating and tinning trade. We also did churches, plating the holy articles (*solarios*), jobs which were open to anyone since these were usually one-time contracts. It would be thirty years or more before they needed to be replaced. Stainless steel has now made the retinning of copper mixing bowls obsolete in Canada but not in Europe, where the *Kalderash* are still working at this trade in France and elsewhere.

Violations of the fortune-telling territory are very common. Each family in the *kumpaniya* has the exclusive territorial right to a certain number of blocks (a radius of from three to five blocks as a rule). Another family cannot open a parlor within this radius without permission from those who own the territory. Unfortunately, not all areas of the city are equally lucrative, accessible, or otherwise attractive in terms of clients. There are always squabbles over this and over who gets the best areas. The case of the polluting of a parlor in London, already mentioned, is one example of the complications that can result from illegal trespassing. In other cases, the established family will bring in the police (or ask the *shato* to do so). Some trumped-up allegation, that the interlopers are running a crack house or a house of prostitution, will be offered in the hope that the police will close down the competition. The interlopers can be brought before the *kris* and ordered to leave the territory, but if they refuse, then other, more underhanded methods are employed. Cases of slander and loss of income can often result. The "stealing" of customers among Rom-Vlach reader-advisers is another issue. Many of the Gypsy women have regular clients who come to them once a week or so, almost like visiting a psychiatrist (which many of the reader-advisers actually resemble). When another reader-adviser "steals" one of these lucrative regulars away from her previous counsellor, the woman will have her husband accuse the family of her competition of "taking bread out of my family's mouth," or loss of family income.

(4) The *kris* acts as the authority concerning the laws of the Rom-Vlach: how they are to be interpreted, retained, and modified, or how new laws are to be introduced to cover areas or situations which were not previously defined or for which there is as yet no legal precedent. Typical are the inroads made into Rom culture from the surrounding host society in the urban environment where most of the Rom now live. Among these issues are birth control, abortion, the use of illegal drugs, women's liberation, and the wearing of non-Gypsy fashions by young Gypsy women, fashions considered to be immodest by the matriarchs.

Another issue is the practice of many younger Rom of taking their interfamily disputes to the non-Gypsy courts. Like most Canadians and Americans, the Rom are catching the disease of "lawyeritis," which means suing everybody and anybody for everything from the neighbor's cat which chews the head off a favorite rose in the garden to his ten-year-old son who scratches the family chariot with his frisbee. This runs from Rom accusing other Rom of kidnapping in cases of elopement to seduction of a minor if the male party is old enough and the woman is under the legal age. Some Gypsy women are also hiring divorce sharks to get a hefty alimony from their former husbands.

Problems may result from *poruyimos* (tattling), where one Rom will inform the police on another Rom. Perhaps this man simply refused to marry his daughter to the tattler, who then informs the police that the other Rom is guilty of some criminal offense such as dealing in illegal drugs. Of course, the victim is innocent of this charge but the resulting arrest and hassle, especially for a Rom, can be devastating. The injured Rom can then take his accuser to the *kris* and charge him with malicious slander. This tattling is also used in other situations; as one patriarch told me: *Vuni Rom si'l mai gordé dushmaya ka'l avrende*—"Some Rom are the worst enemies of the others." Rom who habitually do this type of nastiness soon gain the reputation of *Rom-bedacha* (troublemakers) and eventually become socially ostracized and avoided. Under Rom law they are actually *pukelimé ando mui* (dirty in the mouth).

While the local *shato* is responsible for maintaining smooth relations with the non-Gypsy agencies in the territory, sometimes an issue erupts where the entire community is threatened and the *kris* must be convened to find a solution collectively. This has happened when a city, such as Montreal, suddenly on whim of the mayor, decided to make fortune-telling illegal. In Canada, predicting the future for money has always been illegal under the Criminal Code of Canada, Section 365, which states: "Everyone who fraudulently undertakes, for a consideration, to tell fortunes is guilty of an offense punishable on summary conviction." This law originated in the Witchcraft Act of 1735 (United Kingdom) and deems that nobody has the ability to predict the future. Therefore, anyone who tells fortunes for payment is acting fraudulently, whether or not this person sincerely believes he or she has some "God-given ability."

Today, however, in both Canada and the United States, there exist psychic television hotlines, psychics, gurus, tarot readers, newspaper astrologers, and a host of lesser beings from all races, nationalities, and religious persuasions. This archaic law has almost become meaningless, except when it applies to Gypsies who have always been targets as the arch villains. In Montreal, the loophole was that Rom (or anyone else) could buy a license to practice phrenology and thus open a parlor with a large head painted on the window. In other cities, entertainment licenses were made available. The entertainment exception is used by the television psychics, who as of 1995 grossed over $100 million a year collectively.

In Montreal, the *kris* decided to retain a top attorney to fight the mayor's new ordinance (as did a group of non-Gypsy "seers" who organized a class action) and eventually the law was annulled. Meanwhile, the Rom were forced to leave Montreal.[28]

---

28. One of these non-Gypsy seers was John Manolesco, a famous astrologer, now deceased, who was at that time a resident of Montreal. I interviewed him a few years later after he had relocated to California and had become widely known. He actually thanked the mayor for his crusade against psychics.

The mayor's ordinance had, however, unfortunate results for him. He was a share-holder in an expensive gourmet restaurant. The Rom of Montreal had been servic-ing restaurant kitchens at the time, including the mayor's. Part of this work was to remove the accumulated grease from the stove canopies, a major fire hazard. After the Rom temporarily left, the grease accumulated, and the mayor's restaurant caught fire in the canopy and burned to the ground. To the Rom, this was karmic retribu-tion, the vengeance of *Kali* against one who had created an imbalance of the uni-versal law. As the local patriarch said of the incident: *O Del mardya les*—"God smote him."

When I was living in Streatham, South London, a problem arose among the Canadian and American Rom-Vlach "tourists" which required a *kris* decision. In London, the Rom were renting flats which had two or three floors. The parlor, for obvious reasons, had to be at street level, as was the kitchen and living room. The toilet, however, was upstairs. This meant that Rom women had to walk above Rom men in order to use the bathroom, a defiling offense. Because there was no alter-native to this problem, except for the women to go outside into the backyard in the inclement English climate, the London *kris* ruled that this breach of Rom law was permissible in London. Once back in Canada and the United States, however, these same families had to follow the older ruling since alternative housing was available.

Another recent factor which the *kris* will have to deal with is the emergence of what the Rom refer to as the "Holy Rollers" or "Christian Gypsies." This Pente-costal movement among the Rom appeared in the 1960s in France, where it ini-tially appealed to the Rom because it allowed them freedom to travel to religious rallies without the usual harassment of the police. At this date, the odious *carnet an-thropométrique* was still in force (repealed in 1969).[29] This restricted both traveling and camping, but religious freedom allowed the Rom to travel to and from these Pentecostal meetings (and to do some business along the way). It began among the *Manouche* (French *Sinti*) but later spread to the *Kalderash* around Paris and elsewhere, many of whom became pastors. It has now spread to Canada and the United States, and the "Catholic Rom" who follow the older, traditional folk religion claim that the "Christian Rom," who are Pentecostals, are not following all the estab-

---

29. This French law was enacted in 1912 and was designed to regulate the circulation of nomads as follows: "*All those men, women and adolescents from their fourteenth year who cannot establish that they have a fixed residence or domicile and regular employment must carry this card.*" The identity card issued to the Gypsies car-ried full-face and profile photos, fingerprints, cranial dimensions, and the length of the little finger and left forearm. The law further stipulated: "*All nomads sojourning in a commune at their arrival and departure must present their cards to the superintendent of police or if none, to the commandant of the Gendarmerie, or, in the absence thereof, to the mayor.*" The card was also to be presented on demand to all agents of authority. To be found without an identity card could result in fines and/or imprisonment. Gypsies, including the Rom-Vlach *Kalderash,* who lived in shanty-towns around Paris, were considered to be "sedentary" and thus escaped the need to obtain the card. However, if they travelled on the roads as Gypsies, they were required to obtain one. The central files of these Gypsy identity cards greatly facilitated the job of the Gestapo in rounding up Gypsies after the Nazi occupation of France.

lished Rom laws and customs. I have met Pentecostal Canadian Rom at Sainte Anne de Beaupré performing the same ceremonies as the non-Pentecostal Rom, but some American Rom patriarchs, such as the late Lazo Megel, claimed that some of the Pentecostal Rom beliefs conflicted with the *Romaniya*.

One unprecedented situation a *kris* was convened to deal with, according to Jan Yoors,[30] was whether or not the Rom in Western Europe should unite to combat the Nazi occupation by taking part in the Resistance Movement. This seems rather superfluous at this date since the *Zigeunergeschmeiss* had already been condemned to extinction as part of the Final Solution and the camps were already being prepared in Poland. Nevertheless, it makes for a good novel, like the Rom family head in Yoors' earlier novel (*The Gypsies*), who sat down with the author and conveniently described the breakdown of the Gypsy groups and subgroups with all the academic rhetoric of a member of the Gypsy Lore Society.[31]

In the United States, a *kris* was convened which involved an entire clan of American Rom in Boston, Mass. The *Bimbuleshti*, or Tene clan as they are better known to Americans, had to deal with the aftermath of the book *King of the Gypsies* by Peter Maas and the film which was loosely based on it. Steve Tene, the young Rom informant who had provided the author with much of his material, which was combined with slanted newspaper clippings and police information to create this book and film, was accused in absentia of slandering his people by tattling to outsiders about family skeletons. How much of the actual information contained in the book was true, exaggerated, or apocryphal is known only to the people concerned, but this type of airing of Rom family linen is against Rom law. The book was not all that important to the family/clan since most of the Rom were illiterate, but the film was another story, since it fictionalized the events out of proportion and resulted in the ostracism of the family and clan in the eyes of other Rom. Steve Tene was declared *marimé* in absentia and forced to relocate somewhere far away where he could not be located for his own safety. He was, for all intents and purposes, "vaporized" as a member of the clan.[32]

---

30. Jan Yoors, *Crossing* 82–92 (1971).

31. Yoors, supra n. 10, at 132–35. Gypsies of one specific group generally know little about those of other groups. For example, *Kalderash* elders in Canada can talk about the *Machvaya* in California, but know next to nothing about the European Rom-Vlach groups, the Spanish *Calés*, the English *Romanitchels* or the Albanian Muslim Gypsies. Yoors is practicing artistic license in having his character give him a breakdown of the world's Gypsy groups. At least his character did leave out the Irish Tinkers and other non-Rom travelling groups, which some Gypsyologists include among the "Romani peoples".

32. This sad affair is typical for the sensationalizing of Gypsies for profit. The film, which was loosely adapted from the book, had much more impact on the American Rom because of mass illiteracy. The fiction that "King Tene Bimbo" chose his grandson, Steve, as his successor by promising to give him his hereditary medallion of "kingship" does not make sense. The successor to "King Tene" would have been whoever chose to assume his role after his death. In effect, this proved to be John Tene, a cousin of Steve Tene. Rom-Vlach *shaturia* do not wear any medallions or symbols of leadership except for the mentioned spurious crowns sported by some "swelled heads" among them. In the past, a small emblem called a *pechata* was hung from the shirt pocket by Rom-Vlach family heads and patriarchs, but it had no relationship to a badge of authority.

THE *KRIS-ROMANI* AND TYPICAL CASES

The *kris* can be held in any private location but is not convened in the home of a Rom due to the widespread belief that built-up animosity can linger on the premises, thus disrupting the cosmic balance which could bring misfortune to those living there. Non-Gypsies are never allowed as spectators and Rom women do not attend unless they are called in as witnesses or a woman is on trial. Older matriarchs do attend among some groups. In Montreal, where many Rom families were living during the heyday of the *kris* from the 1960s to the early 1980s, it was regularly convened in a private hall rented from a local "bookie" in what was then a gymnasium owned by a *Gazho*. Since many of the local Rom gambled at this "gymnasium," the owner knew them well and was willing to rent them the hall (poker room). Alternatively, the *kris* could be held in any other rented location agreeable to all concerned, especially the accused who would be footing the bill.

Ideally, the language employed at the *kris* should be only Romani, although today this is not always adhered to. A few Rom do not speak Romani fluently, and immigrant Rom often speak differing dialects of Romani with athematic items (foreign loan words) unfamiliar to Canadian and American Rom. English or some other language commonly known (Spanish in the United States or French in Canada) may then have to be used for clarification. The patriarchs and *Rom-krisunge* are experts at paraphrasing, and a special form of rhetorical Romani was used at the *kris* in my younger days, basically the same style employed in folktales in order to help the narrator remember the story through the rhyming cadence.[33] This rhetorical Romani is also used in solemn invocations, prayers, and other formalized speech. There was much use of proverbs and idiomatic constructions which actually replace the allegedly "missing words" in Romani vocabularies compiled by non-Rom linguists.[34] It is probable that this type of rhetorical Romani is now disappearing in Canada and the United States as the elderly Rom pass away. The language, while still fluently spoken, is now used more as a secondary language and has adopted many borrow-

---

33. Typical of this is the following which I recorded verbatim from a folktale:

Yela sas shé barí,
Tai woi sas buzhanglí,
Tai butender sas piradí.

Yela was an eldest daughter,
And she was very shrewd,
And she had been courted by many suitors.

34. As an example of rhetorical Romani, I can give the following, recorded verbatim:

Standard Romani
Mangav te penav tumenga so kerdyas a Zlatcho kana motodyas kodole swaturia.

Rhetorical Romani
Mangava te penava tumenga, Romale, so kerdyas kako Rom, o Zlatcho, kana motodyas le swaturia kodole.

ings from English and Spanish in the United States and from English in Canada.[35] Immigrant Rom-Vlach, however, often retain the older, rhetorical Romani, and when they first arrive find it difficult to converse fluently with native-born Canadian or American Rom until they learn the current loan words in use.

There are no regular judges on the *kris.* Any Rom is theoretically able to assume this role but, in general, it is reserved for the patriarchs or elders and the well-known *Rom-krisunge.* The supreme judge is usually chosen locally, but in towns with a small Rom population a judge can be invited from elsewhere if this person is agreeable to both parties and the accused is able and willing to foot the bill. Alternatively, depending on the offense, the accused could travel to a large urban center to have his hearing. Usually, all expenses incurred at a *kris* are born by the accused, but the plaintiff will sometimes offer to share the cost. This, again, is a matter of negotiation and agreement.

Each *kris* has a supreme judge, who may or may not be local and a body of advisory elders. Once both litigants have agreed through their spokesmen (*swatasha*) which judge is acceptable, he will suggest a small group of his peers who he feels are best qualified according to their availability to sit with him. Again, these may be local men or they can be invited from elsewhere, provided men are unavailable locally or if the local men are unacceptable to the litigants. As well as the advisory body, any adult male Rom can attend the *kris* and offer suggestions, question witnesses, argue testimony, and offer advice if this is considered constructive by the supreme judge. It is the responsibility of the supreme judge to hear all the evidence, become informed of the facts, and then ask the opinions of his advisory

---

English
I wish to inform you (Gypsy man), what Zlatcho did when he related these words.

Rhetorical Romani also employs many idioms and proverbs. For example, the English expression, "His career is coming to an end," cannot be translated as one would translate this into, say, French or Spanish. Instead, an idiom such as *Pesko kam beshel*—"His sun is setting," would be employed. Actually, Romani is more flexible than most other languages because Romani speakers have a natural skill for fitting loan words from other languages, usually the host culture's language, into Romani in such a way that they are understood. When the group moves to another host-culture, these former loan words are dropped and are substituted with new ones. A Romani speaker temporarily stuck for the existing Romani word can fit English (in Canada) into his Romani without having to use the English word in its original form. For example, if one wanted to say, "My tire blew out," he would have the choice of the following: *Blewisaili muri taiyra*, from English; or *Parulí muri shuna*, from Canadian *Kalderash* Romani. Thus, expressions such as, "I asked my attorney to prepare the necessary documents to procure a license for a reader-adviser parlor for my family," can be easily translated into Romani by converting the English words into their appropriate Romani loan-word forms.

35. Many young Rom-Vlach Romani speakers in Canada will use English loan words. Most of them come from mixed marriages in which English is the main language spoken at home. The process is reversed by intermarriage with immigrant Rom-Vlach, which results in Romani being the only common language between husband and wife. Canada is officially a bilingual country, but there has been no borrowing from French comparable to borrowings from Spanish in the United States.

body before making his final decision. A *kris* can often be a lengthy affair and the defendant usually has to provide food and drink during the proceedings. In their impatience to remain abreast of the trial, often relatives of the litigants will call long distance to a pay phone in the place where the *kris* is being held to learn how the matter is progressing. Once a verdict is reached, it will be known all over the United States and Canada by relatives of those on trial.

During the trial, there is much shouting and it is up to the supreme judge to impose order. The Rom, as a rule, are volatile and emotional, and when pleading issues or trying to elicit support they often get carried away. Often, a judge will ask a Rom to leave the *kris* to compose himself and then return after cooling off outside for a while. The Rom have a saying for this: *Gelotar te avel*—"He departed in order to re-arrive." While some judges will not allow the assembled Rom to drink alcoholic beverages during the trial, some do while others restrict the Rom to beer only. But the Rom are always allowed to smoke and the air soon becomes foul with the reek of cigarettes, pipes, and king-sized cigars. The accused will try to gain as much sympathy and support as he can for his case by turning to face the assembled Rom instead of the judge. Some will go through childish antics to gain support, kneeling down, pleading, and indulging in other theatrical displays of emotion, trying to get the assembled Rom to voice support for their case which they hope will influence the judge.

Periodically some delivery person will arrive with food and drink and there will be a halt in the trial while the Rom refresh themselves. Soon, the floor will be littered with cigarette and cigar remains, food scraps, paper, empty cans, and other debris. Both litigants will have kinsmen and friends who will act as advisers, and periodically they will go into a huddle as the case progresses. Sometimes a teenage boy will enter the room and yell at his father: *Tate, akardyas o Gazho pala o mobili*—"A customer called about the (used) car." This man will then leave to take care of business at the pay phone. When he returns, he will have to be briefed on what transpired during his absence.

When the *kris* was active in Montreal, those I witnessed were very formal. The supreme judge would formally open the proceedings by first invoking the ancestral dead, who would then be assumed to be present. Any Rom giving testimony was obliged first to give a sacred oath (*soláx*) by which he bound himself to tell only the truth. If he should fail to tell the truth, he swore to bring down some terrible punishment on himself: for example, *Te marela man o Del te chi motava me o chachimos*— "May God strike me down if I do not tell the truth"; or, *Te merava me te xoxavava*— "May I drop dead if I lie." At each swearing of a *soláx* the assembled Rom would reply in unison: *Pe amare mulende*—"Let this be on the souls of our ancestral dead," implying that, if the man broke his oath, the ancestral spirits would be given the responsibility of ensuring that he was properly chastised. This was the explanation offered by Russel Demitro and other patriarchs at the time. While this was a very formalized version of the *kris*, it is obvious that without such beliefs on the part of those taking part in it, it would become a toothless tiger.

The *kris* itself is virtually powerless except to impose what modern Rom refer to as a "blackballing." Both the terms *marimé* and *pukelimé* are being replaced by younger speakers with *bawlimé* (blackballed, from English) and *gonimé* (chased out, from Rumanian). Thus, a person who is "blackballed," or *bawlimé*, is to be socially ostracized; and a person declared *gonimé* is penalized by being placed in a *pokala*, or period of defilement, where he must be shunned and avoided by his peers for the length of time determined by the judge. This "contempt of court" sentence is all the *kris* can do to a Rom who refuses to abide by its ruling. This is not the same thing as a period of defilement as a result of pollution (*marimé* offense). In fact, I have been told that the younger generation of Rom in the United States have difficulty in defining just what a *marimé* offense is, other than the obvious skirt tossing. Basically, *bawlimé* means a person is the equivalent of *pukelimé* and *gonimé*, that he has been ostracized for a specific period of time.

When the *kris* is concluded, the litigants are supposed to shake hands and all animosity must be forgotten. There is then a feast of reconciliation. In actual fact, I have often seen the losers storm out of the hall after paying their fines, muttering curses against the "winners." This blackballing or sending to Coventry is the only actual power the *kris* has, and even this is limited to whether or not the Rom in the community adhere to it. Usually, a Rom so sentenced will have trouble functioning in his community as a Rom. What often happens is that the sentenced Rom will simply relocate himself and his family, far away from the local *kumpaniya*, until his period of banishment has ended.

To avoid this type of situation, the supreme judge will attempt to get both litigants to agree beforehand to abide by the decision reached by the *kris*. For this reason, judges are chosen with extreme care, since the refusal of a "loser" to abide by the decision reached by the judge could reflect on the integrity of the judge and be considered a direct insult. Before the *kris* convenes, there is usually much discussion of potential judges by the litigants through their spokesmen. A judge can refuse to accept a case when asked if he has a valid reason. He may feel he is not competent in this particular area or he may be distantly related to one of the litigants. He may have had prior dealings with a member of the family of one of the litigants which might affect his impartiality. It is no wonder that the elders counsel the Rom to settle their differences at a *diwano*. As Lazo Megel put it: "Why go looking for trouble by asking for a *kris?*"

Since so many *kris* cases nowadays are concerned with elopement, this might be an area worth describing in detail. A young couple will decide to elope for any one of many reasons, usually because they feel that the parents of one of them are against the marriage. The father of the young woman will then demand restitution from the father of the male party. Whether or not he gets his daughter back is not relevant to the main issues which concern the *daró*, or bridal dowry. In Canada and the United States, this is usually roughly the price of a new automobile. The actual amount is always stated as so many pounds of gold (*liria*). This is, of course, governed by the current cost of gold on the market. The actual amount is also related to what the father of the young woman may have received as a dowry for a previous daughter. Rom-Vlach women are married off in descending order of age from the eldest (*she barí*). If a younger sister elopes before her next-in-line older sister is married, her parents are usually against the marriage. This would imply to other Rom that the older daughter might be somehow "defective," and this would hinder her chances for marriage in the future. As far as the amount of the *daró* is concerned, a maximum limit is usually adhered to by the local *kumpaniya* and by general consensus among the elders. It is higher for women never-before married, lower for divorcees, and very low for older widows.

There is, however, much room to negotiate. Sometimes two families will make an exchange that does not involve any dowry. One family will take a daughter from another and then give one of its own daughters to the other family as a wife for an unmarried son. Here, the two dowries have canceled each other. Another method of marriage is the *zhamutro ande tsera* or "son-in-law under the tent." In this case, instead of the *borí* (bride) joining her husband's family after marriage, the groom will live with his wife's family and work off the dowry, either by working with his father-in-law or brothers-in-law or for himself. There is even an installment plan where the father of the groom can take the bride into his home and then pay off her father over time. Obviously, all of these marriage arrangements, in the event of a divorce, can raise complicated financial issues that may have to be resolved at a *kris*.

Elopement, however, is the most common problem. The first issue that will have to be decided between the two fathers involved is whether the couple should be separated or whether the marriage should be accepted. The mere fact that the young couple have slept together makes them automatically married in the eyes of the Rom. The actual Rom-Vlach marriage can be either the old bread-salt-wine ceremony or a civil or religious marriage, or both, the last usually for family benefits under Social Assistance programs and for government requirements. If the couple are both under legal age, the civil or religious marriage is delayed until they reach the age of consent. Directly related to this question is the dowry issue. Whatever the outcome of the marital status of the young couple, the father of the young woman will demand recompense since his daughter will be technically "divorced" if the runaway marriage is annulled.

In one such elopement I was involved with (as a newspaper reporter in 1980), the issue became very complicated. Rom A had married one daughter to Rom B. Later, Rom A left his Gypsy wife and lived common-law with a non-Gypsy woman. His wife and her family considered this to be a desertion, although no *kris* action was taken. The man's younger daughter remained with her Gypsy mother, who then placed herself and her daughter under the protection of her father. All Rom-Vlach women must live in the household of a husband or a male relative. When the married daughter became pregnant, she called her mother and asked her to come and help her because she claimed to be sick. Her mother went to stay with her at the home of Rom B, taking her daughter with her. While resident there, the younger daughter eloped with the younger son of Rom B and the couple fled to her grandfather's home, where they asked him, as a patriarch, to negotiate for them with the two fathers concerned.

After speaking to the grandfather, Rom B agreed to pay the full dowry demanded by Rom A, since he already had this man's older daughter in his family and he and Rom A were already *xanamicha* (co-fathers-in-law). The dowry, however, was paid to the young woman's mother, since her father (Rom A) was considered to be *pukelimé* (guilty of disgraceful social conduct). The mother then returned to her father's home, leaving her newly-married daughter at the home of Rom B to serve her apprenticeship as a *borí* (trial bride). Rom A then demanded the dowry from Rom B only to be told that it had already been paid to his wife and her father, since they had been the actual custodians or guardians of the young woman at the time of marriage. He was advised to straighten the matter out with them.

According to Rom law, Rom A had the exclusive right to the dowry, but the issue was complicated by his separation from his wife and by his *pukelimé* status in the eyes of her family and the local *kumpaniya* where his wife lived. This was definitely an issue for the patriarchs to thresh out at a *diwano*. Rom A's wife refused to give him any part of the dowry because, as she said, he was "living in sin with a non-Gypsy woman." Rom A then went to the town where Rom B was living and swore out a charge of "kidnapping" against Rom B. When the police investigated, the woman's mother testified that it was really a case of a Gypsy marriage. Rom B was released and the charges dropped. Angry that his strategy to put pressure on Rom B had failed, Rom A then went to the local newspapers and radio-TV stations and gave them a story worthy of some non-Gypsy author of romantic fiction about Gypsies. This included the "sordid details" of the "bad Gypsies" (Rom B and his clan) who were living in the town. This fabrication now involved the local *kumpaniya*, who demanded that Rom A be summoned before the *kris* to be fined for slander, the amount to be determined by the judge. Rom A then vanished and relocated himself and his non-Gypsy paramour in a far-distant city.

The fictitious story given by Rom A swept through the wire transmitters of the Associated Press and United Press International, with photos of the beautiful young "Gypsy princess" who had been "stolen" from her father by a tribe of "evil Gypsies" through their young "prince" and who were now holding her captive. Even my own hard-nosed editor fell for the story, but after some negotiations, I managed to have it "killed" before publication.[36] Many *kris* cases involve slander related to tattling to the police or other non-Gypsy agencies to put pressure on a specific individual or family. If the slander can be proved, the slanderer will be forced to retract his statements in public before the assembled *kris* and to pay financial damages to the injured party or parties. His reputation will suffer and he will be considered "dirty in the mouth" from then on by his peers.

---

36. Needless to say, those concerned were amazed to be interviewed by a reporter who spoke fluent Rom-Vlach Romani.

One weapon a judge does have at his disposal is the *arman*, or "solemn curse," which he can use when necessary, although this is falling into disuse as younger Rom increasingly refuse to take the old customs seriously. At one trial in Montreal in the 1960s involving slander, the Rom slandered was awarded the sum of $500 in damages by the *kris*. This was paid in full by the slanderer. While the *kris* was dissolving, the victor went to a pay phone in the hallway to tell his family the good news. After removing the telephone number from his wallet, he left the billfold on a ledge near the phone. When he hung up, he reached for his wallet to find it missing along with the $500. He reported this to the judge, who immediately reconvened the *kris* since it was obvious that only a Rom who had been at the *kris* would have stolen the wallet.

The supreme judge then pronounced a formal *arman* (curse) against the unknown thief, asking God, through the ancestral dead, to bring down a *prekaza* (jinx) on the thief unless he returned the money immediately in any way he saw fit. Nobody confessed to the theft and, as far as anyone knows, the money was never returned anonymously. The majority of the older men were visibly shaken and warned of dire consequences for the thief. The late Lazo Megel and other elders have told me that these solemn curses were always taken very seriously by the Rom of their generation in both the United States and Canada. The *arman* can also be used by a judge when he feels a Rom is giving false evidence or claiming to be innocent when he is really guilty. In such cases, the judge then informs the accused that unless he makes restitution or confesses to the crime in the future, the *arman* will take effect and will forever hang over his head like some spiritual sword of Damocles.

In the past, when Canadian Rom were nomadic, *kris* punishments were more primitive. In the 1960s, Russel Demitro, then an elderly patriarch, described a colorful penalty for a male adulterer that he had witnessed as a boy in the early years of the twentieth century. The adulterer was led through the Rom camp in a cart rented for this purpose from a local farmer. The Rom in the camp pelted the sinner with filth collected around the campsite, including animal excrement which was scooped up in shovels. After this ordeal, the adulterer was sent away to live in isolation for the period of his *pokala* (sentence) imposed by the *kris*. In the old days this was three or a multiple of three months, less often years, depending on the offense. Demitro said that the practice with female transgressors was for a group of older women to take the adulteress into the forest, where she was stripped and whipped with switches cut from suitable trees by one or more of the matriarchs. Generally, her cuckolded husband sent her back to her father afterwards. If the husband's mother was among the traveling company, she would administrate the whipping. These punishments were practiced by immigrant *Kalderash* from the Balkans and no doubt reflect the customs of these Rom in their former host countries.

Today, issues arising from adultery revolve more around financial damages, the fining of the adulterer, and the return of the adulterous wife to her father. The male adulterer, if his crime is with a *Romni* (Gypsy woman), is considered *pukelimé* and probably has to relocate far from his *kumpaniya*. A wronged wife can return to her father, who can then demand punitive damages from her philandering husband. A wronged husband can also demand partial repayment of the dowry, depending on the length of the marriage, the age of the couple, and other factors. Related to adultery is wife stealing, another serious matter. The main difference today is that, in the past, crimes like adultery and wife stealing were so rare that they became major issues in the community. Among a closely-knit traveling group or the densely-settled early urban Rom, the effect of such crimes was greater on the community. Today, the Rom are spread out and not as closely scrutinized by their peers, while both adultery and wife stealing are more common than they were in the past. This being the case, they often fail to arouse the same degree of indignation.

Divorces among young couples where the wife is still a *bori* (trial bride) are also issues the modern *kris* must constantly deal with. When a young woman marries, she must spend a period of time at the home of her mother-in-law, who supervises her and trains her to follow the laws and customs of the Rom as she interprets them. The sisters-in-law also contribute, and the position of the *bori* in some Rom households is little better than that of an indentured servant. If, during the trial period, the woman is sent back to her father for some reason, either by the husband or by his family, who might feel she is not suitable, this will then result in a demand for return of all or most of the dowry. The woman's father will naturally contest this and a *kris* will become necessary if they cannot settle the issue among themselves. After the *bori* bears a child of her own, she and the husband are free to leave and set up home together if the mother-in-law approves. If there is then a divorce, the man's father can try to reclaim some of the dowry, but the longer the marriage lasts, the less chance he will have of reclaiming any financial repayment.

Marriage breakups among young Rom today are less likely to revolve around adultery than around spousal abuse, drug addiction, or the fact that the husband feels his wife is not a good reader-adviser and is unable to make as much money as other Gypsy women in her *ofisa* (parlor). A young Gypsy woman with children who is operating a reader-adviser parlor and running a home has little time for or interest in romantic affairs or dates after work. The Rom-Vlach cultures does not have the concept of romantic love to begin with. Marriages are still orchestrated by the parents and there are no fairy tales for little girls about Prince Charming, Cinderella, or Sleeping Beauty. A young Gypsy woman expects her future husband to be a man of respect in the community, to come from an established, powerful family, to be reliable and shrewd with money, and otherwise to conform to the image she expects. A Rom youth looking for a wife is more interested in whether she comes from a good family and is likely to be a successful reader-adviser than he is with her physical anatomy or her beauty. Gypsy girls and women do watch soap operas on television but most of them consider these stories not to be representative of the type of non-Gypsy women they meet in their parlors. They view the soap operas as *Gazhikani rinza-bula* (non-Gypsy tripe), even if they are influenced by the hair styles and make-up they see on television. It is the programs they find ridiculous, not the actors and actresses performing in them.

Love, among the Rom, is more agapic than erotic although, as already noted, young people do occasionally fall in love and elope. Most marriages are still arranged by the parents, although the sons and daughters do have the final say, as a rule, before negotiations for betrothal (*tumnimos*) are initiated.

Sometimes, a family will bend the rules of the *Romaniya* to marry off an eldest or older daughter who is preventing her younger sisters from being married (since daughters must be married in descending order of age). Sometimes, this older daughter, who may have been divorced or for some other reason may not have been asked for by anyone, will be married to a man old enough to be her father or grand-father. This is frowned upon by the community and social censure can often result.

In one such incident, which took place in Canada in the 1960s, the community itself passed judgment, and an informal sentence of *pokala* (disgraceful social be-havior) on the adult Rom and the woman's family was the consequence. A wealthy Rom-Vlach from Cuba visited Canada and made the rounds of the local commu-nities looking for a bride. This widower, in his late sixties, with grandchildren of his own, finally found a family, then living in Montreal, who had an eldest daughter available. She was still unmarried and thus preventing her younger sisters from being asked for in marriage. The problem here was that this eldest daughter was referred to as a *chapladí* (mentally retarded person) among the Canadian Rom-Vlach and, while very attractive, she was definitely mentally impaired. The wealthy Rom mar-ried this woman and returned to Cuba with her. A few months later, she returned to her family after her husband had died of a heart attack. The consensus of the community was that, since this man had acted outside of the balance (*kuntari*), God had struck him down (*O Del mardya les*) for his sin and that the old man had "died in the saddle" (*Mulo ande zin*) and thus received his just desert. He was considered *puke-limé* by the Canadian Rom and nobody but the woman's immediate family attended the wedding feast. The family then went through a fairly long period of social avoid-ance before they were eventually accepted back into the community.

The *kris* was not involved in this issue but public censure accomplished the same result. Older Rom are not supposed to be sexually active, or if they are, to be so discreetly. Any patriarch or matriarch who exhibits public interest in sex, either by marrying or discussing the topic, is usually deemed to be *pukelimé* and then suffers a loss of respect (*pakiv*) among the group. Eventually, the *chapladí* (touched girl) was married to a Rom youth who also suffered from a mental handicap. Rom, as a rule, do not condemn the mentally challenged or the senile. They believe that such peo-ple are *dinó Devlestar*, or "struck by God," and that they should be protected and cared for. Thus, the exploitation of the *chapladí* was seen as *pukelimé* by the Rom community because her father had married her off to a "man without honor" for his own financial advantage (the dowry) and, the potential further dowries from her younger sisters. Under Rom law, he should have made it clear to the commu-nity that his eldest daughter was unable to be married because of her condition.

He would then have been able to marry the second oldest daughter. Instead, he pawned off the eldest daughter onto an elderly lecher in order to obtain the dowry.

This public censure can result in certain individuals being ostracized, not for any blatant act or breach of Rom law they may commit, but simply for their general behavior over a long period of time. One such man, now in his sixties, was always known as a "gay blade" (*kurvari*) among the Rom. He was a sharp dresser and, when young, went through a series of live-in relationships and affairs with non-Gypsy paramours, all of whom eventually left him. He never married a Gypsy woman, and his children ended up with his estranged ex-lovers. Instead of socializing with the Rom of his age group, he hung around with the unmarried or recently married young men, playing pool with them and throwing parties to which he invited them. He also frequented nightclubs and strip joints and was reputed to partake of illegal drugs, which he was also accused of providing for young men of his *kumpaniya*. While this man was able to visit his brothers and stay with them for short periods and to show up at large festive Rom gatherings, he was avoided by those outside his immediate family. As he grew older, almost toothless and bald, but still the sharp dresser, he was looked upon more as an object of pity. He never became a *krizinitori* (patriarch and potential judge on the *kris*) and was not considered to be a Rom *pakivaló* (man of honor). He eventually disappeared into a home for senior citizens and vanished from the Rom community. The Rom who knew him said simply, "*Xalyas peski baxt*" ("He has destroyed his own karmic potential"). All this man's brothers and sisters were respected members of the Rom community in Canada, and he was truly the "black sheep" of the family.

In another example of group censure, a woman from the Canadian Rom-Vlach group took up with a *Gazho* lover and lived with him, operating a fortune-telling parlor and raising a family. She too was ostracized. Marriage between a Rom man and non-Gypsy woman is condoned if the woman learns to follow the Rom customs and the Romani language, but the opposite, which seldom occurs, is not so tolerated. Very seldom is a non-Gypsy man accepted into Rom society and allowed to take part in the culture. The woman and her non-Gypsy husband lived on the periphery of Rom society, and she could visit only her immediate relatives. Even there, her husband had no status. He was an alcoholic who was eventually killed in a barroom fight with another *Gazho*. His widow lived alone for a few years and raised her children with minimum contact with the community at large, although eventually her children married into the Rom community.

The foregoing examples should suffice to show that, even without the official censure of the *kris Romani* and a sentence of ostracism, certain individuals in the Rom community are for all intents and purposes actually censured and ostracized by the community itself because of their behavior. Seen in this light, the *kris* is then not so much a body of lawmakers that exists to punish transgressors (as in non-Gypsy state law) as it is a reflection of the consensus of the Rom community at large. This has its parallel, for example, in the shunning among the Amish and in similar forms of ostracism among other tightly-knit religious groups.

Attempts to integrate the *kris* into the surrounding non-Gypsy legal system have been made, but to date nothing concrete has emerged. In the late 1980s Southern California was divided into eighteen territories, each having its own local *shato* and judges. According to the late John Merino, one of the *shaturia* involved, the *kris* attempted to operate collectively as an integrated body within the state judicial system in areas of civil and domestic law for cases involving Rom and Romani law. The *kris* retained non-Romani attorneys on its behalf, most of whom were familiar with Gypsies and their culture. This was an effort to solve conflicts when Rom levelled false accusations against fellow Rom because of territorial invasions and other squabbles, or when they took cases of kidnapping, which were actually elopements, to the American courts, which were ignorant of Rom culture and Romani law. The *kris* could then submit a report to the American court outlining the trial and the results, thus avoiding prosecution of Rom for kidnapping when elopement was the real offense. It could also settle other problems, such as false accusations.

This type of inter-court liaison is already practiced between Canada's Native peoples and the Canadian courts in the Canadian Northwest Territories, where Inuit and tribal Indian courts work in conjunction with the Canadian courts to administer justice to Natives. This cooperation relates to crimes committed by Natives against other Natives, whose concepts of crime and punishment differ radically from the mainstream non-Indian Canadian justice system. Whether or not this type of liaison could work between the *kris-Romani* and the law of the land is problematic. Apparently the California experiment was not entirely successful. The Canadian system works because there are large communities of Natives, an available group of educated Native administrators, lawyers, and social workers, and a Native police force. Further, Natives in Canada are recognized officially as a genuine aboriginal people with rights to their culture, which is certainly not the case with the Rom, except under the Charter of the United Nations. The understanding of the true culture, history, and origin of the Rom by the average non-Gypsy judge, lawyer, or police officer in any country is deplorable and at the level of a paperback novel about Gypsies, thanks to the constant mythology which appears in the press.

There was another departure for the *kris* in the fall of 1986 when Rom leaders from the southwestern United States, representing Rom communities in many cities, met in Houston, Texas, to reevaluate the role of the *kris* and to discuss the problems now confronting the Rom judicial system. This "seminar" was attended by over two hundred Rom representing twenty-six states, and was the largest such assembly of Rom in living memory in the United States. It was aimed at covering the rules and laws not just of one specific location, but of the geographical area represented by the delegates. The Rom rented an entire hotel and the meeting was held in an ultra-modern setting with a podium, sound system, and other paraphernalia. According to Dr. Ian Hancock of the University of Texas, who attended this meeting, the main topics discussed were Rom divorce and the question of "blackballing," the latter covering mainly the ostracizing and public censure of Rom who failed to abide either by the rules adopted by the *kris* or by those rules already in force. This meeting was convened because Rom leaders felt that the overall effectiveness and structure of the *kris* was being eroded and weakened and that consolidation and reaffirmation of its strength were needed. Women's rights were also discussed, although no women were present, as well as the *marimé* code, which many felt is becoming vague among the younger Rom.

The questions of an umbrella political organization and the role of the International Romani Union were discussed, and while many of the older men rejected the idea of meddling in non-Gypsy politics, many of the under-forty age group agreed that some type of Rom political alliance to deal with external matters was necessary. Plans to form such an organization were discussed. Since then, a fair number of younger Rom leaders have become involved in one way or another with the American branch of the Romani Union, and some have visited international Rom conferences held in Europe, where the problems facing Gypsies of all subgroups are far more serious than they are in the United States or Canada. But the current swing to the right which has affected the European Gypsies is also spreading to both countries, where it is becoming more evident in the so-called "Gypsy squads" and self-appointed "Gypsy criminal experts," or in the special law enforcement officers who have become "Gypsy hunters" by adhering to the Nazi concept that Gypsies, as an ethnic group, are "criminal by heredity" (guilty in principle).

Such organizations have created the mythology that there is a nationwide (even worldwide) network of highly organized "Gypsy gangs" working hand-in-glove with one another, whether they are Rom-Vlach Gypsies, other Roma (such as *Bayash*, Muslim Gypsies, Hungarian Gypsies, and *Romanitchels*) or even non-Gypsy groups such as the Irish Travelers and itinerant rip-off artists from a multitude of ethnic backgrounds who allegedly commit what are erroneously defined as "Gypsy-type crimes." Anyone who has studied the diversity of the Gypsy groups in the United States and their cultural isolation from one another can only find this idea ludicrous, but it is dangerously reminiscent of the Nazi "Jewish conspiracy" theory. The singling out of any ethnic group as "criminal" contravenes both the U.N. Charter and the Canadian Constitution.[37] There are individual Gypsy criminals, and sometimes families of them as there are individuals and crime families among other ethnic groups. Gypsy crime, however, even at its worst, bears no resemblance to the organized crime of the underworld. Rom do not deal in narcotics, run protection rackets, organize prostitution rings, rob banks, extort, commit murder for pay, or do any of the things generally attributed to the "Mafia" and the criminal underworld. Even veteran police officers, who have naturally dealt only with Gypsy lawbreakers, have been reported in the press as saying that "Gypsy crime" is penny ante and consists mostly of confidence games, not dangerous criminal activity.

However, the Rom as a group will be forced to take some action if this trend continues. Even if individual Rom were interested in engaging in dangerous criminal activities, both the *Romaniya* and the *krizinitoria* (elders) who administrate it

---

37. United Nations Declaration of Human Rights.

would condemn such behavior. Violators would be ostracized and forced outside the framework of the Rom community. The Rom economic strategy is to find some legal niche within the framework of the economy of the host culture. In Canada and the United States, this has become mainly fortune-telling for the women and a variety of trades and occupations for the men, such as dealing in new and used vehicles and other surplus commodities, which can be bought and resold or moved from one area where they are plentiful and cheap to other areas where they are worth more. Some Rom have bought businesses ranging from small fairs to laundromats, while a few are even dealing in real estate.

Economic strategies vary from one region to another with the fluctuations of the greater economy around the Rom. Thus, while many Rom run afoul of the law for minor problems such as unpaid parking tickets, working without the required license, illegal fortune-telling, and other misdemeanors, only a small minority from any of the many subgroups of Gypsies in Canada and the United States can be connected with really criminal acts. The infractions most often consist of overcharging, shoddy workmanship, and confidence games connected with spray painting, landscaping, and other work that among non-Gypsy tradesmen would be matters for the better business bureau rather than the police. Scams connected with used car dealing, for example, committed by dealers in general, both Rom and non-Rom, are singled out as part of this "nationwide Gypsy crime problem" when committed by Gypsies.[38] However, since the Rom have no way to combat this type of ethnic stereotyping, some action by a nationwide assembly of elders through the *kris* will probably have to be undertaken.

The *kris* has been inherited from a former, originally more nomadic existence after the end of Rom slavery in Rumania, and functioned principally to administer the *Romaniya* among a closed community of travelling or closely-knit urban Rom. Now the American and Canadian Rom-Vlach are becoming more of an ethnic minority in urbanized North America than a people apart living on the fringes of society as they did in Europe and, in the earlier part of the twentieth century, in Canada and the United States. Some Rom leaders have realized this, like the late John Merino in Los Angeles and those who attended the area *kris* in Houston, Texas. Whether or not this demographic trend will continue remains to be seen. Yet, in order to survive as a culture, the Rom will need to develop some form of representation in the future where they can have a voice in defining who they are. The purpose would be to work constructively with non-Gypsy organizations, instead of simply being victims of these administrations, defined not by themselves but by the surrounding nation-state.

38. When one realizes that these crimes are committed by a minority of Gypsies from any group and that all the groups have been lumped together as one organized group (which they are not and never could be), the concept of a "massive, organized Gypsy crime syndicate" is ludicrous. In reality, Gypsies from one subgroup seldom even know Gypsies from other subgroups, let alone socialize or do any kind of business with them.

TEN

Complexities of U.S. Law and Gypsy Identity

Anne Sutherland

Fundamental differences between sedentary societies and nomadic societies frequently lead to conflicts. Such conflicts stem from the interests vested in the basic social and legal forms of societies organized around individuals being in a fixed place and the interests of societies organized around the flexibility of being able to move from place to place. In sedentary societies (which developed historically with agriculture), each person has an official and personal identity linked to a fixed abode (an address), a name (a legal name), and often documents of proof of identity (birth certificate, identity card, driver's license, passport, etc.). In nomadic societies, individuals do not have a fixed abode, but work and live within a broad territory; they may have several names or identities suitable for each location within which they work; and their official or true identity is based on that which is fixed in their lives, membership in a broad kin group within which they are born or married. Their relationship with the state is therefore often problematic, and government officials frequently view nomadic peoples as a threat to the state. People who are not easily located are hard to control.

The global history of the relationships between emerging states and nomadic peoples (for example, Indians in the United States, Bedouins in Arabia, or Maasi in Kenya) is commonly a history of discrimination, persecution, violence, forced assimilation, or containment in reservations. The Gypsies are a nomadic group with such a history. Persecuted with various degrees of harshness throughout the last millennium during their movement west from northern India, they have been vilified, subject to laws targeting their nomadic ways, forcibly evicted from towns (England, France, United States), expelled *en masse* from the state (present-day Germany), enslaved (Romania), imprisoned and exterminated (Hitler's Germany), and forced to settle (Communist Russia and Eastern Bloc). Some Gypsy groups have stayed in one place (the Spanish *Kale* and Romanian Gypsies being prominent examples), but many have continued to pursue a nomadic life and culture based on large kin groups moving around in pursuit of a living.

GYPSIES IN THE UNITED STATES

There are many different Gypsy groups in the United States. The largest number call themselves *Roma*. They are subdivided loosely into "nations," of which two, the *Kalderasha* and the *Machwaya*, are predominant. These nations are further subdivided into large extended kin groups known as *vitsiya (pl.)*. The *vitsa* is the primary basis of identity for an individual. The source of a man's or woman's personal name, family name, social status, and significant relationships throughout life are based on membership in a *vitsa*. There are, of course, nuances and complications in this system (for example, women over time may take on the identity of their husband's *vitsa*), but in basic terms identity is fixed by birth in a kin group and personal identity is established and determined by that membership.

In the United States, on the whole, Gypsies enjoy more human rights and suffer less persecution than they do in Europe or Russia where their numbers are larger (approximately 10 percent of the population in Central and Eastern European countries, less in Western Europe). In the early part of the twentieth century, when Gypsies migrated in large numbers from the east coast of the United States to the west coast, Gypsies were feared and despised and often arrested for purportedly stealing children (a myth that has amazing persistence, in spite of the lack of any evidence that Gypsies have ever stolen children); they were run out of town amid wild rumors and warnings to the local citizenry published in local papers. Today, however, both the legal system and the attitudes of people towards ethnic minorities presents a much improved picture—improved but not resolved.

This article describes an encounter between a Gypsy and the law of the United States, an encounter that illustrates the more subtle problems experienced by nomadic Gypsies living in a sedentary society.

UNITED STATES V. NICHOLAS[1]

In the fall of 1991, a nineteen year-old Gypsy man, Sonny Nicholas, was convicted of the crime of using a social security number that belonged to his five-year-old nephew.[2] He subsequently served a prison term of six months. The conviction was based on a recent law making the use of a false social security number a federal felony. The law in question was intended primarily to help with the prosecution of major drug-crime syndicates and others who falsify social security numbers in order to commit serious crimes. However, as is sometimes the case a law made for one

1. United States v. Nicholas, No. 4-91-137-CR (D. Minn. Nov., 15, 1991).

2. See Sutherland, "Gypsies, Identity and Social Security Law," in 17 *PoLAR* 74–81 (1994), for an earlier version of this essay. The present essay has been extensively expanded and includes new data.

set of purposes has an unintended impact on a particular ethnic group or minority. This law has a special impact on Gypsies in the United States.

The case came to my attention when I was asked by the defense to be an expert witness on Gypsy culture. Arguments in the case concentrated on three lines of reasoning; (1) the social security law unfairly singled out Gypsies for punishment, (2) there was no intent to commit a crime, and (3) in using the social security numbers of relatives, Gypsies were following a cultural tradition based on the idea of a kin group as a corporate group. This tradition helped them to remain anonymous and separate from non-Gypsy society and is part of their strategy to survive in sedentary societies.

BACKGROUND OF THE CASE

Sonny Nicholas (S.N.) came to St. Paul, Minnesota and, using the social security number of his five-year-old nephew, obtained credit to purchase a car at a local car dealer. Noting the birth date associated with the social security number, a few days later the car dealership asked him to return the car. When S.N. returned the car to the dealership, he was arrested on the felony charge of using a false social security number. The police searched his apartment and found lists of names, addresses, and social security numbers, leading to suspicion of an organized crime ring.

In *United States v. Nicholas*,[3] it was "alleged that the defendant, S.N., while in the process of obtaining a new Ford Mustang from a car dealership, used a social security number that was not his own with intent to deceive." Under statute 42 U.S.C. 408 (g) (2), "a person who, with intent to deceive, falsely represents his or her number to obtain something of value or for any other purpose, is a felon." The defense lawyer noted that there was no allegation of attempted theft. The focus of the charging statute was false representation of numbers. He argued that the "underlying purpose which motivates a person to falsely represent his or her number may be an essentially innocent purpose, but the statute, at least as it has been interpreted, does not appear to impose a burden of proof as to wrongful purpose. The statute punishes the means (false number) which a person may employ to achieve any number of ends and it punishes those means as a felony." Furthermore, he argued that the statute's failure to address the nature of the purpose to which false credentials are used is a serious flaw in the law and may punish those who would use the number for petty misconduct at a felony-level crime. He suggested there is potential for discriminatory impact on Gypsies who use false credentials to conceal themselves from mainstream society. For example, a Gypsy household may obtain

---

3. The following quotes are from a memorandum in support of a motion to declare 42 U.S.C. 408(g)(2) unconstitutional, presented in the United States District Court, District of Minnesota by the defense attorney, Philip Leavenworth. See also United States v. Nicholas, id., including the affidavit of Janet Tompkins.

a telephone by providing a false social security number, and even if they pay the telephone bill without fail for years, they are felons under this law. In this case, S.N. not only made the payments for his car, but he returned it when the number was questioned. Nevertheless, he was still a felon under this law.

The defense lawyer argued that the law is objectionable for two reasons. First, the law's disproportionate impact on the Gypsies is objectionable under the equal protection guarantees in the Fifth Amendment of the U.S. Constitution. The law denies Gypsies equal protection by irrationally and disproportionately punishing at the felony level certain traditional Gypsy conduct which causes no positive injury to anyone. As evidence for this case he called on material from my book, *Gypsies: the Hidden Americans*,[4] for testimony that Gypsies routinely use false social security numbers to acquire credit but do pay their bills and are available for repossession of the chattels in case of default of payment. They obtain phone service, buy houses and cars and other household items on credit, and have a record of payment that is probably better than that of the general population. They do this primarily to remain unknown by mainstream society, rather than to cause loss or injury to any person.

Second, the proceeding conflicted with a Supreme Court decision that requires the government to prove felonious intent when it seeks to punish a person for wrongful acquisition of another's property.[5] The defense lawyer argued that S.N. used a false social security number because of a Gypsy tradition to remain anonymous and because his own number had been used by other Gypsies.

The federal prosecutor, on the other hand, argued that there was a "ring" of Gypsies in the area, with whom S.N. was associated. At S.N.'s residence, a number of false credentials and social security numbers, used to obtain cars illegally, were found. Some of these cars were still missing at the time of the trial. In other words, there was evidence that false identity had been used recently in the area to commit thefts. However, S.N. himself had not stolen anything and was not being accused of stealing, only of using a false social security number.

Because of the evidence of a ring of car thieves in the area, the prosecution hoped to use the threat of prosecution against S.N., the only Gypsy they were able to arrest, to plea bargain for information regarding the other people involved in the alleged ring. These other people had disappeared immediately after S.N. was arrested.

One of the problems in the case was that both the prosecution and the defense had difficulty understanding the situation they faced. Neither could establish com-

---

4. Anne Sutherland, *Gypsies: The Hidden Americans* (1986). See also "The Gypsies of California," in *Face Values: Some Anthropological Themes* 176–207 (1978).

5. See Morrissette v. United States, 342 U.S. 246 (1952) in which the Supreme Court provided an examination of the issue of intent in criminal law. The court ruled that in the absence of an express element of felonious intent, intent will become an element to be proved. Id. at 279. There must be some loss or injury to justify a felony conviction.

plete and accurate information on S.N., beginning with his "real" name, which they never did determine correctly.[6] Although I explained the Gypsy practice of using many "American" names but only one "Gypsy" name (*nav romano*), neither the prosecution nor the defense was satisfied with a "Gypsy" name. For example, the Gypsy name of *o špiro le Stevanosko* (or Spiro, the son of Stevan) uses the noun declension characteristic of the Sanskrit-rooted language (*Romanes*) and does not employ a surname. Spiro's identity can be pinned down by finding out what *vitsa* (a cognatic descent group) he belongs to so that he will not be mixed up with any other Spiro le Stevanoskos. The Spiro of our example is a *Kashtare*, which is part of a larger "nation" of Gypsies or *natsia* called *Kalderasha* (coppersmiths). For his "American" names he may take any of a number of American names used by his relatives such as Spiro Costello, John Costello, John Marks, John Miller, Spiro John or Spiro Miller. His nickname is Rattlesnake Pete.

Also, neither the defense nor the prosecution were able to deal with two issues. First, Gypsies, organized around traditions suitable for a nomadic people, frequently borrow each other's "American" names and social security numbers, viewing them as a kind of corporate property of their kin group (the *vitsa*). Second, Gypsy families who move around the country on a regular basis often lack birth certificates[7] and must somehow create midwife or baptismal certificates to use for identification purposes to obtain a social security number, enter school, or apply for a driver's license.

THE ANTHROPOLOGIST AS CULTURAL BROKER

S.N.'s defense attorney contacted me after reading my book on Gypsies and learning that his confusion about S.N. was helped by understanding something about them. For his case he needed to determine if S.N. really was a Gypsy, find out his name and circumstances and get some cultural information that would help him with his case (such as the use of social security numbers by Gypsies).

---

6. See Price & Price, "Saramaka Onomastics: An Afro-American Naming System," in 11 *Ethnology* 341–44 (1972). They reported that some African-American minorities may use many names as part of a survival strategy. For example, the Saramaka Maroons (also known as "Bush Negroes") in Surinam have three kinds of names: a true or big name (a name associated with their bearers), little or nicknames (names given throughout life marking identifying features of the person, including playful names, romantic names, and insulting nicknames) and a Western name (used when they take 'work trips' in areas other than where they live).

7. Although babies are now frequently born in hospitals, the families may move soon after the birth, before the baby is named, and be unable to remember where or when the children were born in order to obtain a birth certificate, the place of birth being unimportant to them. If they do obtain a birth certificate, the name given on it will not be the name of the child within the *vitsa*, but will be an "American" name for outsiders. This American name is flexible and can change and is unimportant for their purposes. Police and prosecutors are often disconcerted to find that a Gypsy may have many "aliases" and are frustrated at not being able to establish a legal name, leading to suspicion of criminal activity on the basis of so many "aliases." See Sutherland, supra n. 4, at 176–207; Tompkins, "Barvale Revisited," in *100 Years of Gypsy Studies*, 111–16 (Matt T. Salo ed., 1990).

Consequently, one cold fall day I drove up to the prison, one and a half hours from the city, and met S.N. in a room in a federal holding prison. He was a thin young man, scared and nervous, in perpetual fear of pollution from contact with non-Gypsies, and suffering from the effects of several months of what for him was solitary confinement since he had not seen any of his people since being incarcerated. The telephone was his only link with people with whom he could relate, people from his own culture and language. His main contact was with a non-Gypsy woman who lived with one of his relatives. She was his link with the world he had known and hers was the only "American" household he had been in before prison. Since my primary task was to determine if he was a Gypsy, first I talked to him about his relatives in Los Angeles and his *vitsa (Yowane)* and tried to establish what section of the *vitsa* I personally knew. This exchange of information about *vitsa* and Gypsies of mutual acquaintance is a normal one between Gypsies. The purpose is to establish a link between two persons meeting for the first time.

To help the defense collect accurate information on the facts of the case, I asked him what had happened and why he was in Minnesota. He talked about a seasonal expedition he and his brothers and cousins make to Minnesota to buy and sell cars and fix fenders before winter sets in. He claimed not to know where his brothers and cousins had gone or how he got into his present predicament. He was somewhat perplexed at being arrested since he had stolen nothing, and he certainly did not understand the law under which he was charged.

Somewhat frustrated with efforts to facilitate communication between S.N. and his defense lawyer, I sought to take action on his conditions in jail. When I met him, S.N. had lost fifteen pounds in the month that he was held in jail and was suffering demonstrable distress and nervousness. Like many other prisoners, he was distressed because he was incarcerated for the first time in his life. He was also fearful of the other prisoners and worried about his safety while in prison.

But as a Gypsy he had two serious concerns particular to his culture. While in jail he was cut off from his culture and people without any possibility of direct contact. Within his own culture's legal system (the *kris*), the most severe punishment imposed upon a Gypsy who has transgressed an important code of conduct is to be declared "rejected" (or *marime*, in *Romanes*) by the group for a specified period of time. This "rejection" denies the individual access to all other Gypsies (including family), and is viewed as both a kind of solitary confinement as well as a condition of constant moral impurity until readmission to the group.

In addition, confinement in jail meant he had to worry about becoming defiled (also known as *marime*) through the food, close physical contact with non-Gypsies, and exposure to jailhouse germs. He was worried that if he ate food prepared by non-Gypsies who do not follow rules of cleanliness considered essential in the Gypsy culture, he would become *marime*. To avoid this fate, he refused prison food in the hope that when he was released from prison he would be able to return to his family without a period of physical exile (*marime*).

Although there was no remedy for the first specifically Gypsy cultural concern, the second problem was relatively simple to ameliorate. I arranged for his lawyer to provide him with money to buy food from the concession because it is packaged and untouched by non-Gypsies and therefore considered clean by Gypsy standards. He bought milk in cartons, candy bars and soft drinks and other packaged foods that, though they may not have provided balanced nutrition, at least were not defiling and kept him from starvation.

A further complicating factor for S.N. was that he spoke English as a second language. His ability to read was rudimentary, thus straining his grasp of his defense. Also, his only contact with relatives was by telephone since neither he nor they could write with any ease. Even though his limited English made it difficult for him to follow his own trial, the court did not provide a translator.

THE TRIAL

The trial, held in the U.S. District Court of Minnesota, centered around the constitutionality of a law that unfairly targets a particular ethnic group and the question of intent to commit a crime. My testimony was intended to establish that Gypsies may use false identification for a number of cultural reasons which may have no connection with any intent to commit a crime. For a traditionally nomadic group with pariah status in the wider society and a pattern of secretiveness and autonomy, the argument went, concealing identity is a long-established pattern. This pattern, widespread among all Gypsy groups in Eastern Europe, Western Europe, Russia, Latin America and the United States, is a mechanism developed over centuries to protect themselves from a wider society that has persecuted them, moved them on, and treated them as parasites on society.

Both historical and current examples of persecution were presented. The recent case in which the German government paid large sums to Romania to take back Gypsy refugees was only the latest in a historically established tradition of modern nation-states abhorring Gypsies. The persecution of Gypsies in the Holocaust, in medieval Europe, and in the early part of the twentieth century in the United States has been well documented.[8] Recent events in Eastern Europe have shown a resurgence of extreme prejudice against Gypsies. Interviews in New York Times articles point to a hatred of Gypsies so deep that there is talk of extermination.[9] Because

---

8. See Donald Kenrick & Grattan Puxon, *The Destiny of Europe's Gypsies* (1972) and Ian Hancock, *The Pariah Syndrome: An Account of Gypsy Slavery and Persecution* (1987). Because of the attempted extermination of Gypsies during the Holocaust, they are now represented at the United States Holocaust Memorial in Washington, D.C. For accounts of the slavery of Gypsies in Romania, see also Beck, "The Origins of Gypsy Slavery in Romania," 14 *Dialectical Anthropology* 53–61 (1989), and Gheorghe, "Origin of Roma's Slavery in the Rumanian Principalities," 1 *Roma* 12–27 (1983).

9. See "In New Eastern Europe, An Old Anti-Gypsy Bias" by Henry Kamm, *N.Y. Times*, Nov. 17, 1993 and "In Slovak Gypsy Ghetto, Hovels and Plea for Jobs," by Henry Kamm, *N.Y. Times*, Nov. 28,

of the history of violence against them, Gypsies developed elaborate mechanisms of secrecy and hid their identity in order to survive.[10] I argued that they have little motivation to change a pattern that has stood them in good stead for so many centuries.

An additional complication in the S.N. case was the question of identification from photographs. Here we came up against the age-old problem of members from one culture and race having trouble identifying individuals from another culture and race. In simple terms, to many non-Gypsies, all Gypsies look alike. Part of the case involved clearing up erroneous identification of S.N. in photos provided by the prosecution, most of which were photos of other people.

The purpose of my testimony was to establish that S.N. was a Gypsy, and that Gypsies often use false identification without intent to defraud. They do so because as members of a *vitsa*, which is their cognatic descent group, identification is corporate in nature. Members of the group have corporate access to property owned by other members of the group. That property includes forms of identification.

I was also asked to testify regarding my own personal experience with discrimination against Gypsies by the Minneapolis Police Department. This occurred during a talk I gave to some twenty police to help them understand Gypsy culture. When I spoke about the strong sense of family and community among the Gypsies, in particular how important their children are, one officer suggested that since their main problem is how to detain Gypsies long enough to prosecute them, removing Gypsy children from their homes on any pretext would be an effective way to keep the parents in town.

Prejudice against Gypsies often goes unrecognized even by normally culturally and racially sensitive people. The assistant district attorney prosecuting S.N. offered me an article that he used to understand the Gypsies, entitled, "Gypsies, the People and Their Criminal Propensity,"[11] which quotes extensively from my work, including the fact that they have several names and that the same or similar non-Gypsy names are used over and over. The article concentrates on "criminal" behavior and never mentions the possibility that there are Gypsies who may not engage in criminal activities. In one section, there are quotes from my book on the

---

1993 for recent accounts of extreme prejudice against Gypsies. One Catholic parish priest in Slovakia is reported to have said, "I'm no racist, but some Gypsies you would have to shoot" (*New York Times*, Nov. 28, 1993). For a recent book on the plight of Eastern European Gypsies who are returning to a nomadic life after decades of travel restrictions under Communist governments, see David Crowe & John Kolsti, *The Gypsies of Eastern Europe* (1991); Marushiakova, "Ethnic Identity Among Gypsy Groups in Bulgaria," 2 *Journal of the Gypsy Lore Society*, 5, 95–115 (1992), and Marushiakova, "Relations Among the Gypsy Groups in Bulgaria," *The Ethnic Situation in Bulgaria* 7–16 (1993).

10. The literature on this phenomenon is huge. See, for example, Sutherland, supra n. 4; Judith Okely, *The Traveller-Gypsies* (1983); and George Gmelch, *The Irish Tinkers* (1985).

11. Terry Getsay, "Gypsies, the People and Their Criminal Propensity," *Kansas State Fop Journal*, Parts I, II, and III (1982).

ways Gypsies deal with the welfare bureaucracy placed under the title, "Welfare Fraud," although by far most of the practices I described were legal. Part II of the article concludes in the following way and is representative of the tone of the article: "Officers should not be misled into thinking these people are not organized. They are indeed organized and operate under established rules of behavior, including those that govern marriage, living quarters, child rearing, the division of money and participation in criminal acts." These are highly inflammatory statements. Gypsies have a culture, history, language and social structure, but that fact is distorted to imply that their social organization is partly for the purpose of facilitating criminal behavior. The prosecution saw their culture as a "criminal" culture, a viewpoint that Gypsies have been fighting for hundreds of years and still combat in their relations with law enforcement and the criminal justice system.

The American law enforcement and legal systems are, of course, not the only systems to single out Gypsies as a criminal culture, unworthy of basic respect. Indeed, I have personally witnessed far worse examples of legal injustices and police brutality against Gypsies. In Stara Zagora, Bulgarian police broke up marriage celebrations in a public park and brutally beat several men, including one man in his seventies, and then threw them in jail for several days. Gypsy informants and a Bulgarian ethnographer confirmed that such treatment is so commonplace that the Gypsies have come to expect it. In Budapest, Hungary, police stood by while a mob of skinheads ransacked an apartment house occupied by Gypsies and beat several occupants, including women, who were later hospitalized. I have not heard of such instances of brutality by the police in major American cities, but they do train their officers to regard the Gypsies as an organized criminal culture, a "poor man's mafia." This practice has far-reaching implications for the position of Gypsies in relation to the U.S. judicial system.

In spite of the best efforts of S.N.'s attorney and my testimony that use of a false social security number did not necessarily indicate intent to commit a crime, S.N. was convicted of illegally using a social security number and served about six months in jail.

Anthropologists are often called in as expert witnesses in cases involving cultural differences. Most Native American legal cases, such as the Mashpee case reported by James Clifford,[12] center around Indian status versus treaty and land rights. In St. Paul, a number of high visibility Hmong legal cases have involved marriage customs and age status coming into conflict with the legal status of minors in American law. With the Gypsies, there is yet another set of issues in their contact with the law.

The first is the question of the cultural conflict between a historically nomadic group and the state bureaucracy of settled people. Identification, which is a serious legal issue in a bureaucratic society composed of people with fixed abodes and

---

12. See Clifford, "Identity in Mashpee," in *The Predicament of Culture: Twentieth-Century Ethnography, Literature and Art* 277–346 (1988).

a written language, has virtually no meaning for the nomadic Roma, who consider descent and extended family ties the defining factors for identification and whose language is based on orality. The second is the conflict between Roma religious rules regarding purity and prison regulations. The Roma avoid situations, such as working for non-Gypsies or being in school or jail, that require them to be in prolonged contact with non-Gypsies rather than with their own family and Gypsy friends. They particularly avoid having to eat food cooked by non-Gypsies or having to wash in a way that fails to keep upper and lower halves of the body separate, the mixing of which they consider polluting.

Jail presents special problems for the Roma. Prison has its own stigma, which can include the stigma of becoming *marime*. The psychological trauma that results from isolation from their community is compounded if they then emerge from jail and have to undergo a further isolation from relatives because of becoming *marime* in jail. When this does occur, they must submit to another trial, a *kris,* which is held by their own people.

Gypsies in the United States rarely do go to jail; however, it is not uncommon for a *kris* to be held after a jail sentence to "reinstate" a person. Ian Hancock has reported that a *kris* held for a family some time ago in Chattanooga resulted in reinstatement after a specified period of *marime.* Because the case involved rape and incest, several people did not honor the reinstatement, although such a decision should be binding. The severity of the crime may have had an influence on people's feelings about reinstatement.

The most notorious figure to serve time in prison was Barbara Miller, convicted of fraud over thirty years ago with the help of other Gypsies who hoped to break her control over fortune-telling in San Francisco. She had no *kris* when she returned from jail; however, she did not make an appearance with other Gypsies for about five years after her release from prison. This, of course, constitutes a kind of isolation. She also was ostracized by some Gypsies for many years afterwards. Although there is no rule that requires someone coming out of prison to be cleared by a *kris,* some people are isolated automatically if the crime is considered serious. For example, a Gypsy family in Hawaii that had committed a murder had not been welcome at any Machwaya Gypsy event for some time, and it was generally agreed that they would not dare show up. The isolation constitutes a penalty. A *kris* would be appropriate if the criminal gets another Gypsy in trouble or causes so much trouble with the police that they bring the law down on other Gypsies in the area. In these cases, the *kris* is needed to determine a fine or for how long a person is "blocked."

In Minnesota in 1938, Rosa Frank (aka Madame Mary Johnson or Mary Smith) was convicted of defrauding a woman of $3,850 and received an "indeterminate sentence in the state reformatory, not to exceed seven years."[13] Incensed by her conviction, she agreed to an interview with the local newspaper:

13. Information on this case is from the *Albert Lea Tribune,* May 17, 1938. I am indebted to Linda Evenson of the Freeborn County Historical Society for locating this article.

My real name is Mary Smith. I am Romanian. My mother's name is Rosa Frank and she is somewhere in Kentucky. I have been a mind reader for the past five years. . . . I want you to put in the paper that I have been treated fine while in jail. Well, I got seven years, but I don't expect to stay there that long. Your paper said I had a long criminal record. Well, that may be, but this is the first time I have had to go up for anything I ever did. If you want me to tell you more about myself and my people, ask me. I'll tell you everything now—and the truth. I might just as well, for I'll have to go to jail anyway. So what's the difference? Now, be sure to put this talk with me in your paper. If you don't I'll give it to the big-city papers.

This interview is revealing in several ways. According to her, she has "borrowed" her mother's name for her trial, although the "real" name she gives, Mary Smith, is clearly another "American name" for the newspaper, in addition to her fortune-telling name of Madame Johnson. She fully expects her relatives to reimburse the woman she defrauded and her sentence to be reduced.[14] Finally, much of the interview is directed to her relatives and other Gypsies. She emphasizes and wants it published that she is being treated well (presumably in hopes of avoiding 'rejection' after jail), and she threatens to tell "everything now—and the truth." Going to jail places her at risk with her people, so secrecy is negotiable.

Another case[15] in San Francisco involved a girl who ran away from her parents to join the Job Corps, an organization that, to many Gypsies, resembles prison. After a few lonely months she called home, and her parents immediately brought her home. A *kris* was assembled in a park in the center of town composed of all the adult men in the vicinity, with George Merino from San Jose officiating. Women were present to comment, but they did not directly take part in the proceedings. They passed around documents that the girl's mother had obtained with the help of their social worker. Three documents were required: a gynecological exam to determine that she did not have venereal disease, a statement from a psychiatrist that she was sane (he was instructed by her mother to "fix her mind so she would not do it again"), and an affidavit from the social worker that the Job Corps was not a prison. The *kris* accepted all three documents as valid, and the verdict was one-month *marime*, after which the girl was welcomed back into the community and married to a Gypsy boy chosen by her parents.

14. According to the *Albert Lea Tribune*, May 17, 1938, "a brother of Madame Johnson, one George Frank, informed Judge Peterson that he was going to help reimburse Mrs. Cloukey. 'Here is $700 in currency' (laying that sum down on the clerks' desk). 'That is the first payment. I will turn over $300 in the next fifteen days.' He continued, 'I will see the heads of different tribes of gypsies and I am sure I can get all of the money for Mrs. Cloukey.' Archie Tom, another gypsy, addressed the judge, stating that he, too, would help get the money that was taken from Mrs. Cloukey. The move on the part of the gypsies (it was very, very evident) was to persuade the judge to make Madame Johnson's sentence a light one." The gathering of the "heads of different tribes of gypsies" probably refers to a *kris* that would be called to deal with the situation.

15. From personal correspondence with Janet Tompkins.

Finally, these examples illustrate a cultural clash between the Rom value of corporate kinship and the American value of individual rights. The rights and status of an individual Rom are directly linked to his or her membership in the *vitsa*. Furthermore, the status of all members of the *vitsa* is affected by the behavior of each individual *vitsa* member. Since they are so intricately linked, reciprocity between *vitsa* members is expected. Members of a *vitsa* and family share economic resources, stay in each other's homes, help each other in work and preparation of rituals, and loan each other cars, information, identification, and money. They also share the shame of immoral or incorrect behavior by one member and the stigma (*marime*) attached to going to jail. For the Gypsies, the American ideal of each individual having only one name, one social security number, and a reputation based entirely on personal behavior is contrary to their experience and culture.

CONCLUSIONS

The analysis of an event such as a trial, especially an event that brings to the fore cultural differences, can be instructive for both cultures. In this essay I have tried to present fundamental differences between the practices of American culture and law and the practices of Gypsy culture and Roma law. Understanding differences does not necessarily resolve conflict, but it can lead to a more humanitarian application of the law to different cultures. The United States, a country based on immigration and diversity, is in no position to ignore the cultural foundations of different ethnic groups. Of course, different cultures in the United States are not exempt from a law because it is contrary to custom. However, the more aware the legal system is of cultural histories and custom, the greater its capacity for justice.

As the world moves into the next millennium, more people than ever before in human history also are on the move—as migrants, immigrants, guest workers, refugees, and even as tourists. At this time in history, many people are living in places that do not share their cultural and legal traditions. Studies of society and legal systems must search for ways to deal with this cultural encounter. Gypsies have probably the longest recorded history of continuous movement and adaptation to other societies and cultures. Their treatment is a barometer of justice and civilization.

ELEVEN

Oral Legal Traditions of Gypsies and Some American Equivalents

Walter O. Weyrauch

INTRODUCTION

The significance of tribal law for comparative law is not commonly stressed. To the extent that comparisons remain on the level of legal cultures that are historically and politically closely allied to each other, even though they are in appearance "different," an element of unconscious ethnocentrism cannot be eliminated. We tend to compare legal cultures with whose reasoning and results one can identify. The closeness of the parallels, while full identity is missing, tends to be experienced as stimulating. Yet the occasional forays into legal cultures that are "radically different"[1] may be more fascinating and jurisprudentially and even practically rewarding. This will become increasingly apparent as my discussion of Gypsy law and American equivalents proceeds. Indeed, as the extraordinary importance of oral legal traditions within American law is suggested, the distinction between the foreign and local may become blurred, as well as the separation of jurisprudence and legal practice. This journey will take us from the esoteric to questions of legal strategy that finally may gain a legitimate place within legal theory. Since essentially novel territory is explored, I present no firm conclusions, but mere guidelines for further research.

As an example of tribal autonomous lawmaking, Maureen A. Bell and I have examined *Romaniya* or Gypsy law.[2] This having been the first study of Gypsy law

The author is indebted to Frank Allen, Gunther Arzt, Maureen Bell, Martha Duncan, Ian Hancock, Stanley Ingber, Joanna Kinney, Leslie Lieberman, Lynn LoPucki, Ronald Mann, Matilda Montgomery, Rosalie Sanderson, Paul Schwartz, and Robert Summers. Financial support of the University of Florida Summer Research Program is gratefully acknowledged.

1. John H. Barton, James Lowell Gibbs, Victor Hao Li & John Henry Merryman, *Law in Radically Different Cultures* (1983). The foreign jurisdictions chosen in this work, Botswana, the People's Republic of China, and Egypt, are still largely based on written sources, while Gypsy law is wholly based on oral legal tradition.

2. Weyrauch & Bell, "Autonomous Lawmaking: The Case of the 'Gypsies'," chap. 2 in this volume. [hereinafter Weyrauch & Bell, *Gypsy Law*].

published in any legal periodical, it has evoked comments by readers that were not covered in the original effort but are worthy of examination. They may prove to be significant for an understanding of our law in its possible "tribal aspects." Three points that were raised are important in this context: first, the purposes of studies of legal anthropology of this kind; second, the ethics of uncovering a legal system meant to be secret; and third, the charge that the Roma violate human rights because they supposedly treat half of their population, namely women, as impure.[3]

The first two points are necessary for a full discussion of the third point that cultural practices of the Gypsies violate human rights. A charge of this gravity requires some level of self-examination. If this element is neglected, unresolved problems of one's own culture may be inadvertently projected into the culture whose practices are critically analyzed. Introspection, recommended in section one, leads to multiple questions of ethics, discussed in section two. The research on Gypsy law itself raises the question whether it is appropriate to give information, confidentially obtained from Romani sources, wide circulation, if publicity may result in damage to the Gypsy culture. In evaluating what constitutes "damage," weight must be given to the perception of the Roma themselves, rather than imposing the host culture's views that inevitably are quite different.

The idea that human rights are violated because Gypsies consider women to be "polluted" as a result of menstruation, discussed in section three, may conceivably involve a misplaced projection of Western values. One can hardly speak of *universal* human rights in regard to whether menstruation is "polluting" or has perhaps some more positive meanings. Caution may be required in analyzing notions common among the Roma, especially if they are essential for the efficacy of their autonomous legal system. Human rights violations may, of course, occur in any nation or ethnic group. Even the United States, as President Reagan once publicly acknowledged, has not been immune to such charges in regard to racial strains and the plight of the homeless.[4] Yet such official acknowledgments are exceedingly rare and are likely to come from within a powerful nation that has a tradition of public dialogue and freedom of expression and the means and will to bring about change. The situation of alleged human rights violations of the Gypsies is different.

The Roma are a dispersed and defenseless people who have survived against all odds by cultural practices that, to outsiders, may be offensive. They have no central government and little, if any, power or sympathy in their "host nations." For

---

3. Reisman, "Autonomy, Interdependence, and Responsibility," 103 *Yale L.J.* 401, 416–17 (1993). See also Diane Tong, *Gypsies: A Multidisciplinary Annotated Bibliography* 335 (1995) (citing subordination of Gypsy women and possible human rights violations).

4. Steven V. Roberts, "President Praises Soviet on Rights: Cites U.S. Failings," *N.Y. Times,* May 5, 1988, at A-1 (responding to Soviet charges of human rights violations in the United States that in turn were prompted by earlier American charges of human rights violations in the former Soviet Union).

centuries they have been maligned and subjected to severe and often ferocious persecutions, culminating in the Nazi holocaust.[5] World support has been, and continues to be, conspicuously absent. The objection that the Gypsies have brought these persecutions upon themselves has little persuasive power. From time immemorial this reasoning has been used to justify racial and religious persecutions in any part of the world. Misgivings that xenophobia may be involved cannot be easily dismissed.[6]

Within this historical background of victimization, the charge that the ethnic group of Gypsies as a whole violates human rights because of its views of menstruation demands close scrutiny, for customary practices that may similarly subordinate women, although of different origin and legal consequence, are not unknown in Judeo-Christian cultures, including our own. Thus a discussion of seemingly similar gender-related problems among the Roma may shed light on perspectives and practices closer to home. I will take up the three topics in the order in which they are stated, culminating in a discussion of the alleged human rights violations and showing, in summation, that these themes are interrelated.

In the concluding section four, I will try to show, based on two illustrations from judicial processes taken from a county court and hypothetically from the U.S. Supreme Court, how the seemingly esoteric discussion of the law of the Gypsies may yield insight into the working of American law. As with the Gypsies, questions of scholarly ethics relating to cultural taboos may determine how far such an inquiry may be pressed. Finally, I suggest that so-called lawyer strategies gain their persuasive power from untapped resources of oral legal traditions.

I. OBJECTIVES OF STUDYING GYPSY LAW

Essential features of Gypsy law must be shortly summarized as a foundation for analysis. It is based on ancient oral traditions, some of them dating back to India which the Roma left a millennium ago. Law is perceived as a state of balance and wholesomeness (*kintála*) that can be disturbed by acts perceived to be polluting.[7] A unique feature of Gypsy law is that it is closely tied to the human body, including aspects of intimate life and procreation. The human body is both pure and impure.[8] The upper body is fundamentally pure and clean, while the lower body is *marime* or impure. Functions relating to the lower part of the body, regardless of

5. See, e.g., Alan Cowell, "Attack on Austrian Gypsies Deepens Fear of Neo-Nazis," *N.Y. Times*, Feb. 21, 1995, at A-1. See also infra n. 59. The commonly used term "host nation" is objectionable to some Roma because of possible negative connotations. Cf. Katrin Reemtsma, *Sinti and Roma: Geschichte, Kultur, Gegenwart* 69 (1996) (questioning the propriety of treating the Sinti and Roma as "foreign" after six hundred years of presence in Europe).

6. See infra nn. 30–35 and accompanying text (discussing alleged Gypsy criminality).

7. Hancock, "Glossary of Romani Terms," chap. 8 in this volume, at 176 (defining *Kintála*).

8. Anne Sutherland, *Gypsies: The Hidden Americans* 258 (Reissue 1986) (1975); Hancock, "Gypsies," in *Harv. Encyc. of Am. Ethnic Groups* 440, 443 (1980).

gender, are matters of intense concern to the Roma and must be regulated by law in minute detail to prevent contamination.[9]

While most of these regulations have direct consequences for conducting daily life and relations to other people, their strict observance determines whether one is not merely law-abiding, but in a deeper sense a just person. Essentially they are self-executing, more comparable to the function of our conscience, and do not require the threat by any outside authority. Violation, however, may result in being ostracized and shunned, in severe cases even expelled from the community of Gypsies. The intensity of these internalized commands and the fear of losing communal respect and support is sufficient to prevent many forms of deviancy among Gypsies.

Distinctions between law, ethics, and custom, problematical even in American law, cannot be made in the Romani legal culture in these respects. Moral behavior, as understood among Gypsies, determines the content of law. Consequently, law cannot be merely an ethical minimum. It would not make sense for Gypsies to argue that their conduct was legal, although it may have violated the mandates of good morals. In other words, in their view morality is a matter of law, and disputes are likely to concentrate on whether particular facts alleged have taken place. This does not foreclose the possibility of a deliberation whether a past controversial incident was morally wrong and therefore illegal.

As far as Gypsy women are concerned, menstruation is given special significance, in accordance with contemporary Indian customs, thus giving them symbolic power over others, including men, for example, by tossing their skirt.[10] Yet the genital aspect should not be overemphasized. A woman may throw her shoe at another person with the same polluting effect.[11] Nonsexual matters, such as stealing from another Gypsy or not paying a debt when due, may also be seen as polluting.[12] From a non-Gypsy (*gajikano*) perspective much of the Gypsy concern with cleanliness seems to be more metaphorical than real, at least to the *gaje* (non-Gypsies), perhaps because the Roma are concerned with inner purity regardless of external appearances.[13]

The legal significance of the human body, rather than of abstract concepts, also seems to be a distinctive feature. Thus it is the person who is the primary source of

---

9. Weyrauch & Bell, *Gypsy Law*, supra n. 2, at 30–32. The highly private nature of Gypsy law, as well as the sanctions in case of violation, help also to minimize conflict with the host country's legal order. Letter from Robert S. Summers, William G. McRoberts Research Professor of Law, Cornell University, to Walter O. Weyrauch, at 1 (March 20, 1995) (on file with author).

10. Isabel Fonseca, *Bury Me Standing: The Gypsies and Their Journey* 80, 130 (1995).

11. Miller, "American Rom and the Ideology of Defilement," in *Gypsies, Tinkers and Other Travellers* 41, 51 n. 20 (Farnham Rehfisch ed., 1975).

12. Weyrauch & Bell, *Gypsy Law*, supra n. 2, at 000.

13. Rena C. Gropper, *Gypsies in the City: Culture Patterns and Survival* 91 (1975); Okely, "Gypsy Women: Models in Conflict," in *Perceiving Women* 55, 60–61 (Shirley Ardener ed., 1975). Okely describes the Romanichals (English Gypsies), whose laws on purity and pollution are in many respects similar to those of the Vlax Gypsies and other Romani groups.

law and not a body of theoretical constructs originating from an elite or the state. To the extent that there is a leadership, it finds its authority in a Gypsy having adhered to the unwritten code and thereby over time earned the respect of others. Significantly, a primary criterion for leadership among Gypsies is that a man has a wife who is strong and capable of aggressively asserting her authority within the family and toward outsiders, a factor that speaks against a subordinate position of Gypsy women.[14]

While all Roma adhere to notions of purity and pollution in various degrees, some groups, in particular the Vlax who were enslaved in Rumania for five hundred years and who are the largest group of Gypsies in the United States, have a formal method of adjudication called *kris*.[15] Elected judges decide on specific controversies. Although the Vlax Gypsies have no standing courts, it is useful to refer tentatively to these decisionmaking bodies as courts.[16] They are no more or less judicial in their functions than American courts that, in contemporary practice, are often merely rubberstamping settlements in criminal and civil cases. In these instances the actual decisions have been bargained out in attorneys' offices, and the approval of the court is more administrative in nature than judicial.[17]

To speak of courts invokes, however, powerful myths that lend themselves to comparisons as such. To the extent that law is largely based on myths, both in the

---

14. Sutherland, supra n. 8, at 102.

15. Ronald Lee, "The *Kris Romani*," *Roma*, July 1987, at 19; Liégeois, "La Kris," 19 *Études Tsiganes*, Sept. 1973, at 31; Nemeth, "Field Notes from 1970: A Kris in River City," in *100 Years of Gypsy Studies* 117 (Matt T. Salo ed., 1990); Weyrauch & Bell, *Gypsy Law*, supra n. 2, at 42–48. The proceedings are entirely conducted in Romani, the language, rooted in Sanskrit, common to all Gypsies, Lee, supra, at 28. See also infra nn. 65, 66, and 94 and accompanying text (noting that translation into English is difficult, but important for comprehending *Romaniya* or Gypsy law).

Other Gypsy groups, such as the Kaale in Finland and the Romanichals in England, have informal means of dispute resolution. Some of the practices have evolved into benign derivatives of the original "blood feud." The culprit and his kin move to an area that is distant from the location of the victim. Since both parties mutually refrain from further contact, the remedy has been called "institutionalized avoidance." It implies a legal fiction that treats the parties as if guilt had been admitted and further retaliation is not possible or desirable. The wrongdoer has to live with his shame. Grönfors, "Social Control and Law in the Finnish Gypsy Community: Blood Feuding as a System of Justice," 1986 *J. Legal Pluralism & Unofficial L.* 101, 120–21; Acton, Caffrey & Mundy, "Theorizing Gypsy Law," chap. 3 in this volume. But see Elena Marushiakova & Vesselin Popov, *Gypsies (Roma) in Bulgaria* 155–65 (Studien zur Tsiganologie und Folkloristik No. 18, 1997) (maintaining that judicial proceedings similar to the *kris* of the Vlax exist also, under different names, in other Romani groups).

16. But see Reisman, supra n. 3, at 405–6 (suggesting that reference to the *kris* as "court" may lead to the untested assumption that it is the actual arena of decision).

17. Weyrauch, "American Law as a Bargaining System," *U. Fla. Law.*, Fall 1989, at 14, 15 (stating that the vast majority of all controversies, even outside of criminal law, divorce, and personal injury, are resolved by an essentially invisible process of bargaining). Id., "Aspirations and Reality in American Law," in *Law, Morality, and Religion* 217 (Alan Watson ed., 1996). The availability of formal adjudication in courts, even when not used, is likely to influence the bargaining process, as well as the content of settlements. Summers, supra n. 9, at 1–2.

United States and with the Gypsies, the comparisons should stay on the same level in order to be fair. It would be inappropriate, for example, to compare the alleged reality of a foreign legal system with American legal myths, as often happens. Myths should be compared with myths, and realities with realities. To seek out an assumed reality in Gypsy legal processes and measure them with myths about American legal processes can only lead to a validation of idealized American values.

These considerations were relevant for the purposes of our previous essay (chapter 2 in this volume) on Gypsy law. That essay was meant to stimulate curiosity, in other words, it was concerned with enlightenment.[18] The more alien the described culture appears to be to the prevailing American value system, the stronger the sense of fascination about the assumed difference.[19] Yet this fascination is ultimately meant to be directed toward the American culture. The readers may ask questions, such as, "Why did we not know about these people living among us?" and "Are there identifiable reasons why we are attracted or repelled by the Gypsies?" Because the article's primary value was enlightenment, it was not concerned with criticizing the Roma or changing their attitudes about themselves and about non-Gypsies. Instead, the references to any form of private lawmaking and tribal aspects of American law invited readers to look at their own legal system, for example, in regard to alternative methods of dispute resolution or as a means to determine whether the treatment of the Romani people can be used to measure the general level of tolerance in society.[20]

In a similar vein, long ago I examined the attitudes of German lawyers, without intent to moralize about Germans or German lawyers, but with the express purpose of stimulating readers to think about American lawyers.[21] The references

18. Harold D. Lasswell & Myres S. McDougal, *Jurisprudence for a Free Society* 453 (1992) (referring to enlightenment as an end in itself); Mead, "Research with Human Beings: A Model Derived from Anthropological Field Practice," 98 *Daedalus* 361, 362 (1969) (pointing out that, in final analysis, intellectual curiosity of the public supports and complements anthropological research).

19. Whether one approves or disapproves of the Romani culture, including its legal aspects, depends on one's own value preference. Cf. Reisman, supra n. 3, at 410 (objecting to descriptions of the Romani culture in terms used by the Roma, because that would make it difficult for the [non-Romani] reader to react in anything but a negative way). See also Tong, supra n. 3, at ix (suggesting that genuine objectivity is hardly possible in the field of Gypsy studies).

20. Summers, supra n. 9, at 2. Our article suggests respect for private lawmaking beyond the Gypsy experience. It points out the oral legal traditions that govern our institutions and groups, even the ways we apply written law. Weyrauch & Bell, *Gypsy Law*, supra n. 2, at 19–20, 68–74 (role of interpretation and strategy in the outcome of litigated cases). See also discussion infra part IV.

A broad definition of law is used: "Law can be found any place and any time that a group gathers together to pursue an objective. The rules, open or covert, by which they govern themselves, and the methods and techniques by which these rules are enforced is the law of the group." Thomas A. Cowan & Donald A. Strickland, *The Legal Structure of a Confined Microsociety*, at i (University of California, Berkeley, Space Sciences Laboratory, Working Paper No. 34, 1965). For the full text of the definition, see Weyrauch & Bell, *Gypsy Law*, supra n. 2, at 15.

21. Walter O. Weyrauch, *The Personality of Lawyers: A Comparative Study of Subjective Factors in Law, Based on Interviews with German Lawyers* (1964) [hereinafter Weyrauch, *Lawyers*].

to American lawyers, while unsupported by the data, were meant as sign posts for further inquiry. As illustration I referred then to Jonathan Swift's *Gulliver's Travels* and his fictional account of seemingly odd customs in imaginary countries.[22] His ironical descriptions, although in his own words designed to "vex the world rather than divert it,"[23] were meant to stimulate his contemporaries, in this case Englishmen, to think about themselves. His readers found out that what appeared to be fantasy had a bearing on their reality. As the Yahoos in Gulliver's voyage to the Houyhnhnms, the *gaje* in our Gypsy law article may come to realize that all standards of measurement are relative and that indeed they themselves may look strange, perhaps even inhuman, from some other perspective. At no point is this clearer in Swift's account than when he brilliantly describes the moment when Gulliver realizes in shock that he himself is a Yahoo and has the features of the species that he despised and that he had thought lacked human characteristics:

> . . . I hope the reader will pardon my relating an odd adventure.
>
> Being one day abroad with my protector the sorrel nag, and the weather exceeding hot, I entreated him to let me bathe in a river that was near. He consented, and I immediately stripped myself stark naked, and went down softly into the stream. It happened that a young female Yahoo, standing behind a bank, saw the whole proceeding, and inflamed by desire, as the nag and I conjectured, came running with all speed, and leaped into the water, within five yards of the place where I bathed. I was never in my life so terribly frightened; the nag was grazing at some distance, not suspecting any harm. She embraced me after a most fulsome manner; I roared as loud as I could, and the nag came galloping towards me, whereupon she quitted her grasp, with the utmost reluctancy, and leaped upon the opposite bank, where she stood gazing and howling all the time I was putting on my clothes.
>
> This was a matter of diversion to my master and his family, as well as of mortification to myself. For now I could no longer deny that I was a real Yahoo in every limb and feature, since the females had a natural propensity to me, as one of their own species.[24]

Comparisons in a study of Gypsy law reach beyond the individual realm and find an echo in a societal dimension. Questions can be asked on that level too. How accommodating is society, including its branches of scholarship, if groups are examined that do not embrace the prevailing myths? To what extent do conceptions of democracy include groups, like the Roma, that do not fit into societal arrangements? If problem areas can be identified, how many of these are projected under what theories into alien cultures with what results? Within the local dimension, what groups are actually tolerated and up to what point? What legal standards are

---

22. Id. at 25–26.

23. Letter from Jonathan Swift to Alexander Pope (Sept. 29, 1725), quoted in Quintana, "Jonathan Swift," 11 *New Encyc. Brit. Micropaedia* 443, 444 (15th ed. 1987).

24. Jonathan Swift, *Travels into Several Remote Nations of the World by Lemuel Gulliver, part IV: A Voyage to the Houyhnhnms* 303 (1950) (1727).

used to justify intervention? Does unrecognized autonomous lawmaking within American groups and institutions reflect ancient oral legal traditions that find parallels in tribal law?[25]

These problems are universal and by no means endemic to the United States. They have a bearing on determining whether Gypsies engage more frequently in criminal behavior than other segments of the population, a common assertion. The comparative data on an alleged innate criminality of any ethnic group are as suspect as similar enunciations of higher or lower degrees of intelligence.[26] They are based on unproven cultural assumptions that are likely to contain veiled forms of discrimination. All cultures, including the Gypsies, change standards, if it comes to judging those who differ from the dominant norms. German studies have maintained on the basis of empirical investigations that 80 to 90 percent of the prison population belongs to the lower classes (*soziale Unterschicht*), while at the same time about the same percentage, namely 80–90 percent of the total population, have violated criminal law but for a variety of reasons have not been detected, prosecuted, or convicted (*Dunkelzifferforschung*).[27]

The situation in the United States may differ only in degree. It seems to reflect ethnic tensions, at least in significant part, that are likely to have an incidental impact on Gypsies, who may find themselves classified as another nonwhite minority. According to a report of the Department of Justice the inmate population in state and federal prisons, disproportionately nonwhite, has almost tripled since 1980.[28] Compared to other nations the numbers of incarceration are exceedingly high. The nation with the next highest figure, South Africa under its old apartheid regime, was in terms of percentages one-third lower than the United States.[29]

25. Weyrauch & Bell, *Gypsy Law*, supra n. 2, at 19–20.

26. See, e.g., Lane, "The Tainted Sources of the 'Bell Curve'," *N.Y. Rev. Books*, Dec. 1, 1994, at 14 (reviewing Richard J. Herrnstein & Charles Murray, *The Bell Curve* [1994] a controversial book asserting that African Americans are supposedly inferior in intelligence to whites or Asians).

27. In literal translation: dark-figure research. See Winfried Hassemer, *Strafrechtsdogmatik und Kriminalpolitik* 13 (1974); Klaus Lüderssen, *Kriminologie* 70–93 (1984) (discussing the concept of *Dunkelziffer*, methodology, and specific estimates); Kreuser, "Kriminologische Dunkelfeldforschung," 1994 *Neue Zeitschrift für Strafrecht* 10; Frehsee, "Zur Abweichung der Angepassten," 23 *Kriminologisches Journal* 25 (1991). See also Thomas Gabor, *Everybody Does It! Crime by the Public* (1994), reviewed by Jolanta Juszkiewicz, "We've Met the Criminals, and They're Us!," *Fed. Probation*, Mar. 1995, at 85 (maintaining that crime, as far as Canada and the United States are concerned, is not confined to an identifiable class of criminals, but is a common occurrence in all segments of the population).

28. Darrell K. Gilliard & Allen J. Beck, U.S. Dep't of Justice, "Prisoners in 1993," *Bureau Just. Stat. Bull.*, June 1994; id., "Prison and Jail Inmates, 1995," *Bureau Just. Stat. Bull.*, Aug. 1996; Dubber, "Recidivist Statutes as Arrational Punishment," 43 *Buff. L. Rev.* 689, 719–24 (1995) (suggesting racial discrimination in the contemporary "war on crime").

29. "State, U.S. Inmate Total Hits Record: '93 Incarcerations Nearly Triple 1980's, Data Show," *Dallas Morning News*, June 2, 1994, at A-1; Michael J. Sniffen (AP), "Inmate Levels Rise to Record: There Were Nearly a Million Americans Behind Bars in State and Federal Prisons in 1993—Almost Three Times the 1980 Number," *Gainesville Sun*, June 2, 1994, at A-1. See also Becker, "The Politics of Women's Wrongs and the Bill of 'Rights': A Bicentennial Perspective," 59 *U. Chi. L. Rev.* 454, 506 (1992) maintaining that the

Comparisons of Gypsy criminality with general American crime statistics are, however, not necessarily disadvantageous to Gypsies. A study by Zimring and Hawkins indicates that, contrary to common assumptions, criminality in the United States, as distinguished from incarceration rates, is generally in line with Australia and England. Yet the emphasis in the United States is on crimes of violence, such as murder, robbery and rape. The rate of homicides in New York and Los Angeles is more than ten times as high as in London or Sydney. Americans, the authors maintain, are in greater danger than their counterparts elsewhere to be shot in a traffic or domestic altercation. Crimes of violence furnish the political incentive for tough crime legislation, but the resulting mass incarceration of nonviolent offenders aggravates rather than solves the problem. Zimring and Hawkins conclude that the issue is violence, not crime.[30] The described political situation parallels the concern about Gypsy criminality that prompts calls for action, although the latter crimes appear to be minor by comparison. They involve allegations of theft and fraud, but hardly any crimes of violence.[31]

Studies have also shown that cultural and economic factors affect criminal proceedings. The probability of a prison term is twice as high if a criminal defendant appears in court in working clothes rather than in a jacket and tie.[32] If the Gypsies, as the group of persistently lowest status in the United States, in fact substantially lower than any other ethnic minority,[33] escape to some extent a skewed application

United States has the highest incarceration rate known in the world, followed, with distance, by South Africa and the former Soviet Union). Current statistics confirm this trend. Henry Stern (AP), "Up 8.6 Percent: Crowded Prisions Add Record Number," *Santa Barbara News Press*, Aug. 10, 1995, at A-3; Dubber, supra n. 28, at 719 n. 122; "Violence, Drugs Hike Prison Population," UPI, Aug. 19, 1996, available in LEXIS, Nexis Library, UPI File.

30. Zimring & Hawkins, "Is American Violence a Crime Problem?" 46 *Duke L.J.* 43 (1996); id., *Crime is Not the Problem: Lethal Violence in America* (1997).

31. John B. McLaughlin, *Gypsy Life Styles* 86 (1980) (noting absence of crimes of violence, such as murder, robbery, and rape by Gypsies).

32. Bell, "Racism in American Courts," 61 *Cal. L. Rev.* 165, 180 (1973) (referring to Donald I. Warren, "Justice in the Recorder's Court of Detroit: An Analysis of Misdemeanor Cases During the Months of September to December 1969," at 34 [1970] [typescript, mimeographed]). The impact of clothing on outcomes of criminal cases is now widely known. Public defenders have closets of donated clothes they put on defendants. According to an unwritten rule the closer the appearance of the defendant corresponds to the looks of the jury, the more he has an advantage. Judges are less likely than jurors to be influenced by clothes. Telephone Interview with Richard Parker, Public Defender, Alachua County, Florida (June 24, 1994). Any consideration of clothing and styles of dress clearly puts those Gypsies at a disadvantage who insist on their traditional style of dress.

33. In national opinion polls in 1964 and 1989 Gypsies had persistently the lowest rating of 58 ethnic minorities in their estimated social standing. In a nine-rung ladder Native White Americans were rated in 1989 with a mean of 7.03; American Indians, 4.27; African Americans, 4.17; and Gypsies, 2.65. The comparable ratings in the 1964 poll were Native White Americans, 7.25; American Indians, 4.04; African Americans, 2.75; and Gypsies 2.29. Tom W. Smith, *What Americans Think of Jews?* 29–30 (1989 poll), 34 (1964 poll) (Working Papers on Contemporary Anti-Semitism, American Jewish Committee, 1991). The report lauds the decline of prejudice, but does not comment on the continued low rating of Gypsies.

of criminal sanctions, it may be due more to their ingenuity than to a high level of tolerance of the dominant society. From these perspectives the standards promulgated by criminal law lack objectivity. They are suitable only with reservation in formulating policy.

Gunther Arzt has observed that the proportionately high number of arrests of Gypsies may be artificially inflated by two social factors. First, some behavior is perceived to be socially acceptable, although of more-than-questionable veracity, for example, promises made by the cosmetic industry in their advertisements. In these instances charges of fraud are unlikely. Comparably damaging but socially unacceptable activities by Gypsies are likely to result in arrests, for instance, the selling of love potions or fortune-telling. Second, a self-fulfilling prophecy is involved if a shopowner closely watches Gypsies whom he suspects of shoplifting. Ordinary middle-class customers are not subjected to the same scrutiny, although they may engage in shoplifting too. The result may be an inflated number of criminal charges against Gypsies.[34] Other distortions may result from what is mistakenly perceived as criminal behavior. Fortune-telling, to give an illustration, is often characterized as a fraudulent activity, engaged in by Gypsies. Yet a Gypsy woman who practices as a psychic may apply ancient healing functions. These traditional skills are religious in origin going back to Indian sources and are constitutionally protected in some jurisdictions.[35]

A way to change attitudes of the Gypsies, if this had been the objective of the previous article on Gypsy law (it was not), would consist in bringing about a change from within, rather than imposing it from the outside. The Roma might, for example, look at the *gaje* as if they were the inhabitants of a strange place, similar to

34. Letter from Gunther Arzt, Professor of Criminal Law and Criminology, University of Bern, Switzerland, to Walter O. Weyrauch (June 9, 1994) (on file with author). See also Angelika Pitsela, *Straffälligkeit und Viktimisierung ausländischer Minderheiten in der Bundesrepublik Deutschland* 146–51 (1986) (discussing increased criminal prosecution of members of foreign minorities due to xenophobia, easy identification, intense observation, and greater willingness of the host population to inform the police on alleged infractions by anybody who looks and behaves differently). See also Fonseca, supra n. 10, at 180 (suggesting that the supposedly innate criminality of Gypsies is a label attached to them by the dominant society).

35. Spiritual Psychic Science Church of Truth v. Azusa, 703 P.2d 1119 (Cal. 1985) (holding that municipal ordinance prohibiting fortune-telling and any related activity violated Cal. Const. art. I, §2). Although arrests for fortune-telling are now less frequent in California than before *Azusa*, they still occur. In San Diego four women belonging to the same Gypsy family were recently charged with theft by false pretense. As a condition of bail they were prohibited from engaging in fortune-telling or from being in locations of psychic activities. Perry, "Gypsy Clan Facing Test as Psychics," *L.A. Times*, Feb. 27, 1995, at A-3. Legal problems of fortune-telling may have been partly aggravated by an erroneous translation from the Sanskrit *dravya*, meaning "medication," which is the root of the Romani verb *drabar. Drabar* is often translated into English as "to tell fortune," but actually means "to make well." Many Gypsies prefer the term "advising" to "fortune-telling." Hancock, supra n. 7, at 174 (defining *drab, drabaràv, drabarni, drabèngro*).

Many activities that are related to fortune-telling, such as reporting of horoscopes in the media, are tolerated. Furthermore, not all fortune-tellers and palm-readers are Gypsies. The possibly fraudulent practices of these non-Gypsies are likely to be charged to the Roma.

the people described in *Gulliver's Travels*. The Gypsies could conceivably conclude that the world of the *gaje* is not that alien after all and thereafter rearrange some of their conceptions. Recent political activism of Gypsies and the Romani women's movement, evolving in many countries, may be illustrations of cultural changes from within, as distinguished from charges of human rights violations that originate from outside of the Gypsy culture. Persuasion is hardly possible by coercively imposing values on others through external sanctions.[36]

The Romani women's movement has emerged within the last ten years and is too young to evaluate its impact on the traditional Gypsy culture. In part it could contain an adaptation to the corresponding women's movements in the host countries and, to that extent, might be a reaction to external influences. It also appears to be more organized and effective among the Romanichals (English Gypsies) and the Spanish Gitanos than among the Vlax group in the United States. The possibility of transference cannot be entirely discounted in a critical analysis, namely that justified disapproval of gender discrimination in one's own culture may influence in discreet ways how seemingly corresponding discriminatory behavior among Gypsies is perceived.

An admitted problem of the objective to stimulate self-examination is that such effort might be too subtle to be effective. Similarly, Jonathan Swift probably had little effect on English society. His work tended to be taken as an amusing but unduly ironical fantasy or, heavily edited and abridged, as entertainment for children.[37] Our original Gypsy law essay may be perceived as an exposé of an ethnic group whose ways ought to be changed rather than as an invitation to the reader to change his or her own premises. The essay deals also with real people, not with fiction and irony. Yet allusions that may be understood if a work originates from an English department may not be noted or may be misunderstood if it is addressed to a legal readership. Lawyers by training and practice are not conditioned to engage in introspection.

On the other hand, our objective contained some degree of ambiguity. Comparison was not our only goal; a detailed description of the laws of the Gypsy culture

36. For Romani political activism and the women's movement, see Hancock, "The East European Roots of Romani Nationalism," in *The Gypsies of Eastern Europe* 133 (David Crowe & John Kolsti eds., 1991); Tong, supra n. 3, at 255, 335; Mossa (no first name given), *La Gitane et son destin: Témoignages d'une jeune Gitane sur la condition féminine et l'évolution du monde Gitan* (Bernard Leblon ed., 1992) (containing taped statements of a 28-year-old Gypsy woman, with comments by Leblon). Relating to the effectiveness of persuasion and coercion, see Lasswell & McDougal, supra n. 18, at 1118–28.

37. "Jonathan Swift," *Colum. Encyc.* 2668 (5th ed. 1993). Some legal authors have tried, while describing ancient or foreign cultures, to keep the attention of their readers on problems of immediate concern. See, e.g., David Daube, *Collaboration with Tyranny in Rabbinic Law* (1965) (implying contemporary relevance of collaboration with oppressive regimes); Ross, "Tû-Tû," 70 *Harv. L. Rev.* 812 (1957) (describing the taboo of *tû-tû* among a tribal culture on the Noîsulli Islands in the South Pacific, while in fact being concerned with Western legal concepts such as rights, duties, ownership, and territory). Ross leaves no doubt about his true intentions. Id. at 817 ("But perhaps it is now time to drop all pretense and openly admit what the reader must by now have discovered, that the allegory concerns ourselves").

was also attempted. Thus the article can indeed be read and criticized on several levels that include taking our descriptive account at face value. Still, a comparative quest for self-examination should not be entirely overlooked whenever policymakers are faced with incompatible foreign cultures and legal systems.

II. ETHICS OF UNCOVERING FACTS MEANT TO BE SECRET

The question of ethics came up in a specific way. Is it appropriate in scholarship to expose facts about a legal system that, according to the studied population, are possibly not meant to be known?[38] The Gypsies have prohibitions against articulating matters of their law toward outsiders. Some of their rules relating to purity and pollution, especially those that deal with the consequences of menstruation, are adhered to but not talked about, perhaps not even conscious, among Gypsies.[39] Roma ordinarily do not discuss these tabooed body functions among themselves. They also have elaborate ways to avoid reference to urination, defecation, and sexual intercourse.[40] Even the suggestion of going to bed and the act of yawning are avoided because they may infer a desire for sexual activities.[41]

One Romani informant who read the original manuscript of our previous essay prior to its publication mentioned that, strictly speaking, no Gypsy could read the portions relating to the legal significance of intimate activities and life without the risk of being polluted by the mere act of reading. Verification through Gypsy sources, consequently, poses formidable problems. Any shocked reponse would be inherently ambiguous. It could be a reaction of anger or denial at disclosure of factors not to be acknowledged or discussed. It could also mean disagreement with a report considered inaccurate and disparaging of the Romani community. Many non-Gypsy readers, on the other hand, who were not subject to this particular taboo, voiced concern that the essay would be "too Gypsy-friendly."

Even in our culture some aspects of life are sufficiently taboo that they are rarely fully articulated, although they may have legal consequences, for example, matters that question or disprove widely accepted myths about ourselves and our society. Studies could try to establish that hallowed concepts, such as

38. I am indebted to Stanley Ingber and Lynn LoPucki for raising the point that any exposition of Romaniya or Gypsy law may ultimately prove to be destructive to the Romani culture.

39. Okely, supra n. 13, at 65 (noting that information on the significance of menstruation is difficult to obtain, especially by male fieldworkers); Thompson, "The Uncleanness of Women Among English Gypsies," 1 *J. Gypsy Lore Soc'y* 15, 38 (1922) (mentioning of menstruation is a punishable offense for Romani men and women, regardless of whether the person addressed is a *Rom* or a *gajo*). See also Jean-Paul Clébert, *The Gyspies* 132 (Charles Duff trans., 1963) (discussing the secrecy in which Gypsy law is wrapped).

40. Sutherland, supra n. 8, at 265–66; Jan Yoors, *The Gypsies* 30 (1967) (relating that even implied reference to toilets is polluting). Many euphemisms are also used in the English language, e.g., menses or period for menstruation, facility or restroom for toilet. In fact the term "toilet" is a euphemism too.

41. Miller, supra n. 11, at 42 n. 3.

democratic government, freedom, and equality, are illusory in the United States, or operate in a form that is different from what is commonly believed and communicated to the world.[42] There can be little doubt that an uninhibited discussion of taboos, regardless of freedom of speech guarantees, could be damaging to accepted values.

The unconscious restrictions that govern us in these respects are really part of an unwritten code that, similar to tribal Gypsy law, is based on oral legal traditions. In case of violation of this internalized code, the culprit may face being socially ostracized, comparable to the shunning among Gypsies. Loss of credibility among peers is a powerful sanction. Perhaps the sophisticated language of the transgressing scholar may alleviate some of the more stringent informal consequences. Violation of a taboo may also have repercussions of differing severity, depending on whether a statement is made toward insiders or is directed toward the outside. Character and content of communications, whether among the Roma or members of any other culture, including our own, are largely determined by their purpose and indirectly by the person to whom they are addressed. Constitutional protections do not reach this level because the participants in discourse are not fully conscious of the regime of unwritten legal tradition. Still one should withhold judgment on whether sanctions of unwritten law, in spite of their highly effective nature, are inherently wrong. They may protect cultural ideals.

Evidence relating to taboos in one's own culture is difficult to obtain. Exposing Gypsy taboos is much easier because the scholar involved in such activities has little to fear. The only restraints result from empathy and ethical concerns about the consequences of exposure to others. Discussing taboos in one's home culture is infinitely more complex. The essence of any taboo is to prevent discussion. The matter is perceived to be self-evident and beyond proof. Any attempt at a detached examination is likely to be dismissed as speculative, if not offensive. A distinguished German legal scholar, Konrad Zweigert, has considered it to be the primary objective of any scholarship, regardless of discipline, to combat taboos and advance knowledge. Yet he concludes his analysis with a paradox that taboos can be refuted only if actual contact with them is avoided.[43] Zweigert does distinguish between different kinds of taboos and acknowledges that they can have beneficial functions.

---

42. The clash between myth and reality may lead to embarrassing situations. German lawyers and judges, upon being readmitted after World War II by the American Occupation Forces, took an oath to apply *the law* without regard to race or creed. A difficulty arose because German conflict of laws referred family-law matters relating to the requirements and validity of marriage to the laws of the nationality of the parties concerned. This often meant racially discriminatory laws, still existing at that time in many American states, which prohibited interracial marriages and declared them null and void. The German judges solved the dilemma by declaring marriages between African American soldiers and German women valid because application of the racist American laws would be against German public policy. For further discussion of a dichotomy between myth and reality, see infra part IV. B.

43. Zweigert, "Tabus in Deutschland," *Zeit,* Jan. 8, 1965, at 8 (quoting Stanislaus Letz, while discussing taboos in Germany).

These positive elements are difficult to recognize if they belong to and are effective in a fundamentally foreign value system.

The effectiveness of the sanctions provided for in *Romaniya* or Gypsy law could be damaged if Gypsies, because of past disclosure of taboo matters, were to start to talk freely about intimate matters, as is commonplace among the *gaje*. Romani objections to schooling may be related to this danger because of exposure of their children to courses on sex education and uninhibited communications with non-Gypsy children.[44] Gender and ethnic limitations of *Romaniya* are meant to prevent free communication of intimate matters among Gypsies and from Gypsies to the outside.

Gypsy women, for example, conceivably may talk about menstruation among themselves, but in earlier times even child birth was such a taboo that a Romani woman may have gone into the forest to have the child by herself, unassisted. Upon returning home she may have said, "look what I found."[45] It is inconceivable that in a traditional Gypsy family a woman would communicate about these matters to her husband, much less to any male non-Gypsy scholar. Because these intimate spheres are the foundation of Gypsy law, the integrity of legal rules is protected by taboos that appear to be unrelated to conceptions of law as understood in our culture.

Interestingly, many aspects of purity and pollution in Gypsy law have become known only in recent years. As the gender barriers in academic life have been partly overcome, women anthropologists have succeeded in communicating with Gypsy women who confided in them matters of intimate feminine concern.[46] Had the Gypsy women known that this information would be published, they might have refrained from telling their story. Women scholars were sufficiently concerned to include their ethical dilemma in their accounts.[47] Yet their misgivings were not strong enough to overcome the desire to make their discoveries known. Still, their scholarly descriptions were essentially only disseminated to a limited readership, mainly consisting of other anthropologists. Our description was designed to be read by a wider circle of people, in particular by lawyers. It may even have reached persons in law enforcement.

---

44. Vogel, "The Least Known Minority," *Civ. Rts. Dig.*, Fall 1978, at 37 (discussing Gypsy attitudes toward schooling as a source of pollution, in particular toward eating in lunchrooms, use of public bathrooms and shower facilities, close contacts between boys and girls, and programs of sex education). Vogel is a member of the Sinti group of Gypsies, located for centuries in Germany and France.

45. Miller, supra n. 11, at 42 n. 3 (noting that Gypsies prefer a query "Where were you found?" to the question "Where were you born?"). See also Elwood B. Trigg, *Gypsies, Demons and Divinities* 59–60 (1973) (Gypsy mother goes into some remote location to have her child unassisted rather than expose her family to contamination).

46. Sutherland, supra n. 8, at xiii (discussing the role of women scholars in uncovering secret information).

47. Gropper, supra n. 13, at ix ("There are also promises made to Gypsy informants, long since become friends, of things to be explained to the outside world—and also of things to be kept secret"); Sutherland, supra n. 8, at xii (reporting misuse of scholarly information by the police).

Some readers of our essay on Gypsy law raised the question whether our publishing these intimate matters for a legal readership could be damaging, perhaps even destructive, to the Romani culture. Lawyers are more prone than anthropologists to intervene actively in a foreign culture. They may even feel a moral obligation to change the ways of the Gypsies. Many of the severe reservations that anthropologists have in these regards may never occur to lawyers who, as advocates of particular viewpoints, have been professionally trained to intervene in other people's lives. From a professional perspective, lawyers, when apprised of aspects of Gypsy law, could possibly be more dangerous to the continued peaceful existence of that culture than many other non-Gypsy groups. The lawyers' concern with policy making may find some aspects of Gypsy culture intolerable to contemporary life.[48]

Similarly, another group of *gaje*, the police authorities, have proven in the past to use anthropological information to the detriment of Gypsies under the heading of "effective law enforcement."[49] The legal reader may find this to be permissible, but anthropologists have been concerned. They have deplored that their data were misused.[50] They were disturbed that individual informants could be harmed, for example, by being sanctioned by government forces or members of their tribal group for having violated prohibitions against talking to outsiders.[51]

---

48. Reisman, supra n. 3, at 414 (suggesting that the legal scholar may explicitly have to change roles and become a citizen-advocate). Different disciplines of learning may emphasize different approaches. Lawyers and political scientists, while concerned with enlightenment, may legitimately stress power processes and policies. See Lasswell & McDougal, supra n. 18. Anthropologists may emphasize enlightenment. Legal anthropologists may lean toward enlightenment, although power continues to be of interest as a subject of inquiry. Even within the discipline of law, basic approaches may vary. International law may favor intervention, in other words, power, while comparative law is more concerned with introspection and enlightenment. See Weyrauch, *Lawyers*, supra n. 21, at 284–86 (emphasizing enlightenment rather than power, persuasion over coercion, and a continuing process of introspection).

49. Sutherland, supra n. 8, at xii (reporting how her discussion of close family ties and love of children among Gypsies was used by a police detective who, upon this information, endeavored to take Gypsy children into custody to induce their parents to stay long enough within the jurisdiction for criminal prosecution). A Houston police sergeant recommends Sutherland's "Gypsies: The Hidden Americans" to his colleagues as "fairly accurate." Roy House, "Introduction to Investigations Involving the Rom (aka Gypsies)" 13 (n.d.) (unpublished typescript, mimeographed, on file with author) (suggesting that the Gypsies "delight in misleading those formally studying them"). For a discussion of police attitudes toward Gypsies, see Grönfors, "Police Perception of Social Problems and Clients: the Case of the Gypsies in Finland," 9 *Int'l J. Soc. L.* 345 (1981) (noting a law and order orientation, with comparative references to the United States, England, and Scandinavia).

50. Allan J. Kimmel, *Ethics and Values in Applied Social Research* 118–23 (Applied Social Research Methods Series No. 12, 1988); Wax, "Some Issues and Sources on Ethics in Anthropology," in *Handbook on Ethical Issues in Anthropology* 4–10 (Special Publication of the Am. Anthropological Ass'n No. 23, Joan Cassell & Sue-Ellen Jacobs eds., 1987) (noting misuse of data for governmental and intelligence purposes).

51. See, e.g., Jacobs, "Cases and Solutions," in *Handbook on Ethical Issues in Anthropology*, supra n. 50, at 27–28 (discussing a case of governmental intimidation). See also Martin Block, *Gypsies: Their Life and Their Customs* 13 (Barbara Kuczynski & Duncan Taylor trans., 1939) (Gypsy informant receiving a deep cut on the cheek for assisting in the compilation of a dictionary of the Gypsy language).

Future communications to Gypsies could be impeded because investigating scholars would now be exposed to legitimate suspicion. The Roma could be confirmed in their age-old fears that any *gaje*, no matter how seemingly benevolent, would have to be distrusted. Furthermore, the leaked information could prove to be destructive to Gypsy law, because the taboos protecting the law had been violated with impunity. Cultures whose taboos have been violated by invaders, such as the Aztec, have lost vitality and have been virtually wiped out.

Legal scholarship may increasingly face these dilemmas, for instance, if it involves empirical research and if confidences of informants are disclosed. As legal research sometimes deals with issues that question traditionally accepted values, if only for the pragmatic purposes of advocacy in specific cases, questions of professional ethics are likely to be raised by those who have a vested interest in defending commonly held conceptions of law and legal processes. On the other hand, even raising a question of ethics may occasionally come too close to areas that are taboo. Scholarly inquiry into forbidden territories may in such cases be challenged by disputing the qualification of the scholar or the merits of the results. Here, too, as with the Gypsies, the boundaries of permissible inquiries are set by unwritten law.

Anthropologists cope with related problems constantly. They have developed "Principles of Professional Responsibility" that contain statements on ethics.[52] Potential damage to individuals and to the community observed, which may even include segments of our culture, is of prime interest. Damage to individual informants, however, was not involved in our studies, which primarily involved piecing together amorphous and scattered information from various publications. But protracted damage to the Romani culture is a realistic possibility that should be examined.

The charge that cultural practices of Gypsies, supposedly subordinating women, violate human rights and ought to be changed is only an illustration. Whether this charge is legitimate, and if so under what standards of interpretation, theoretically should not retroactively affect the question of scholarly ethics of an earlier time. However, problems of ethics arise when the scholar examines these practices and contemplates how far the inquiry should be pushed in the light of possible detriments to the culture whose confidences are the substance of the study. In practice, this means that a scholar might be impeded in his or her quest for enlightenment by knowing that, as a result, charges of human rights violations could be leveled against the subjects of the inquiry. One cannot assume that the values of the scholarly investigator and of subsequent potential actors are identical.

The mere fact that much of the information about Gypsies is already published, although not always in reliable form, is not necessarily a justification as far as ethics are concerned. Within a legal context much espionage is conducted by assembling data from dispersed sources, such as seemingly innocuous news reports, thereby

52. *Statement on Ethics: Principles of Professional Responsibility* (adopted by the Council of the Am. Anthropological Ass'n, May 1971, amended through Oct. 1990).

uncovering secrets that in their totality were not yet known.[53] If such activity that can be likened to the solution of a jigsaw puzzle is to the detriment of a nation-state, it can be subject to legal sanctions.[54] Possibilities in this realm have caused misgivings to anthropologists. State agencies involved in gathering intelligence have sometimes tried to use anthropologists for gaining access to information that would be inaccessible if more direct means of investigation were employed.[55]

While these surreptitious activities fall squarely under the prohibitions of anthropological professional ethics, standards also have been developed concerning what scholarly conduct is still permissible. Obviously, any scholarly intervention, in fact the mere presence of a scholar, somehow influences those who are studied. That in itself is unavoidable. More broadly, scholars should consider foreseeable repercussions against the population studied, and "[i]f they anticipate the possibility that such violations might occur they should take steps, including, if necessary, discontinuance of work. . . ."[56] Yet there is something sinister in an assumed power of academics to withhold information from the public for whatever reason, even that in some form or another revealing the information may hurt a foreign culture. Some form of prior restraint could be involved in the notion that one should not even try to find out what ultimately may cause harm.

The idea of powers of censorship is antithetical to the traditional pursuit of truth that has been a hallmark of scholarship. Even though there may be parallels between the pursuit of truth and spying,[57] scholarship may have a license that intelligence gathering for the state may not possess. Anthropologists have tried a solution, although perhaps self-serving, by weighing harms and benefits against each

53. Blair S. Walker, "CIA Role in Business Spying Debated," *USA Today,* July 2, 1992, at B-9 (discussing intelligence techniques of sifting through information from the public domain, such as annual reports and newspaper clippings).

54. See, e.g., United States v. Progressive, Inc., 467 F. Supp. 990 (W.D. Wis.), *appeal dismissed,* 610 F.2d 819 (7th Cir. 1979), *mandamus denied sub nom.* Morland v. Sprecher, 443 U.S. 709 (1979) (temporary injunction against publication of data detailing method for constructing hydrogen bomb, although the information was compiled from public sources). See also Powe, "The H-Bomb Injunction," 61 *U. Colo. L. Rev.* 55, 68 (1990) (reporting threatened criminal prosection of the Washington Post in a related case); "CIA Head Threatens Espionage Charges: Casey Seeks Criminal Charges Against Post, NBC Over Coverage of Pelton Case—Claims Stories Harmed National Security Even Though Russians Already Had Data," *News Media & the Law,* Summer 1986, at 4, col. 1; Stephen Engelberg, "U.S. Aides Said to Have Discussed Prosecuting News Organizations," *N.Y. Times,* May 21, 1986, at A-18, col. 1.

55. *Statement on Problems of Anthropological Research and Ethics* (adopted by the Council of the Am. Anthropological Ass'n, Mar. 1976) (prohibiting clandestine activities and regulating government sponsorship). See id. at II(6) ("There also is good reason to believe that some anthropologists have used their professional standing and the names of their academic institutions as cloaks for the collection of intelligence information and for intelligence operations").

56. *Statement on Ethics,* supra n. 52, at I(5). An earlier version of the *Statement on Ethics,* as amended through November 1976, merely stated: "There is an obligation to reflect on the foreseeable repercussions of research and publication on the general population being studied." Id. at 1(e).

57. Weyrauch, "Gestapo Informants: Facts and Theory of Undercover Operations," 24 *Colum. J. Transnat'l L.* 553, 594–95 (1986).

other to determine whether on balance publication may more likely be beneficial.[58] In regard to the Gypsies, their culture could be benefited by spreading among non-Gypsies, especially lawyers, some greater understanding of Romani standards of morality, different from ours as they may be. It would become more difficult for the dominant culture to justify persecutions under conceptions of alleged criminality, if prevailing stereotypes are contravened and corrected. Enlightenment, as discussed, can be the base for introspection and thus may affect power processes that in the past have been used to persecute Gypsies in often ferocious and wholly indefensible ways.[59]

The Roma themselves are by no means uniform in their strategies to cope with scholarly inquiries originating from their host cultures. Increasingly they maintain that cultural adaptation is permissible and beneficial.[60] Such adaptation requires some cooperation and mutual recognition to be effective. While efforts to use information to change or control the Gypsy culture should be viewed with reservation, on balance the benefits from increased knowledge probably outweigh the detriments that may result from ignorance. Anthropologists have recognized their own frailty in a touching way that is wholly applicable to the legal scholar who ventures into their field:

58. *Statement on Ethics,* supra n. 52, at II(A)(B) (stating that, after carefully considering social and political implications, anthropologists have a professional responsibility to contribute to the informational resources upon which public policy may be founded).

59. According to a law passed by Hapsburg Emperor Charles VI in 1726, any male Gypsy was to be executed without trial. The ears of Gypsy women and children were to be cut off. Ian Hancock, *The Pariah Syndrome* 58 (1987). Gypsies were killed in Bohemia and their mutilated bodies hung along the border to discourage migration. Willy Guy, historical postscript to Josef Koudelka, *Gypsies* (1975). See also Angus Fraser, *The Gypsies* 146–53 (2d ed. 1995) (listing similar legislation). An undetermined number of Gypsies, possibly more than one million, were murdered in Nazi concentration camps or were executed on the spot. Many were summarily shot as alleged partisans at the Russian front. Ulrich König, *Sinti und Roma unter dem Nationalsozialismus: Verfolgung und Widerstand* 87–88 (1989). After the collapse of communist regimes in Eastern Europe severe persecution of Gypsies took place, especially in Rumania, where unfounded rumors circulated that the disposed communist ruler, Nicolae Ceauşescu, was a Gypsy. Pavel, "Wanderers: Romania's Hidden Victims: New Assaults upon the Gypsy Minority," *New Republic,* Mar. 4, 1991, at 12 (Juliana G. Pilon trans.); Williams, "Gypsies Feel Curse of Hatred," *L.A. Times,* Dec. 20, 1991, at A-1; Fisher, "The Bosnia War: Religion, History & the Gypsies," 17 *Whittier L. Rev.* 467, 472–75 (1996). Christopher H. Smith, "Foreigners in Their Own Land," *Christian Sci. Monitor,* July 17, 1996, at 20 (reporting severe persecution of Gypsies in the Czech Republic).

The situation in the United States is less favorable than one may think. Numerous statutes and local ordinances, some of them still in effect in the absence of constitutional challenge, single out Gypsies for discriminatory treatment. Hancock, supra, at 105–14. Police practices follow the same pattern. See, e.g., State v. Marks, 790 P.2d 138, 142 (Wash. 1990) (mentioning "egregious behavior" of the police); Claudia G. Dowling & Linda Gomez, "Gypsies," *Life,* Oct. 1992, at A-16 (reporting the incidents that underlie the litigation in *Marks*).

60. Hancock, "The Romani Diaspora Part 2," 1989 *The World & I* 644, 651–52; Silverman, "Negotiating 'Gypsiness': Strategy in Context," 101 *J. Am. Folklore* 261, 266–71 (1988).

In the final analysis, anthropological research is a human undertaking, dependent upon choices for which the individual bears ethical as well as scientific responsibility. That responsibility is human, not superhuman, responsibility. To err is human, to forgive humane. This statement of principles of professional responsibility is not designed to punish, but to provide guidelines which can minimize the occasions upon which there is a need to forgive.[61]

III. POWER OF GYPSY WOMEN

The problem of whether Gypsies violate human rights because they treat half of their population, namely women, for most of their lives as impure raises questions of great complexity.[62] It is also of concern to the comparatist. The original essay on Gypsy law was perhaps misleading in these respects. It contained a heading *Contamination by Women*,[63] an editorial change from the earlier heading *Role of Women*. The change inadvertently accentuated a seemingly negative aspect of the way in which Romani law characterizes women. It may also have conveyed a one-sided meaning of menstruation and procreative functions as a source of contamination, as it is perceived in Jewish and Christian religious traditions.[64] In retrospect it would have been preferable to have retained the original heading that presented the status of women in a neutral way that included the possibility of positive interpretations. At the source of the problem is language.[65] None of the terms in the English language relating to pollution or contamination capture the multiple conceptions

---

61. Earlier version of the *Statement on Ethics*, supra n. 52, as amended through November 1976, Epilogue. The current version stresses professionalism and has deleted references to broader aspects of human concern.

62. Reisman, supra n. 3, at 416–17 (referring to Universal Declaration of Human Rights, G.A. Res. 217A, U.N. GAOR, 3d Sess. pt.1, at 71, U.N. Doc. A/810 [1948]; International Covenant on Civil and Political Rights, Dec. 16, 1966, G.A. Res. 2200, U.N. GAOR, 21st Sess., Supp. No. 16, at 52, U.N. Doc. A/6316 [1967] [entered into force Mar. 23, 1976]; International Covenant on Economic, Social and Cultural Rights, Dec. 16, 1966, G.A. Res. 2200, U.N. GAOR, 21st Sess., Supp. No. 16, at 49, U.N. Doc. A/6316 [1967] [entered into force Jan. 3, 1976]).

In regard to the emerging Romani women's movement, see supra nn. 36–37 and accompanying text.

63. Weyrauch & Bell, *Gypsy Law*, supra n. 2, at 32.

64. Gen. 3:16 ("the curse of Eve"). See infra nn. 81, 100–01. See generally Carmichael, "Romani Law and Jewish Law," chap. 5 in this volume.

65. 1 K.N. Nayak, *Cultural Relativity: A Unified Theory of Knowledge* 300–01 (1982) (concluding that three-dimensional languages, such as English, cannot grasp the meaning of ideas expressed in a five-dimensional language, such as Sanskrit, without being forced into distortion). A similar problem exists, however, when ideas expressed in German are translated into English. Weyrauch, "Limits of Perception: Reader Response to Hitler's Justice," 40 *Am. J. Comp. L.* 237 (1992). To the extent that language mirrors cultural expectations, distortions of meaning may occur within the same language, as illustrated by the statement attributed to George Bernard Shaw: "England and America are two countries separated by the same language."

of impure (*marime*) behavior in Romani, the Gypsy language that descends from Sanskrit.[66]

Since, as stated at the outset, the human body is regarded as the source of Gypsy law, the upper part being pure (*vujo*) and the lower part impure (*marime*), to strike a balance between these two extremes (*kintála*) would be an ideal that is hard to achieve.[67] Just as the parts of the human body, the Romani conceptions of *vujo* and *marime* have to be seen as integral parts of a whole. The concept of purity, also in its metaphorical meaning of behaving in accordance with law, would be impossible without the presence of the seeming opposite of being contaminated or in a *marime* state. Both concepts permeate each other and are preconditions to aspire for *kintála* or wholesomeness. Thus all legal rules, no matter how specific and removed from the physical aspects of the human body, are aspirational in nature.

Women have a unique role in this system of beliefs.[68] The Romani culture commingles notions of Christianity and Hinduism in a way that sometimes can be misleading. A report from the Camargue (Rhône Delta) in southern France may illustrate this. Each year in May festivities take place in Saintes-Maries-de-la-Mer, a small fishing village on the Mediterranean coast.[69] Thousands of Gypsies from all over the world make a pilgrimage to honor Ste. Sara. According to local folklore Ste. Sara was a dark-skinned servant woman, closely allied with the Holy Family. Her statue in the twelfth-century church of Saintes-Maries, being of dark complexion, has led to the Romani belief that she was a Gypsy and to her adoption as the patron saint of all Gypsies. In a procession to the sea, the statue of Ste. Sara is symbolically immersed in the Mediterranean waters and thereafter returned to the crypt.

The ceremony in Saintes-Maries closely parallels the annual processions in India, the country in which the Roma originated, when statues of the Indian goddess Durga, also named Kali, are immersed into water.[70] Durga, the consort of Shiva, usually represented with a black face, is the goddess of creation, sickness, and death. Shiva, equally awe-inspiring, holds in his hand a trident that symbolizes emanation, stability, and death. It appears that the Indian mother-goddess cult (Shaktism) has survived in contemporary Gypsy beliefs. Even Shiva's trident has been transformed into a Christian symbol, as evidenced by the Sanskrit word *triśula* for trident and the Romani word *trušul* for cross.[71]

---

66. Fraser, supra n. 59, at 15–20 (comparing words in Sanskrit, Hindi and Romani).

67. See supra n. 7 and accompanying text.

68. Miller, supra n. 11; Okely, supra n. 13.

69. "Saintes-Maries-de-la-Mer," 10 *New Encyc. Brit. Micropeadia* 339 (15th ed. 1987).

70. Pashmari W.R. Rishi, *Roma: The Panjabi Emigrants in Europe, Central and Middle Asia, the USSR and the Americas* 58–64 (1976) (describing the festivities and the connection between the worship of St. Sarah and Durga or Kali).

71. Id. at 61. I am indebted to Ian Hancock for bringing this linguistic comparison to my attention. See also Fonseca, supra n. 10, at 106.

Gypsy women do not convey an image of being the victims of male dominance. They exude self-confidence in posture and speech.[72] Indeed, their assumed state of impurity because of menstruation can more properly be understood as a power that they have over men. A Gypsy man may take his wife along to a troublesome negotiation with another Rom. Her presence and her power to pollute the adversary by tossing her skirt is more effective than brandishing any weapon.[73] Similarly, a Gypsy woman may have the power to break up any fight among men by lifting her skirt. The men would immediately disperse in panic.[74]

Murder, rape, or sexual abuse of a Gypsy woman by a Gypsy man is unlikely to occur and exceedingly rare because such unspeakable crimes under Gypsy law would lead to the automatic pollution of the perpetrator.[75] Yet these are common offenses in the United States. The legal concept of sexual harassment might well be peculiar to Western cultures that seemingly have freed women but continue to subject them to abuse. Conceivably, problems of misogyny could be more serious at home than among the Roma. At the least, a comparative analysis of an alleged subordination of Gypsy women should include efforts to determine whether continued and pervasive gender discrimination in Western cultures subtly influences scholarly perspectives on Gypsies.[76]

Cultural attitudes toward women are reflected in perceptions on menstruation. It may have multiple and sometimes contradictory meanings, since women are viewed as having the power to create and to destroy. Similarly, menstruation can be seen as a manifestation of creative power because it signals that conception and birth are possible.[77] It can also be understood as a symbol for death because it demonstrates that life has not been conceived.[78] The taboo of menstruation in many cultures, including the culture of the Gypsies, comprises both the positive and the negative aspects. Indeed the conception of taboo, originating from Polynesia, embraces positive and negative connotations, while Western languages tend to create

72. Okely, supra n. 13, at 72 (fighting prowess and capacity to take care of themselves are valued in Gypsy women, while an appearance of frailty and other attributes of "femininity" are discouraged). See generally Silverman, "Pollution and Power: Gypsy Women in America," in *The American Kalderaš: Gypsies in the New World* 55 (Matt T. Salo ed., 1981) (discussing superior power of Gypsy women).

73. Miller, supra n. 11, at 51. The resulting pollution is theoretically permanent, but it can be removed by resort to a legal fiction. After amends the Gypsy woman may forgive the offending man by pretending that the whole incident never happened. Id. at 52.

74. Id. at 51–52 n. 20 (describing an incident in which a young Gypsy woman stopped a fight among men by disrobing and yelling at them).

75. McLaughlin, supra n. 31, at 86.

76. See supra nn. 36–37 and accompanying text. Cf. Tong, supra n. 3, at xv, 335 (noting problems of non-Gypsy researchers in dealing with sexism).

77. Buckley & Gottlieb, "A Critical Appraisal of Theories of Menstrual Symbolism," in *Blood Magic: The Anthropology of Menstruation* 26 (Thomas Buckley & Alma Gottlieb eds., 1988).

78. Id. at 38. Among the Maoris menstrual blood signifies the demise of a person who could have been born. The blood accordingly "has the impossible status of a dead person that has never lived." Mary Douglas, *Purity and Danger: An Analysis of the Concepts of Pollution and Taboo* 96 (1978).

a dichotomy and to force thought into pairs of opposites.[79] To speak of women and of menstruation in terms of contamination or impurity creates the impression that they have been victimized by a misogynic male society.[80] While this may be true in Western societies, it is at least subject to question in the case of the Gypsies.

A closer examination of how a taboo operates in a given society is needed. A taboo can have multiple functions that can be viewed positively, negatively, or both at the same time. It may also be ambiguous. A differentiation may show that menstruation, for example, is desirable rather than a curse. It may be perceived as a sign of femininity and even, as in case of the Gypsies, as a power over men.[81] A critical question for analytical purposes is whether a woman, by violating a menstrual taboo, harms herself or someone else.[82] Many of the regulations of Gypsy law dealing with women, menstruation, and childbirth seem to be designed to give women an area of protection and power over those who could pose a threat or danger.[83] Their power to pollute can be viewed simultaneously in positive and negative terms without need to dichotomize, while in our culture the negative signals seem to prevail. The contemporary uses of "pollution" and "contamination" to describe damage to the environment are illustrations.

In response to our article on Gypsy law, parallels have been suggested by Reisman between the *marime* practices of the Roma and female mutilations in East Africa.[84] According to estimates of the World Health Organization, the latter pro-

79. Buckley & Gottlieb, supra n. 77, at 8 (stating that in Polynesian languages the term taboo implies a fusion of "holy" and "forbidden," while Western cultures insist on polarity). In discussing the tendency of the English language to dichotomize concepts, Nayak argues that the procedural insistence to answer questions by "yes" or "no" creates a polarity where none may exist. Counterquestions or qualifications are unacceptable. The mandated choice between two seeming opposites is viewed as a sign of exactitude. Nayak, supra n. 65, at 225.

80. See, *e.g.*, Andrea Dworkin, *Intercourse* (1987) (giving numerous illustrations how women are subjugated in Western cultures); id. at 183–84 (describing menstruation); Kubie, "The Fantasy of Dirt," 6 *Psychoanal. Q.* 388, 396, 422 (1937) (discussing unconscious fantasies viewing women as dirtier than men).

81. Silverman, supra n. 72; Fonseca, supra n. 10, at 40 (suggesting that Romani culture is really a matriarchy and that men are in effect relegated to child status); Sutherland, supra n. 8, at 102–04 (describing how Gypsy women, because of their innate power to pollute, are feared and sometimes have more authority than their men); Miller, supra n. 11, at 51 (noting Gypsy women's power to penalize by pollution). The negative view of menstruation as "the curse of Eve," or in short form as "the curse," has been characteristic of Judeo-Christian cultures. Buckley & Gottlieb, supra n. 77, at 32. Ambivalent views on menstruation are expressed among feminists in regard to menopause. Pamela Warrick, "Feminists Face Off in War Over Menopause," *L.A. Times,* Aug. 9, 1994, at E-1, E-5 ("At the heart of the debate is . . . the very question of what makes a woman a woman").

82. Buckley & Gottlieb, supra n. 77, at 10.

83. Id. at 12 (describing menstruation as enhancing solidarity among women and providing a sanctuary); id. at 14 (suggesting that "female oppression" models of menstrual taboos are inadequate).

84. Reisman, supra n. 3, at 416–17. For an exhaustive discussion, see Lewis, "Between Irua and 'Female Genital Mutilation': Feminist Human Rights—Discourse and the Cultural Divide," 8 *Harv. Hum. Rts. J.* 1 (1995).

cedure is performed on more than two million Muslim women and children annually.[85] It is referred to as female circumcision, but is more properly called clitoridectomy because it often involves removal of the clitoris. Being of unknown ancient historical origin, the practice is meant to preserve female chastity and is perceived in the respective cultures as an essential condition for being marriageable.[86] The custom has the support of most women in the regions concerned, especially those who are older. Women also perform the surgery and the required examinations prior to marriage, while men often purport not to know about these matters.[87]

Although the comparison of mutilation of women by clitoridectomy and the alleged impurity of women because of menstruation appears to be strained, it finds some support in the psychoanalytic literature. Speaking of our culture, Lawrence Kubie has linked contamination fears caused by menstruation with fantasies of mutilation.[88] The bleeding in menstruation is said to trigger fantasies of castration in men and women alike. The differences between menstruation and clitoridectomy become apparent, though, if one compares the realities of how they come about— menstruation as an inevitable and natural incident of life, although subject to a variety of interpretations; clitoridectomy as a mutilation inflicted in some cultures on women regardless of their consent.

Children and young women are forcibly subjected in clitoridectomy to a surgical procedure that, aside from the removal of the clitoris, may also involve cutting of the labia and infibulation, the stitching together of the open wound. In the African

---

85. "WHO Discusses Female Circumcision," UPI, May 5, 1994, available in LEXIS, Nexis Library, UPI File; "Genital Mutilation: Stop the Butchering," *Ariz. Republic*, Apr. 4, 1994, at B-4. The estimates of the World Health Organization may be too low.

According to structured interviews with a sample of Nigerian women, 85.71% were circumcised and 75.23% indicated their continued readiness to have female children circumcised. Religion, whether Christian or Muslim, and literacy did not significantly influence the attitudes of the respondents. Lola Irinoye', "Attitude of Women Toward Female Circumcision: A Case Study of Women Attending a Comprehensive Health-Centre in Ile-Ife, Nigeria" (unpublished paper, presented during the Sixth Int'l Conf. on Women's Health Issues, June 27 to July 1, 1994, in Gaborone-Sun, Botswana, on file with author). I am indebted to W. Jape Taylor, Distinguished Service Professor of Medicine, University of Florida, for bringing this paper to my attention. See generally Toubia, "Female Circumcision as a Public Health Issue," 331 *New Eng. J. Med.* 712 (1994).

86. Mary Ann French, "The Open Wound: At Last, the World Comes Face to Face With What Is Being Done to All Little Girls, in the Name of God and in the Service of an Ancient Ideal of Chastity," *Wash. Post*, Nov. 22, 1992, at F-1 (interviewing a forty-year-old man originating from Somalia: "In Somalia, circumcision is a good thing. . . . If a lady is open, her chance of marriage is lost, because anybody can marry her and divorce her the next day. I'm serious. The next day, you're gone. . . . When a lady is married, they call about 20 or 30 women to check her to see if she's okay or not. They will come, and the girl's mother and the man's mother, they will open her like a gift").

87. William Raspberry, "Barbaric 'Tradition' Is Really Torture Aimed at Females," *Chi. Trib.*, Nov. 29, 1993, N-19 (suggesting complicity of women in the regions concerned); French, supra n. 86 (noting that, in most African countries, usually women insist on and carry out female circumcision).

88. Kubie, supra n. 80, at 399, 422. But see Buckley & Gottlieb, supra n. 77, at 15–18 (criticising psychoanalytic theories of menstruation).

tribal context the operation is performed with any sharp instrument, such as a piece of broken glass, and without anaesthesia. Sometimes herbs or ashes are rubbed into the wound.[89] Infections, lifelong trauma, and impairments are frequent. Claims of human rights violations associated with these cultural practices are understandable, even if one removes oneself from the cultural perspectives of the West.

On the other hand, as far as psychoanalytical comparisons of menstruation and castration are concerned, one should realize that these theories are based on cultural constructs that originate in the West. The limitations of scientific theories become apparent in the light of the rapid changes that they have undergone. Clitoridectomy, for example, was widely practiced by the medical profession in England and the United States in the nineteenth century.[90] Scientific theories at the time perceived it to be a valid treatment of hysteria in women and a cure for female masturbation, referred to as "peripheral excitement," which was seen as a sign of mental illness.[91] Although disparaged by medical authorities, these surgical procedures still occur in England and the United States if persons of foreign origin are concerned, but efforts are under way to outlaw them.[92] When we condemn cultural practices elsewhere, we should keep our own history and behavior in mind.

The legal discussion of human rights violations finds an echo in the anthropological literature. Ruth Benedict and Melville Herskovits started out with premises of cultural relativity that, in the absence of any overriding general standards, inevitably led to a quest for tolerance of the beliefs and practices of other cultures.[93]

---

89. A.M. Rosenthal, "On My Mind: The Torture Continues," *N.Y. Times,* July 27, 1993, at A-13; French, supra n. 86 (describing surgical procedure); Colleen O'Connor, "Victory in Deportation Fight Offers Hope to Other Women," *Dallas Morning News,* May 22, 1994, at F-1 (describing the use of herbs, earth, or ashes to stop bleeding).

90. Ann Dally, *Women Under the Knife: A History of Surgery* 159–84 (1991); Alice Walker, *Possessing the Secret of Joy* 185–88 (1992).

91. Dally, supra n. 90, at 164–69 (referring to Baker Brown, *The Curability of Certain Forms of Insanity, Epilepsy, Catalepsy, and Hysteria in Females* [1866]); id. at 161 (quoting from Samuel Ashwell, *A Practical Treatise on the Diseases Peculiar to Women* 708 [1844]).

92. Federal Prohibition of Female Genital Mutilation Act of 1995, H.R. 941, 104th Cong., 1st Sess. (1995), sponsored by Representative Patricia Schroeder; S. 1030, 104th Cong., 1st Sess. (1995), sponsored by Senator Harry Reid. See also Dally, supra n. 90, at 212–15 (reporting recent clitoridectomies performed by British gynecologists on young Arab girls); Jane Hansen & Deborah Scroggins, "Special Report, Female Circumcision: U.S., Georgia Forced to Face Medical, Legal Issues," *Atlanta Journal & Constitution,* Nov. 15, 1992, at A-1 (reporting recent clitoridectomies in the United States).

A contemporary legal issue is whether threat of female mutilation in their countries of origin entitles women to asylum in the United States. See In re Kasinga, Interim Decision (BIA) 3278, 1996 WL 379826 (B.I.A.) (asylum granted). For a discussion of the case, see Celia W. Dugger, "Woman's Plea for Asylum Puts Tribal Ritual on Trial," *N.Y. Times,* Apr. 15, 1996, at A-1. See generally Kelly, "Gender Related Persecution: Assessing the Asylum Claims of Women," 26 *Cornell Int'l L.J.* 625 (1993).

93. Elvin Hatch, *Culture and Morality: The Relativity of Values in Anthropology* 35–81 (1983). An extreme expression of cultural relativity, perhaps showing its inherent limitations, is contained in a statement by Herskovits, as quoted by Hatch: "There is, indeed, some reason to feel that the concept of freedom should be realistically defined as the right to be exploited in terms of the patterns of one's own culture." Id. at 101.

Western cultures in particular, the argument went, should not use their own values to judge whether other cultures were of supposedly high or low status. Even judging the quality of conduct as good or bad depends, according to this view, on preconceived notions that are taken from the culture of the person who passes judgment. Language itself is seen as a reflection of culture.[94] It carries its intrinsic limitations that prevent us from validly perceiving what takes place elsewhere. There is, as it were, a no-man's land between different cultures, including their different legal systems, in which ideas, in the absence of means to express them, may get lost.

The ideal of cultural relativism was severely shaken by the events of this century. The Nazi theories of racial superiority led to the concomitant murder of millions of people who did not conform to this image.[95] Thus the need to draw a line between acceptable and nonacceptable beliefs and behavior could no longer be denied. Cultural relativism was increasingly criticized for supporting the oppressive regimes of this world.[96] The query remained, What factors should be used to determine unacceptable cultural beliefs and practices? Any form of severe human suffering is perceived to be universally bad, regardless of whether it is caused by oppressive regimes, sickness, or economic conditions. Nevertheless, a rule of evidence might be needed. In case of doubt, principles of tolerance should prevail and mandate nonintervention.

In respect to Gypsy laws of impurity that seemingly give women a lower status because of menstruation and child birth, although the contrary can be argued, the doubts prevail. In the case of the gruesome practices of female circumcision, as performed in some cultures, the level of tolerance is exceeded. The line is somewhere in between. Yet, a cautionary suggestion that I made twenty-five years ago is still valid:

> Language follows the myths of culture, and it is difficult to perceive of universal thoughts, ideas and conditions without feeling the need for qualifications. Cultural patterns assure also that self-interest is not neglected, and self-interest is likely to play some role in the definition, justification and identification of universal human rights. Like civil rights in the United States, human rights in general are likely to be discussed and recognized in times of crisis when previously deprived segments of humanity have increased in power and begin to pose a threat. It is natural that a threat of this kind stimulates the more privileged to new thought and new efforts at control.
>
> May I state in conclusion . . . that I do not consider this account, if accurate, to be dismal or even discomforting. Chances for survival may be endangered by chaos as much as by forces that try to bring order in reality. On the other hand, those ad-

---

94. A comparison of characteristics of Sanskrit, which is the source of the language spoken by the Romani people, with Western languages may help in understanding Gypsy law. Nayak, supra n. 65, at 201–309 (discussing the impact of linguistic comparisons on comprehension, in particular in regard to Sanskrit and the English language).

95. Hatch, supra n. 93, at 103–04.

96. Id. at 130.

vocating greater respect for mankind than has been given in the past deserve our sympathy, even if they have difficulty articulating and defining human rights, and even if they are partly moved by unconscious self-interest.[97]

In summation, I suggest that the topics of this article are interrelated. The objective of the original article on Gypsy law[98] was less concerned with changing the Roma in any way and more with creating an awareness of submerged patterns of private lawmaking in the American legal culture. In other words, the objective was to increase knowledge. A likely effect of any increased enlightenment is to raise doubts about one's own motives. Questions of ethics may be raised concerning to what extent it is appropriate for scholarship to give information wide circulation that, at its inception, was meant to be kept secret. These concerns are deepened if publication of confidential information may lead in one form or another to sanctions against the described alien culture, especially if human rights violations are alleged.

Positively, comparisons may encourage the host society to reexamine its own cultural values, for example, in regard to sexual taboos and the status of women, and to initiate change. While introspection seems to emphasize local reforms, it does not resurrect the more extreme manifestations of cultural relativity that leave other cultures alone under any circumstance. Still, there remain large areas of human behavior in any culture, including our own, that need to be sheltered from outside interference, even if they are perceived to be strange and perhaps objectionable. Within limits cultural integrity should be presumed to be protected.

Menstruation, for example, is of universal concern, and attitudes relating to menstruation and the concomitant pollution are likely to affect the status of women in any culture. Menstrual taboos have also been widely considered to be oppressive to women.[99] Traditional Jewish laws on menstruation, purity and pollution, although of entirely different origin and meaning, outwardly resemble in many respects those of Romani law.[100] Many of the remainders of these traditions in our own culture are controversial. Even feminists are not in agreement on how men-

97. Weyrauch, "On Definitions, Tautologies, and Ethnocentrism in Regard to Universal Human Rights," in *Human Rights* 200 (Ervin H. Polack ed., 1971).

98. Weyrauch & Bell, *Gypsy Law*, supra n. 2.

99. Buckley & Gottlieb, supra n. 77, at 6.

100. See, e.g., Isaac Klein, *A Guide to Jewish Religious Practice* 509–22 (1979) (discussing family purity and menstruation); Jacob Neusner, *The Idea of Purity in Ancient Judaism* 108–30 (1973); Evelyn Kaye, *The Hole in the Sheet: A Modern Woman Looks at Orthodox and Hasidic Judaism* 146–66 (1987) (discussing orthodox laws on menstruation); Anne Lapidus Lerner, *"Who Has Not Made Me a Man": The Movement for Equal Rights for Women in American Jewry* (American Jewish Committee, 1977). Jewish tradition also includes a daily prayer by the husband thanking God that he was not born a woman. Hayim Halevy Donin, *To Pray as a Jew: A Guide to the Prayer Book and the Synagogue Service* 193–96 (1980); Becker, supra n. 29, at 464 (critiquing the prayer). See also Carmichael, supra n. 64.

struation and menopause should be viewed.[101] In the light of these gender problems, that may well call for reform, perhaps some restraint should be exercised when legal traditions of the Gypsies are subjected to a critical analysis. Not reform as such is questionable, but changes suggested by non-Gypsy critics may require caution.[102] It goes without saying that this fundamental recommendation to exercise some restraint before interfering with others is of benefit to any culture, the Gypsies' as well as the culture in which we live.

IV. APPLICATION OF ANTHROPOLOGICAL INSIGHT TO AMERICAN LAW

Throughout this essay it has become apparent that much of the discussion contains comparative pointers on contemporary society. We are surrounded by institutional structures that in many ways share tribal characteristics. They have their own legal systems, based on oral traditions, complete with unwritten norms, taboos, and sometimes severe sanctions in case of violation. Clear divisions between facts and opinion, procedure and substance are missing, and due process is largely absent. Standards of relevance are perceived in the broadest terms, and communal values are emphasized over individual rights.[103] Although we tend to be aware of these structures as such, their underlying unwritten legal traditions escape our consciousness to a large extent. We adhere to their commands, but their tribal aspects remain as much hidden from our conscious vision as the presence of Gypsies among us. Their articulation may result in stunned surprise. What is involved may be shown by two illustrations from the realm of law.

In Metropolitan County Court

The first example relates to a crowded metropolitan court having jurisdiction over misdemeanors, such as open container violations, disorderly conduct, prostitution, and other minor crimes.[104] The court may be governed by unwritten rules of procedure. The participants, although changing from day to day, out of self-interest tend to adhere to these unwritten rules, even though they may be in contradiction to the official laws of the state. There is indication that the most important rule is "Don't interfere with the speed of the proceedings." Making a

---

101. See Dworkin, supra n. 80, at 118–19, 183–84 (discussing traditional negative views of women and menstruation); Schroeder, "Feminism Historicized: Medieval Misogynist Stereotypes in Contemporary Feminist Jurisprudence," 75 *Iowa L. Rev.* 1190–1201 (1990) (discussing medieval theories of sex and women as polluting); Warrick, supra n. 81 (noting controversy among feminists relating to menstruation and menopause).

102. See supra nn. 36–37 and accompanying text.

103. Weyrauch & Bell, *Gypsy Law,* supra n. 2, at 19–20, 82–85.

104. Mark B. Carroll, "The County Courtroom Group: Unspoken Rules of Procedure," (Dec. 1989) (unpublished paper, University of Florida College of Law, on file with author).

legal argument, for instance, or being represented by an attorney inevitably may slow down the proceedings and thus constitutes a breach of the basic rule, inviting sanction.[105]

The rule of "speed" appears to be largely enforced by court clerks or secretaries who are responsible for the paperwork, such as scheduling proceedings and recording dispositions. Although their educational level rarely reaches beyond high school, their presence is more durable than that of other participants, such as judges and prosecutors, who are regularly rotated. These participants are, however, aware that the staff members are the repositories of the unwritten procedures. The clerks or secretaries are consequently treated with utmost deference, even by the judges. They have the power of sanction by granting or withholding information on the oral legal tradition. Cases are won or lost on this level. In extreme cases the staff may even alter the disposition of cases by the way they record them.[106] If dispute arises, the problems of evidence are almost insurmountable, because the official record tends to prevail.

Trying to explain why the rule of "speed" is accepted and working may be difficult. Any attempt at explanation is, by definition, a violation of the unwritten laws that support a taboo. From a law enforcement perspective, certain categories of persons may have created a problem by being sufficiently conspicuous to be detained and charged.[107] The relatively large number of persons so characterized, who often may be ethnically or socially different from the mainstream of the population, must be processed rapidly through the courts in a proceeding that, at least to the outside, appears to maintain due process and important cultural myths, while in fact a presumption of guilt prevails. The conventional explanation of limited resources and budgetary constraints, while not untrue, stays more on the surface.

Although the research behind the above observations did not deal with Gypsies, it is easy to surmise how this group might fare in a crowded metropolitan court.

---

105. Id. at 9 (discussing the role of the public defender who is not considered to be a member of the courtroom group and, essentially, is perceived to be superfluous); id. at 15 (discussing sanctions against uncooperative defense attorneys). See also President's Commission on Law Enforcement and Administration of Justice, *Task Force Report: The Courts* 30 (1967) (stating that speed is the watchword in misdemeanor cases). The situation has been unchanged for decades. In the fifties the following exchange took place in a Philadelphia court, the defendant being charged with drunkenness and convicted for vagrancy:

> Magistrate: "Where do you live?" Defendant: "Norfolk." Magistrate: "What are you doing in Philadelphia?" Defendant: "Well, I didn't have any work down there, so I came up here to see if I could find. . . ." Magistrate (who had been shaking his head): "That story's not good enough for me. I'm going to have you investigated. You're a vagrant. Three months in the House of Correction."

Foote, "Vagrancy-Type Law and Its Administration," 104 *U. Pa. L. Rev.* 603, 611 (1956).

106. Carroll, supra n. 104, at 18–20.

107. See, e.g., Patricia J. Williams, *The Alchemy of Race and Rights* 56–57 (1991) (reporting an incident in an all-white restaurant involving a law student who was an African American woman).

Their ethnic difference, appearance, and demeanor would be prejudicial. The rule of speed would require that they are disposed of immediately and that any form of argumentation, even if made by counsel, would be held against them. More likely than not they would plead guilty without a true understanding of what this means and pay their fine, thus providing documentary evidence for the cultural assumption of their criminality. They would pay lip service to any condition the judge may impose and try to escape the environment as soon as possible. Conceivably they could also be "cantankerous" and difficult, thus inviting official sanctions beyond the original charge, unless the court released them in an effort to avoid further complications and delays.

In U.S. Supreme Court

The second illustration is taken from the other end of the spectrum. As any court, the U.S. Supreme Court is subject to an infinite number of oral legal traditions that may affect the outcome of litigation, sometimes perhaps critically so.[108] We deal here, of course, with matters that may be as taboo in our society as some of the rules about purity and pollution among the Gypsies. I am submitting them merely hypothetically, since any true validation, at this stage, is missing and perhaps not even possible. A scanning of any number of opinions will disclose "ritualistic words" that are commonly used by the Court. I have come up with the following list, which could be expanded:

flagrantly and patently unconstitutional, justiciable controversy, balancing, ripeness, rational basis, unreasonable burden, supersede, chill, preempt, minimum connection,

---

108. Some of the more visible unwritten rules are described in H. W. Perry, *Deciding to Decide: Agenda Setting in the United States Supreme Court* (1991); Walter F. Murphy, *Elements of Judicial Strategy* (1964); Bob Woodward & Scott Armstrong, *The Brethren: Inside the Supreme Court* (1979). See, e.g., Perry, supra, at 218–20 (discussing presumption against granting certiorari); Woodward & Armstrong, supra, at 179–80 (quoting a memorandum from Justice William O. Douglas to Chief Justice Warren E. Burger of Apr. 24, 1972, in reference to the traditional rule that the Chief Justice assigns the writing of an opinion, if he is in the majority; if the Chief Justice is in the minority, the assignment is made by the most senior justice in the majority).

Some unwritten rules can be inferred: e.g., justices may remind clerks about their duties of confidentiality circuitously. See Perry, supra, at 142 n. 5 (reporting that a justice assigned close reading of *The Brethren* to the clerks, understood by them as a hint not to breach confidentiality). Some rules have no direct relation to the decision process: e.g., clerks are not supposed to date staff members. Woodward & Armstrong, supra, at 244 (noting that in one instance the male staff member, but apparently not the female clerk, was fired). The same unwritten rule applies in large law firms. Erwin O. Smigel, *The Wall Street Lawyer* 228 (1964) (noting prohibition against socializing across status lines).

The Brethren is criticized for being more interested in gossip than in the workings of the Court. Perry, supra, at 142–43. Its index abounds with references to names of individual persons, at the expense of concepts. The unwritten rule that may have been violated is that references to persons should, if possible, be avoided, especially if they are negative in content. Journalism has, of course, its own unwritten laws that are more permissive.

nexus, penumbra, wholly arbitrary and capricious, invidious, clear and present, imminent, compelling, vague, precisely, unfettered, prurient interest, redeeming social importance, patently offensive, benevolent neutrality, three-pronged test, divisive, accommodate, all deliberate speed, color of law, most rigid scrutiny, inherently suspect[109]

The mere reading of these words invokes the image of the Court and, through it, of constitutional law. The words are sometimes even emphasized in the opinions by putting them in quotation marks.[110] One could view these and similar expressions as parts of a specialized vocabulary or as inevitable incidents of normative language.[111] Clearly, the words are not all in the same category. Some terms, such as "precisely," are used for emphasis or, perhaps, sometimes as a means to strengthen a weak line of reasoning. Some other expressions, such as "justiciable controversy," are terms of art that are meant to invoke a whole range of associations.[112]

Independently of these considerations, the words could acquire ritualistic, perhaps even magical, meaning to the extent that they *must* be used. If it could be demonstrated that litigation depends on exact usage of words, as distinguished from the "fundamental legal conceptions" of Hohfeld,[113] these words would be shown to have some of the quality of *passwords*. The Supreme Court in that respect would assume some of the functions of a sentry. I am not prepared to say that these functions, if they could be proven, are necessarily bad.

There is also the question of what "exact usage" means. It could mean merely that specific words must be uttered.[114] It could refer to correct usage in a wider con-

109.   The words are so commonly associated with numerous opinions of the U.S. Supreme Court that no specific citations to the Court appear to be necessary. However, some of these words, plus additional examples, are included with citations in Park, Comment, "Human Rights and Basic Needs: Using International Human Rights Norms to Inform Constitutional Interpretation," 34 *UCLA L Rev.* 1195, 1208–11 (1987) (mentioning "strict scrutiny," "suspect classes," "fundamental right," "compelling state interest," "substantially related," "rational basis," and "wholly irrelevant"). The list in the text was first compiled in a letter from Walter O. Weyrauch to John H. Merryman, Stanford Law School (Dec. 30, 1976) (copy on file with author).

110.   See, e.g., Roe v. Wade, 410 U.S. 113, 163 (1973) (multiple references to the word "compelling," each time in quotation marks).

111.   Pyle, "Law, Ritual and Language," 8 *ALSA F.* 381 (1984) (describing how ritualistic use of words may transform them from tools of communication into instruments of power). The Vlax Gypsies have such a formalized oratory, which may influence outcomes in their judicial proceedings (*kris*). Weyrauch & Bell, *Gypsy Law,* supra n. 2, at 44.

112.   Laurence H. Tribe, *American Constitutional Law* 67 (2d ed. 1988) (quoting Flast v. Cohen, 392 U.S. 83, 94–95 [1968]).

113.   Wesley N. Hohfeld, *Fundamental Legal Conceptions as Applied in Judicial Reasoning* (Walter W. Cook ed., 1919).

114.   See Balkin & Levinson, "Constitutional Grammar," 72 *Tex. L. Rev.* 1771, 1772 n. 5 (1994) (including "vocabulary" in their definition of grammar as "knowledge or usage of the preferred or prescribed forms in speaking or writing," quoted from *The Random House College Dictionary* 573 [rev. ed. 1975]); Benedict, "Magic," 10 *Encyc. Soc. Sci.* 39, 41 (1933) (defining magic as an attempt to control the universe by an exacting incantation of words); Weyrauch, "Taboo and Magic in Law," 25 *Stan. L. Rev.* 782,

text, which implies the influx of notions of substantive law. Furthermore, to use the Court's mode of expression, the nexus between the written opinion and the arguments and considerations that led to its formulation may be rather tenuous. In other words, the opinion may only reflect in a limited way what actually took place. Although any of these factors may affect proof about the significance of specific words, no doubt those who address the Court, or any student of constitutional law, would be well advised to adhere to the proper words. If technically correct synonyms were used, the argument may lose persuasiveness.

To say that the vocabulary used by the U.S. Supreme Court has some of the characteristics of passwords does not mean that the success of litigation depends exclusively on its use or that the reasoning is incorrect or specious. Obviously, if both parties are equally adept at proper usage, the ultimate outcome must rest on reasoning other than the correct utterance of words. Still, proper usage could be an essential element in the credibility of an argument. Thus adherence to a language ritual, although not essential for winning or losing a case, may give access to the realm of those who argue with credibility. The Court might perform some of the functions of a sentry in these respects, but the extent would be difficult to verify by empirical means. Although law examinations in constitutional law are not comparable to argument before the Court, a student could hardly expect a passing grade if none of the ritual words were used in the response to the test question. Yet how is one to prove this assertion? Such an experiment raises problems of design and ethics. The grading professor must lack knowledge of the experiment and the student must be willing to fail.

Lawyers face in these respects an odd phenomenon that, as far as they are concerned, eliminates the need for evidence. Whatever the suggested unwritten code of the Court may be, it is complemented by very real rules of the legal profession. The bar is subject to its own unwritten codes of conduct. An important rule is that advocates must take cognizance of even remote probabilities that may affect the outcome of pending cases. They should not care whether scientific evidence is missing. If it is possible, no matter how speculatively so, that the use of specific words before the Court may aid their cases, they are bound to use them in an effort to maximize the chances of their clients. Whether nonuse of ritual words would constitute malpractice or violate professional ethics is besides the point. The sanction for having violated the unwritten rules of advocacy consists in living with the stigma of having been an ineffective lawyer and thus, similar to the Gypsy who has violated the taboos of his culture, being impaired in self-respect.[115] Shunning by colleagues and potential clients are likely consequences. Thus a merely hypothetical and unprovable unwritten rule of the Court may nevertheless be fully effective as if it were proven and real.

798–800 (1973) (describing parallels between magical reasoning and efforts in legal processes to control events by an exacting use of language). Pyle, supra n. 111, at 384 (commenting on "precision" of legal vocabulary, as it relates to recognizing and using terms of art).

115. See supra text following note 9.

On the other hand, at least some factors support the lawyers' custom to treat as proven what may be unprovable. Observation may reveal that the ritual words are used uniformly by the justices, regardless of passage of time and change in the composition of the Court. Whether a majority opinion or a dissent is involved, or whether a plurality opinion is issued, seems to have little impact on the efficacy of the words. Their existence appears to be independent of individual ideology and the substance of the cases.[116] To explain this phenomenon in terms of "form over substance" may not be quite accurate. A special kind of form is involved that may have its own functions and unwritten rules. To continue the hypothesis, perhaps we are close to the functions of tribal rituals. One of the objectives of such rituals may be to create the appearance of continuity, although it may be missing in fact. Uniformity of ritual may cover up severe and persistent substantive clashes. It thus may have substantive functions that would be damaged if they were openly acknowledged.

To come back to the metaphors of passwords and sentry. The rigidity of the passwords that allows for no variation whatsoever assures that hostile elements are kept out and cannot infiltrate the camp of the tribe. Those who do not know or refuse to utter the critical words, although their arguments may be perfectly plausible, are likely to be distrusted or perhaps be kept out altogether and lose their case. Similarly, a potential justice who could not be trusted in maintaining ritual and decorum might not be nominated or confirmed. If confirmed, he may create a continuing problem in adjudication. Traditional references to the presence or absence of judicial temperament may be veiled invocations of an assumed adherence, or the lack of it, to the demands of unwritten law.

Nevertheless, similar to the problems of research exposing Gypsy law,[117] the hypothetical illustration raises questions of scholarly ethics that so far have not been addressed. Conceivably such research into the taboos of our legal culture could be problematical, and one may ponder whether it should be undertaken at all.[118] If it were to be shown, for example, that the outcome of cases may indeed be critically

---

116. Perry, supra n. 108, at 18, suggests that, in spite of apparent ideological differences among the justices, "clerks from all chambers were often saying exactly the same thing." Similarly, the mode of judicial reasoning, regardless of differences in outcome, may be identical.

117. See discussion supra part II.

118. Ronald J. Mann, based on observations while clerking at the U.S. Supreme Court, agrees with the suggested presence of traditional rituals and that their examination could sometimes be harmful to the Court. He is less persuaded by the specific illustration of the significance of language rituals, although "the Court's discourse, particularly in constitutional cases, offers an unusual sameness of vocabulary." Letter from Ronald J. Mann, Washington University, St. Louis, School of Law, to Walter O. Weyrauch (June 19, 1995, at 1 [on file with author]).

For an ethics discussion, see "Recording of Jury Deliberations: Hearings Before the Subcomm. to Investigate the Administration of the Internal Security Act and Other Internal Security Laws of the Senate Comm. on the Judiciary," 84th Cong., 1st Sess. (1955) (reprimanding a group of distinguished legal scholars for their research methods).

In contrast to the ethics codes in anthropology and medicine, I am against a formal code regulating legal research. The choice whether to proceed with research should be left to the legal scholar.

influenced by the exact use of words, to the detriment of the substantive "merits" of the case, it could conceivably damage the institution of the Court within the commonly accepted tenets of our culture. The question, as in the case of research about some exotic tribe, could be, What weight should be given in scholarship to the established myths of a culture? What may appear to be a myth or commonly shared belief could be an unrealized but vital aspiration that, like any ideal, could be damaged or even destroyed by showing what actually takes place. Again, this insight may demand some level of tolerance toward actual practices, and there is really, on that conceptual level, no difference between the Gypsies and us.

At the outset I suggested that there may be a link between oral legal traditions and strategies. Strategies are commonly disparaged as detracting from the "merits" of a case.[119] Legal scholarship neglects them as of mere vocational concern. Yet strategies may owe their persuasive powers to an underlying vast body of unwritten law.[120] Direct invocation of that body may be scorned as prejudicial or even as a breach of ethics. The practicing lawyer, in an effort to be more effective, is likely to resort to allusions which, if skillfully presented, may determine the outcome of a case.[121] Since legislation and case law of the state can cover the multitude of controversies only incompletely, the written law may indeed need the support of unwritten oral legal traditions.[122] Any legal scholarship that neglects these aspects is bound to be equally incomplete and flawed. On the other hand, there may also be a competing need for scholarly restraint because smooth operation of the legal culture as a whole, as with the Gypsies, may depend on a low level of awareness of what moves us and according to what hidden standards we make decisions.

Possible sanctions could remain with unwritten law. See supra n. 52 (Statement on Ethics, Am, Anthropological Ass'n); Council on Ethical and Judicial Affairs, American Medical Association, *Code of Medical Ethics: Current Opinions* (1992).

119. Lynn M. LoPucki, *Strategies for Creditors in Bankruptcy Proceedings* at xxix (1st ed. 1985).

120. Weyrauch & Bell, *Gypsy Law*, supra n. 2, at 17–18, 70–74.

121. Id. at 398. For illustrations of successful strategies, see Ansaldi, "Texaco, Pennzoil and the Revolt of the Masses: A Contracts Postmortem," 27 *Hous. L. Rev.* 733 (1990) (large-scale commercial litigation); Lynn M. LoPucki, *Strategies for Creditors in Bankruptcy Proceedings* (2d ed. 1991); Walter O. Weyrauch, Sanford N. Katz & Frances Olsen, *Cases and Materials on Family Law: Legal Concepts and Changing Human Relationships* 840–43 (1994) (child custody disputes).

122. Weyrauch & Bell, *Gypsy Law*, supra n. 2, at 87; Michael Allen Weeks, "Student Strategic Parking: The Culture That Dictates When, How, and Against Whom the Parking Laws Promulgated by the State Will be Enforced," 25 (May 1996) (unpublished paper, University of Florida College of Law, on file with author) ("Without an extensive body of informal law in the area of parking, the written rules could not serve their intended purpose. . . .").

Contributors

Thomas Acton is Professor of Romani Studies, School of Social Sciences, University of Greenwich.

Maureen Bell is an attorney at law. She practices in Orlando, Florida.

Susan Caffrey is Senior Lecturer, School of Social Science, University of Greenwich.

Calum Carmichael is Professor of Comparative Literature and Adjunct Professor of Law, Cornell University.

Sir Angus Fraser is the author of *The Gypsies* (second edition, 1995). He formerly worked in the U.K. government service.

Martti Grönfors is Professor of Sociology, University of Kuopio, Finland.

Ian Hancock is Professor of Linguistics and English, University of Texas at Austin. He is Director of the Romani Archives and Documentation Center.

Angela P. Harris is Professor of Law, Boalt Hall, University of California, Berkeley.

Ronald Lee is an author and journalist. He is Executive Director of the Roma Community and Advocacy Centre in Toronto.

Gary Mundy was a Research Associate at the University of Greenwich at the time of writing his contribution to this book. He currently works on research issues for the Department of Education and Employment in the U.K.

Anne Sutherland is Professor of Anthropology, Georgia State University.

Walter O. Weyrauch is Distinguished Professor of Law and Stephen C. O'Connell Chair, Levin College of Law, University of Florida. He is also Honorary Professor at Johann Wolfgang Goethe University, Frankfurt.

Index

Compositor:	Impressions Book and Journal Services, Inc.
Text:	10/12 Baskerville
Display:	Baskerville
Printer and binder:	Maple-Vail Manufacturing Group